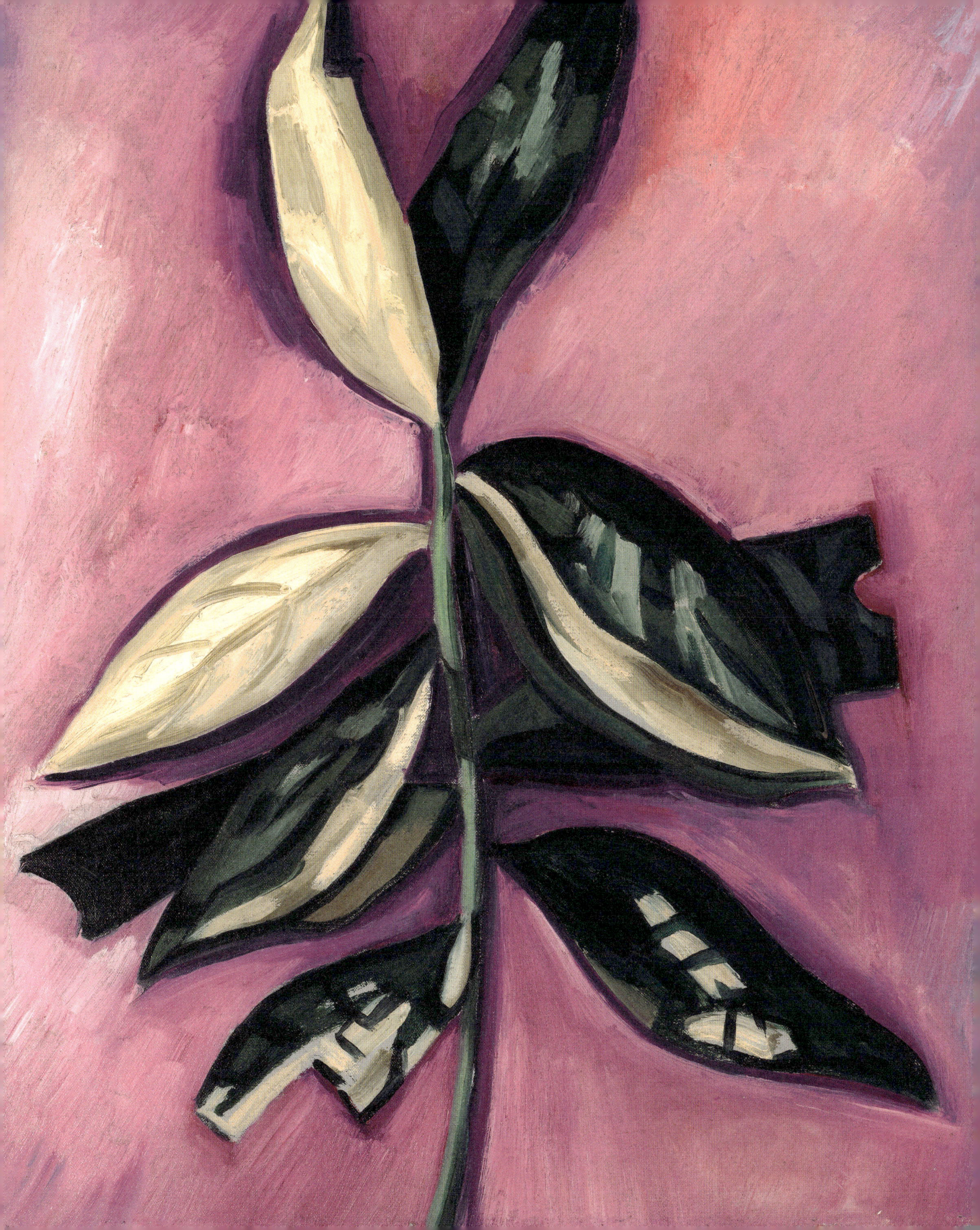

MARSDEN HARTLEY
THE EARTH IS ALL I KNOW OF WONDER

Foreword

It is with great pleasure and excitement that the Louisiana presents an absolute classic, the little known American painter Marsden Hartley (1877-1943). We do so because we are always looking to expand our shared horizons. Moreover, it is a privilege to take on such an endeavour – unpacking an artist's work on a grand scale, while showing the museum in full expansion, with the support of major partners. Hartley is ripe for discovery on the map of art history, as seen from a European perspective. Despite his prominent position in the history of American art, and the fact that he spent a great deal of his life in Germany and France, Hartley remains virtually unknown in this neck of the woods. Which may not be so strange, after all: there hasn't been a single retrospective presentation of Hartley's work in Europe since the early 1960s.

In the European awareness of American art, it might seem like a paradox that we know so much about the art that followed World War II and so very little about the art that predated it, as if the two realms had nothing to do with each other. While key figures of postwar art, like Jackson Pollock (1912-1956) and Mark Rothko (1903-1970), are seen as original, universal artists who appeared out of the blue, Hartley and his contemporaries tend to be subordinated to a narrative of provincialism and a general inferiority complex about European art at the time. Designed to shake up that perception, this exhibition introduces the work of a profoundly original artist, while showing its importance to the celebrated Americans of the postwar period. Through Hartley, we also gain a better understanding of the Louisiana's collection.

The Hartley exhibition follows in the footsteps of a number of related projects at the Louisiana, revisiting historical modernism to introduce important positions that, for various reasons, have been overlooked. Two recent examples are the German artists Paula Modersohn-Becker (1876-1907) and Gabriele Münter (1877-1962), who belonged to the same generation as Hartley (Münter even knew him). While the exclusion of women from the great canon of art can be described as a product of gender roles and the derived concept of artists as male, the omission of Hartley is more complex. Throughout his work, in various ways and degrees of overtness, Hartley alluded to his own homosexuality. This situates his oeuvre on the margins of the established canonic view of genius, which typically cast male artists as heterosexual seducers of women. Apart from its great, purely artistic qualities, Hartley's work was also pathbreaking in its thematizing of gay desire.

The Louisiana presents Hartley's work retrospectively, from his earliest efforts in 1905 to his death in 1943. The exhibition has been put together with a nod to major American shows of Hartley's work in the past, and with the ambition of adding to the existing knowledge about the artist by including works that have not previously been shown within the framework of a retrospective.

The result is an exhibition featuring a string of established masterpieces from the greatest American museums and collections alongside works that are very rarely shown. A few works in the exhibition are completely unknown, and so are having their world premiere in Humlebæk. This includes *Geometric Figure* (c. 1914), a previously unknown addition to one of the most documented and best known periods of Hartley's life, his Berlin years from 1913-1915.

In addition to his art, Hartley left behind hundreds of poems and essays, most of which were left unpublished during his lifetime. The Louisiana's exhibition includes a selection of Hartley's essays on his time and art, and a number of his poems, which often directly related to his paintings. While Hartley's main legacy remains his paintings, his writings help flesh out the portrait of an artist who divided his time equally between writing and painting. Sadly, there is a limit to how much of Hartley's writing can be included in this catalogue, though a number of his poems are featured in the catalogue essays.

Supplementing the retrospective format, the museum has sought to show how Hartley's work continues to live and breathe, not only as art-historical material but as grist and inspiration for many artists today. In turn, we asked eight painters to write a few words about their personal relationship to Hartley's work. You will find them in this catalogue. Seven of the artists also contributed their thoughts to a film, which will be screened at the exhibition and is also available at channel.louisiana.dk.

In his autobiography, the German painter George Grosz (1893-1959) wrote that Hartley was one of the few American painters who were known in Germany when Grosz immigrated to America in

1933. The catalogue for the first retrospective exhibition of Hartley's work – at New York's Museum of Modern Art in 1944, a year after the artist's death – reveals that he was planning an exhibition in Copenhagen in 1916, which was cancelled because of World War I. So, it seems more accurate to say that we in Europe have forgotten Hartley, rather than that we never knew him. Simply put, the aim of the present exhibition is to restore Hartley from oblivion, showcasing the wonderful qualities of his work and his importance in both American and European art history, while reinforcing the transatlantic tale of art's evolution. Now, more than a century after it was first planned, Hartley's works will finally be coming to Denmark.

Mathias Ussing Seeberg, Curator
Poul Erik Tøjner, Director

Acknowledgments
The Louisiana is thankful to the many institutions and individuals without whom this exhibition would not have been possible.

Above all, thanks to all the museums in the US and Europe who deemed this exhibition worthy of support by making invaluable loans. Likewise thanks to the many private lenders who agreed to let wonderful works of art temporarily leave their homes. Thanks as well to the Marsden Hartley Memorial Collection and Archive at the Bates College Museum of Art in the artist's hometown of Lewiston, Maine, for their tremendous graciousness and generosity.

Thanks to Adam Weinberg, Director, and David Breslin of the Whitney Museum of American Art and Randall R. Griffey of the Metropolitan Museum of Art for invaluable instruction and advice. Thanks, as well, to Marc Porter, Jim Reinish and Phil Alexandre for their great help in locating works in private collections.

The Louisiana would like to acknowledge the enormous amount of research and scholarship that others have done and from which we have benefitted. A posthumous thanks to Elizabeth McCausland (1899-1965), the first great Hartley scholar, who was instrumental in Hartley's work being exhibited in Europe in the early 1960s.

We thank the contributors to this catalogue, Edyta Frelik, Elizabeth Finch, Jonathan D. Katz and Randall R. Griffey, for their acute observations on Hartley's work. A big thanks to the artists who contributed their thoughts about Hartley to this catalogue and to the film for the exhibition: Alex Katz, David Hockney, David Salle, Karin Mamma Andersson, Tal R, Dana Schutz, Shara Hughes and Sam McKinniss.

Finally, we are deeply grateful to the Augustinus Foundation and the Terra Foundation for American Art for their generous support for this exhibition.

A very special thanks to the Weisman Art Museum in Minneapolis, home to the largest collection of Hartley's work anywhere, which went above and beyond by lending no fewer than 19 works to the exhibition.

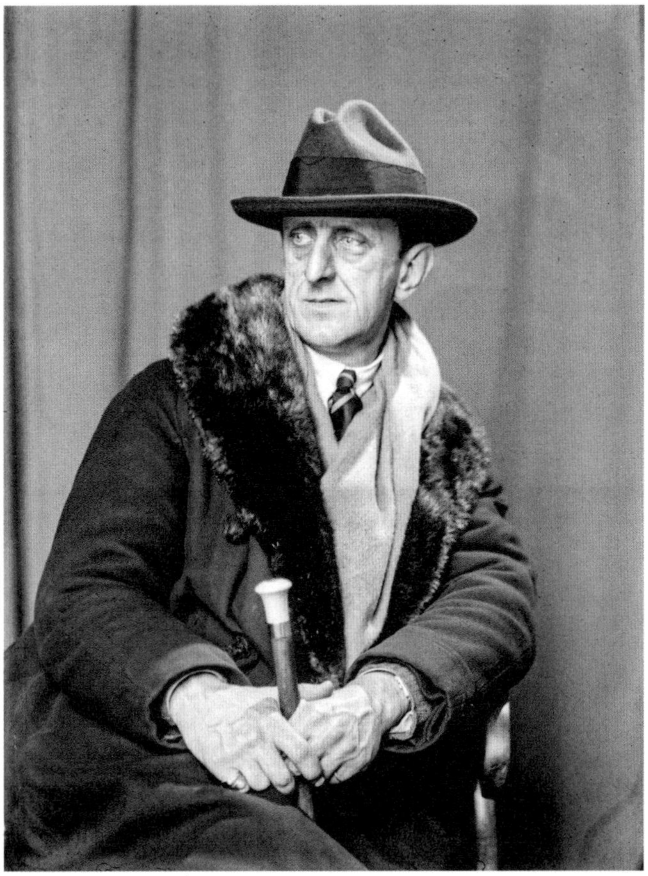

Man Ray: *Marsden Hartley*, 1926. Centre Pompidou – Musée national d'art moderne – Centre de création

Introduction to Marsden Hartley's life and work

By Mathias Ussing Seeberg

The American painter Marsden Hartley (1877-1943) has a unique position in the history of American art. At once insider and outsider, he captured aspects of the zeitgeist, both in Europe and the US, but he always went his own way. Besides his painting, he wrote poetry and essays on art all his life.[1] Even if Hartley had never painted a single picture, he would still be part of the story of American modernism.

Wherever he went, Hartley joined prominent circles of writers and artists, but he was never a leading figure, a fact that haunted him his whole life. Lack of recognition and success was a major reason why Hartley was always moving on – in his adult life, he never lived in one place more than ten months. This restlessness in his personal life was clearly reflected in his paintings. Every new trip, every new place, meant more pictures. Throughout his life, the character and expression of his paintings regularly changed. All the same, as several of the artists contributing to this catalogue note, Hartley's oeuvre is unmistakably the product of one hand – a special Hartleyesque touch that has nothing do with any isms but is simply the artist's profoundly personal imprint.[2]

Hartley was gay at a time when it was illegal, though it was generally accepted in the bohemian circles in which he moved. The artist's restlessness is also tied to his position as a sexual outsider, which made it harder for him to settle down and feel as part of something. In his paintings, we sense discreet attempts at revealing his identity and expressing himself about himself across the various genres he mastered. At times, the results were plainly homosexually loaded. Other times, the artist dealt with the body and sexuality or feelings like longing, loneliness and alienation that are universally valid but can also be tied to a homosexual identity at the time.

When he was 30, the artist changed his given name, Edmund, to his stepmother's maiden name, Marsden. In his autobiography, Hartley describes the name change as a gesture of devotion to his father's new wife, who took charge of the family after the death of his mother in 1885.[3] His work, meanwhile, offers a different explanation: Hartley wanted to create an artist's persona embracing a greater unity of his inner and outer identities. He did so discreetly, and he had an alibi.[4]

Linking the body and sexuality to seemingly innocuous subjects like landscapes was not uncommon in Hartley's day.[5] The circle of artists around Hartley's gallerist Alfred Stieglitz (1864-1946) included a number of similar exponents, notably Georgia O'Keeffe (1887-1986) and Arthur Dove (1880-1946). In that respect, Hartley was a child of his time. But in many other ways his work stands apart, not least in his efforts to express love and desire in a different constellation than the one familiar from the established canon, which mainly aimed its Freudian brush at women.[6] Hartley manifested this shift in his painting *On the Beach* (1940) (cat. 90), which shows a vanishingly small female figure next to two mammoth, hunky males.

Viewing the entirety of Hartley's work from a curatorial bird's-eye view affords one striking observation: his late work, from 1938-1943, includes many paintings of men, several even in various stages of undress. Before that, paradoxically, there were practically no human figures in his art. Where landscapes and still lifes once made up the lion's share of his subject matter, now male figures were everywhere. Examining the back of Hartley's earliest known abstract painting, *Abstraction* (1911) (cat. 12, p. 22), reveals a section of a nude study, apparently a woman (fig. 1). Hence, Hartley did try his hand at figurative painting at least once before. It is remarkable that a body is literally hidden behind the abstraction, even if this is probably a coincidence and not an artistic device. For the absence of bodies does not equal the absence of corporeality in his work. While Hartley did not actually paint figures until late in life, there are numerous allusions to the body, gender, masculinity and sexuality in a lot of his work. In *Landscape No. 20* (1909) (cat. 7, p. 19), one of the earliest works in the exhibition, a body even appears to be embedded in a rock in the landscape, which can here be regarded as a didactic point. Over the course of time, Hartley paints (or chisels) the body out of the rock. This observation – first the absence of bodies, then, all at once, bodies everywhere – is the overarching point of departure for this introduction. Moreover, I want to single out Hartley's gay identity as essential, not only to reading individual works but to understanding the eclectic nature of his oeuvre.

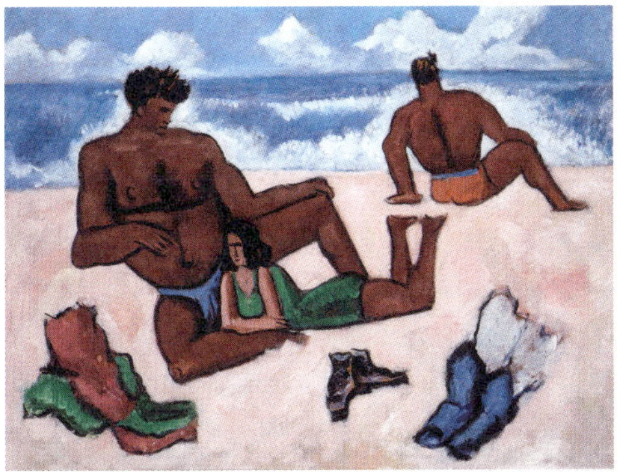

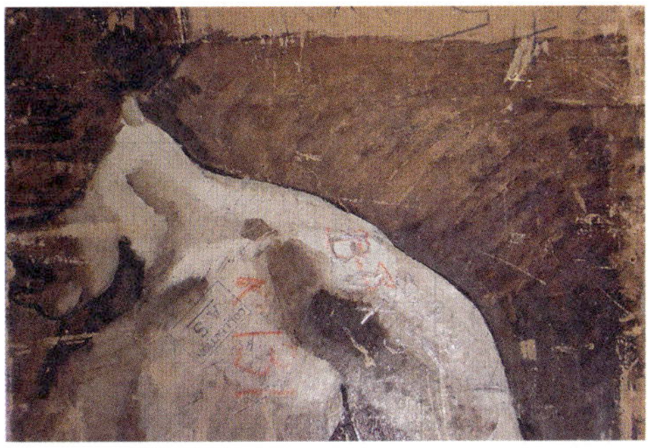

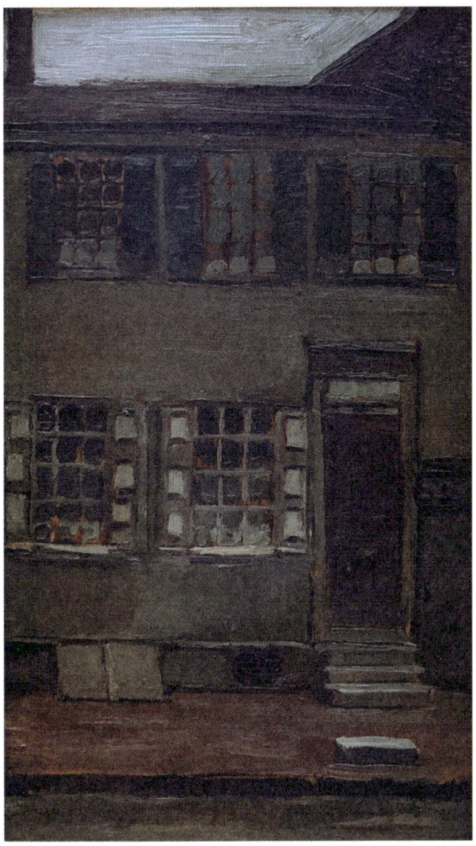

90 *On the Beach*, 1940
Fig. 1 Detail of a nude on the back of *Abstraction*, 1911
1 *Walt Whitman's House*, c. 1905

Maine and New York, 1905-1912

The earliest work in the exhibition, the seminal *Walt Whitman's House* (c. 1905) (cat. 1), shows the house in Camden, New Jersey, where the great American poet Walt Whitman (1819-1892) died. In his youth, Hartley was deeply influenced by Whitman and idolized him together with other equally devoted "Whitmanics."[7] The young artist's strong interest in Whitman was fed, in part, by the assumption that the writer had intimate relations with men, as described indirectly in Whitman's books and more directly in his letters. In Hartley's copy of Whitman's magnum opus, *Leaves of Grass* (1885), he even marked a number of passages hinting at forbidden passions.[8]

Whitman provided Hartley with a model for incorporating his gay identity into his painting without making it plain. In *Walt Whitman's House*, Hartley presents us with a house but does not reveal the reason, apart from its famous occupant, for his fascination with it. The house has an unapproachable air, as if harbouring secrets that are barred to us.[9] This is a consistently applied device in the artist's work. Subject matter is displayed and presented, but remains secretive. There is a double movement of revealing and concealing. We receive only coded or oblique references to Hartley's gay identity – the doors and windows of the house are kept shut.

In general, Hartley's beginnings as an artist are defined by literature. Early on, he took the American philosopher Ralph Waldo Emerson's (1803-1882) *Essays* with him everywhere.[10] A Transcendentalist, Emerson wrote about humanity's spiritual connection to nature. Emphasizing the subjective experience of the world, he regarded divinity as inherent in both nature and humans. It seems obvious to assume that this worldview offered a mirror for Hartley's identity as a gay man: if we have divinity within us, homosexuality cannot be wrong. Emerson regarded artists as "prophets" capable of fixing on canvas their transcendental experience, their connection to the spirit of life.[11]

Transcendentalism provided a language for the spiritually searching Hartley. Through Emerson, and Henry David Thoreau (1817-1862), nature became the main subject of Hartley's early paintings, added a substantial dash of Whitmanesque zing. Specifically, Hartley painted landscapes from his home state of Maine, in New England, north of New York. In

Cosmos (1908-1909) (cat. 5), a cross-like treetop reaches into the sky. The painting's distinctly soft and rounded forms ooze corporeality. Two clouds split in the middle of the picture, while a stream in the centre bisects a range of mountains. Trees are bursting with life. Hartley's cosmic image here merges the sexual and the spiritual.[12]

While Hartley located a foundation for his spirituality and identity in literature, the formal qualities of his works were more variable, inspired by his encounters with the New York art scene, in particular his gallery, the 291, so known because of its address on 5th Avenue. Stieglitz, who ran the gallery, was a key player in raising local awareness of trailblazing French art by exhibiting artists like Pablo Picasso (1881-1973), Paul Cézanne (1839-1906) and Henri Matisse (1869-1954), who all clearly influenced Hartley's painting. In addition, Stieglitz promoted a number of young American artists who today are considered leaders of American modernism. Apart from Dove and O'Keeffe, this includes names like John Marin (1870-1953) and Charles Demuth (1883-1935). Hartley often felt that Stieglitz neglected him in favour of these other artists.

Not surprisingly, he strongly identified with the great American outsider artist Albert Pinkham Ryder (1847-1917). Hartley visited Ryder in New York in 1909 and was influenced by the much older artist's dark, mystical rendering of the human relationship to nature. This is evident in a work like *Deserted Farm* (1909) (cat. 8, p. 20), which mimics Ryder's images of moonlit skies. Ryder had a lifelong impact on Hartley, owing as much to Ryder's position on the margins of the art world as to his painting.

It is clear even in his early works that, while Hartley was inspired by these artistic heavyweights, his pictures never look like copies. *Pears* (1911) (cat. 13, p. 22) is based on a black-and-white reproduction of a Cézanne painting. Heavily outlined, Hartley's two pears have an almost bulging physicality. Purposefully and pronouncedly uniform, one repeats the other – they are the same shape. *Pears* is a prime example of what can be hidden in even the most innocent-looking still life. It is one of the most obviously homosexually charged works that Hartley produced in his breakthrough years, right down to the two pear stems that, in a manner of speaking, cross swords.

Paris and Berlin, 1912-1915

Hartley's enormous interest in European contemporary art took him to Paris, then the epicentre of art. He was hardly the first American to make the journey. One place to be was Gertrude Stein's (1874-1946) famous salon, at 27 Rue de Fleurus. There, Hartley saw the latest art, including a room full of "staggering pictures,"[13] and met several of its creators. Stein had a big hand in Hartley's European debut, not least thanks to the world that she opened up to him.[14] In the artist's telling, Stein concluded after looking at his work, "at last an original American."[15]

What really moved Hartley on as an artist, however, was his encounter with German art and culture. Above all, it was his close friendship in Paris with the German sculptor Arnold Rönnebeck (1885-1947) and his cousin, Karl von Freyburg (1889-1914),[16] a Prussian soldier, that compelled him to go to Germany. For Hartley, it was a revelation – artistically, spiritually and personally. In Germany, he met Wassily Kandinsky (1866-1944), whose art theories he cultivated, as well as Gabriele Münter (1877-1962) and Franz Marc (1880-1916).[17] Meanwhile, like many other artists of his day, he read Christian mystics, like Jakob Böhme (1575-1624) who described everything in nature as being part of God, and the Bhagavad-Gita, an ancient key work of Hindu scripture prescribing a way of living for humankind and defining the recognition of God as a personal affair. Moreover, the writings of the American philosopher William James (1842-1910) were crucial to Hartley in terms of giving his encounter with Berlin – and sexual liberation – painterly form.[18]

Hartley's painting quickly evolved away from the Cubist stringency of works like *Musical Theme No. 2 (Bach Preludes et Fugues)* (1912) (cat. 15, p. 24) towards freer, more dynamic compositions virtuosically mixing styles and symbols. In *Portrait Arrangement No. 2* (1912-1913) (cat. 16), a small, circular emblem of a white horseman at the top of the picture is framed and elevated in large part by a Shunya Mudra, the characteristic Hindu hand sign. The horseman is from Kaiser Wilhelm II's regiment, which often paraded through the city. In his autobiography, written years later, Hartley describes the sight of the soldiers: "those huge cuirassiers of the Kaiser's special guard – all in white – white leather breeches skin tight – high plain enamel boots – those gleaming blinding medieval breast plates of silver and brass ... There were the inspiring helmets with the imperial eagle and the white manes hanging down – there was six foot of youth under all this garniture – everyone on a horse – and every horse white."[19]

Hartley made a number of similar paintings, notably *Berlin Ante War* (1914) (cat. 21, p. 28), pivoting around the white soldiers of the Kaiser's army, putting them on a pedestal. These pictures can very easily be misinterpreted as glorifying war. However, as the above quote testifies, Hartley's fascination with the subject was uniquely tied to the physical attraction he felt for the soldiers. Highlighting both the soldiers' masculinity and their fancy dress, he undermines the notion of pure masculinity.[20] Meanwhile, in a letter to Franz Marc, he described the ideas of Walt Whitman.[21] It would seem that Whitman's notion of "the manly love of comrades"[22] was still with Hartley in Berlin, in his friendship with Rönnebeck and von Freyburg, who were both military men, and that he saw the soldiers as symbols of his own lifestyle. Hartley called these paintings "cosmic cubism." As in the aforementioned, aptly titled *Cosmos*, these early military images elevate earthly, carnal life by appropriating a religious and spiritual vocabulary.

While Hartley's first pictures of Berlin were marked by the city's liberating effect on him – same-sexers were able to live more freely there than anywhere else – the pictures he painted after the outbreak of World War I offer a stark contrast. Hartley's two German friends from Paris were called up when war broke out in August 1914, and von Freyburg was killed already in October. The loss was unbearable for Hartley.[23] In his grief, he began a series relating to von Freyburg – gloomy abstract and symbolist paintings on black grounds.[24] A major work, *Portrait of a German Officer* (1914) (cat. 22, p. 33), a military heraldry of sorts, is composed of emblems, decorations, pennants and other fragments which almost all can be traced to the departed von Freyburg's uniform and regiment. Not unlike his earlier Cubist works, Hartley here, too, used writing to provide clues about the content. In the lower left-hand corner, we see the initials Kv.F., while Von Freyburg's age of death, 24, is written on the canvas. There are references to Rönnebeck, as well, via the triangle, which denotes the friendship between the three men and is also a mystical symbol, and the yellow

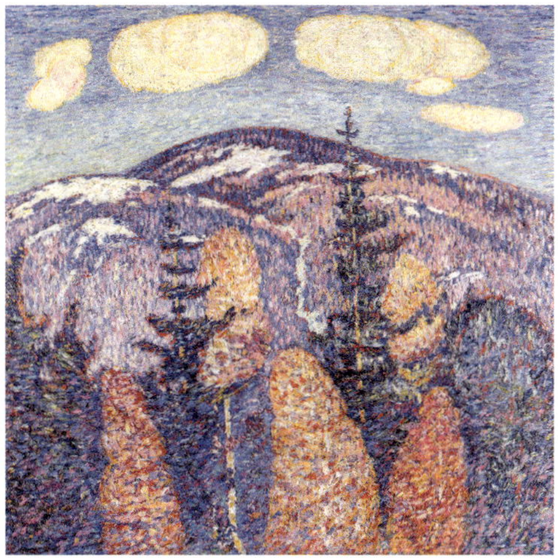

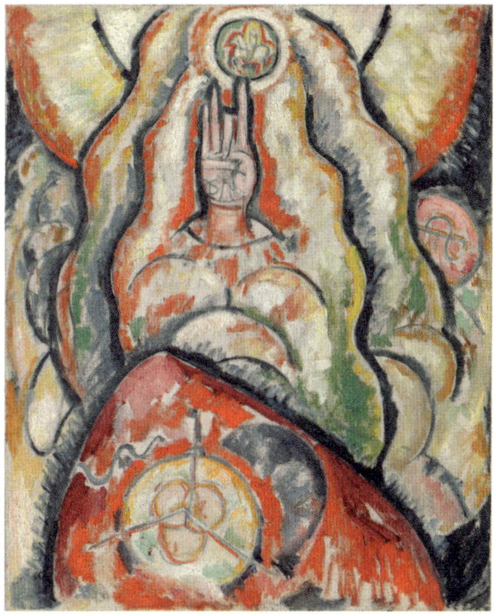

5 *Cosmos*, 1908-1909
16 *Portrait Arrangement No. 2*, 1912-1913

shoulder board with a red E, which, Rönnebeck later said, derived from his regiment.[25]

Hartley called the painting a portrait. Curiously, no body or person is portrayed, though the picture's vertical format and arrangement indirectly allude to a body.[26] As a conglomerate whole, the many components resemble a reliquary. The iconography is forceful and militant, though the painting seems more concerned with its coded and wistful allusion to another man than with glorifying war. It idolizes an absent body. The heraldic fragments can be seen as images of masquerade and disguise, hiding the subject's identity from us. As in *Walt Whitman's House*, Hartley shows us something we cannot see or access.

Throughout his career, it seemed, Hartley burned the bridges to his past artistic projects with remarkable speed. Thus, while the *War Motifs*, as his military series is called, are among his most successful works, they occupied him for only a relatively short while. This consistent trend in his life can mainly be attributed to his great restlessness and ambition, though his lack of success in terms of art sales and fame also prompted frequent changes of track.

After his return to New York, Hartley toned down the meaning and content of his Berlin pictures, in part to avoid appearing pro-German at an unpropitious time, as many have noted.[27] But it can also be seen as an attempt to tone down their homosexual content.[28] In turn, this offers an opportunity to examine the generally eclectic nature of Hartley's work as reflecting a gay man's need to keep a low profile at the time. Just as his travelling from place to place can be seen as a way to protect himself from being unmasked, his changing styles can be seen as disguises allowing Hartley to maintain sexual anonymity.

Provincetown, Bermuda and New Mexico, 1916-1921

Returning to America, Hartley spent the summer of 1916 in Provincetown on Cape Cod with a number of other leading creative people, including the playwright Eugene O'Neill (1888-1953) and the painter Charles Demuth.[29] While the paintings Hartley made there, and later in Bermuda, contain no immediate references to his Berlin pictures and their powerfully loaded masculine iconography, they are compositionally related to them.

Elsa Kobenhavn (1916) (cat. 34) features a number of overlapping, flat geometric figures in much more muted colours than those of the *War Motifs*. Reminiscent of Russian Suprematism,[30] the figures in this context resemble sails because they are combined with various nautical references. Writing the name "Elsa Kobenhavn" (Elsa Copenhagen), incorporating the Danish flag and adding a mooring point, Hartley is clearly making a Cubist rendition of a ship.[31]

Curiously, *Elsa Kobenhavn* and similar works have not been thoroughly discussed within a gay thematic,[32] despite Hartley's investment in expressing this aspect of his identity in past groups of works. In this period, Hartley even made a large number of clearly sexualized still lifes, including *Flower* (1916) (cat. 33, p. 39) and *Still Life with Eel* (c. 1917) (cat. 38, p. 38), which both employ phallic symbols. The pictures from Provincetown and Bermuda are not commonly considered in that light because of their stringency and seemingly non-emotional character, as compared with works like the *War Motifs*. Nonetheless, we need to consider the role of harbour environments in gay culture at the time as places of sexual encounters between sailors and other men. The many photographs of sailors in Hartley's archives[33] only confirm this notion.[34] In his abstractions of ships, the artist may have been experimenting with a new, understated way of expressing his homosexuality by referring to another hyper-masculine milieu known for sexual relations between men.

In 1918, Hartley was invited to join an art colony in Taos, New Mexico, and set out with the intention of discovering "a new, authentic American modernism there."[35] Like many other American artists, he momentarily turned away from his engagement with European art in order to cultivate the idea of an American art,[36] encouraged by his gallerist, Alfred Stieglitz, among others. Breaking with Europe was partly a result of the extremely bloody World War I, which made many Americans question European culture.[37] In his first book publication, *Adventures in the Arts*, a 1921 collection of essays on art, Hartley writes, "Art, like life, has had to begin all over again, for the very end of the world had been made visible at last. The artist may look safely over an utterly new horizon, which is the only encouragement the artist of today can hope for."[38]

Hartley's New Mexican landscapes recall the rolling hills of his early paintings of Maine. Forging an artistic link between the two landscapes, he even titled one of the paintings *The Last of New England – The Beginning of New Mexico* (1918-1919) (cat. 41, p. 42). Another work, *New Mexico No. 2* (1919) (cat. 44), clearly shows Hartley's fascination with Cézanne in the use of parallel brushstrokes. Even as the painting approaches realism, Hartley takes a symbolist view of the landscape, emphasizing the round shapes of the hills, which look like body parts squeezed together. In the middle of the landscape, a graveyard full of crosses recalls the emblematic character of Hartley's *War Motifs*, as if von Freyburg and other victims of the recent Great War lay buried there. The corporeal reference and the image of death create the sense of an afterimage, with a wistfulness that Hartley would return to and underscore years later, back in Berlin, in his series *New Mexico Recollections.*

After Hartley's return to New York in late 1919, it quickly became clear that his farewell to the European avant-garde – "I am an American discovering America,"[39] he had proclaimed – had only been temporary. Hartley met the New York Dadaists of the Société Anonyme, founded by Katherine Dreier (1877-1852), Marcel Duchamp (1887-1968) and Man Ray (1890-1976). As secretary, he contributed to panel discussions and gave lectures, while creating a series of still lifes in the Cubist style. *Rubber Plant* (1920) (cat. 45, p. 43), which once belonged to the Société Anonyme, is characteristic of his new experiments with an avant-garde European vocabulary. Perhaps this representation of a rubber plant is Hartley's version of Dadaist playfulness, the subject underscoring the picture's fabricatedness, artificiality and rubbery character. For Hartley, Dadaism equalled intellectualism and anti-expressiveness. It was the direct opposite of Stieglitz and his artists. Even so, it was Stieglitz who brought Duchamp and Hartley together, in 1917, when he used one of Hartley's military paintings, *The Warriors* (1913), as a backdrop for his photograph of Duchamp's famous urinal, *Fountain* (1917). Not coincidentally, Hartley and Duchamp both described a fluid sexual identity in their art.[40] Duchamp's female alter ego, Rrose Sélavy, first appeared in 1920, at the exact time that Hartley and Duchamp were most involved. Duchamp's way of playing with his masculinity

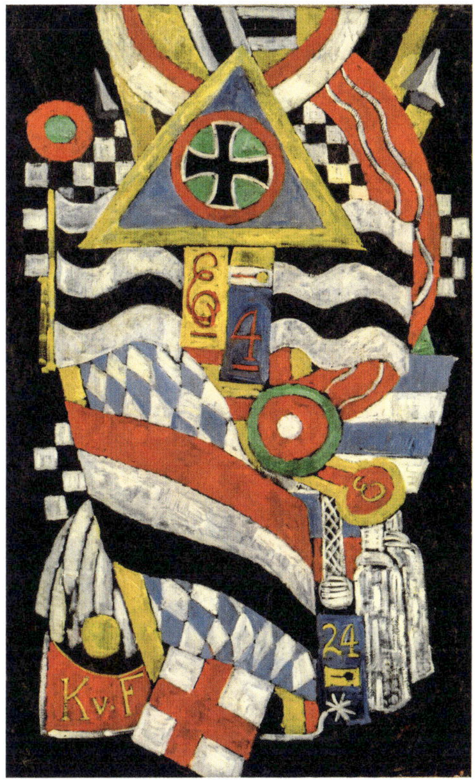

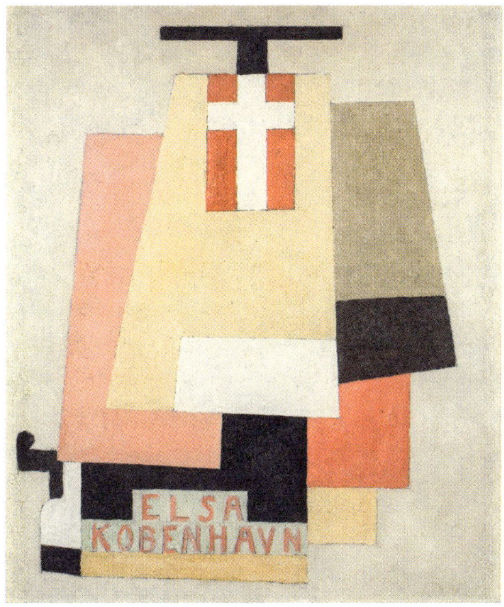

22 *Portrait of a German Officer*, 1914
34 *Elsa Kobenhavn*, 1916

would have appealed to Hartley, and undoubtedly the Société Anonyme was a social safe space for the artist.

Berlin, Provence, Paris and New England, 1921-1931
It was a changed city that met Hartley on his return to Berlin in late 1921. Gone was the Wilhelmine order, the military pomp and splendour that he had so admired during his first visit. However, the permissiveness was, if possible, even more pronounced now than before the war. Leading a freewheeling lifestyle, Hartley "went to immense costume balls where in exotic dress he was worshipped by young men."[41]

Unlike his last stay in Berlin, Hartley's pictures during this period show nothing of the city. His thoughts were still going back to New Mexico. Based on photographs of his works from New Mexico, Hartley painted a great number of landscapes, collectively known as the *New Mexico Recollections*,[42] which are far more dream-like and surreal than the ones he actually painted in New Mexico. *Landscape Fantasy* (1923) (cat. 46) is gloomy and severe, with a forbidding sky and landscape. The clouds and mountains come together like two sets of teeth, rendering the picture claustrophobic and unoccupiable. While the symbolism of the earlier New Mexico landscapes derives from the representation of a present, external world, *Landscape Fantasy* is a projection of an internal world.

Many of Hartley's *New Mexico Recollections* look like they were made of flesh and blood, rather than of stone, soil and sand. Surpassing any of his past efforts in landscape painting,[43] they are suffused with feelings of loss and longing. Marked by loss and longing, they are executed in a palette that evokes the body. Two pastels – *Seated Male Nude* and *Standing Male Nude* (both c. 1923, cats. 117-118, pp. 45, 48) – made in Berlin around the same time as the *New Mexico Recollections*, reinforce the interpretation of Hartley's landscapes in this period as particularly corporeal.[44] Hartley's first actual studies of human figures since an early series of drawings,[45] they are classical life drawings of a young man, exaggerating his physical appearance. Moreover, his genitals are missing (or, at least, obscured) in the drawings, suggesting an idealized and, for the artist, unattainable masculinity, much like the soldier in *Portrait Arrangement No. 2*. Hartley never portrays men as conquests; like his mountains and

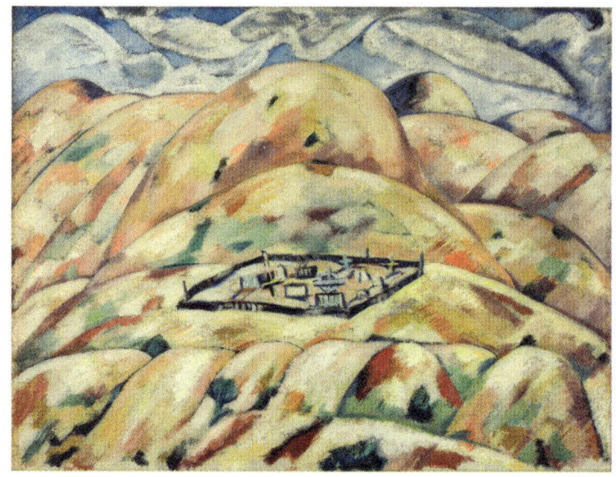

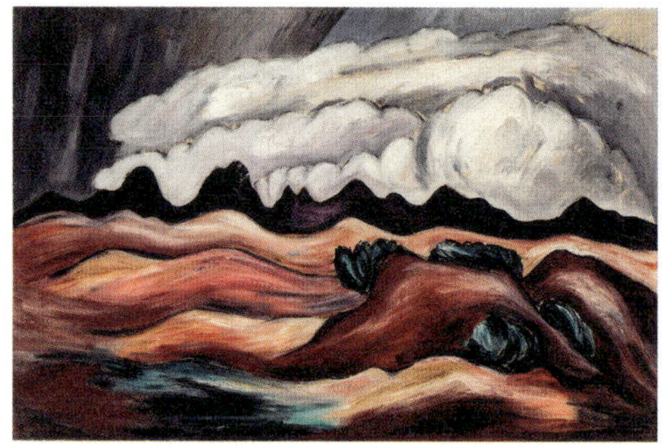

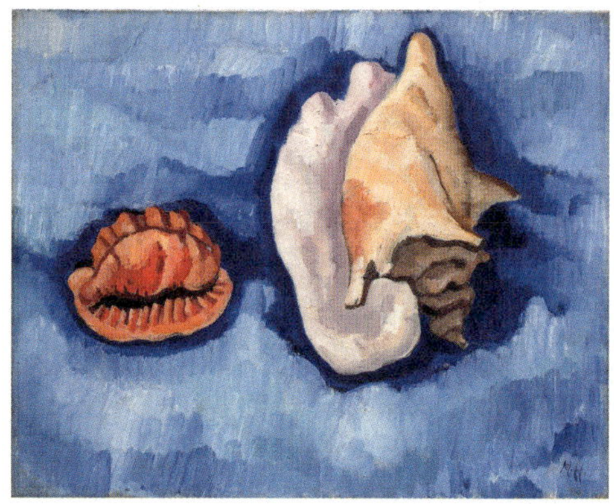

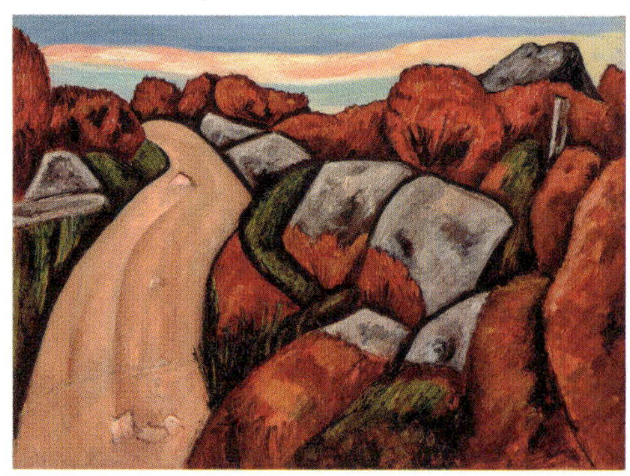

44 *New Mexico No. 2*, 1919
46 *Landscape Fantasy*, 1923
55 *Two Shells*, 1928
60 *Blueberry Highway, Dogtown*, 1931

landscapes, they are impossible to scale and possess. They can only be admired.

In New Mexico, Hartley had tried to imitate the style of Cézanne in a subject of his own choice. In 1927, however, he took on Cézanne's own mountain, Mont Sainte-Victoire, near Aix-en-Provence. *Mont Sainte-Victoire* (1927) (cat. 54, p. 50) is one of a number of paintings Hartley made following his idol's example. But while his procedure is like Cézanne's, the product looks nothing like a Cézanne. The colour scheme of Hartley's painting is wilder and more synthetic than anything his role model ever did – less delicate, more massive and flatter than the many versions Cézanne painted. *Mont Sainte-Victoire* is the first time Hartley actually portrays a mountain, which is represented as a singular object, its silhouette rendered iconic. He subsequently repeats this device with several other mountains. Perhaps, in fact, Hartley's attempt at imitating Cézanne was more of an exorcism. Trying to paint Cézanne out of his system, he paved the way for a more personal painting style in the years to come.[46]

In art history, the years that Hartley spent in Europe in the 1920s have often been called "a lost decade."[47] I would argue, however, that, in several respects, a key development occurs in Hartley's painting during this period. This is particularly evident in a series of still lifes made in Paris in 1928 and 1929.[48] *Two Shells* (cat. 55) and *Still Life No. 4* (cat. 57, p. 53), depicting seashells that Hartley had brought over from Paris to Maine,[49] are landmarks in the artist's still-life production. Overtly experimental, *Two Shells* shows its subjects inhabiting an indefinable space, appearing to be pressed against the front of the canvas. These paintings foreshadow Hartley's male portraits, which are often depicted in a similar monochromatic space. *Still Life No. 4* even looks corporeal in its predominantly flesh-coloured tones.

After returning to America in 1930, Hartley painted his first pictures of New England since the 1910s.[50] This period is important because it marks the beginning of his long journey back to Maine. In New Hampshire, his first subject, he painted works like *Landscape No. 35 (Beaver Lake, Lost River Region)* (1930) (cat. 59, p. 55). His decision to paint there was motivated in part by yet another lukewarm reception of his European pictures on the New York art scene, and in part because "a strong nationalistic pride had seized the country at large and the avant-garde artistic community in particular."[51]

As for so many other American artists, landscapes were a catalyst for Hartley.[52] He mirrored himself in landscapes, and the clarity of this mirroring was essential to his paintings' vitality. One of the landscapes with which Hartley strongly identified, Dogtown Common near Gloucester on Cape Ann, Massachusetts, is strewn with huge boulders, like a naturally occurring Stonehenge. Hartley described the landscape as "majestically lonely, as if nature had at last formed one spot where she can live for herself alone."[53] In his autobiography, he remarked almost contemptuously that most other painters preferred the picturesque harbour in Gloucester proper.[54] In that regard, Dogtown lived up to Hartley's self-image as an original artist who did not kowtow to popular taste. Less than a year before his death, Hartley wrote to his niece Norma Berger, " I am not a 'book of the month' artist, and I do not paint pretty pictures."[55] This statement and his identification with the Dogtown landscape can be seen to reflect his position as a sexual outsider, for whom beauty took other forms. Gloucester Harbor was the conventional, normative choice for those who paint "pretty pictures," in light of which Dogtown Common can be seen as Other. Hartley cultivates the Otherness of the landscapes to an extent that his subjects, including those of the paintings *Blueberry Highway, Dogtown* and *Altar Boulder, Dogtown* (both 1931) (cats. 60-61, pp. 56-57), end up looking plastic and unnatural or – as the first great Hartley connoisseur, Elisabeth McCausland (1899-1965), described the series – "as if confected for stage sets."[56]

Mexico, Bavaria and Bermuda, 1932-1935

In order to travel, Hartley throughout his life relied on the kindness of others. In 1931, he received a Guggenheim grant enabling a one-year stay abroad. The following year, he travelled to Mexico, where he had a chance to study the work of leading Mexican artists. At the time, painters like Diego Rivera (1886-1957), David Alfaro Siqueiros (1896-1974) and José Clemente Orozco (1883-1949)[57] were making frescoes depicting historical events of importance to the Mexican people. Hartley did not care for Mexico, but his stay there proved significant nonetheless. Hartley's late male figures have obvious parallels to heroic depictions of the Mexican people by artists like Siqueiros, whose figures, like Hartley's, tend to be earthy and a bit awkward. Furthermore, some of Hartley's impetus for creating his own mythology in and around Maine originated in Mexico.

Inspired by Mexican history painting, Hartley's works from Mexico illustrate both history and mysticism. Rereading mystics like Richard Rolle (c. 1300-1349) and Jakob Böhme, Hartley painted pictures, especially landscapes, featuring mystical symbols like the octagram. *Morgenrot* (1932) (cat. 64), specifically referencing Böhme's *Morgenröte im Aufgang* (1612), shows six golden spheres floating behind a hand rising like the sun, with a seventh sphere on its wrist.[58] Other works, like *Tollan, Aztec Legend* (1933) (cat. 66, p. 60), were based on the mythology embedded in the Mexican landscape. The Mexican pictures remind us of Hartley's continued interest in mysticism and spirituality combined with indigenous cultures, folk art and primitivism.

All along, Germany remained in Hartley's thoughts. That much was clear in 1933, the landmark year of Adolf Hitler's (1889-1945) rise to power, when Hartley made his final trip there – specifically, to the Bavarian Alps, at a time when artists and intellectuals were leaving Germany. Hartley was attracted to Hitler's new regime and even expressed a desire to meet the Fuhrer.[59] This fascination was, at least in part, born of a dream of seeing resurrected the glorious Germany, the Wilhelmine Empire he had been longing for since he first visited the country. Although Hartley later distanced himself from the Third Reich, his initial interest cannot be dismissed as mere naive nostalgia.[60] All the same, his works from Bavaria show no clear traces of the crucial period in world history in which they were painted.

Hartley did a series of pictures of the Bavarian Alps. Several of them, including *Bavarian Alps, Garmisch-Partenkirchen* (1933-1934) (cat. 69, p. 64), have a cathedral-like appearance, an effect underscored by the vertical board.[61] Tellingly, Hartley described his Alpine paintings as portraits. This idea is even more pronounced in his late works from Maine, which display "a virtual interchangeability of human ... and landscape images."[62]

In 1935, a year after returning from Bavaria, Hartley made his last real trip abroad, spending the summer in Bermuda.[63] *Red Flowers and Sailboat*[64] (cat. 72) is a view out of a window that is almost completely obstructed by a vase of flowers.[65] The demonstrative way in which Hartley cuts himself off from the outside world by filling the picture plane with flowers lends the painting an autobiographical air. We might here recall Hartley's statement about picturesque Gloucester Harbor as representing a world he could not belong to even if he wanted to. The painting describes the feeling of distance between Hartley and the world around him, which is viewed voyeuristically. The image of the painter as observer is a basic one, of course, but the painting's subject can also be seen as expressing an insurmountable distance in terms of Hartley's sexual identity, complicating the sense of belonging and reinforcing the feeling of isolation.

Nova Scotia and Maine, 1935-1943

The last years of Hartley's artistic life were marked by another tragedy. In his 1940 poem, "Fishermen's Last Supper," he writes,

For wine, they drank the ocean –
for bread, they ate their own despairs;
counsel from the moon was theirs
for the foolish contention.

Murder is not a pretty thing
yet seas do raucous everything
to make it pretty –
for the foolish or the brave,
a way seas have.[66]

In Nova Scotia, Hartley stayed twice, in 1935 and 1936, with the Masons, a family of fishermen, consisting of the parents, a daughter and two grown sons, Alty and Donny. During Hartley's second stay, the two young men and a cousin died on their way home from a night on the town. Before the accident, Hartley's restlessness had finally calmed down with the Mason family. As he put it, he had been a de facto orphan since the age of eight when his mother died: "a lone left thing to make its way out for all time after that by itself."[67] The artist's relationship to the two sons was brotherly but also fuelled by sexual attraction. In a letter to a friend, Hartley wrote, "one must love what one loves to the end & so I shall love these boys as long as I have memory of them ... and the biggest one [Alty] wanted to build a little shack with me & live in it with me."[68]

In the wake of the boys' death, Hartley painted a number of very gloomy pictures, notably the Pinkham Ryder-inspired *Northern Seascape, Off the Banks* (1936-1937) (cat. 76, p. 86), with its forbidding and ferocious ocean and cliffs. A triangle in the sky recalls the one from *Portrait of a German Officer*, where Hartley was alluding to the trinity of Rönnebeck, von Freyburg and himself. In the Mason brothers, Hartley saw a parallel to his youthful delights in Berlin – a trinity of Whitmanesque comrades.

It was only after he had left Nova Scotia for Maine that Hartley started painting actual portraits of the family, situating them within a Christian iconography. But not because he was religious. Rather, Hartley used the proverbial idiom to say that this family, to his mind, was *like* the holy family. They had come to represent a personal and artistic ideal. *Fishermen's Last Supper* (1940-1941) (cat. 98) shows the family enacting the last supper, with the brothers at the far left and right. The whole painting lists to the left, as if the family were on a capsizing ship. The picture is one of impending doom. Once Hartley had begun painting figures by portraying the Mason family, he never stopped.

It seems obvious to view Hartley's late figure paintings through the lens of coming out. As described in this introduction, the artist's work is full of more or less subtle references to bodies, corporeality and his gay identity. Three paintings of the young *Madawaska – Acadian* (all 1940) (cat. 91-93, pp. 97, 98, 101) all portray the same local boxer sporting an impressive beefcake physique.[69] The paintings show Hartley's heritage from European modernism, in particular Cézanne's rigid figures, which are often mentioned in this context. Picasso, whose *Self-Portrait with Palette* (1906) also drew on Cézanne, is another obvious influence. A related work by Hartley, *Finnish-Yankee-Sauna* (1938-1939) (cat. 83, p. 94), shows similar figures derived from European modernism, whose "physical closeness ... might seem to go beyond the decorum of heterosexual male bonding."[70] This is also evident in *Canuck-Yankee Lumberjack at Old Orchard Beach, Maine* (1940-1941) (cat. 96, p. 105) and *On the Beach* (1940, p. 104). In the latter, Hartley paints the men as boulders with waves crashing against them, while

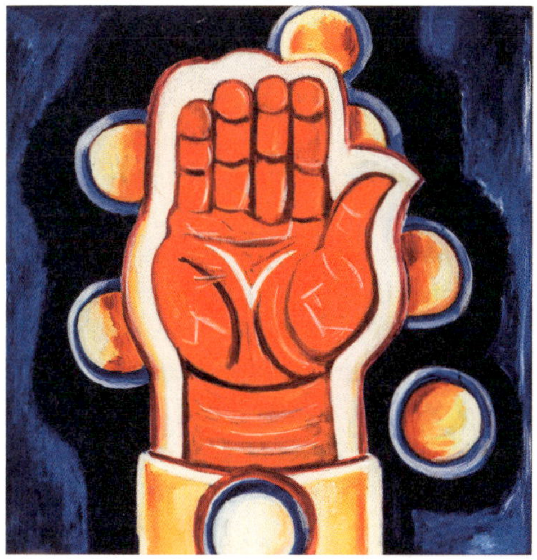

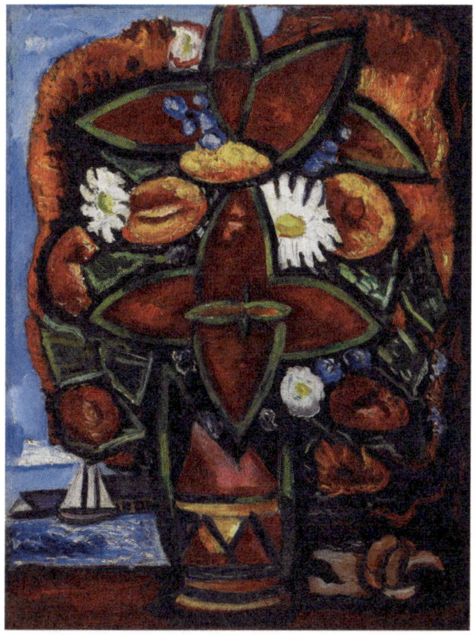

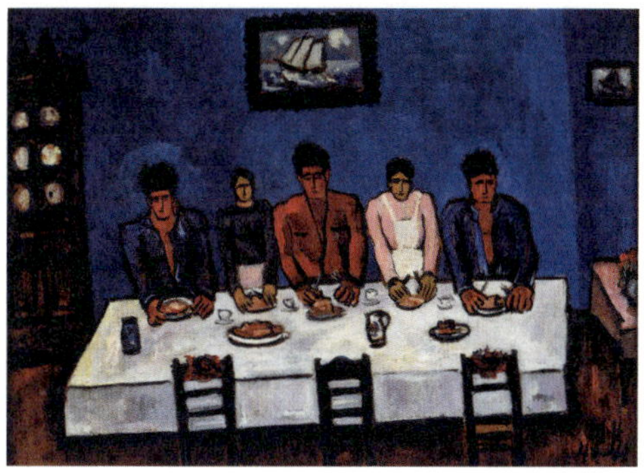

64 *Morgenrot*, 1932
72 *Red Flowers and Sailboat*, c. 1935-1936
98 *Fishermen's Last Supper, Nova Scotia*, 1940-1941

the female figure, as mentioned, is small and insignificant. What all these works have in common is unconditionally casting the viewer and the painter in the role of voyeur. There is still no suggestion that these men were conquests.

Hartley's frank depictions of male bodies in the last years of his life came after decades of veiled allusions to his sexuality. This, moreover, at a time of heightened surveillance and criminalization of homosexuals in America.[71] Indeed, Hartley took pains to paper over or tone down the homosexual content. As several scholars have noted, Hartley, in connection with an exhibition of these pictures, declared that they were intended for gymnasiums. This would place them in a context where their intense idolization of the male body would seem normal. Likewise, the men, and the situations in which Hartley portrayed them, are clearly alibis. They appear in places where men can be unclothed – a sauna and the beach, where men are expected to be nude together, while it is also not unusual for a boxer to be nearly undressed.[72]

The standard narrative of Hartley's late return to Maine is that of a prodigal son finding himself, once back in his natural surroundings. He even proclaimed that he wanted to be "the painter from Maine." Indeed, apart from the male figures, Hartley's paintings from Maine are mainly landscapes of rivers, Mount Katahdin, woods and coastlines. But the paintings speak of more than Maine. Painting the sea also represented the painterly gesture itself. Witness *Evening Storm, Schoodic, Maine No. 2* (1942) (cat. 106), which anticipates the Abstract Expressionist crystallization of the phenomenon. Hartley was from Maine, of course, but earlier in life he told Stieglitz, "I come as near being a man of no land as anyone I know, spiritually speaking."[73] Positioning himself as "the painter from Maine" was in large part a marketing stunt, as several art historians have noted.[74] Hartley, so to speak, gave the American art public what it wanted, which brought him some success late in life. However, as his portrayals of the local landscape and the people show, he was a newcomer, whose outlook and visual vocabulary were shaped by a lifetime of experiences in Europe and Mexico, as well as in other parts of America, even if the subjects he painted in his last years were plainly American. Hartley's paintings from Maine can be likened to Paul Gauguin's (1848-1904) depictions of landscapes

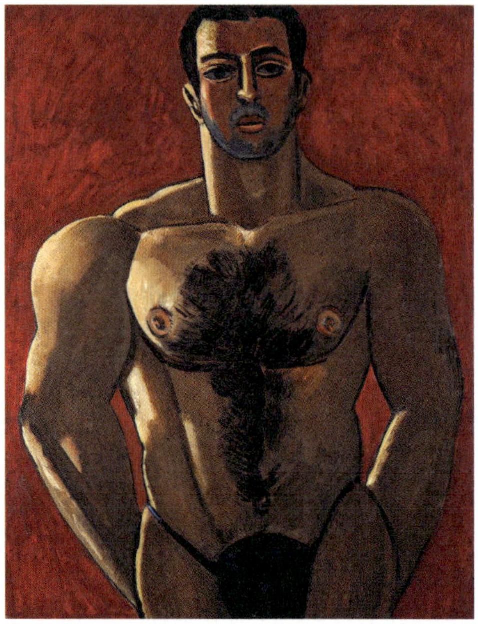

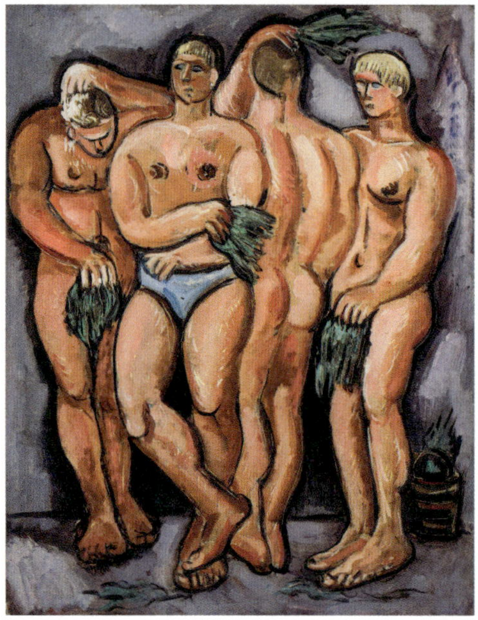

91 *Madawaska – Acadian Light-Heavy*, 1940
83 *Finnish-Yankee-Sauna*, 1938-1939

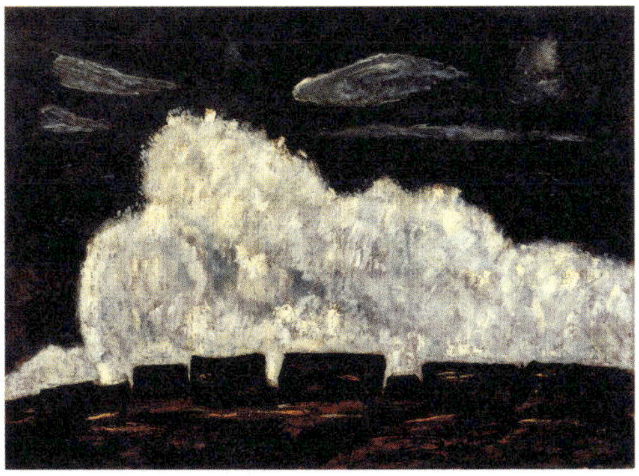

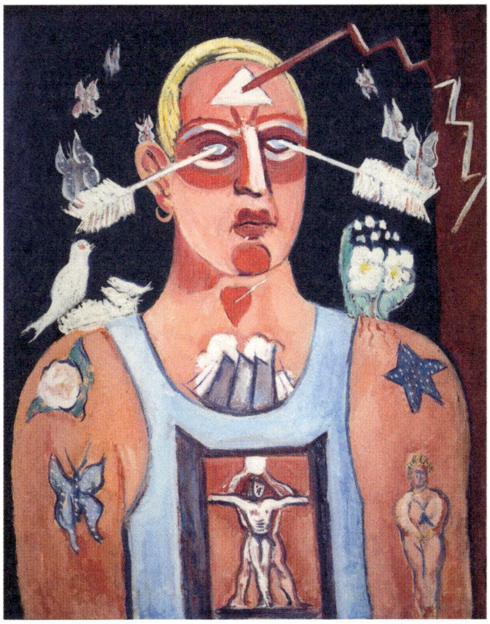

and indigenous people in Tahiti. There is something archaic, exotic and attractive yet unapproachable about Hartley's male figures that is not unlike Gauguin's many paintings of indigenous women – he was a newcomer observing the locals. Perhaps it is more to the point to say that Hartley's lifelong interest in indigenous cultures and primitivism found a natural language in the Maine he discovered upon his return.

Around the same time that Hartley painted his first portraits of the Mason family, he also made his first real self-portrait since his youth. *Sustained Comedy* (1939) (cat. 85) depicts the artist as an idealized martyr, in the figure of a young, muscular sailor, body emblazoned with tattoos referring variously to his life history and work, nature, personal tragedy, etc. Like a clown or an Indian, he wears a mask or makeup – he is in disguise. His blue eyes are pierced through with arrows, a thinly veiled reference to St. Sebastian, "who has traditionally served in the gay subculture as a kind of patron saint of homosexuality."[75] In a sense, the painting serves as a kind of artistic last will and testament, neatly tying a bow on his work and unpacking it for us. It links a number of Hartley's motifs to himself and his journey, which culminated here. Nature is even seen to grow on a potent, sexualized body once hidden away in flowers, hills and trees. Located on his neck, his heart is pierced through, as well, as if grief and love were continually overwhelming him.

Most canonized artists are known for a particular style. This is often seen as artistic conviction – steeliness and confidence about a project's validity. That road was never open to Hartley. He struggled with life, so he struggled with painting. The two were interdependent. His eclectic oeuvre is shot through by a symbolist, spiritual vein that elevates earthly life, as seen from his unique perspective. In a late poem, "To the Nameless One" (c. 1940-1943), he writes,

> I want nothing in the way of artificial
> heavens –
> The earth is all I know of wonder.[76]

106 *Evening Storm, Schoodic, Maine No. 2*, 1942
85 *Sustained Comedy*, 1939

Mathias Ussing Seeberg is a curator at Louisiana Museum of Modern Art, Denmark, where he has curated exhibitions like *William Kentridge: Thick Time*, *Being There* and the Marsden Hartley exhibition.

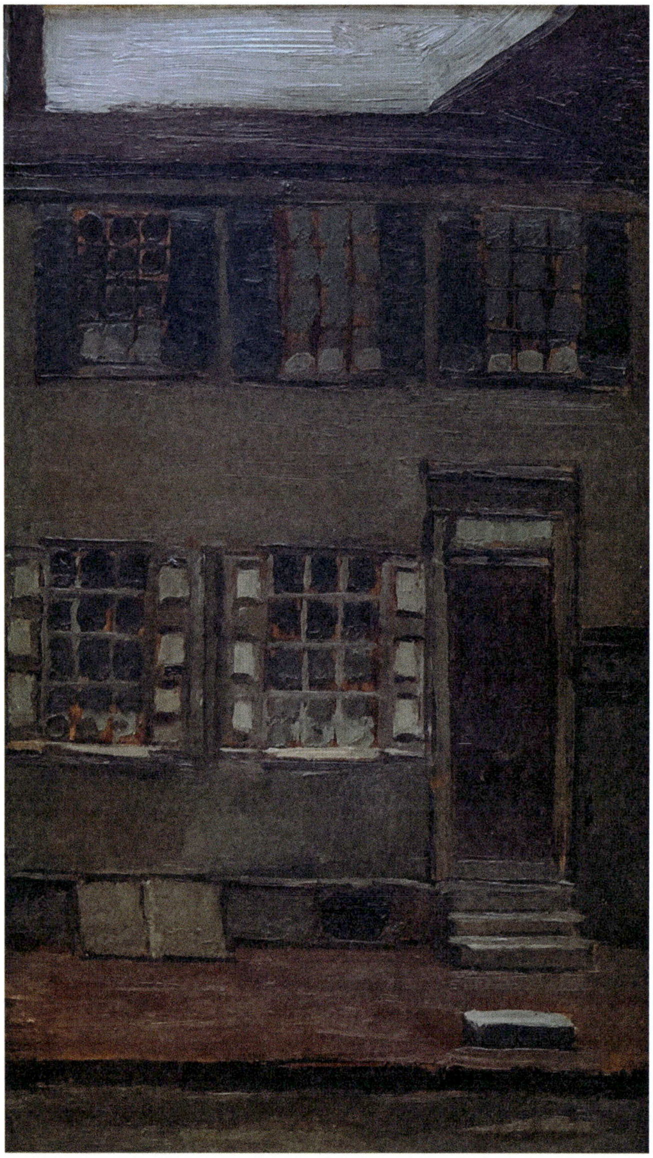

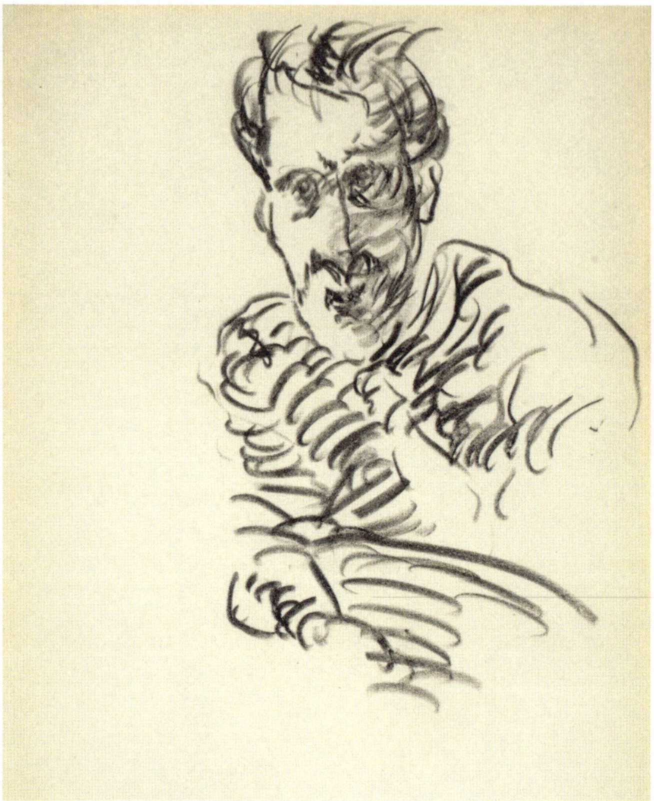

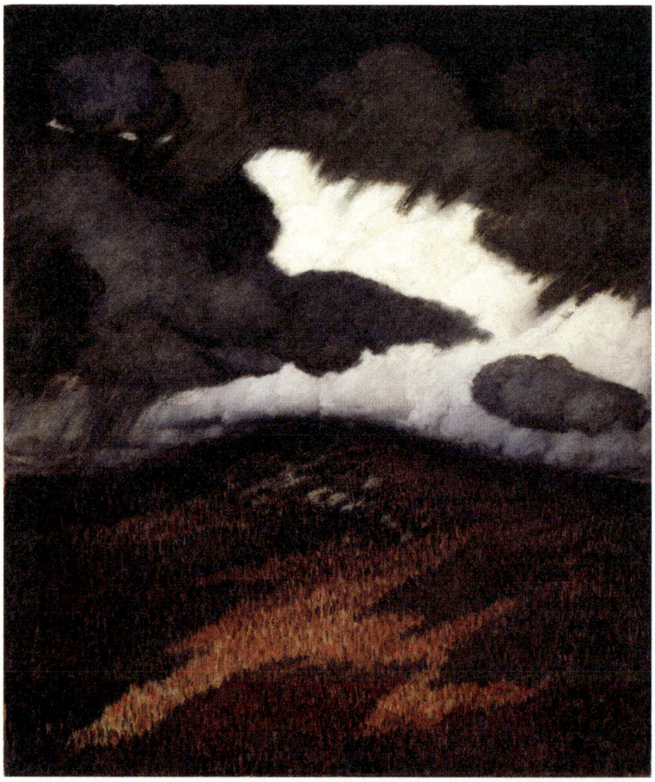

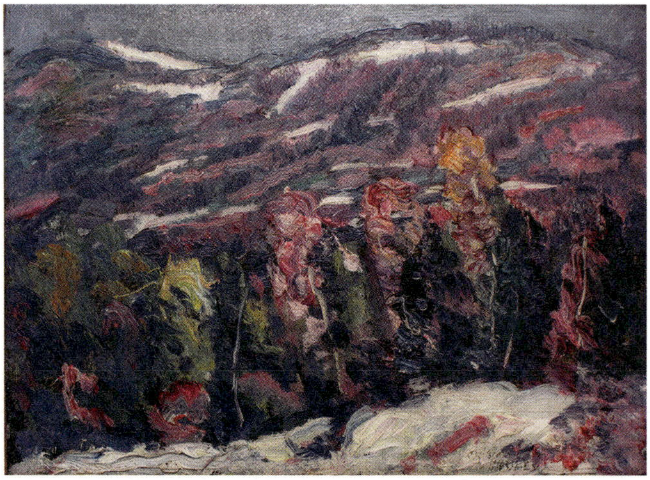

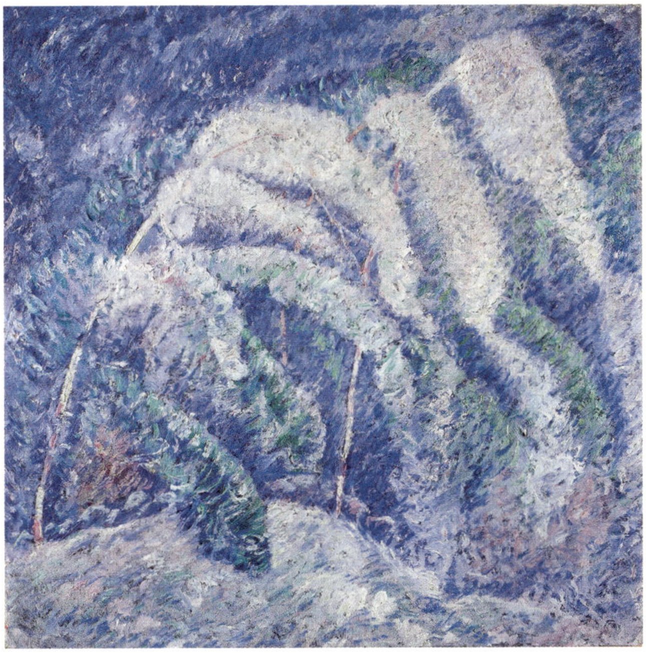

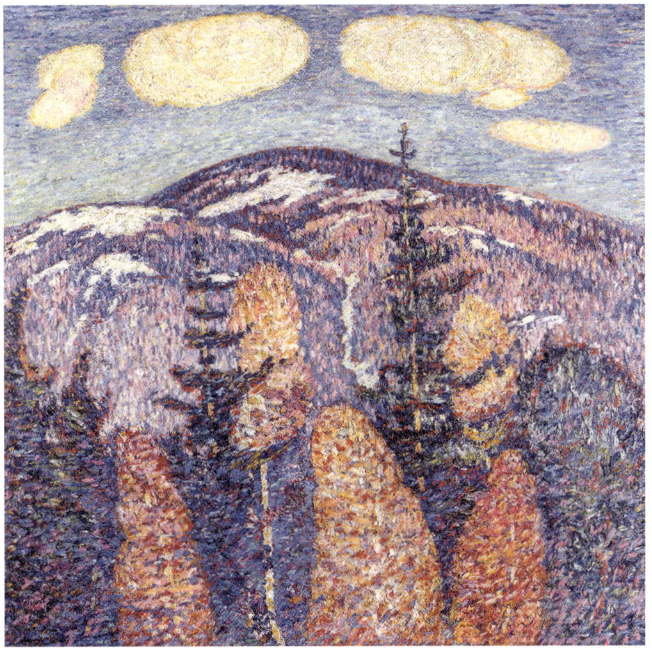

1 Walt Whitman's House, c. 1905
114 Self-Portrait, 1908

4 Song of Winter, 1908
2 Storm Clouds, Maine, 1906-1907

3 Maine Snowstorm, 1908
5 Cosmos, 1908-1909

6 Landscape No. 36, 1908-1909
7 Landscape No. 20, 1909

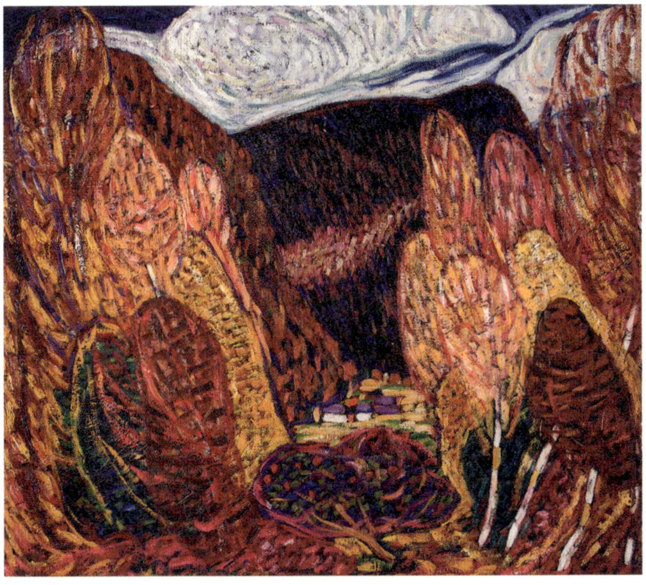

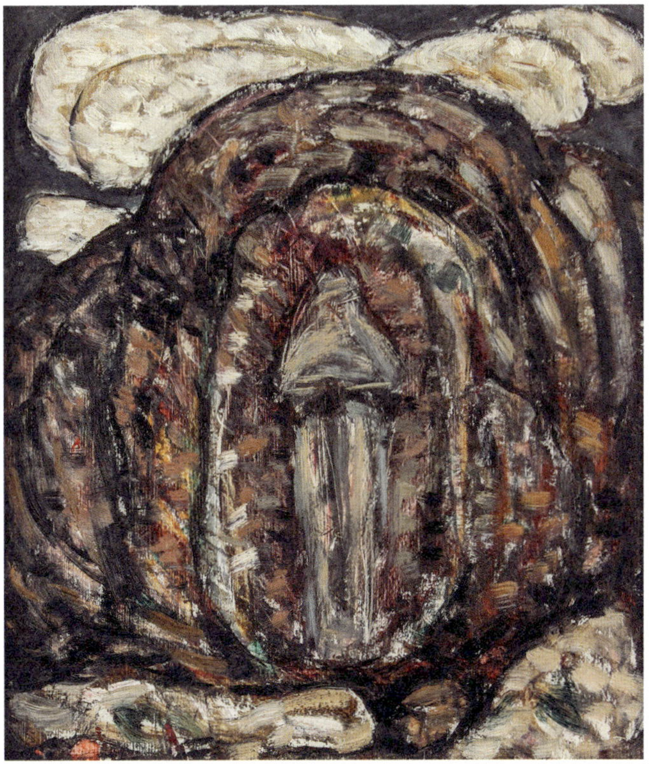

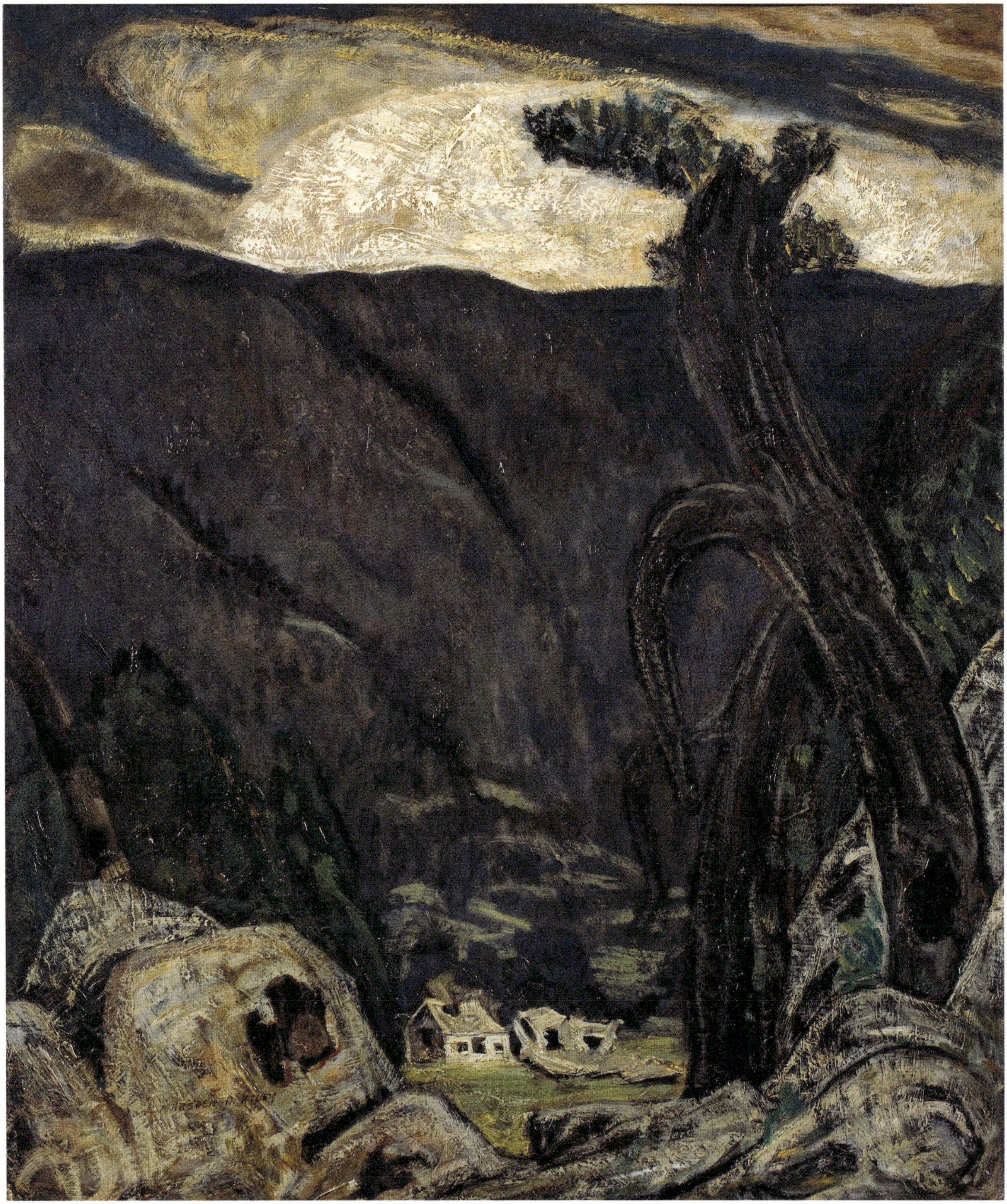

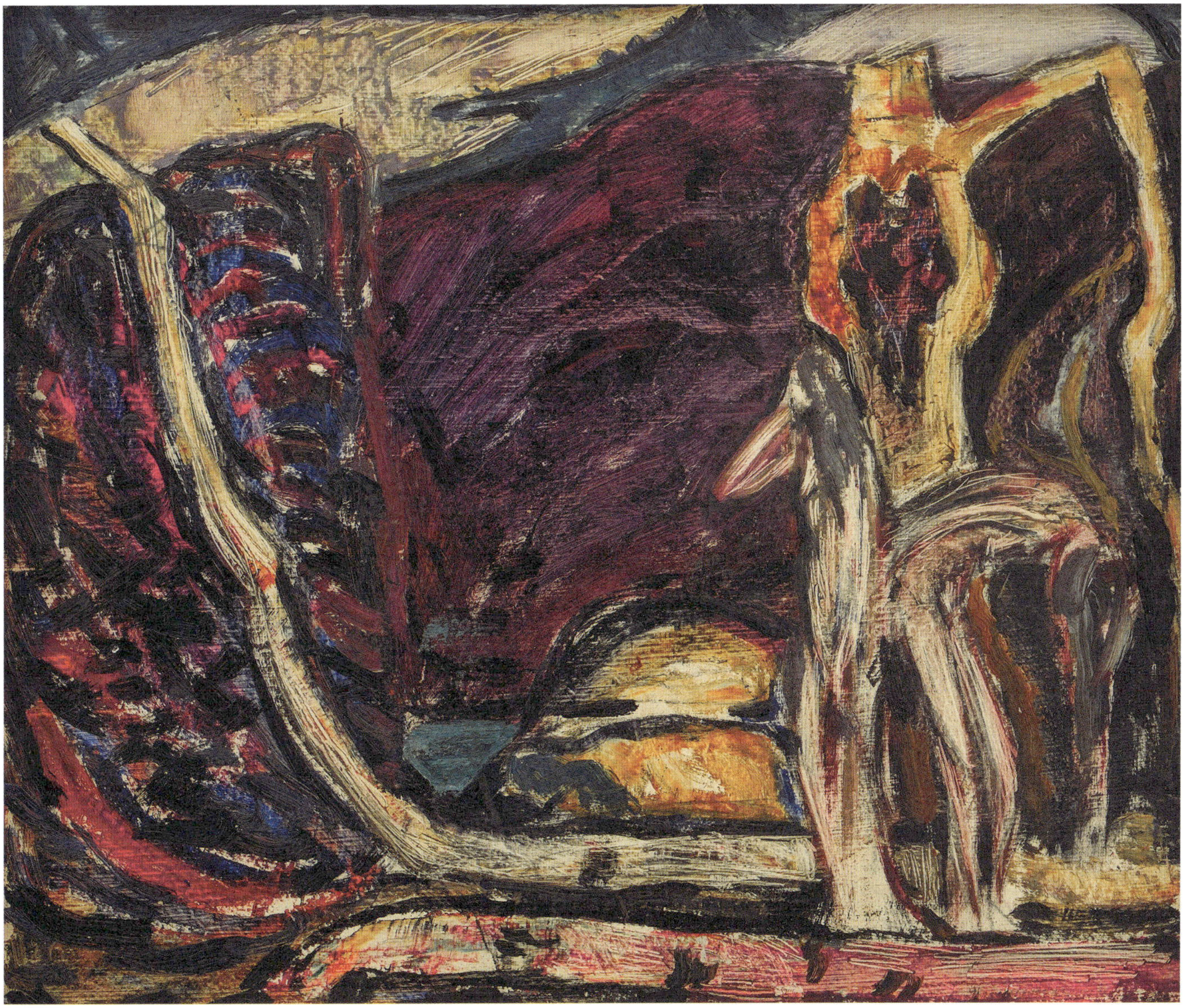

8 Deserted Farm, 1909
9 Landscape No. 24, 1909-1910

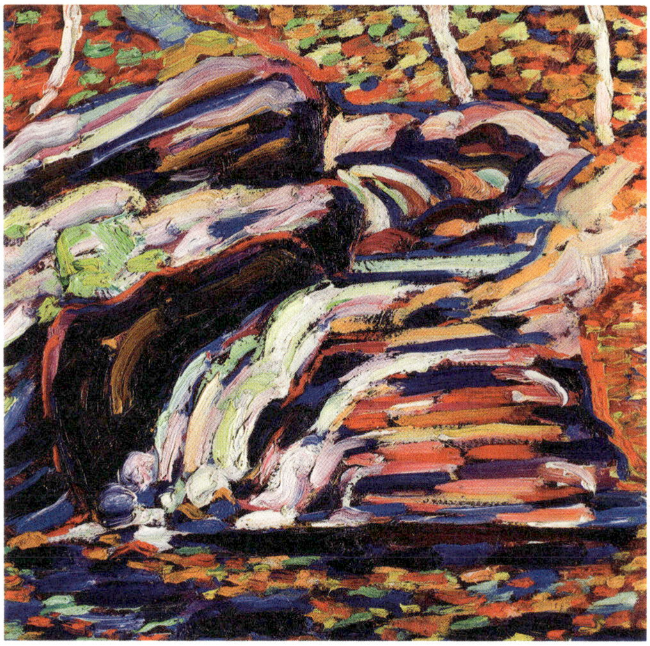

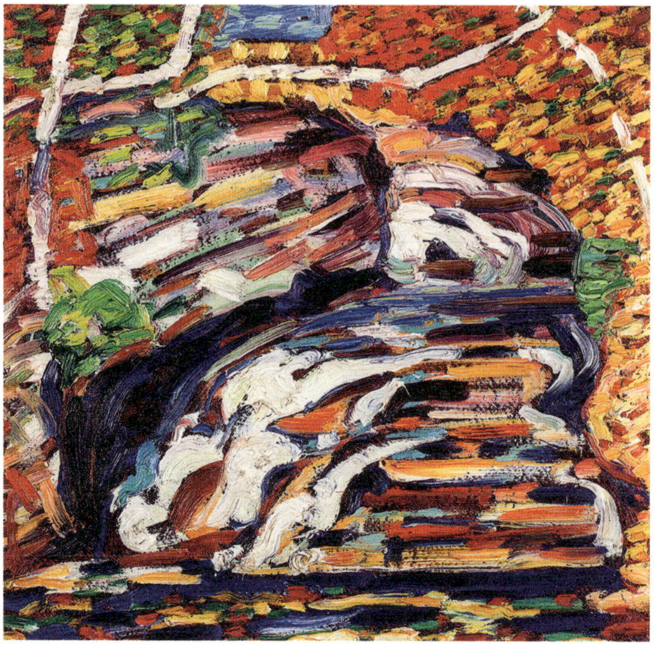

10 Waterfall, 1910
11 Autumn Cascade, 1910

12 Abstraction, 1911
13 Pears, 1911

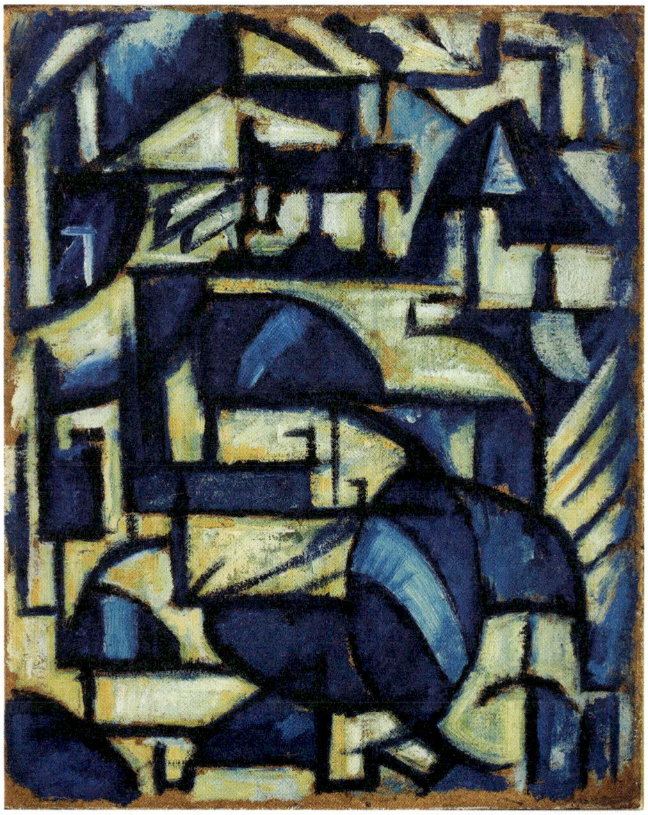

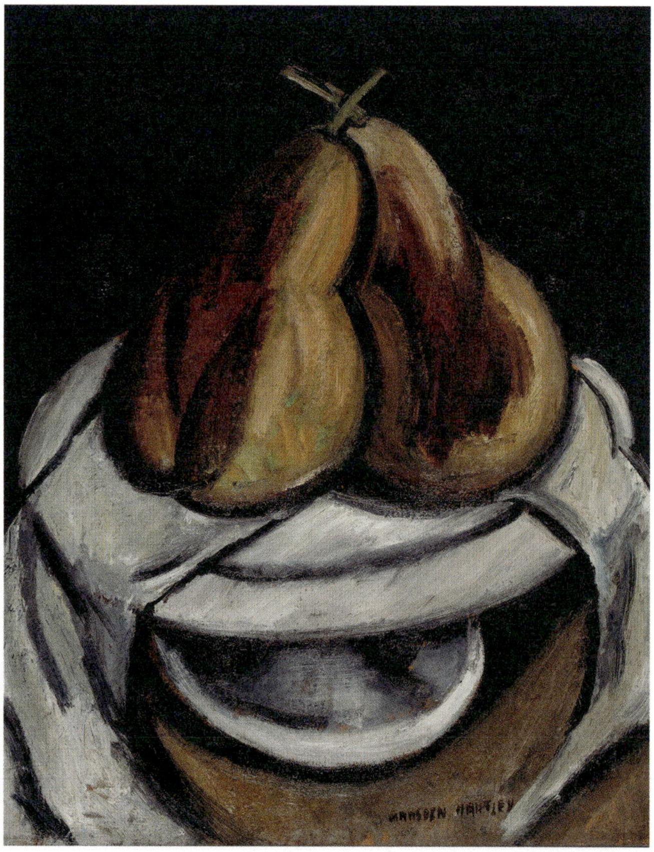

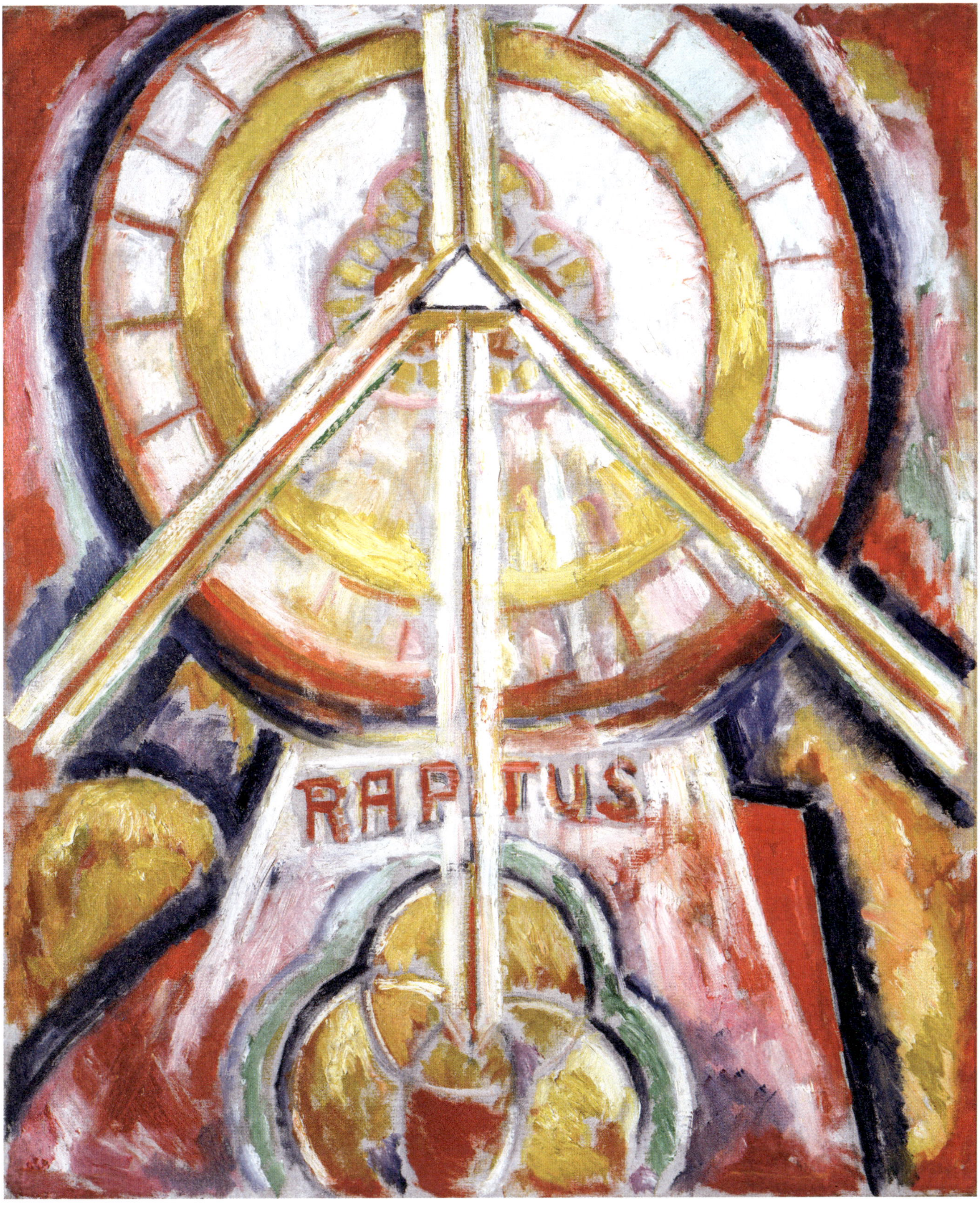

19 Raptus, c. 1913

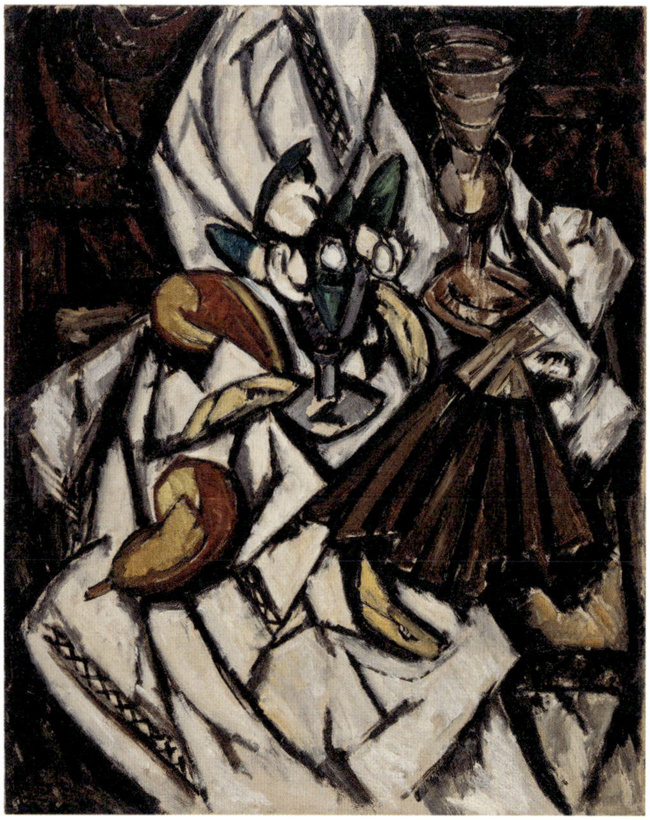

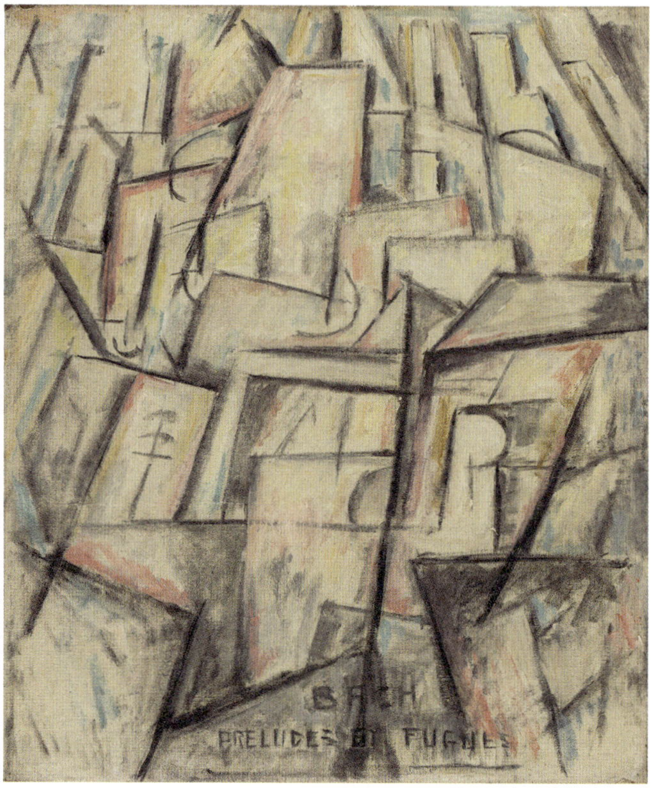
BACH
PRELUDES ET FUGUES

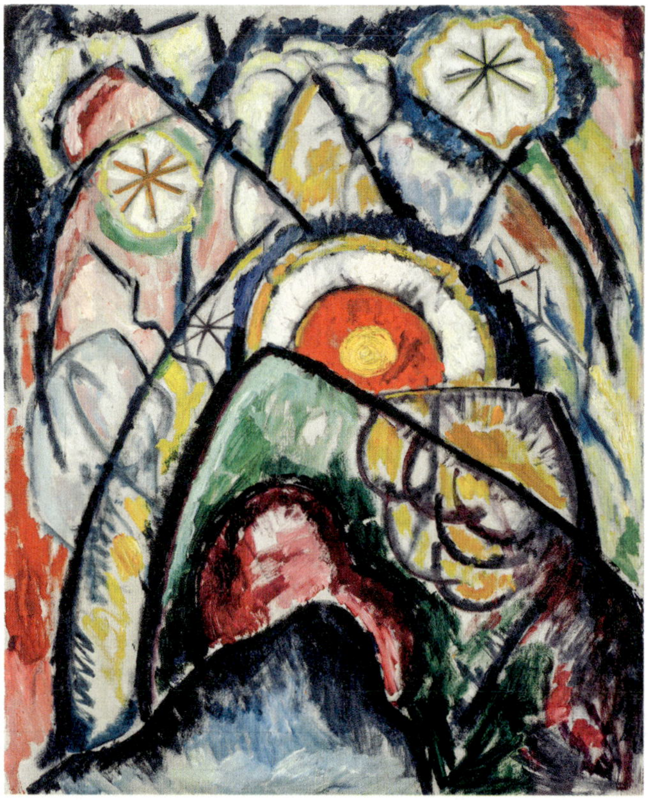

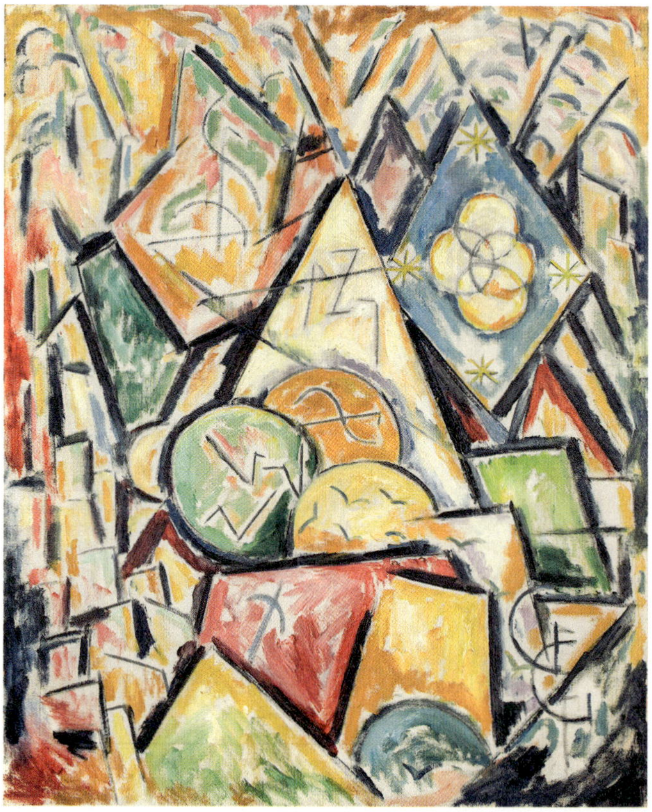

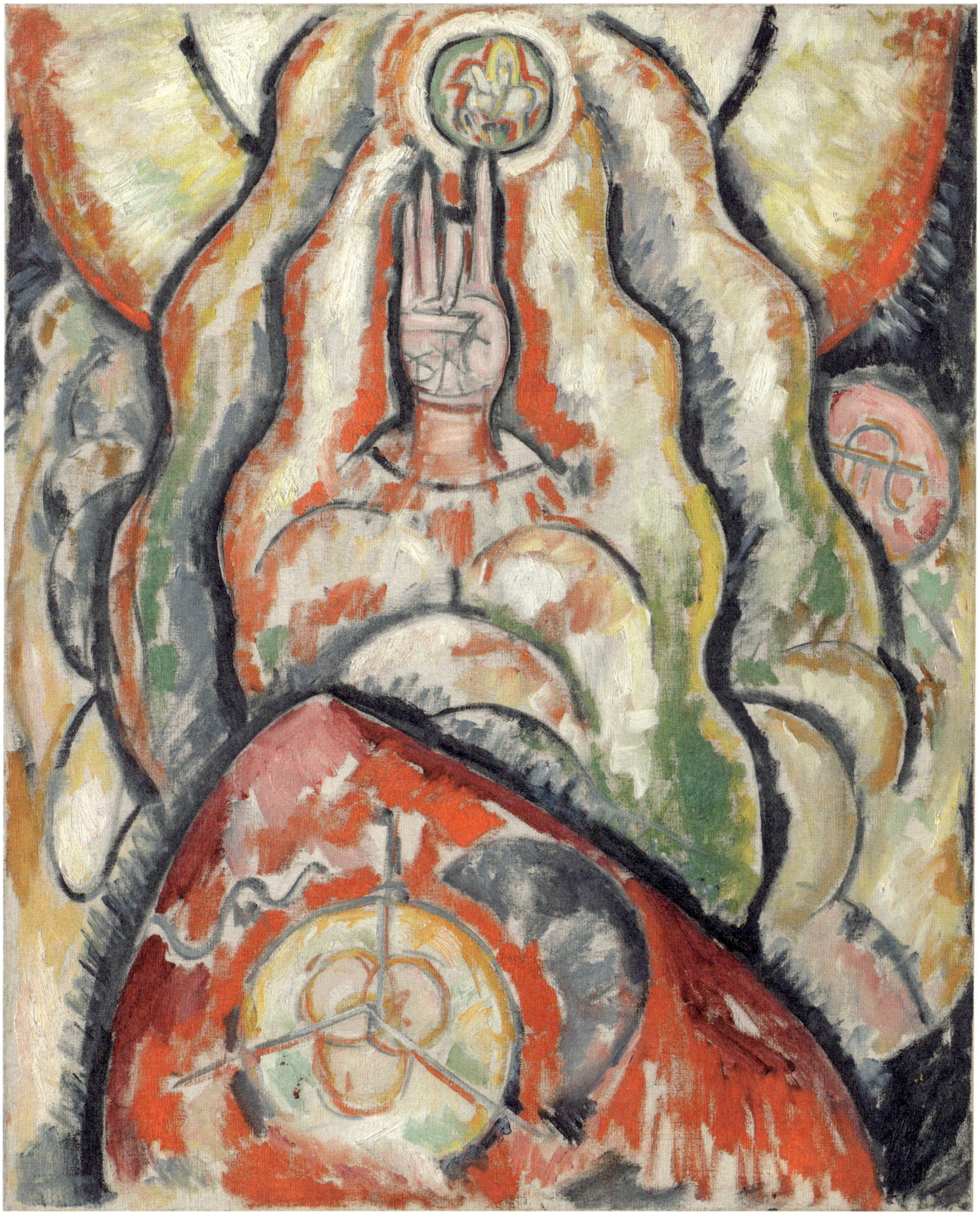

14 Still Life with Fan, 1912
15 Musical Theme No. 2 (Bach Preludes et Fugues), 1912

17 Painting Number One, 1913
18 Painting No. 2, 1913

16 Portrait Arrangement No. 2, 1912-1913

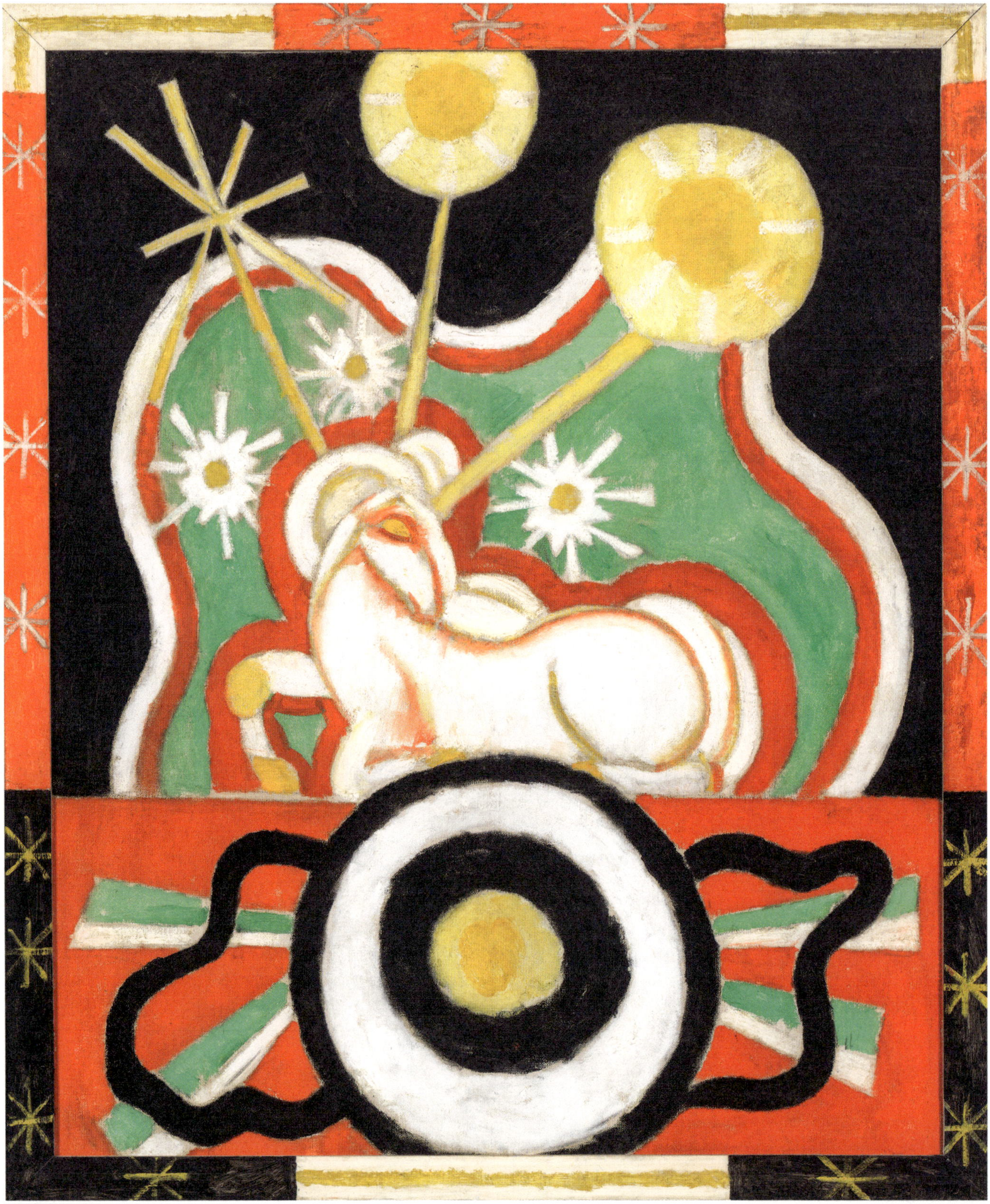

20 Forms Abstracted, 1914
31 Schiff, 1915

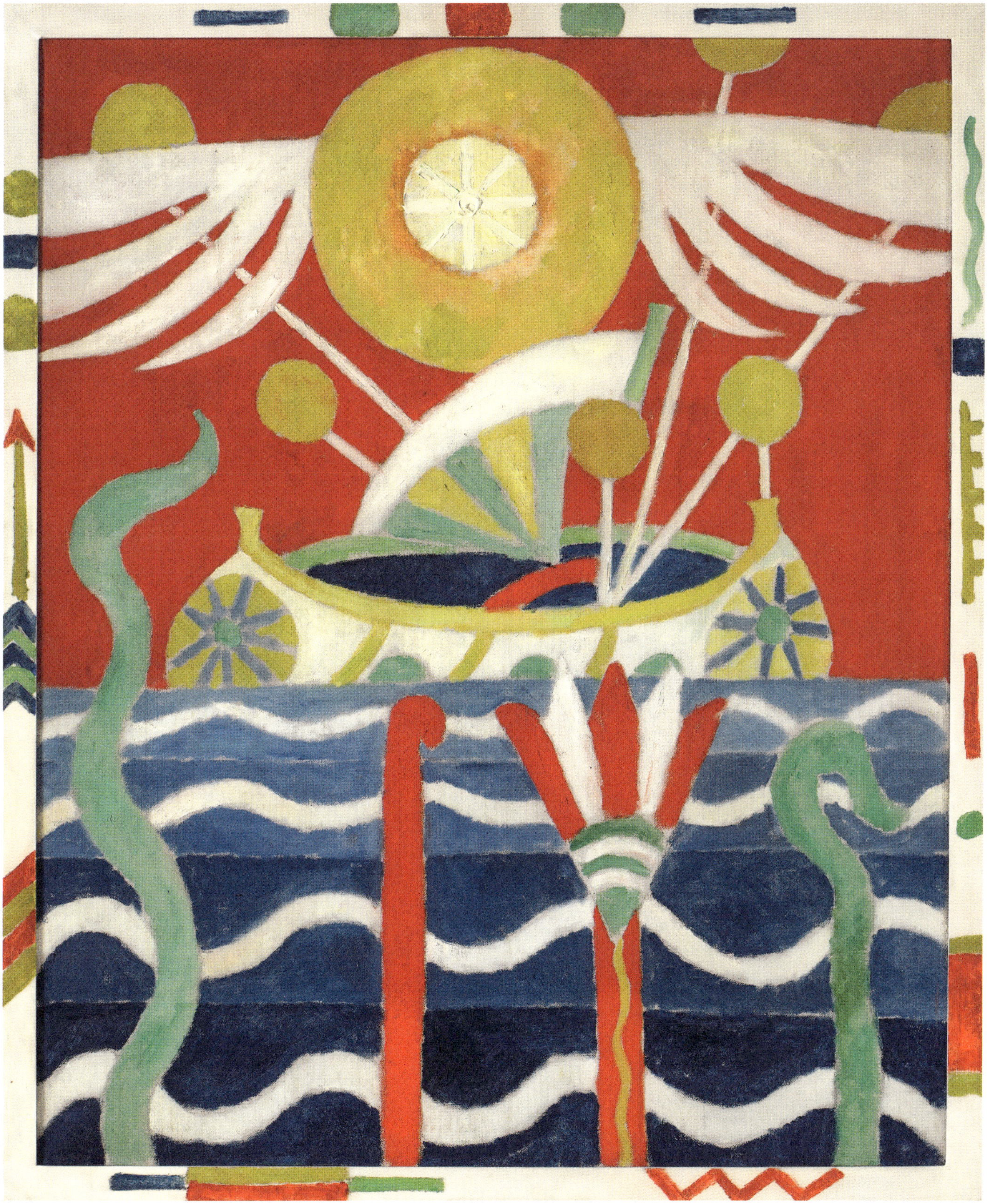

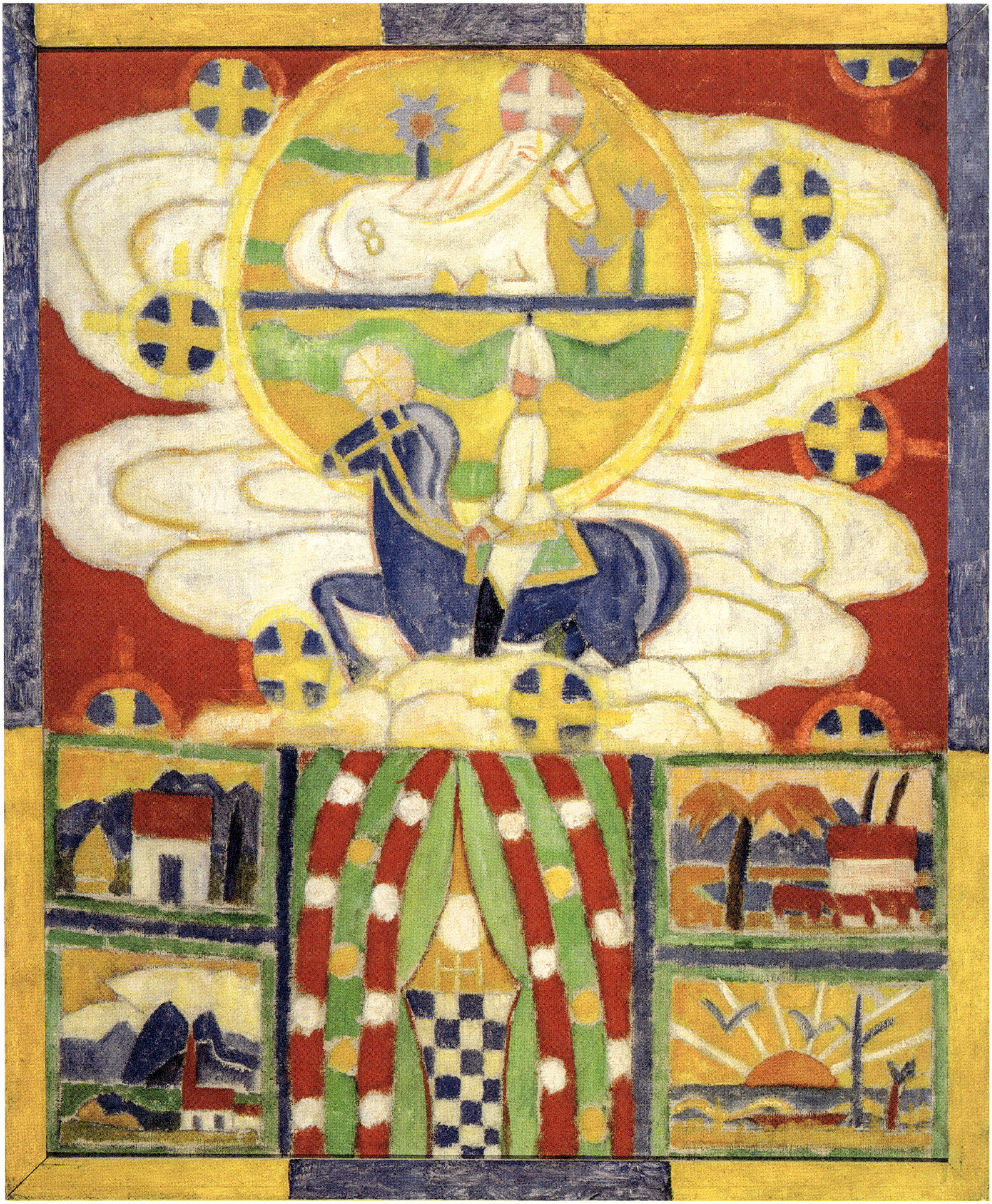

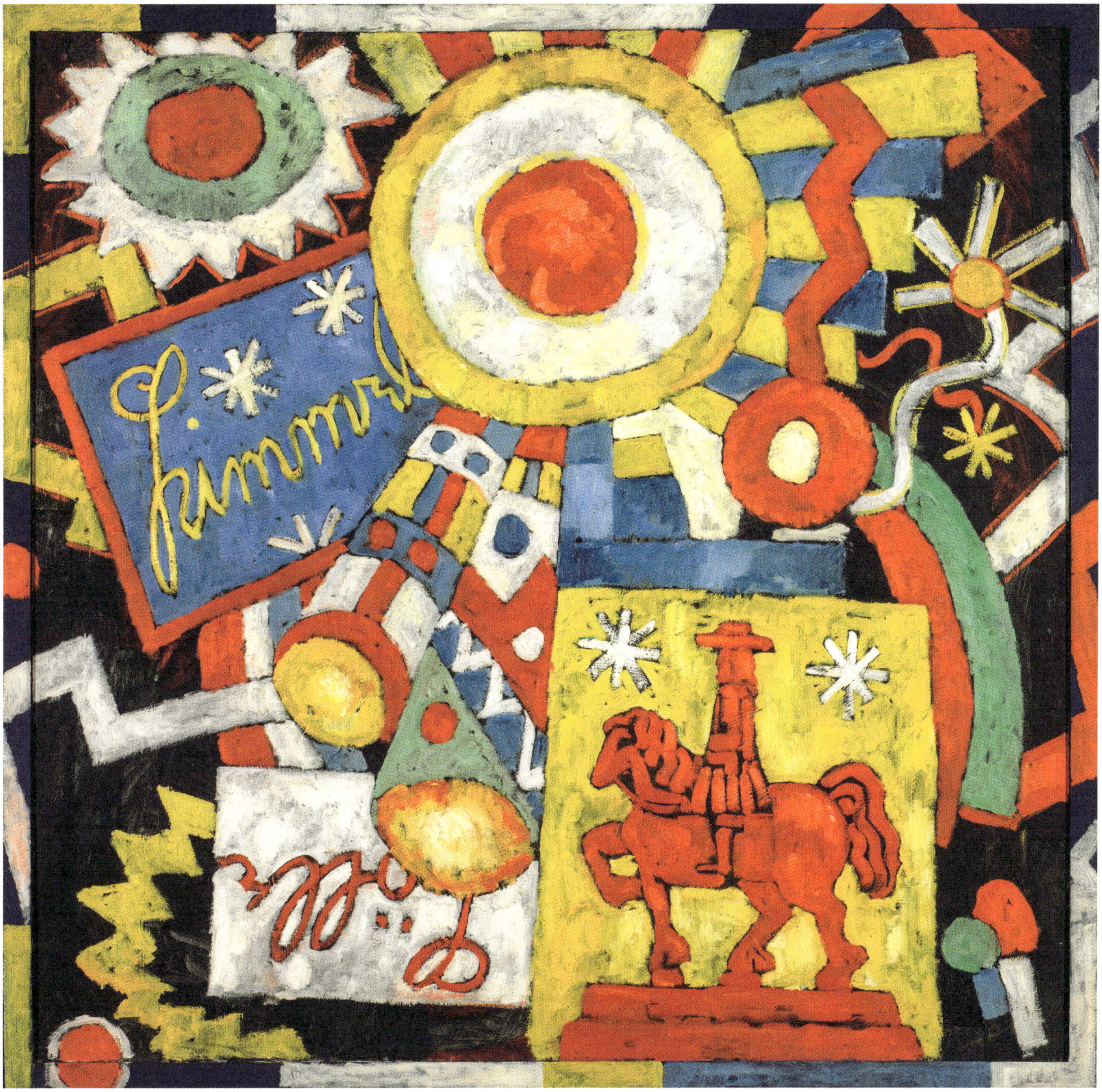

21 Berlin Ante War, 1914
29 Himmel, 1914-1915

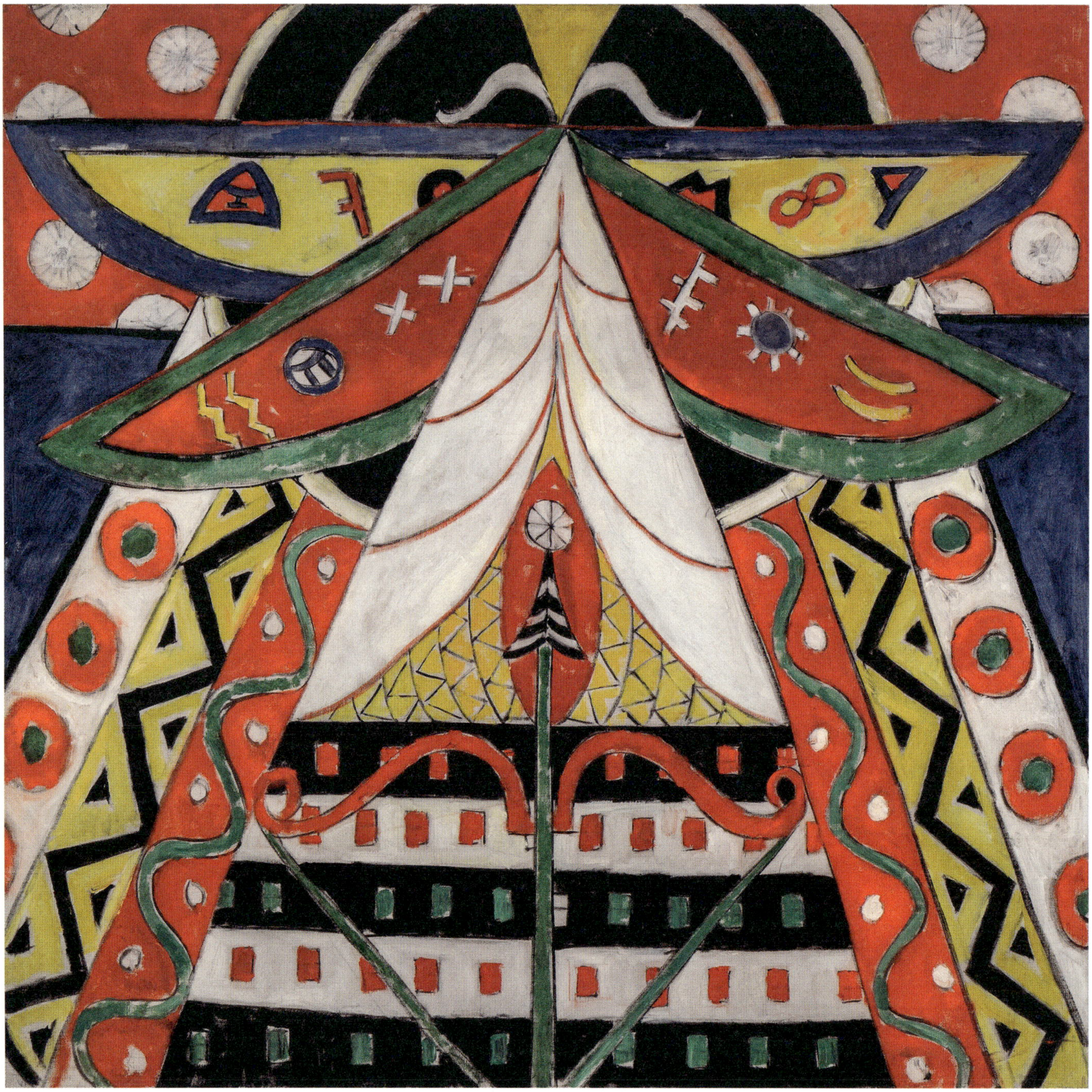

25 Painting No. 50, 1914-1915

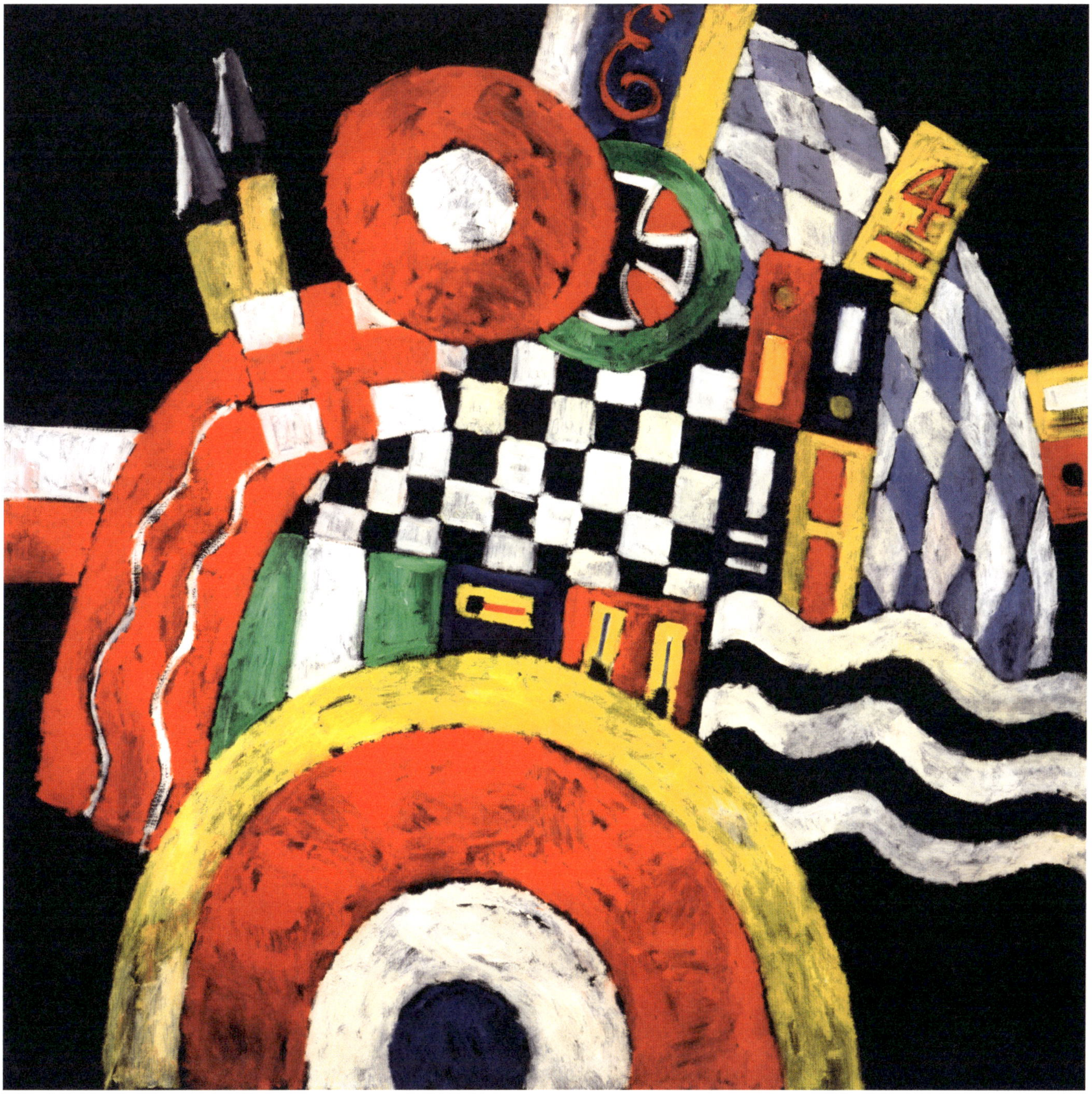

30 E, 1915

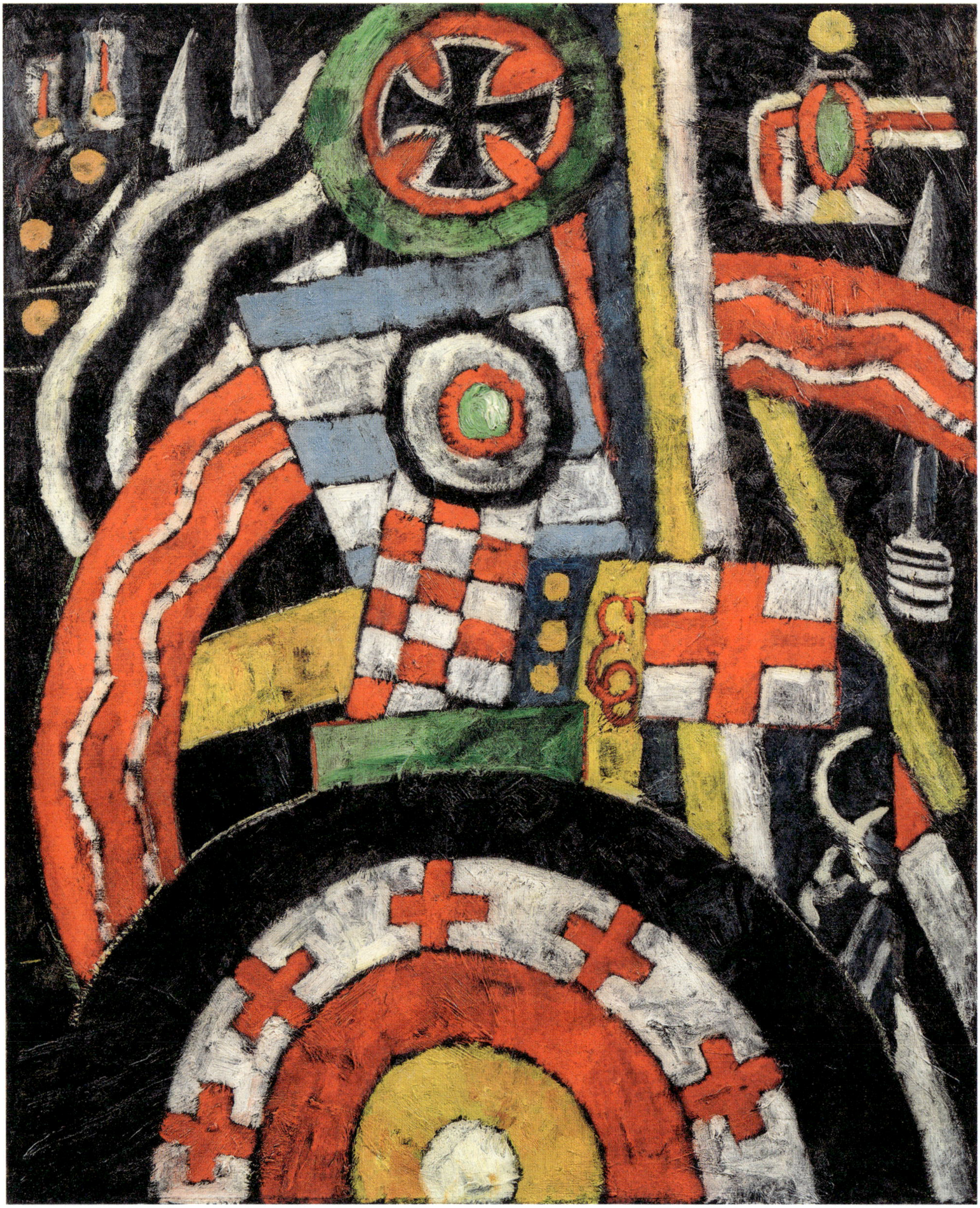

26 Abstraction (Military Symbols), 1914-1915
22 Portrait of a German Officer, 1914

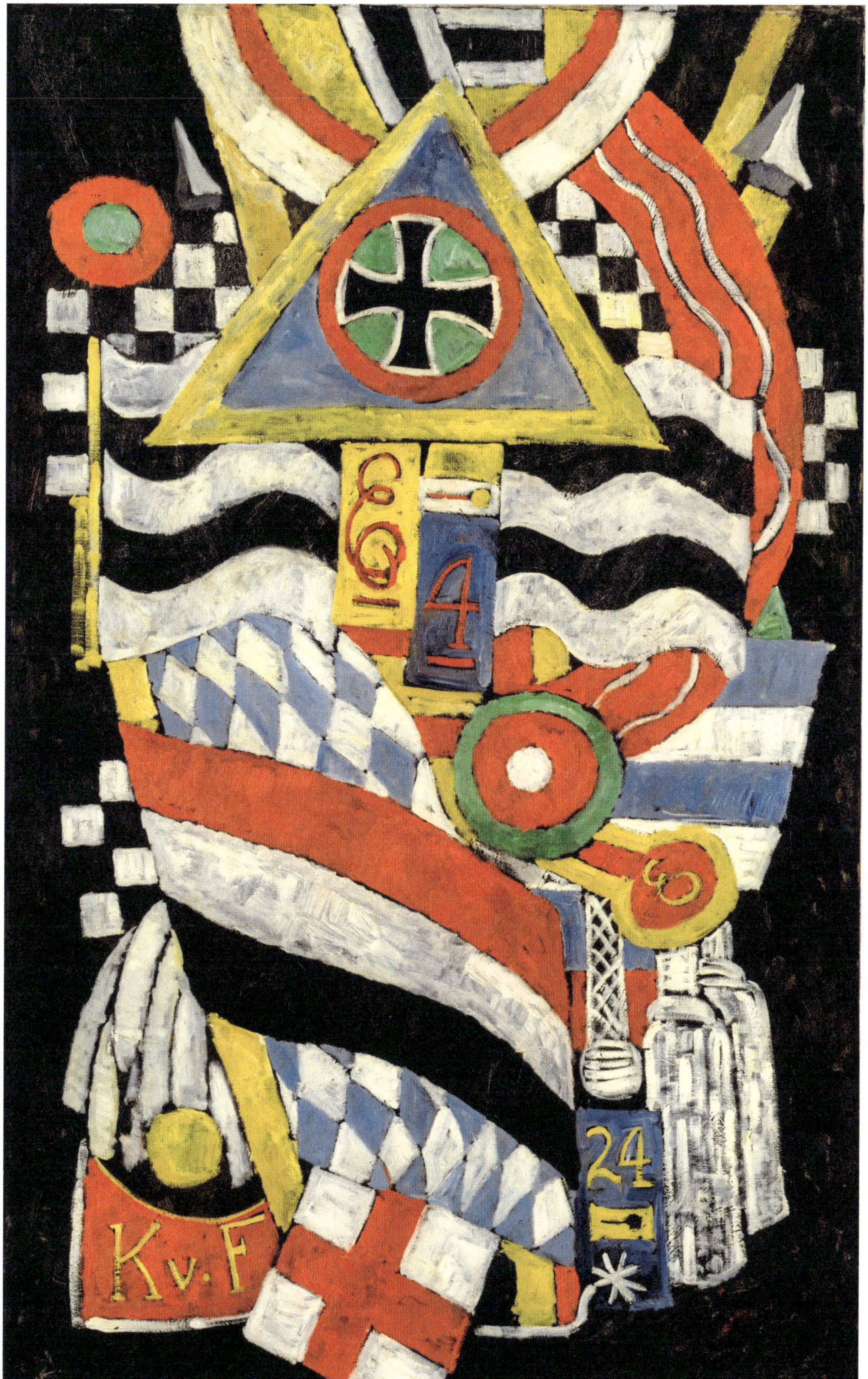
Kv. F
24

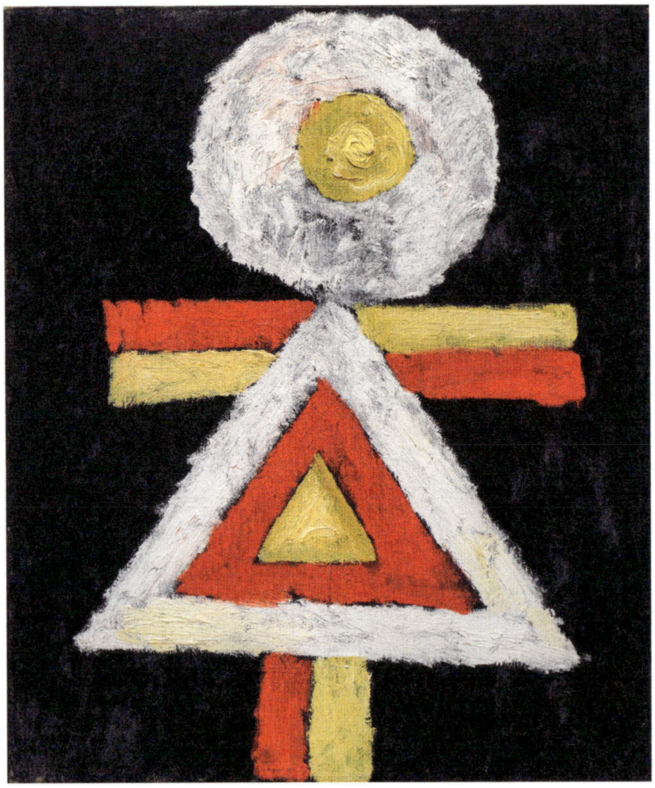

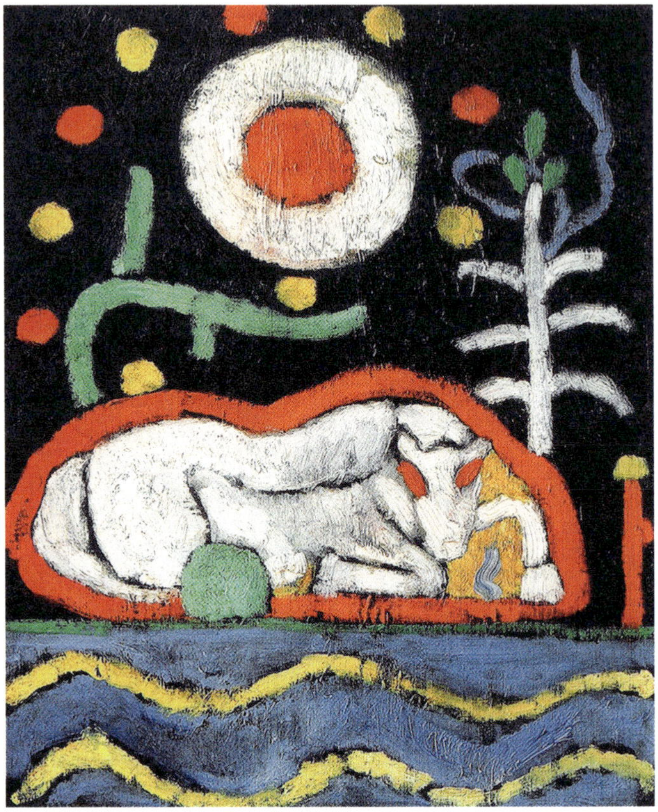

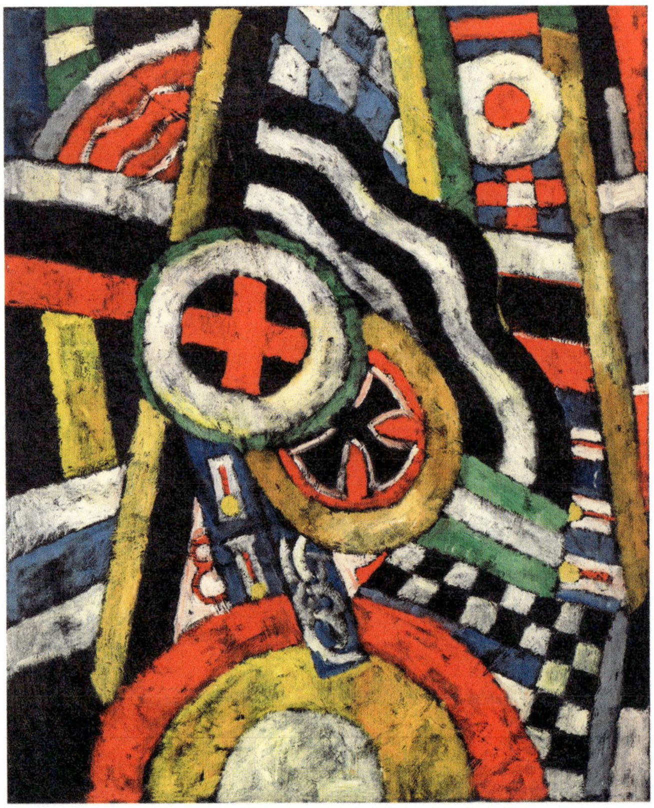

24 Geometric Figure, c. 1914
23 Berlin Series No. 2, 1914

27 Painting, Number 5, 1914-1915

28 Painting No. 47, Berlin, 1914-1915

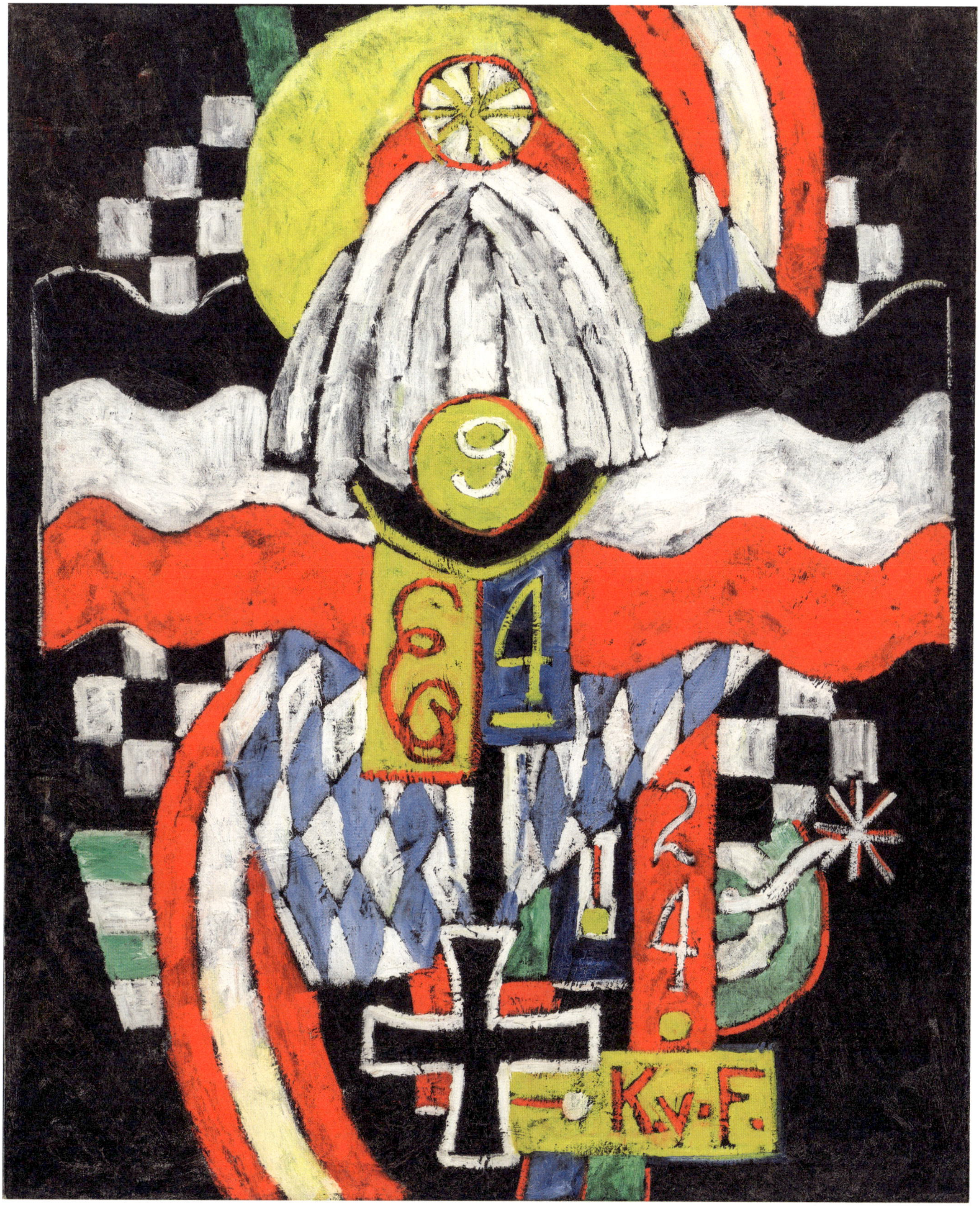
9
8
4
2
!
4
K.v.F.

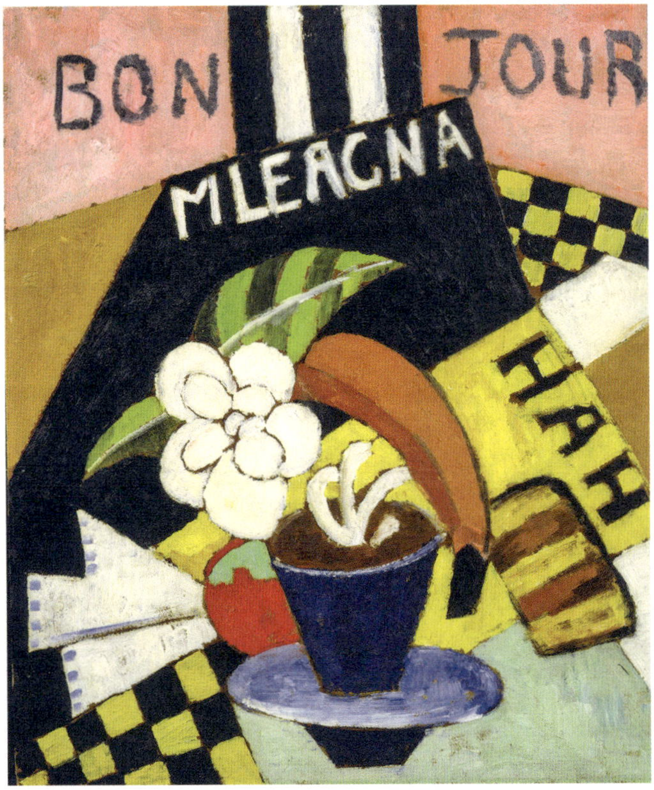

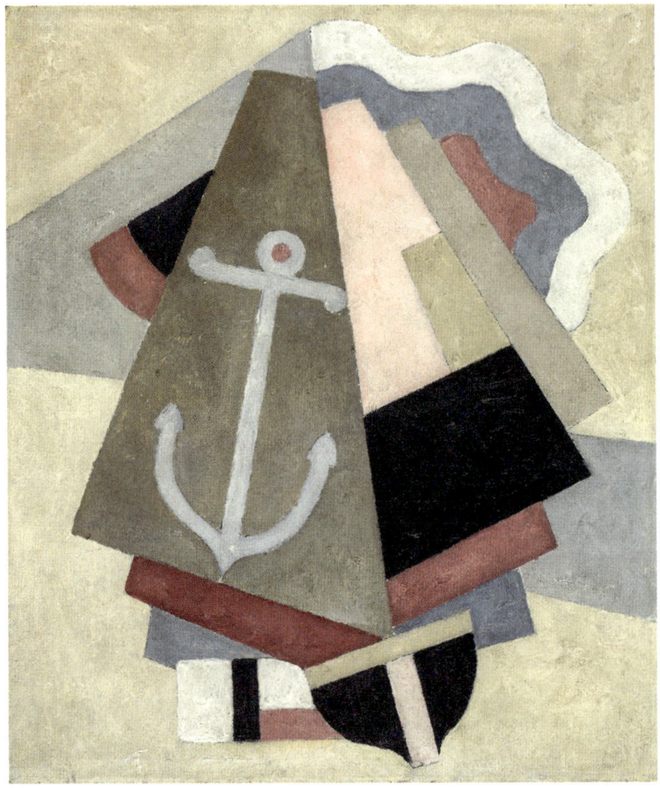

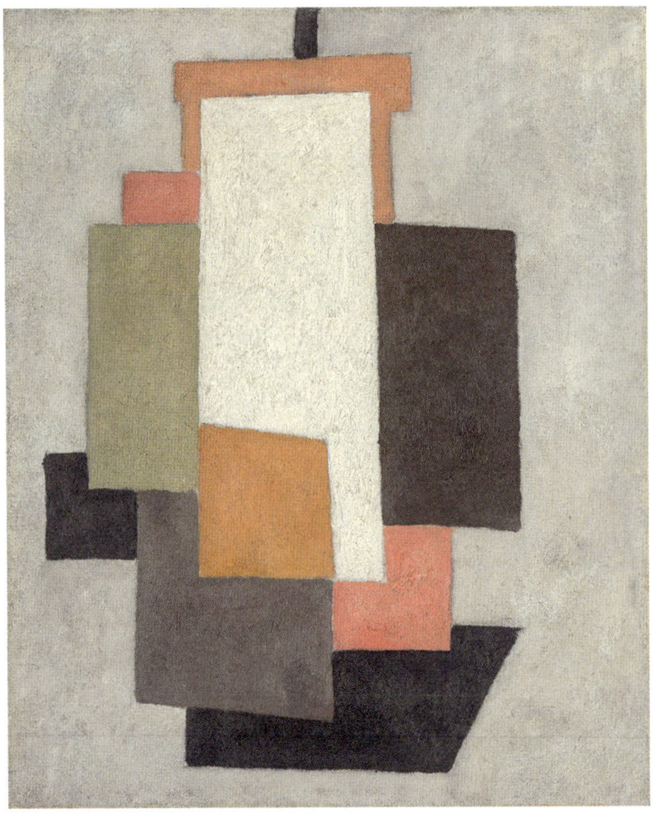

32 A Nice Time, 1915
35 Movement No. 7, Provincetown, 1916

36 Provincetown, 1916

34 Elsa Kobenhavn, 1916

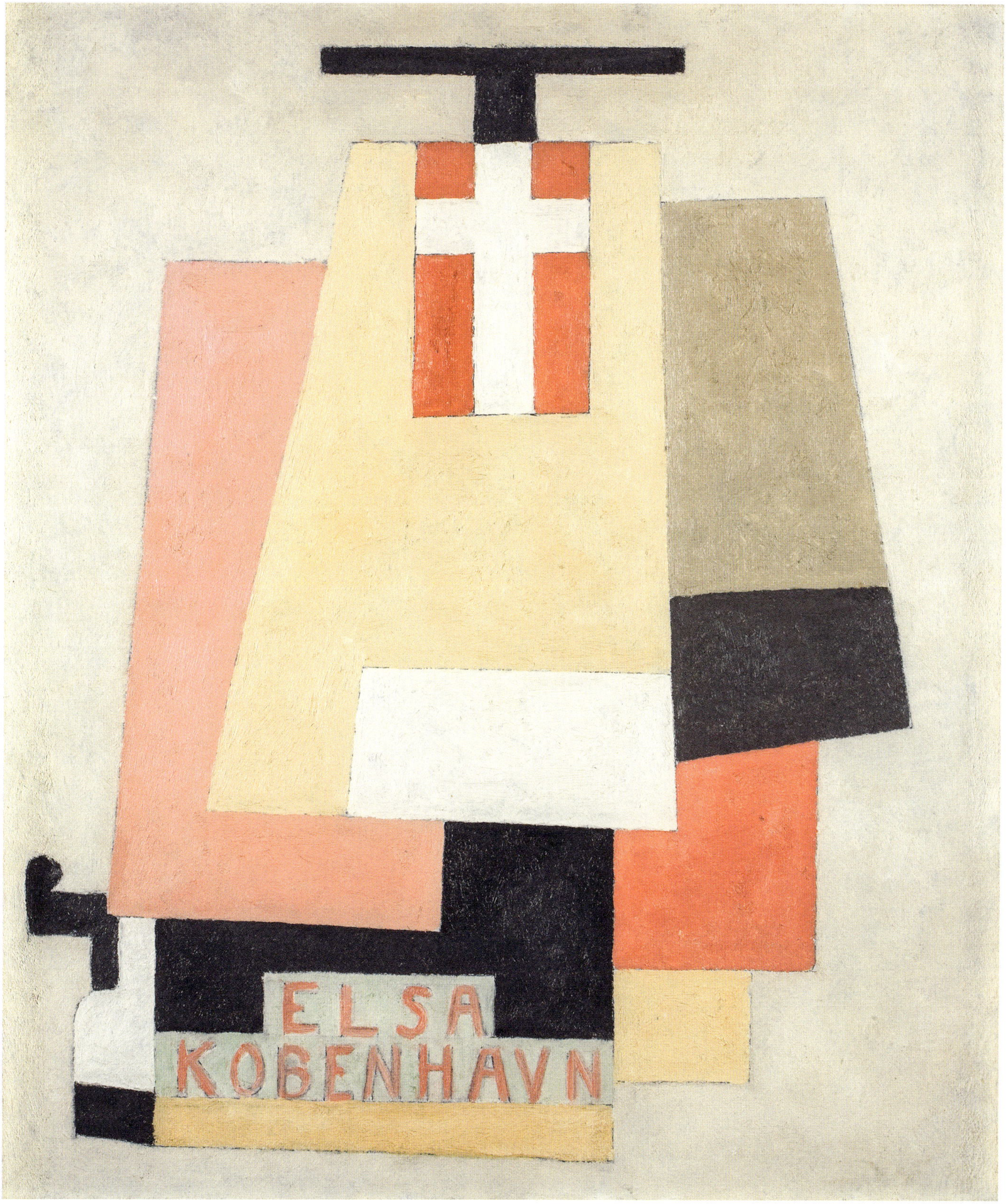
ELSA
KOBENHAVN

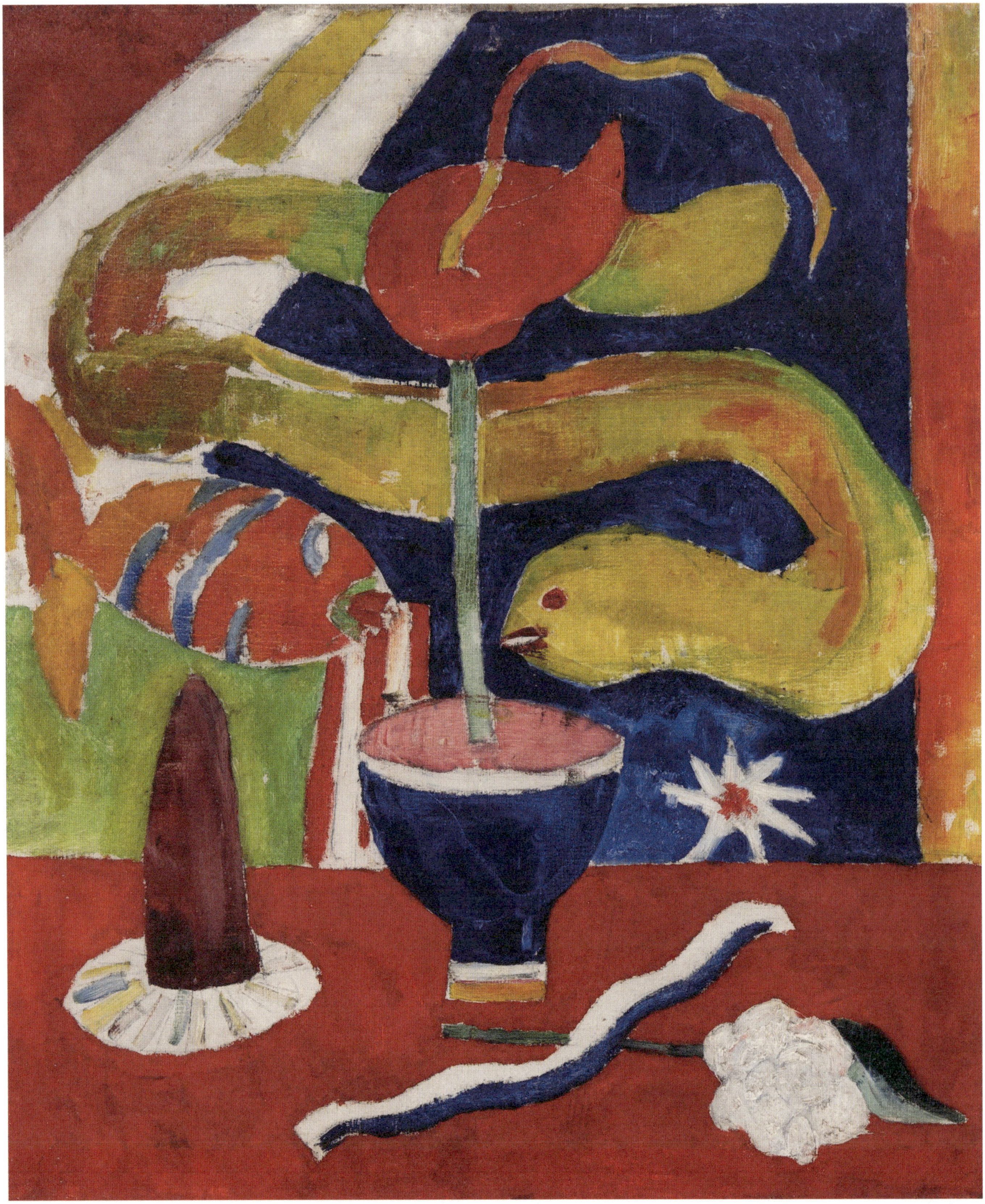

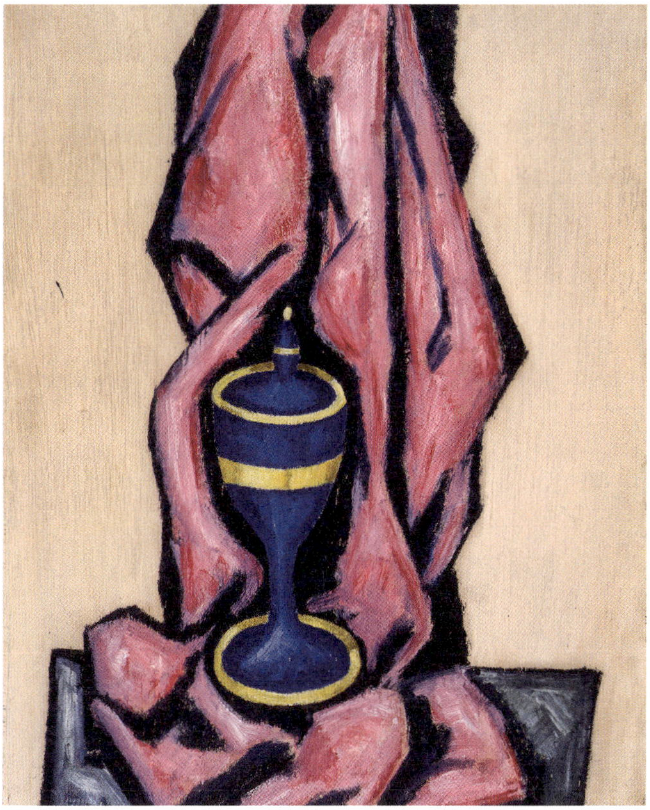

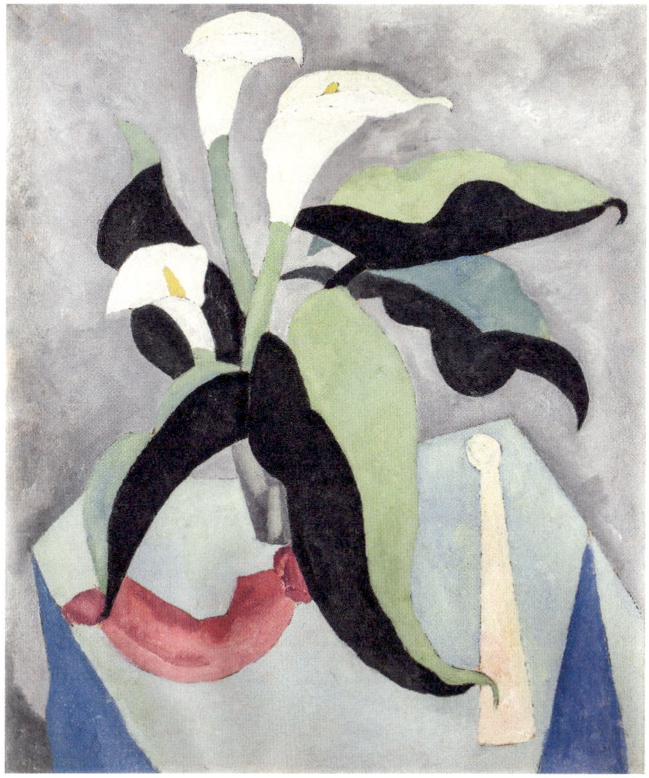

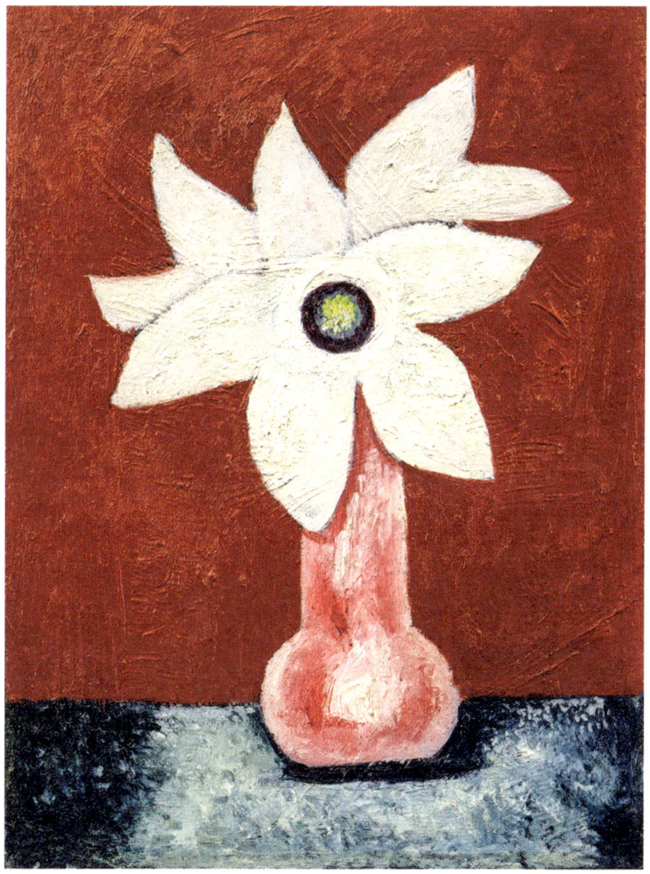

38 Still Life with Eel, c. 1917

39 The Blue Cup, c. 1918
37 Still Life No. 9, 1917

33 Flower, 1916

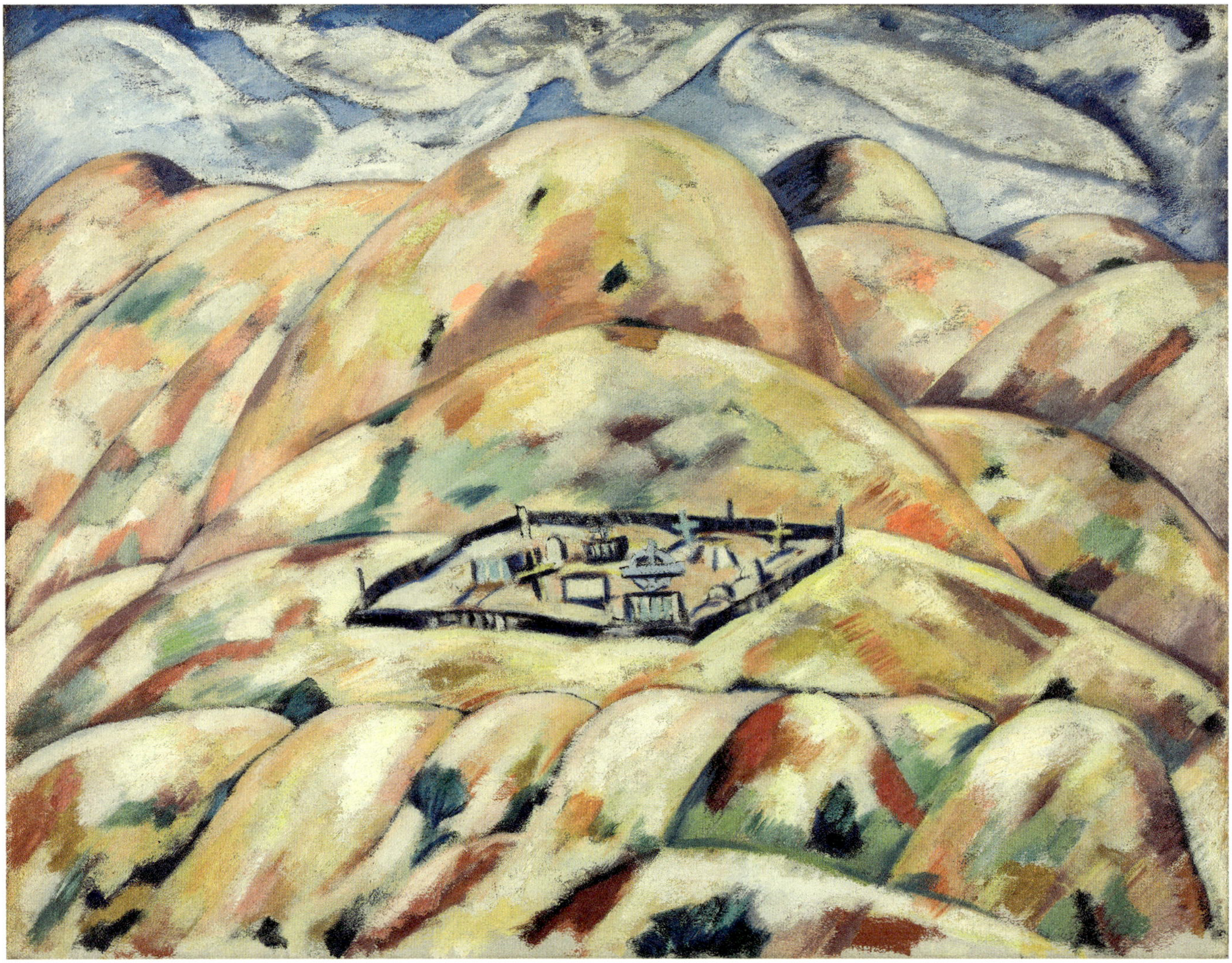

44 New Mexico No. 2, 1919

116 Valdez Hills, 1918
115 New Mexico Hills, 1918

40 Santos, New Mexico, 1918-1919

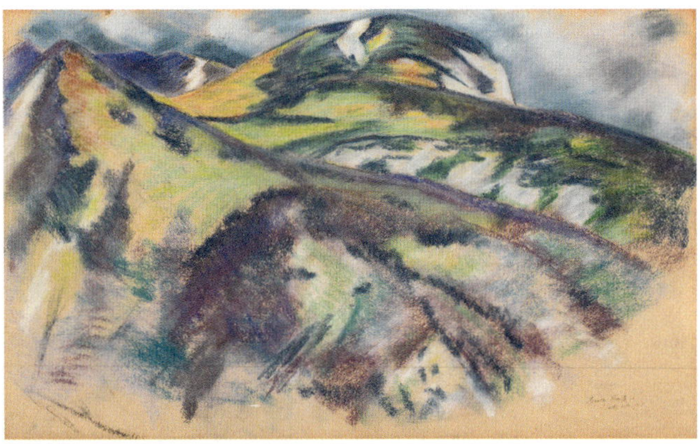

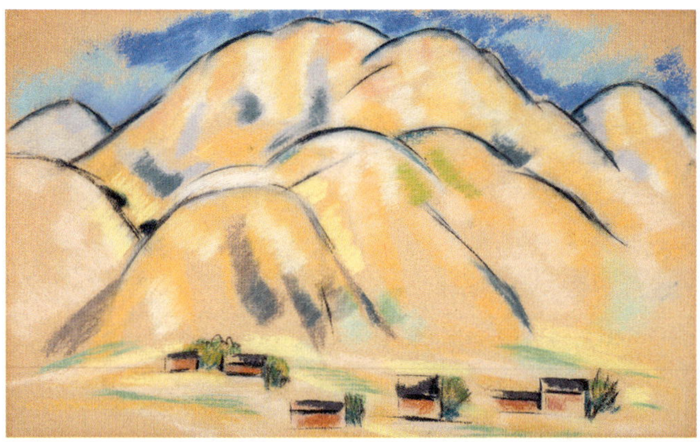

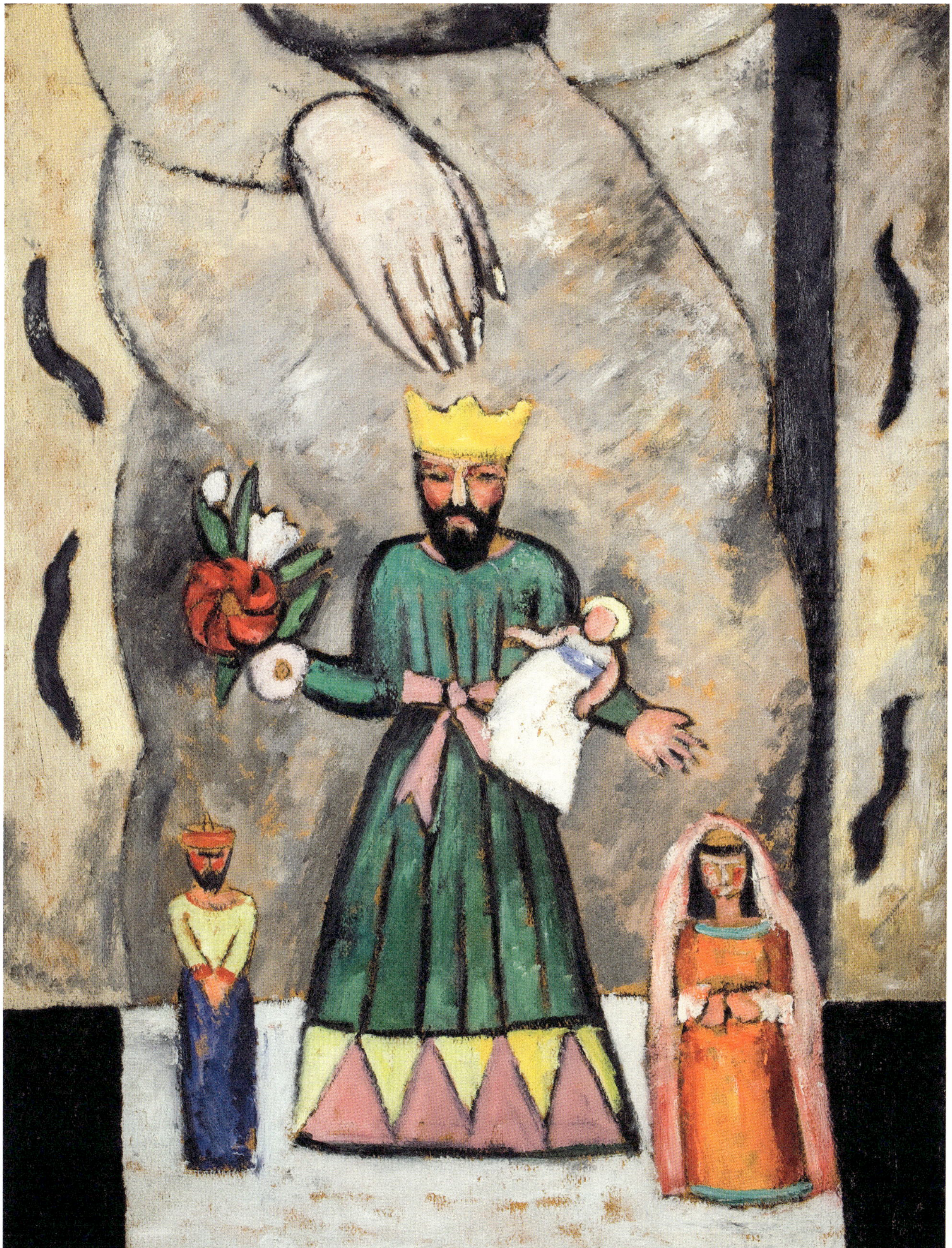

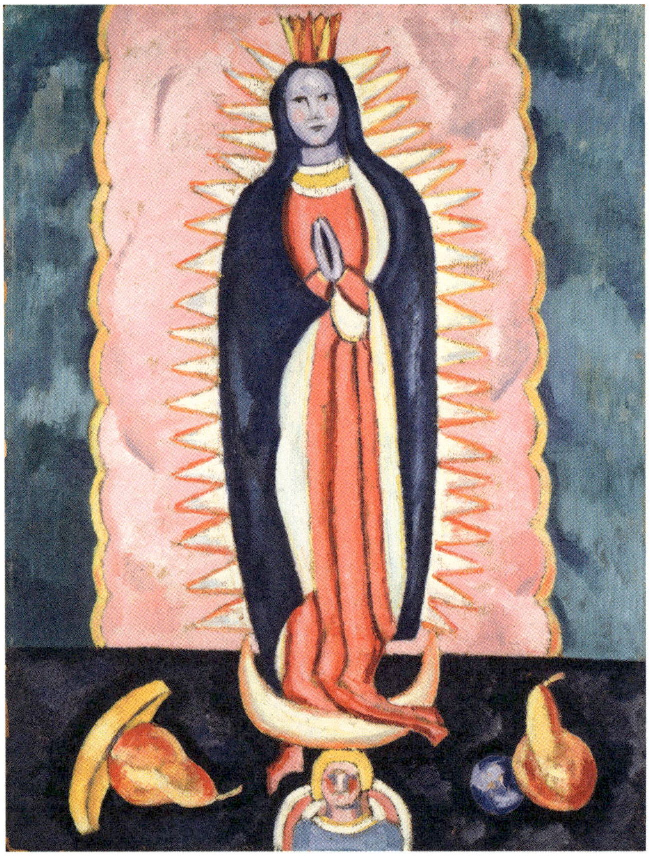

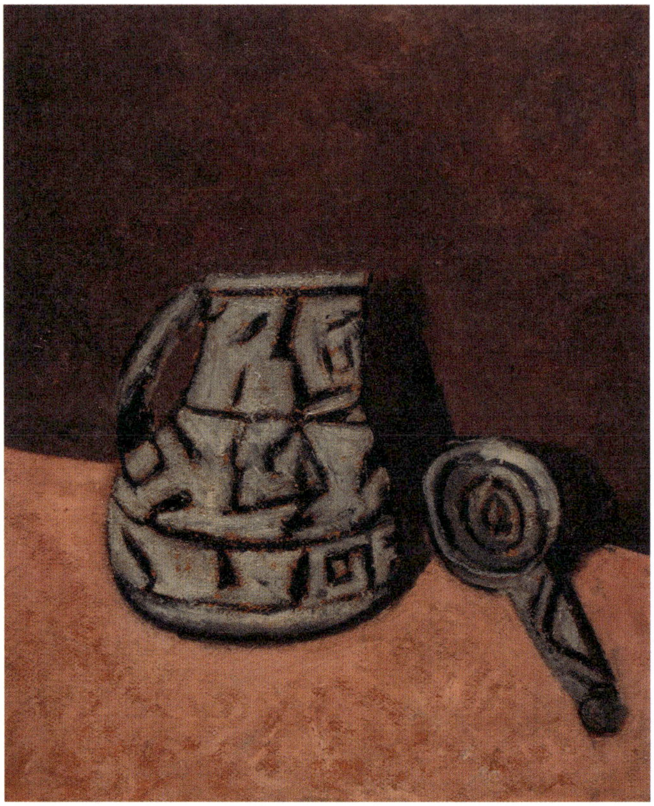

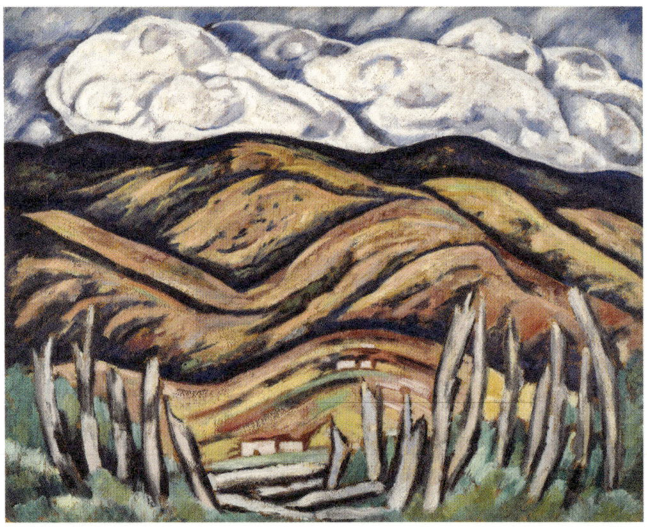

42 The Virgin of Guadalupe, c. 1918-1919
43 Pitcher and Dipper, 1918-1921

41 The Last of New England – The Beginning of New Mexico, 1918-1919

45 Rubber Plant, 1920

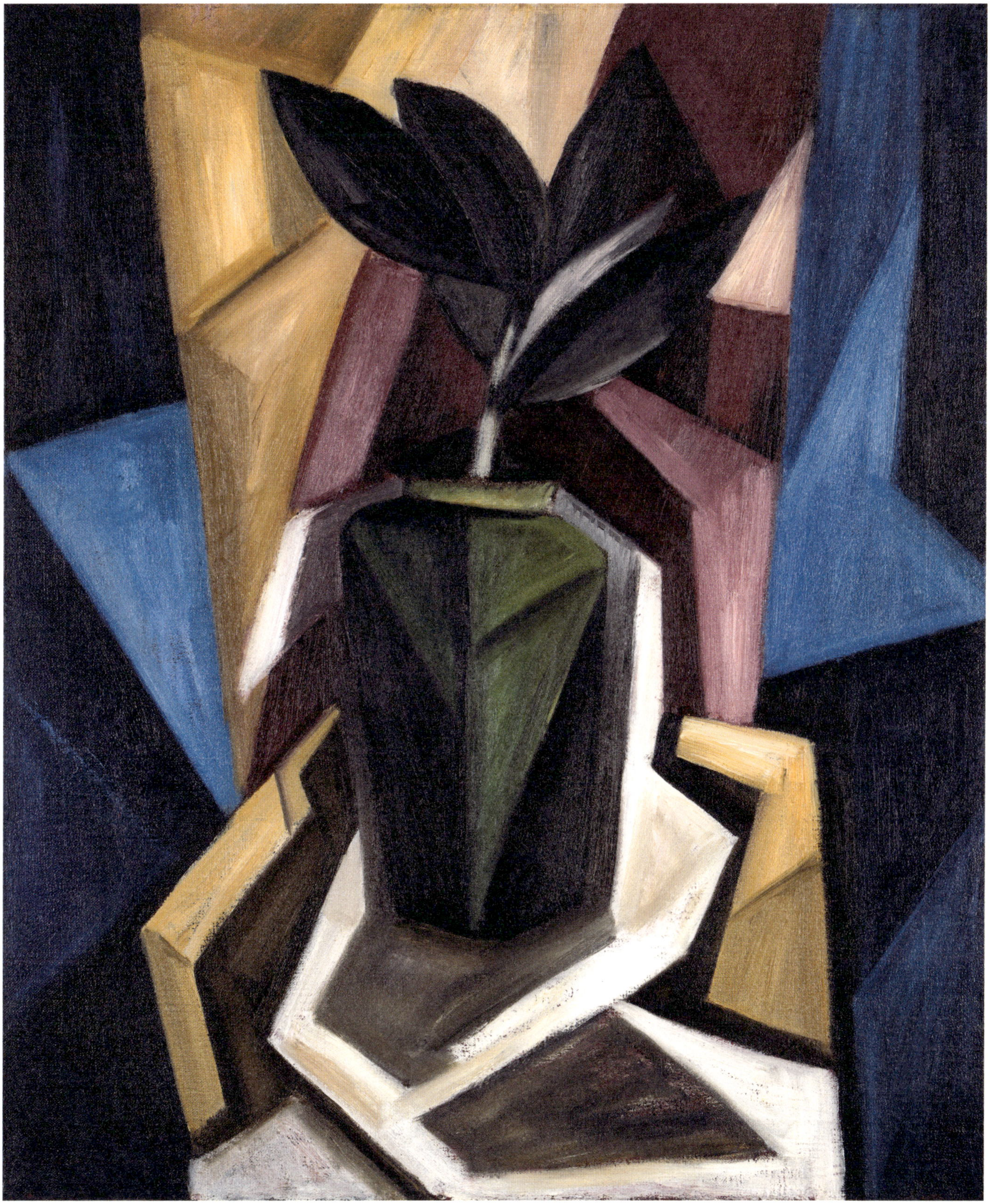

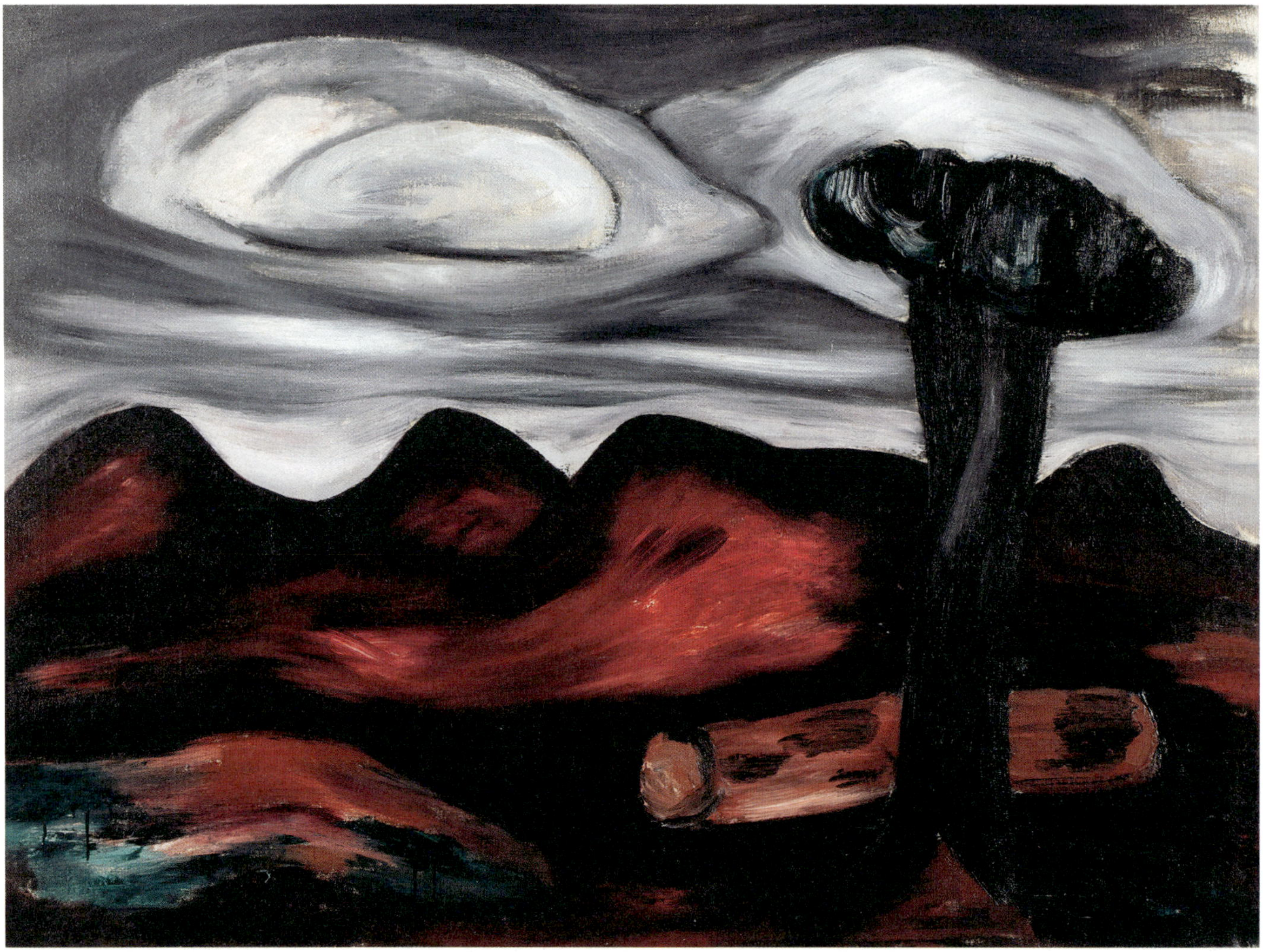

48 New Mexico No. 3, c. 1923
117 Standing Male Nude, c. 1923

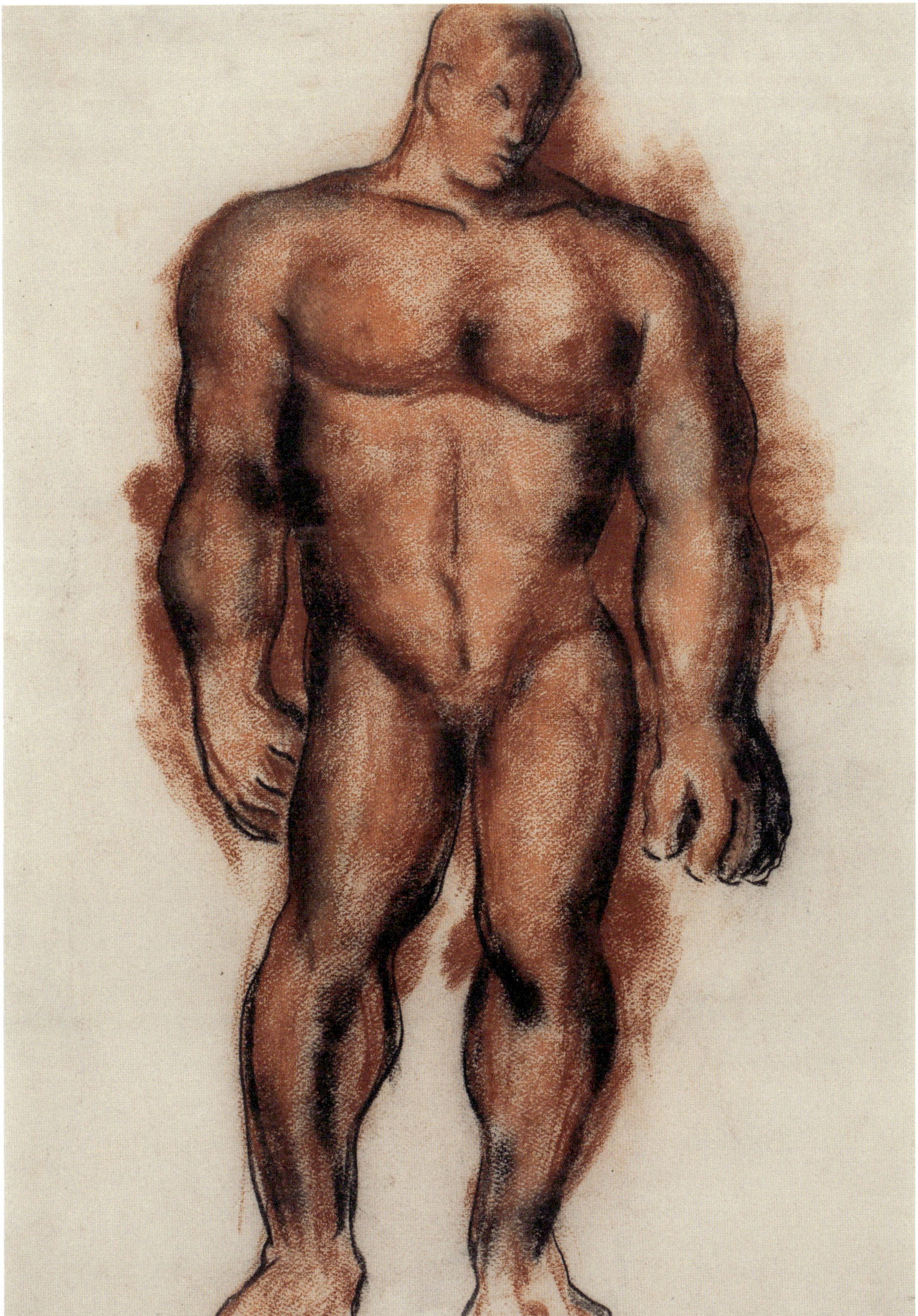

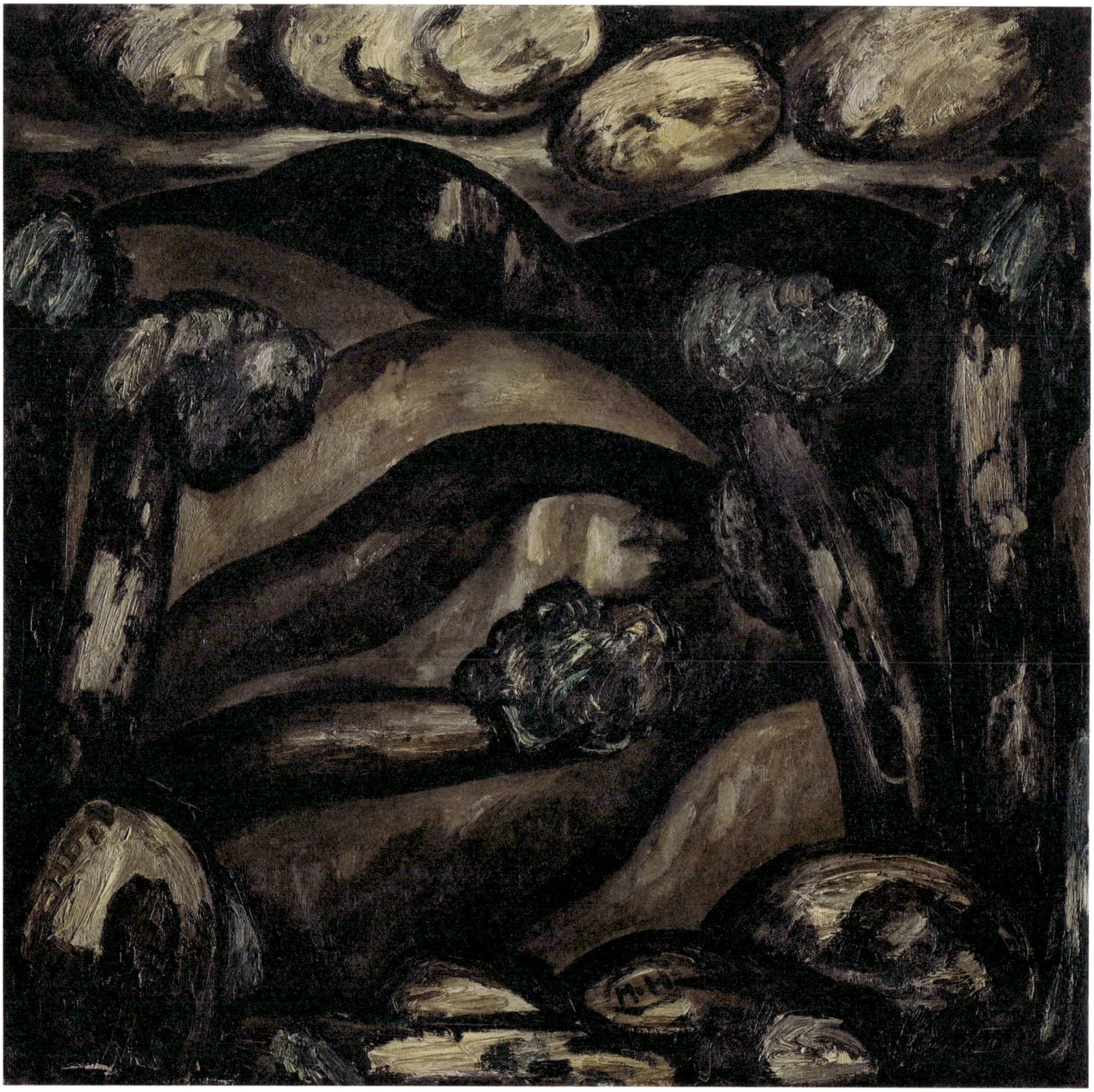

49 Paysage, 1924

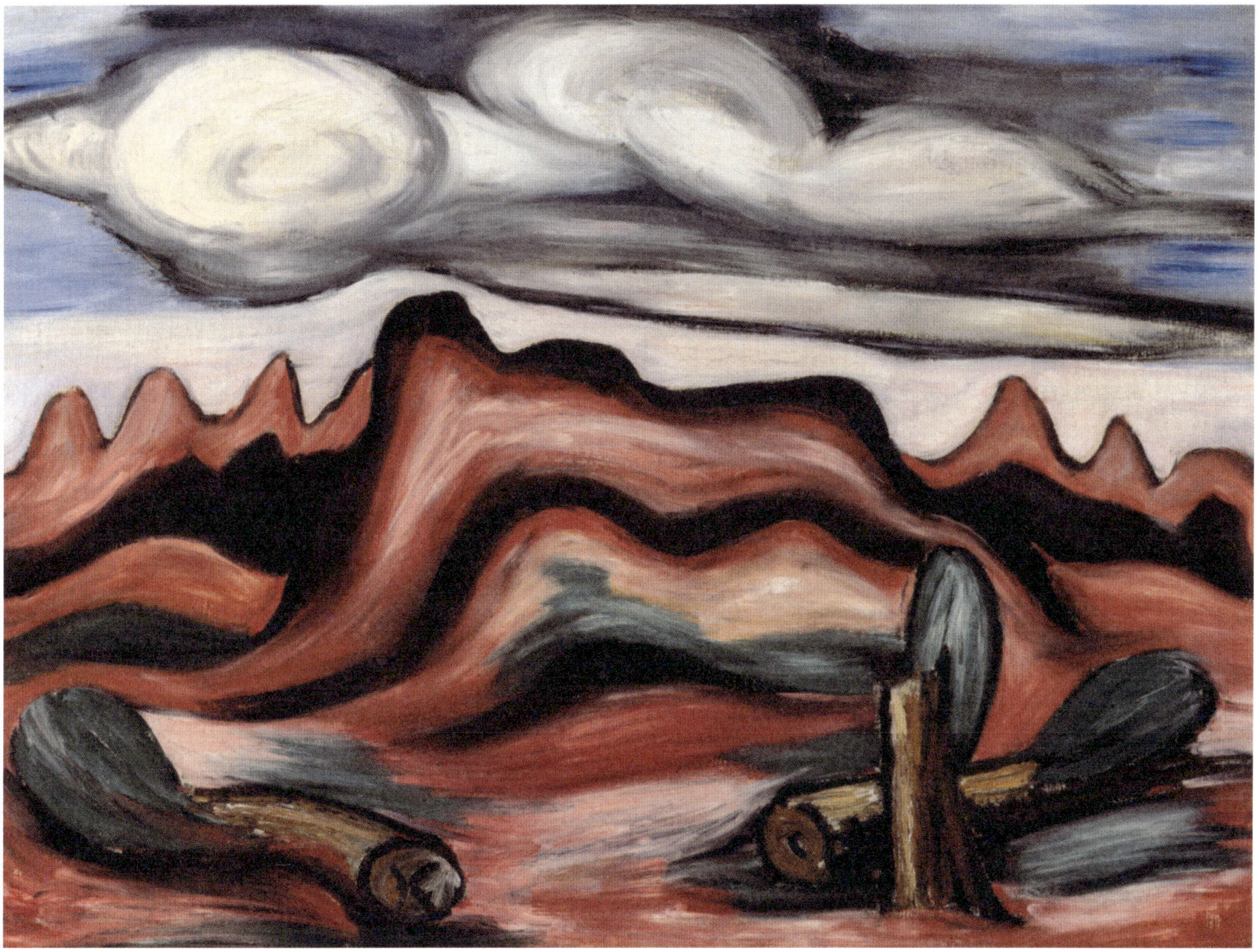

47 New Mexico Recollections No. 13, 1923

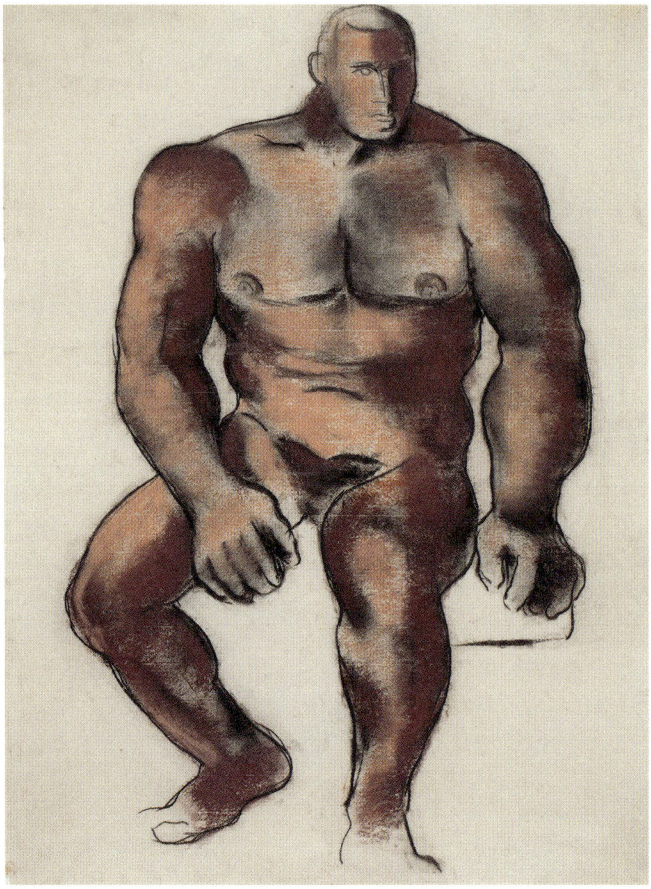

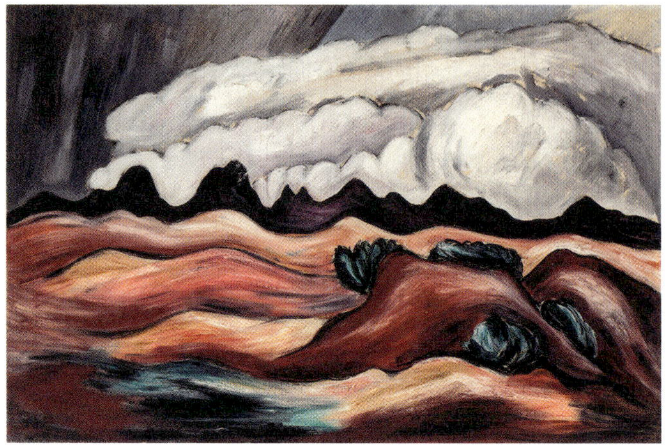

118 Seated Male Nude, c. 1923
46 Landscape Fantasy, 1923

50 Alpes Maritimes, Vence, 1925
53 Landscape No. 1 (Trees, Vence), c. 1925-1926

51 Motif from African Textile I, 1925
52 Motif from African Textile II, 1925

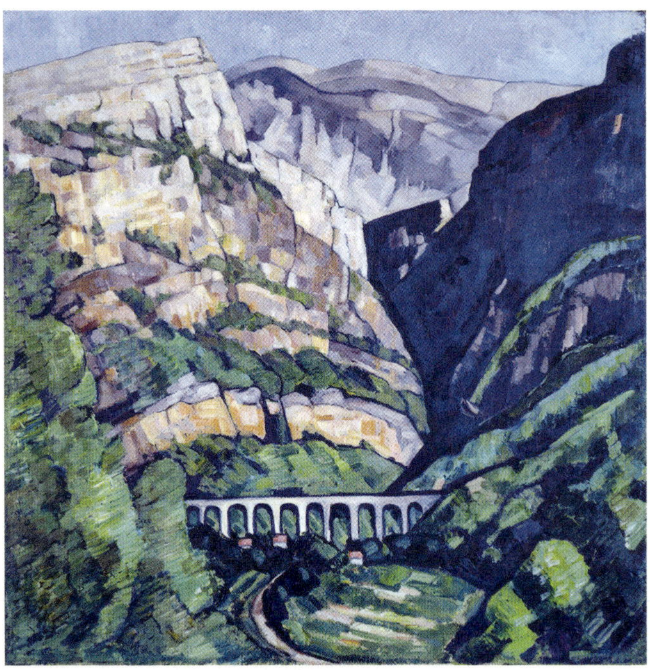

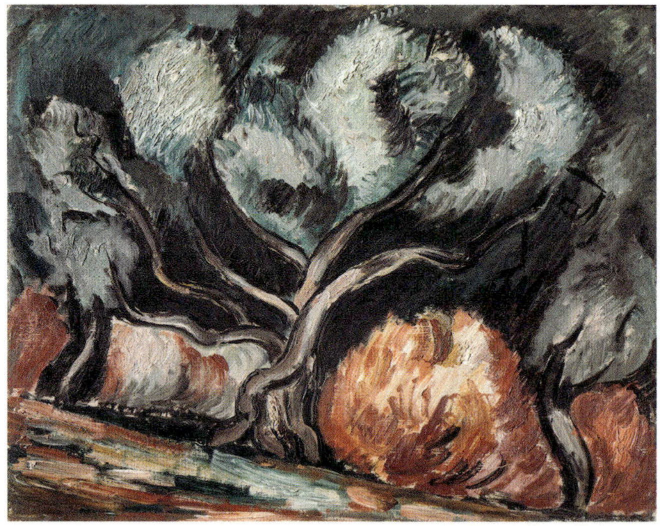

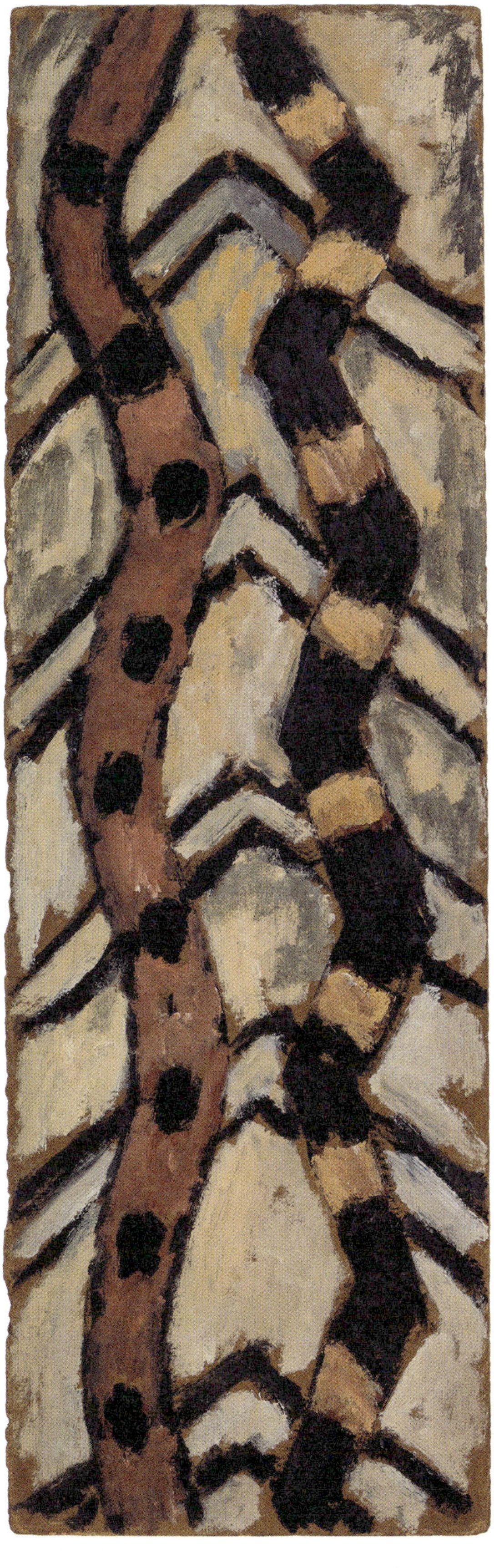

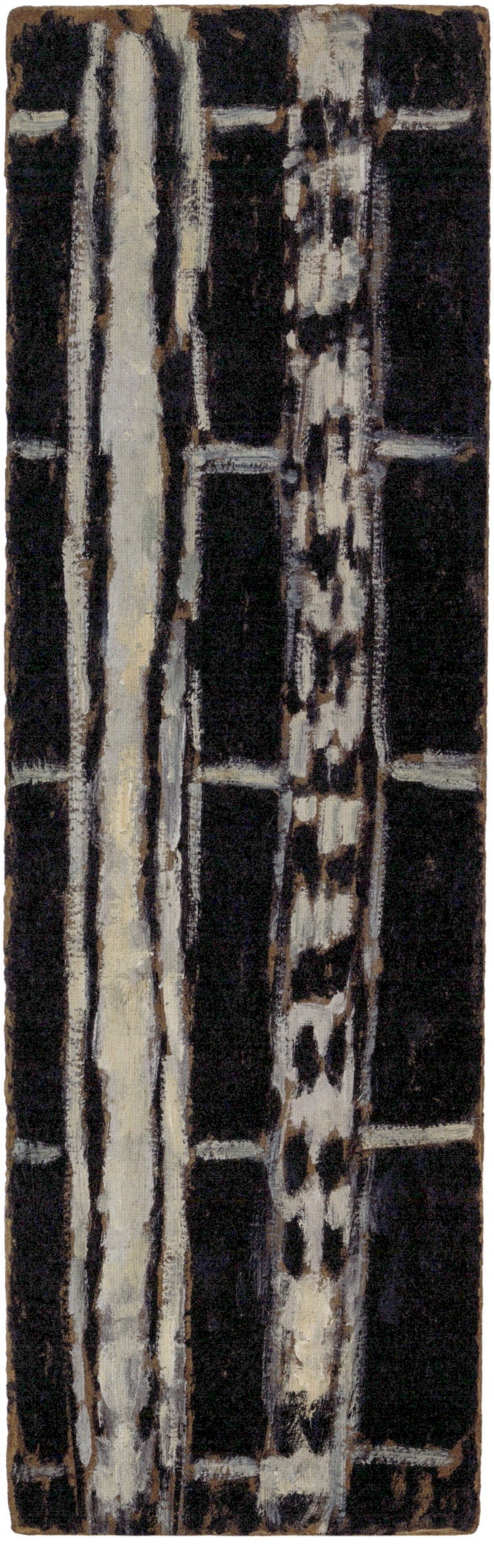

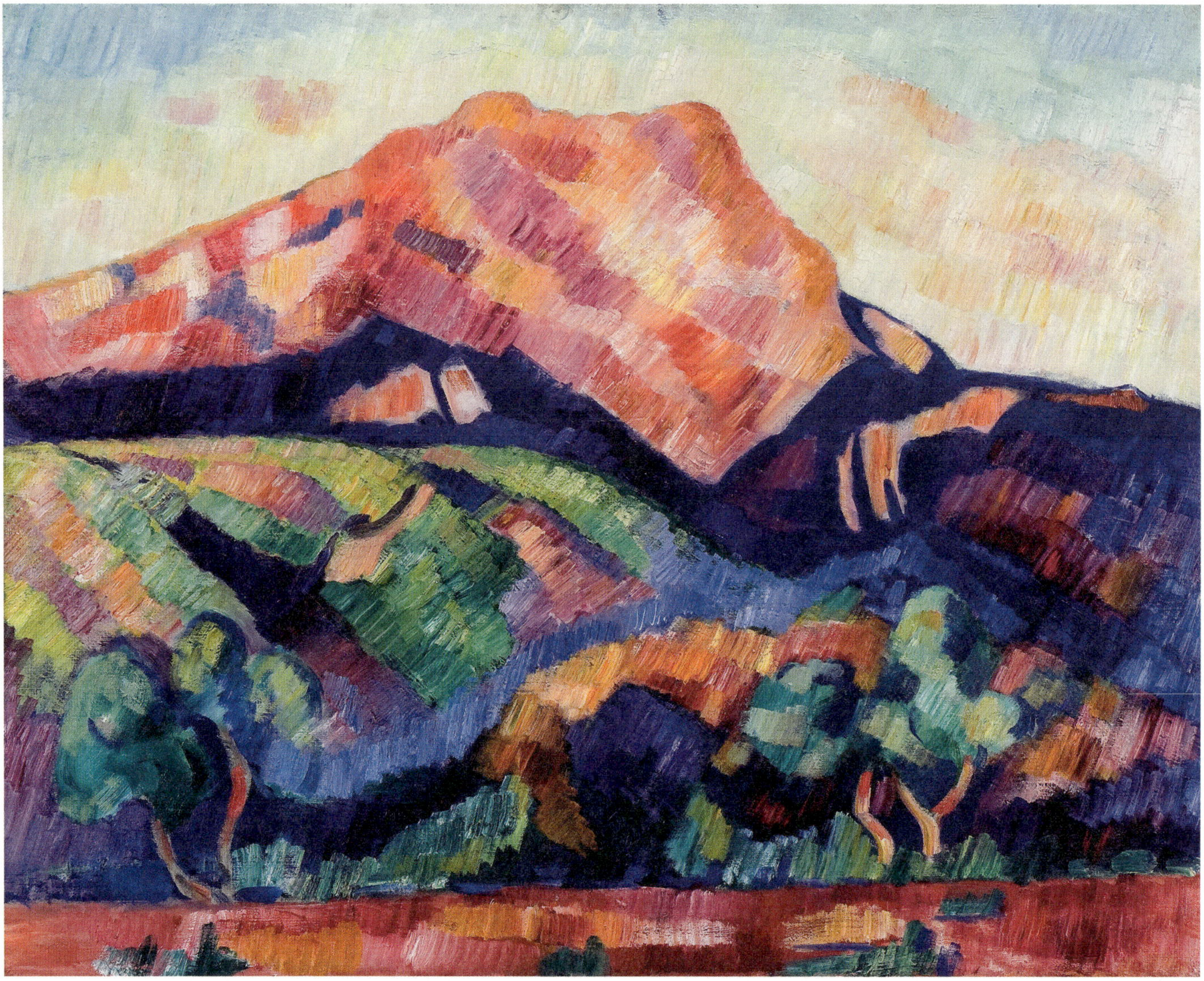

54 Mont Sainte-Victoire, 1927

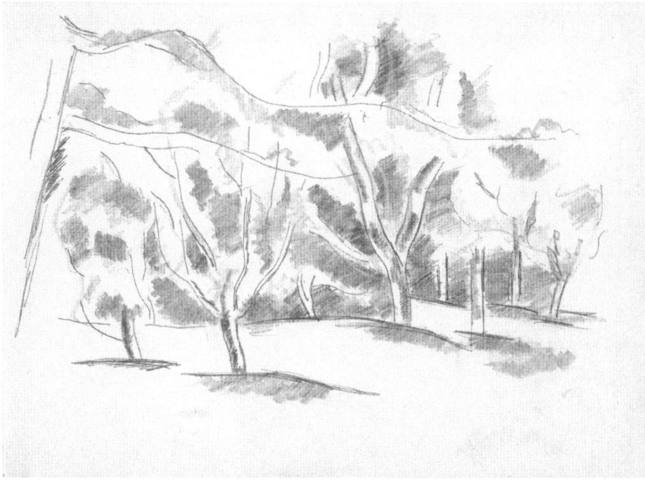

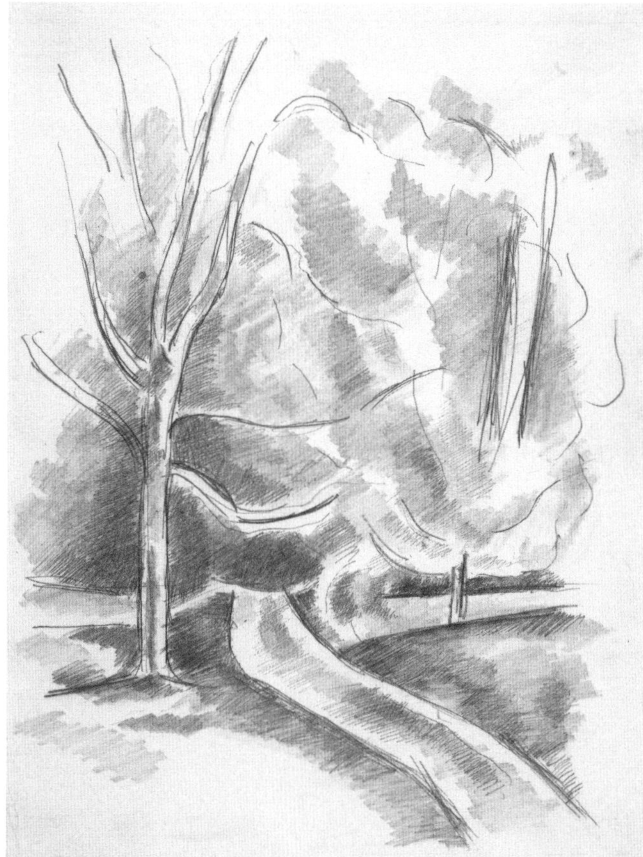

121 Untitled (Landscape with Trees), 1927
119 Untitled (Landscape with Forest Road), 1927

120 Untitled (Still Life Flowers), c. 1927

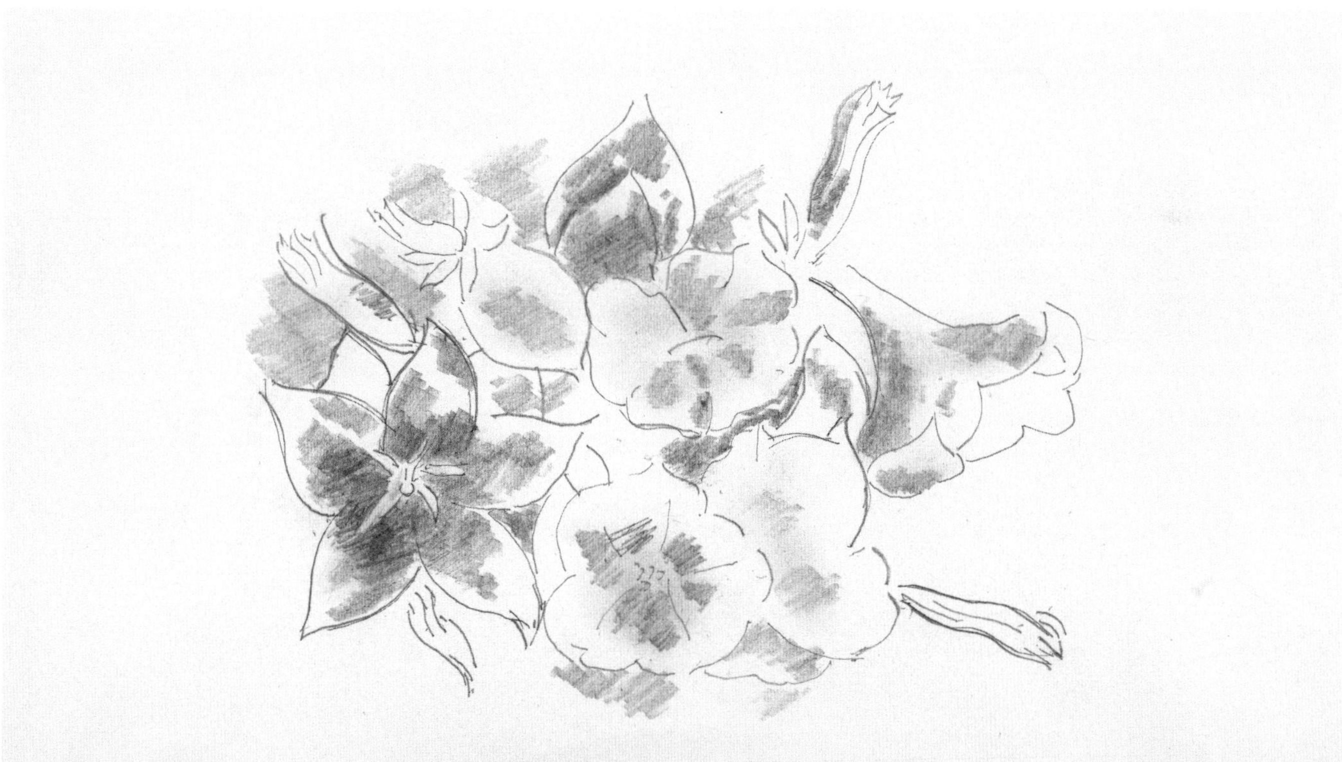

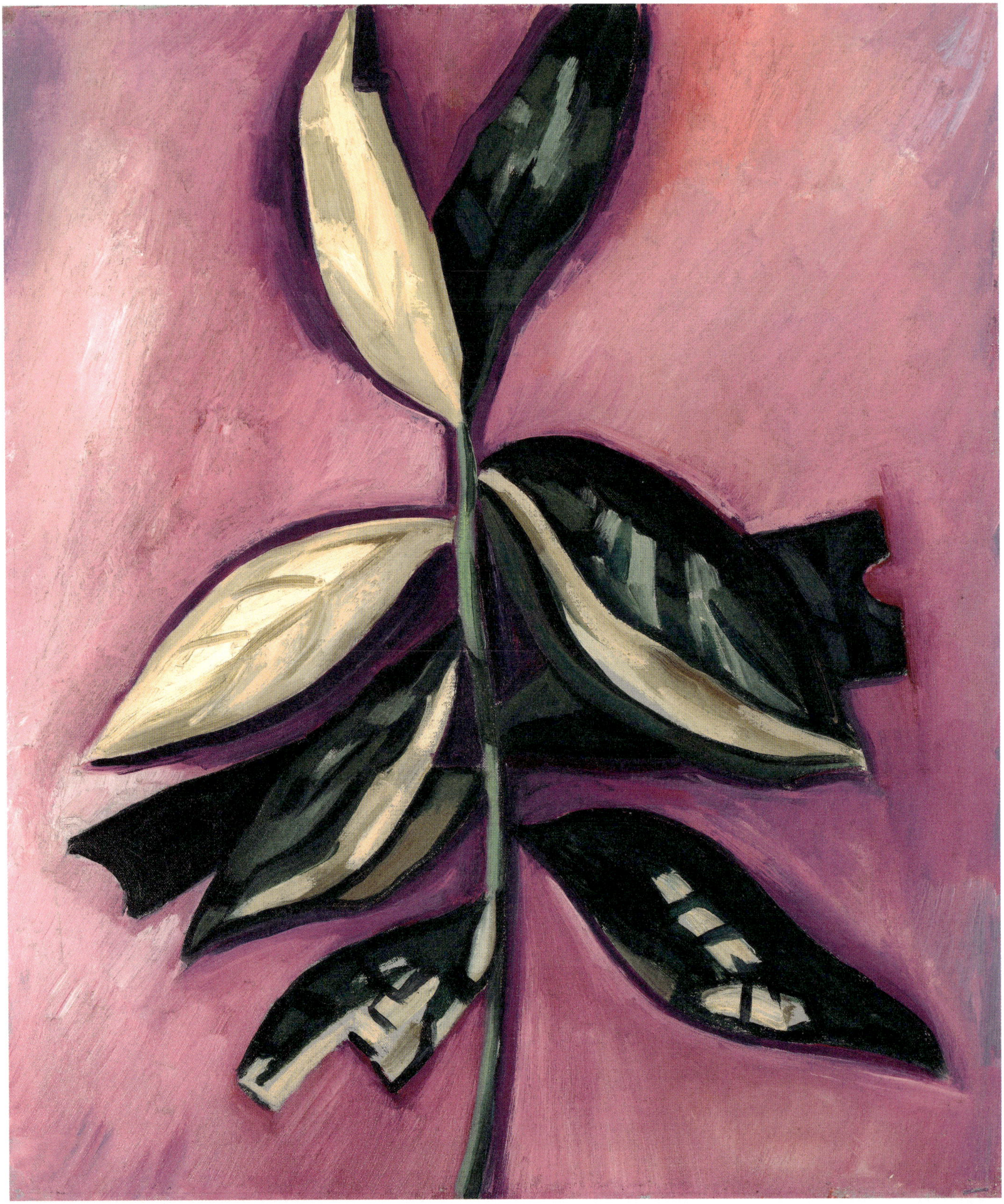

56 Leaves, 1929

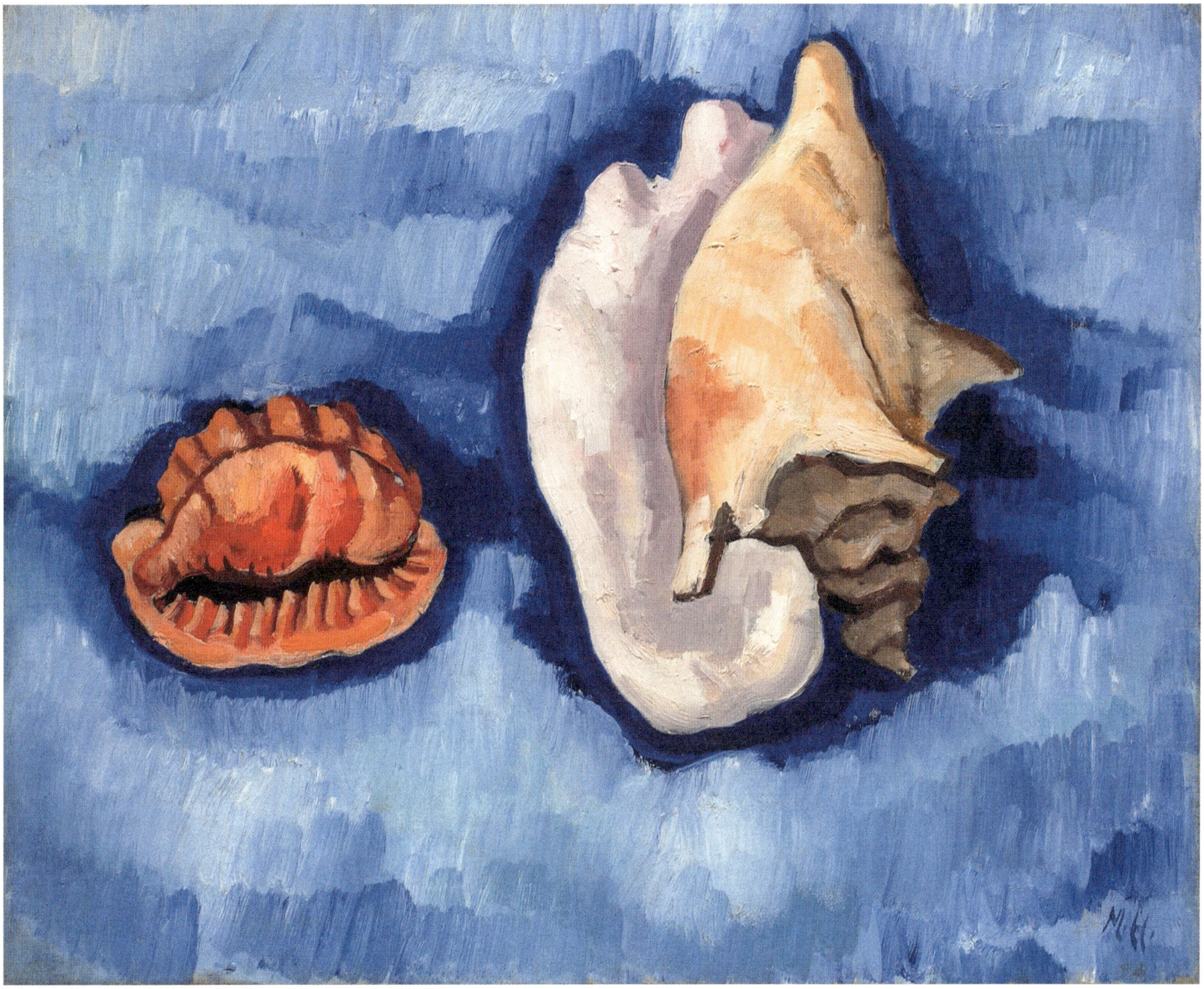

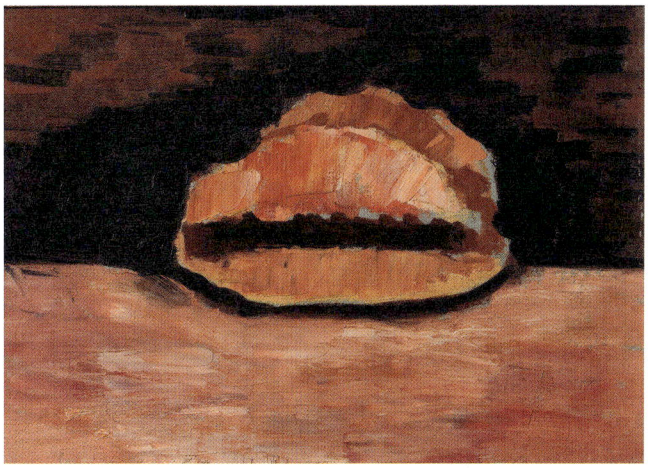

55 Two Shells, 1928
57 Still Life No. 4, c. 1929

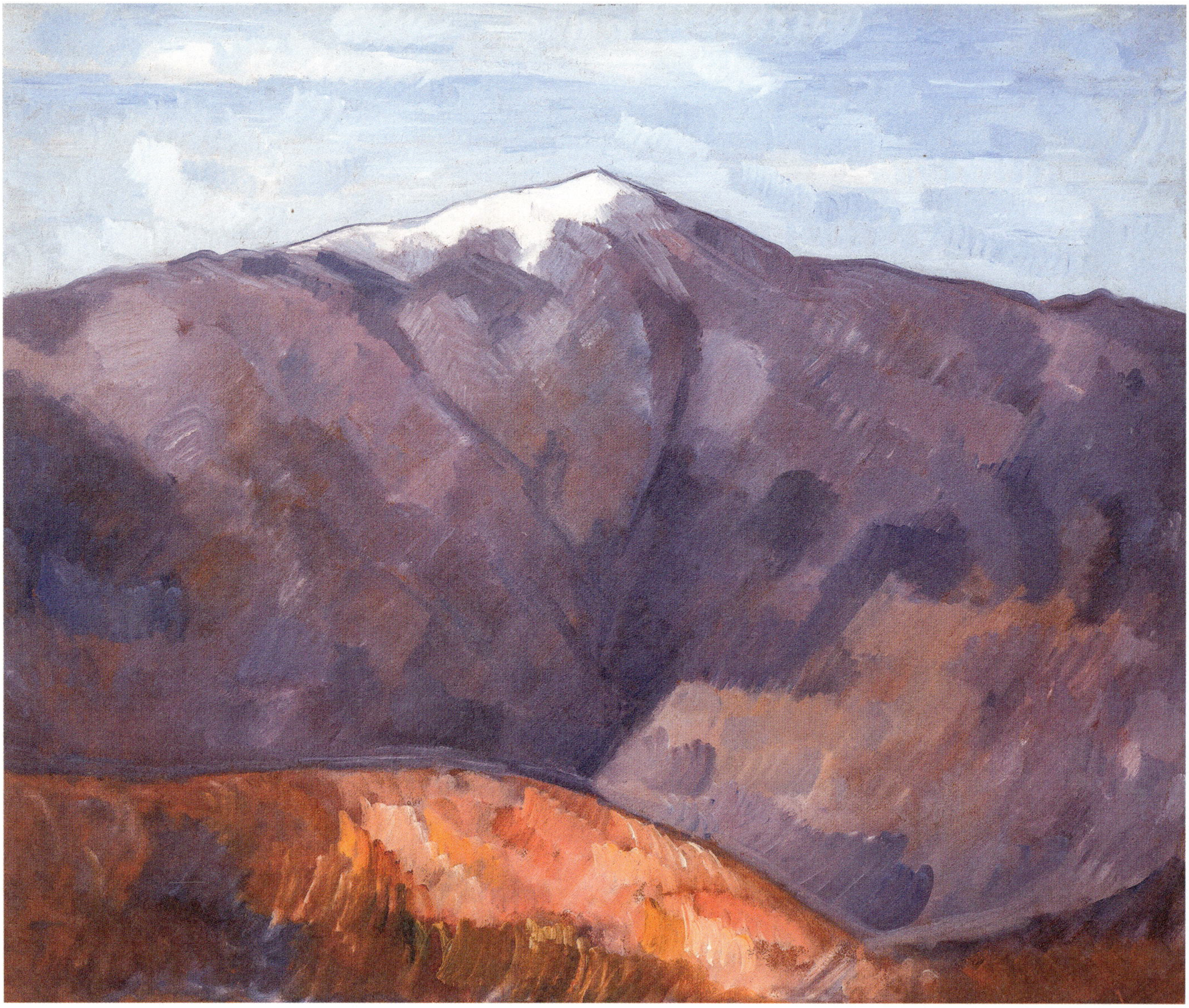

58 White Top Mountain, 1930

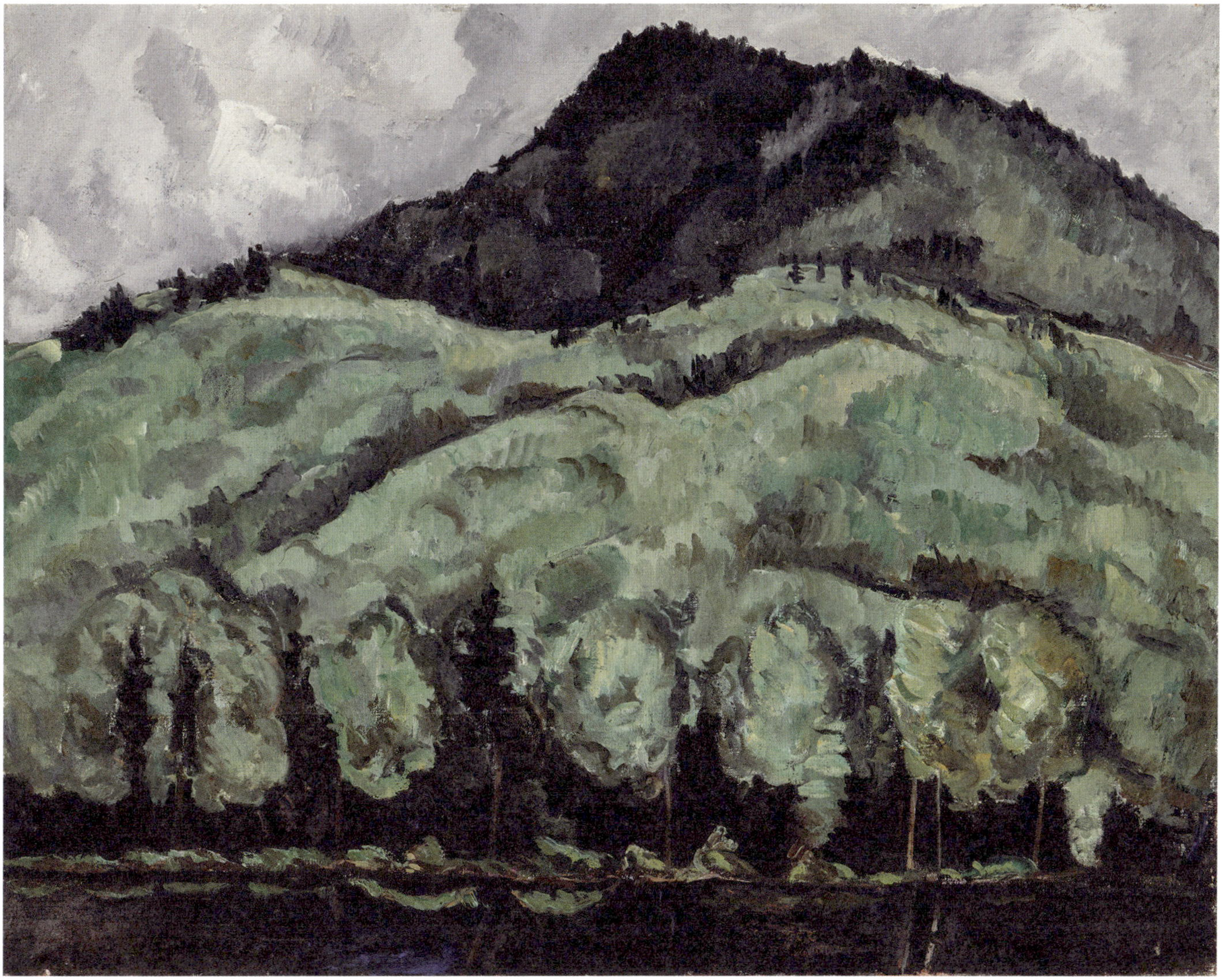

59 Landscape No. 35 (Beaver Lake, Lost River Region), 1930

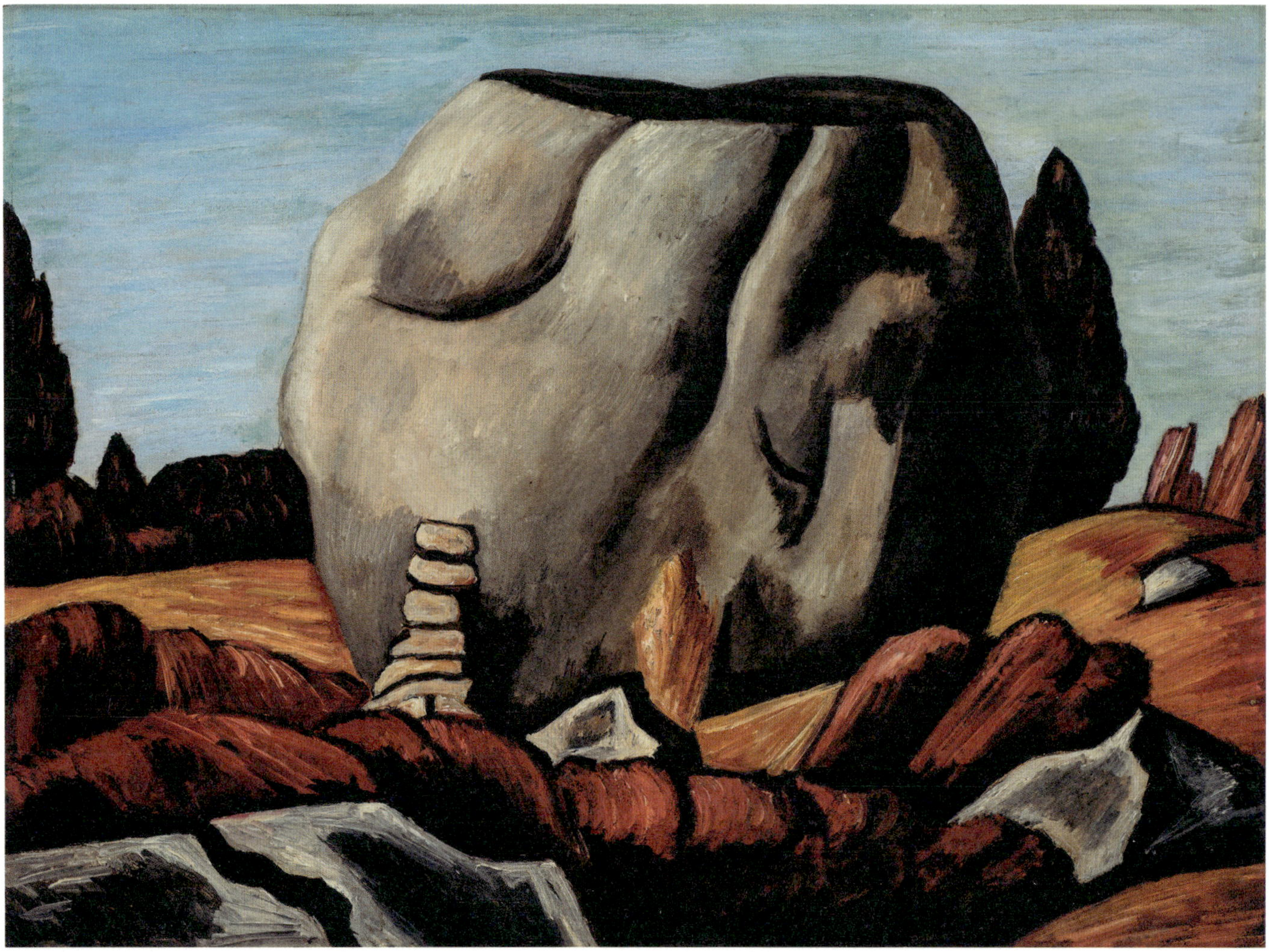

61 Altar Boulder, Dogtown, 1931

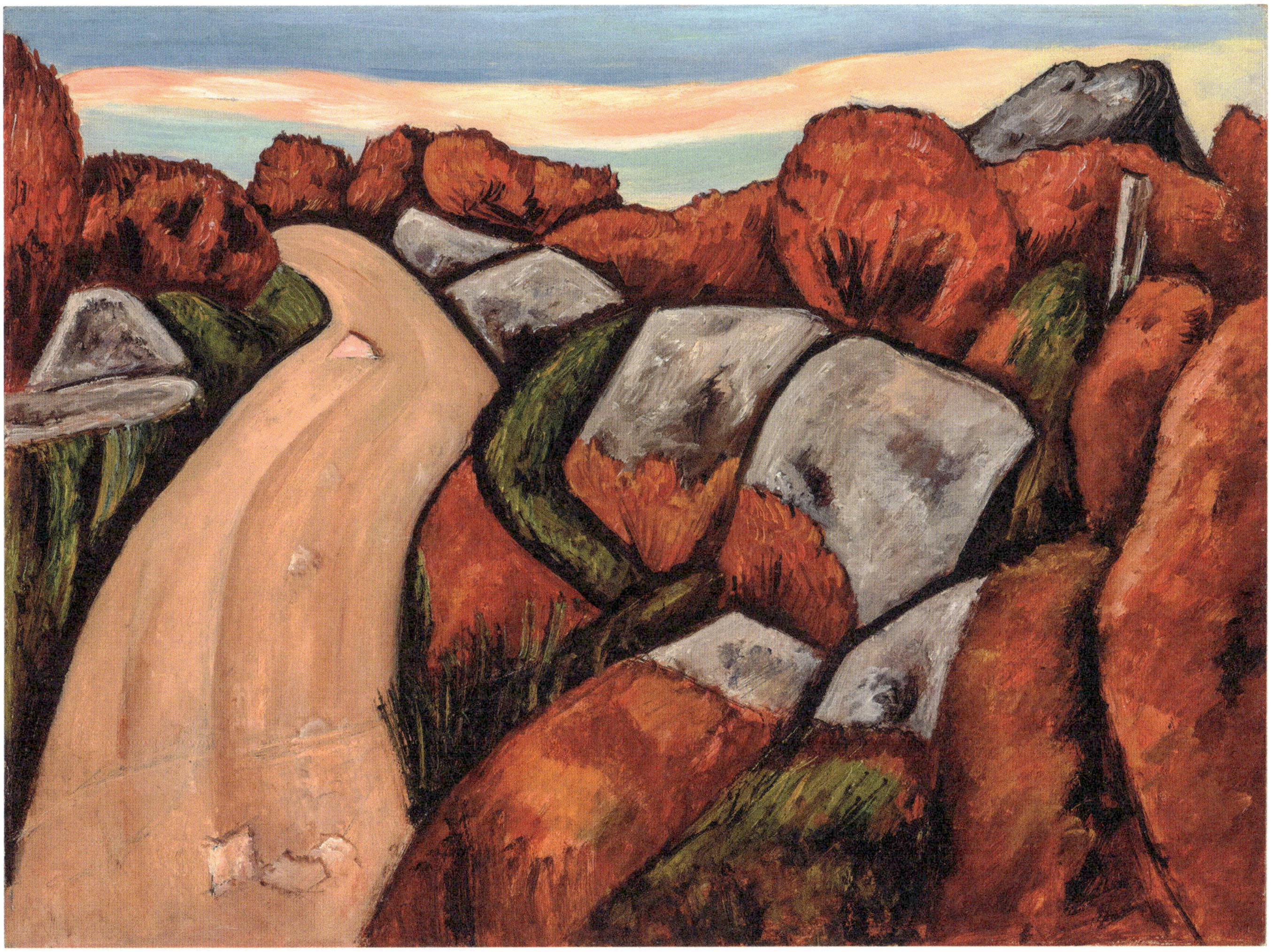

60 Blueberry Highway, Dogtown, 1931

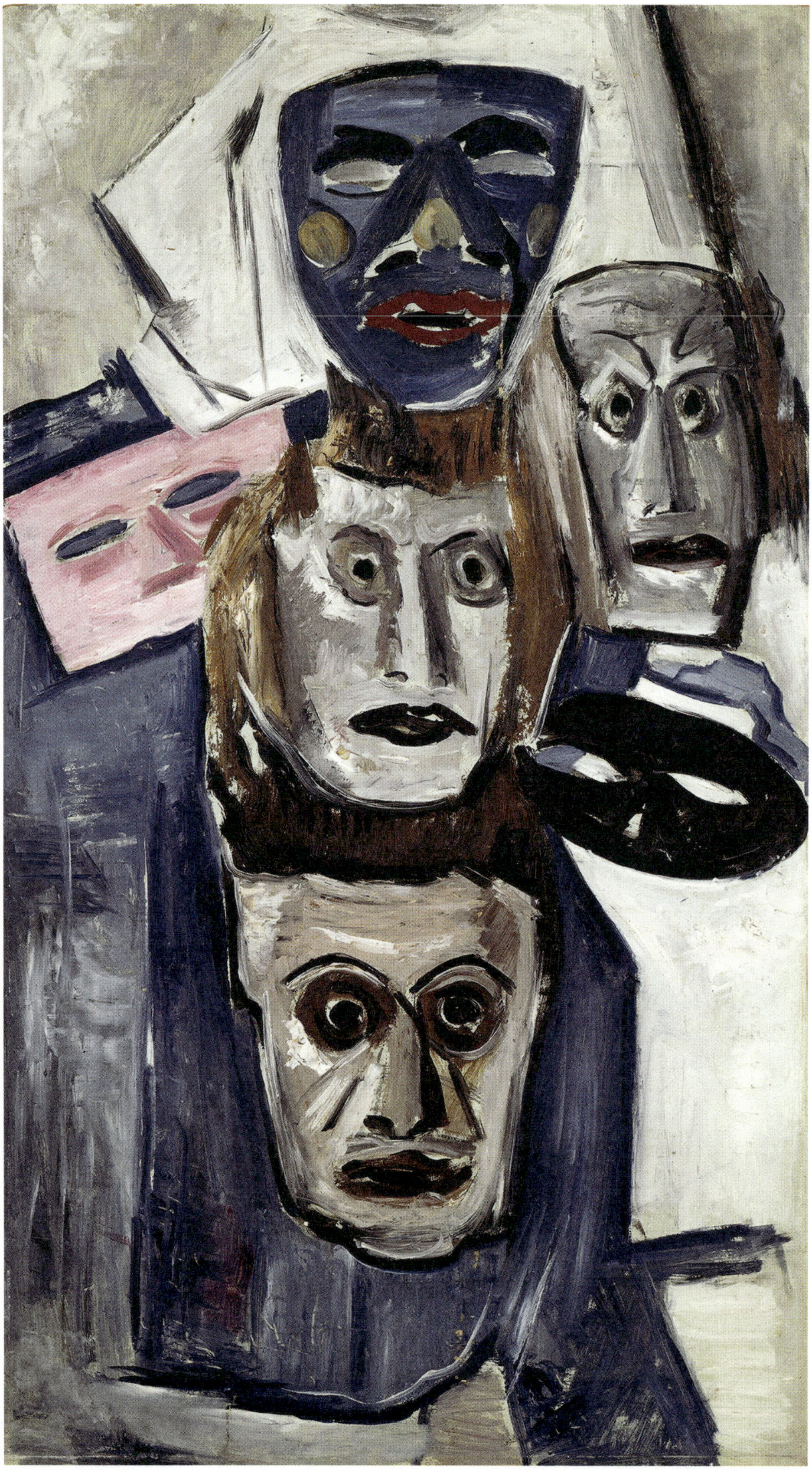

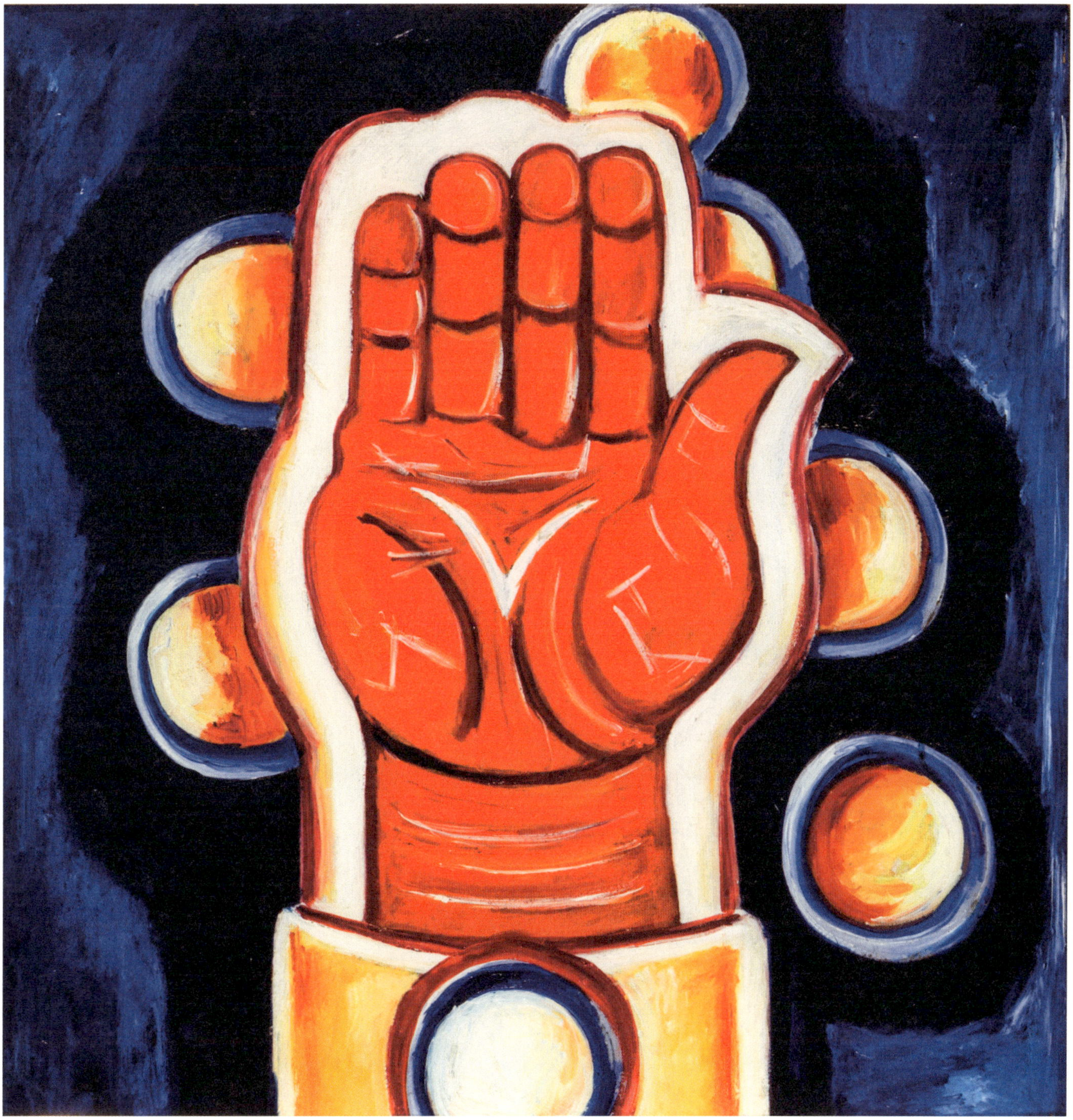

62 Masks, 1931-1932
64 Morgenrot, 1932

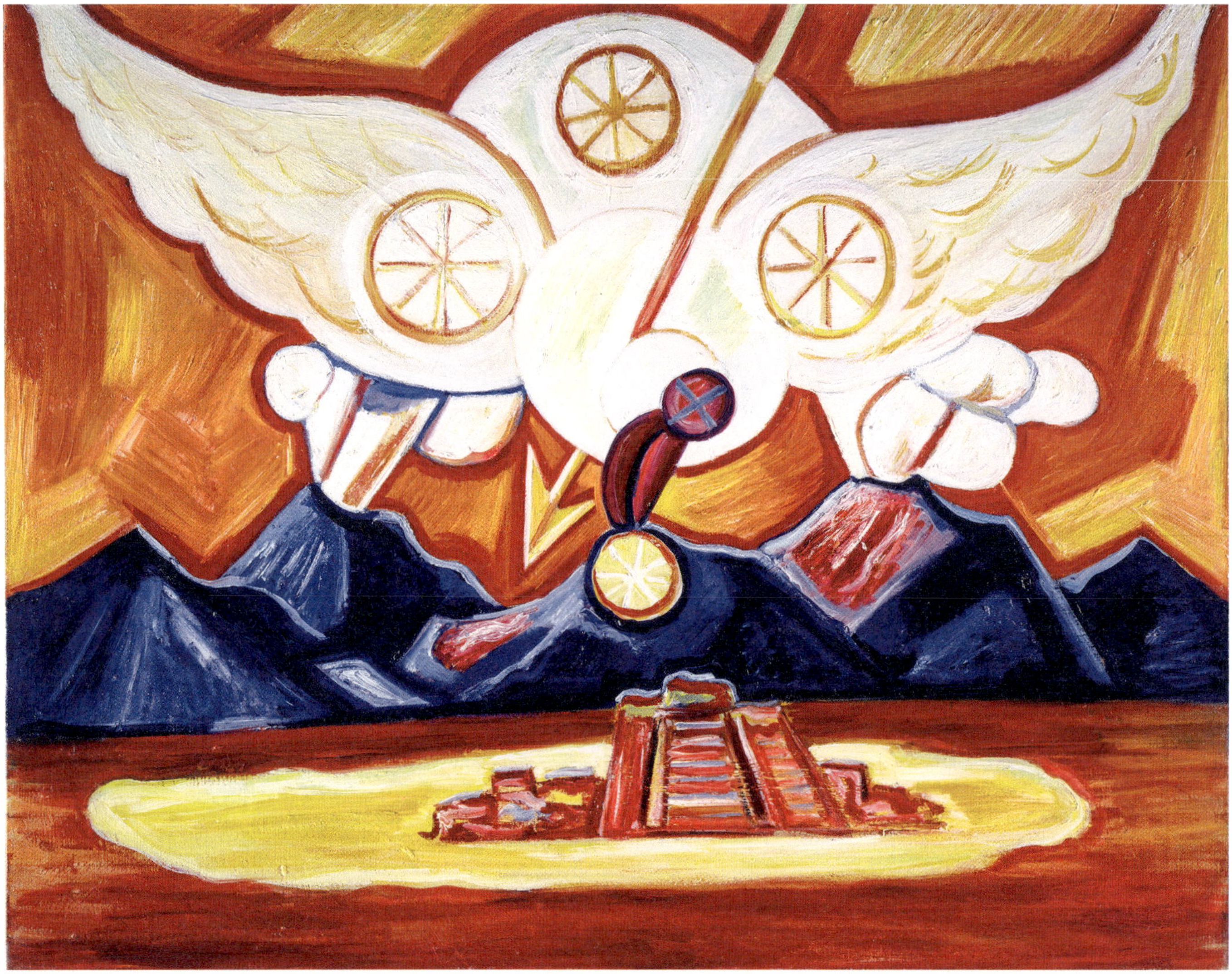

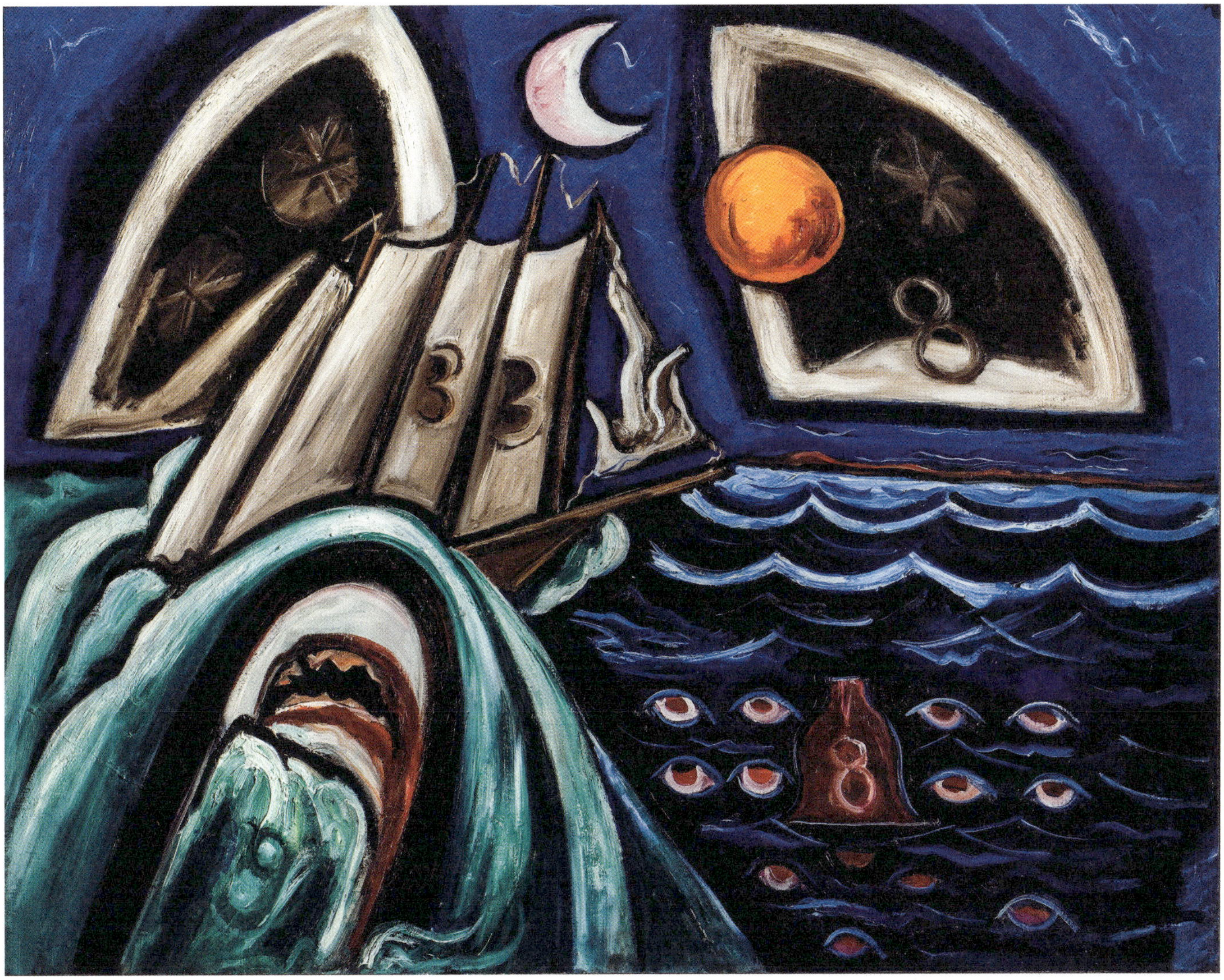

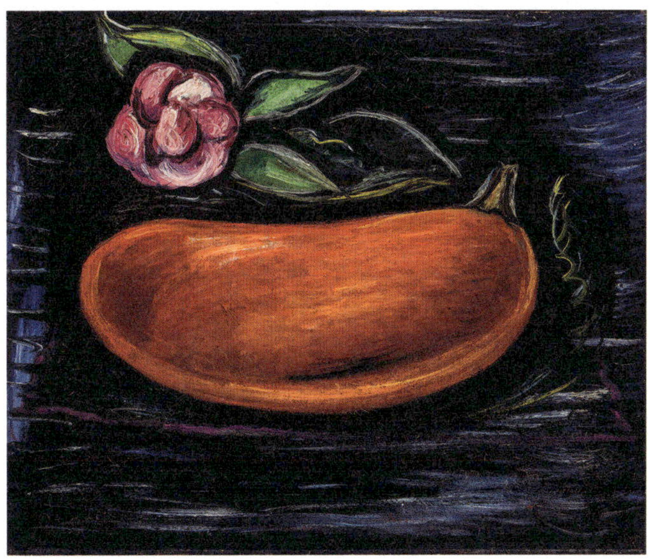

66 Tollan, Aztec Legend, 1933

67 Eight Bells Folly: Memorial to Hart Crane, 1933
65 Still Life, 1932-1933

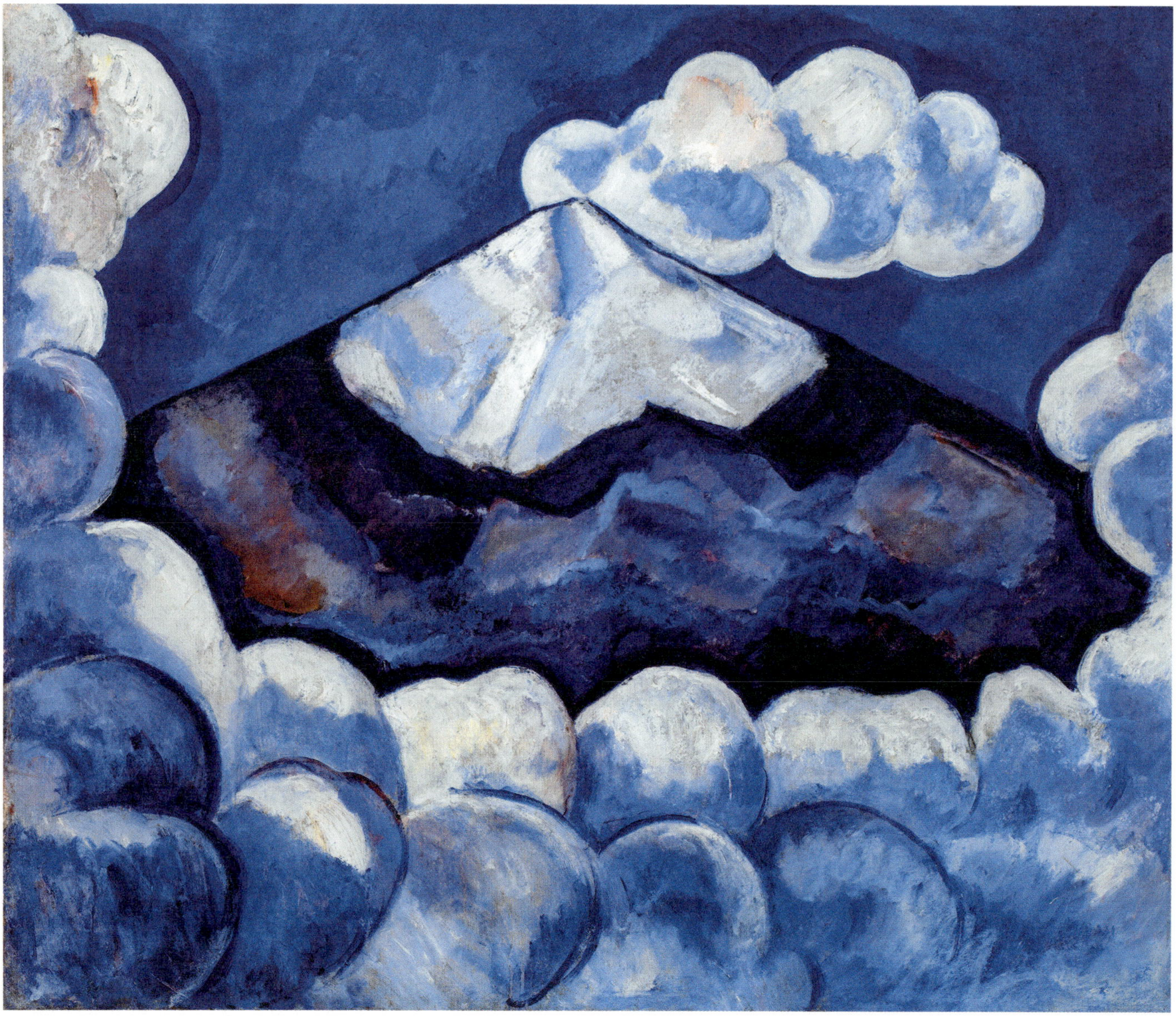

63 Popocatepetl, Spirited Morning – Mexico, 1932

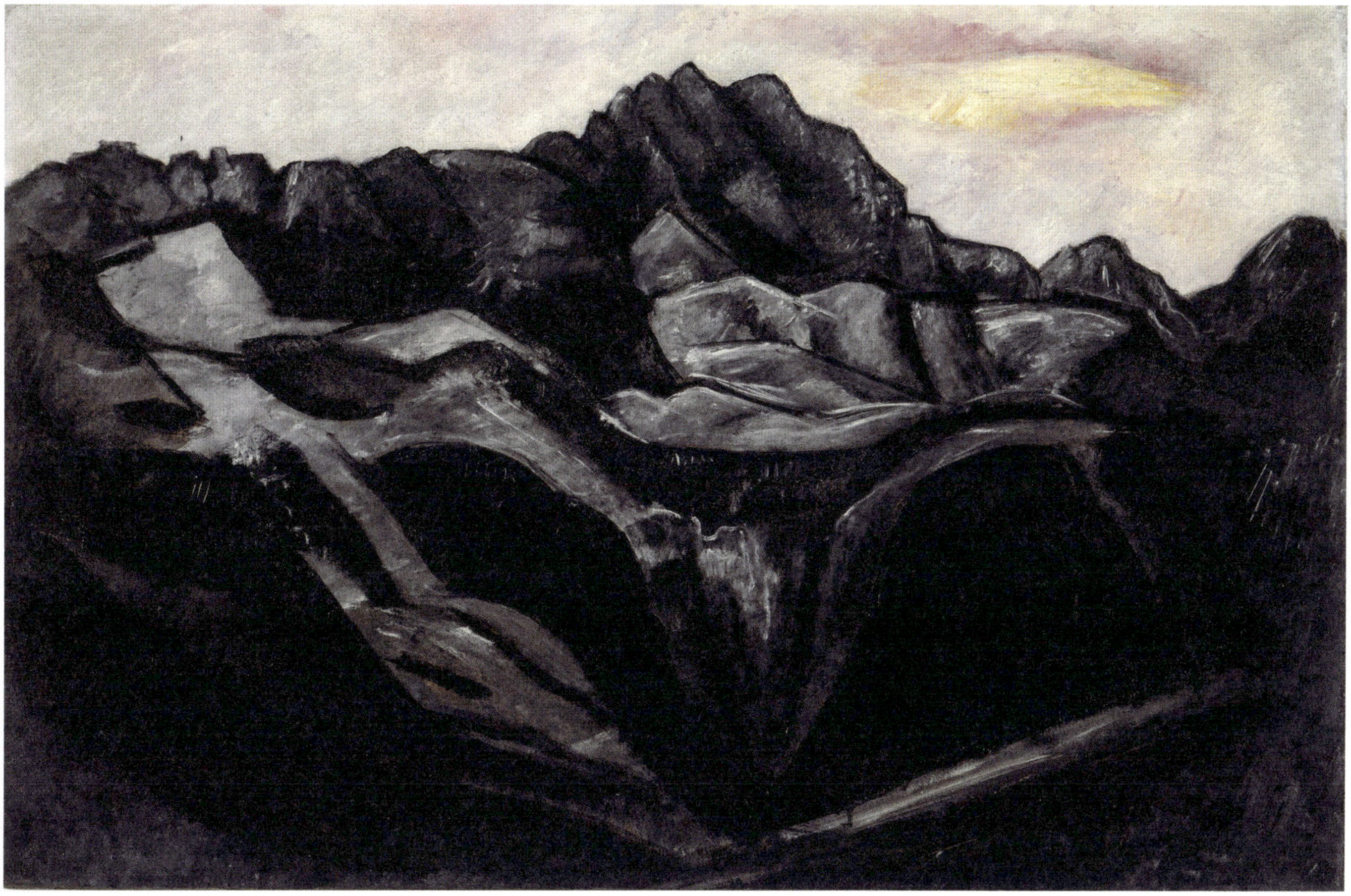

68 Garmisch-Partenkirchen II, 1933

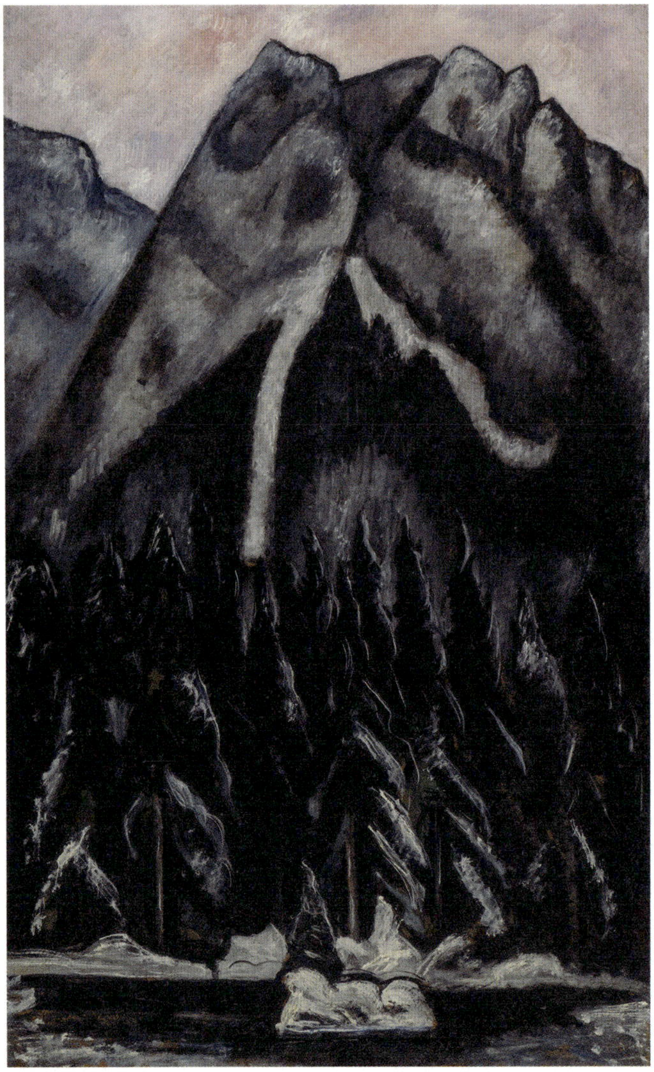

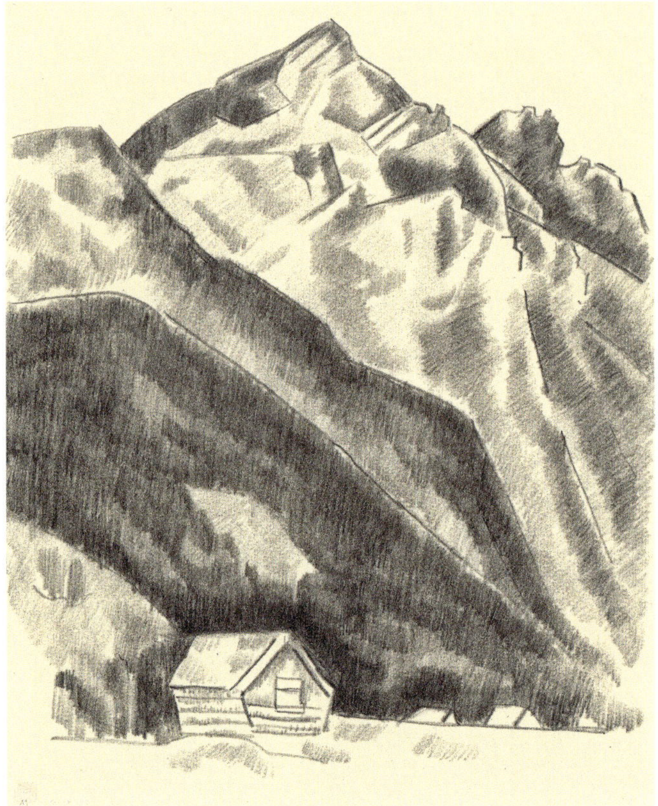

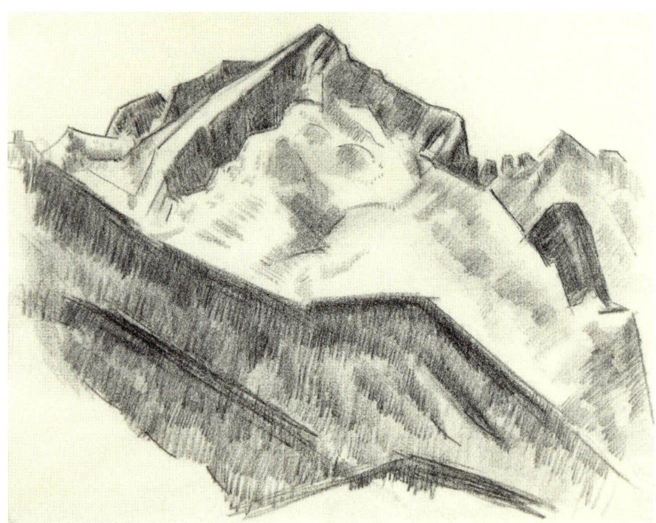

69 Bavarian Alps, Garmisch-Partenkirchen, 1933-1934
126 Mountain Landscape (Garmisch-Partenkirchen), c. 1933

125 Mountain (Alpspitze), c. 1933

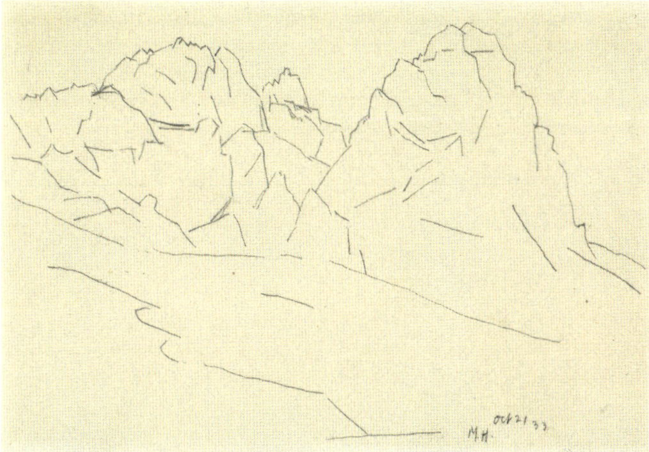

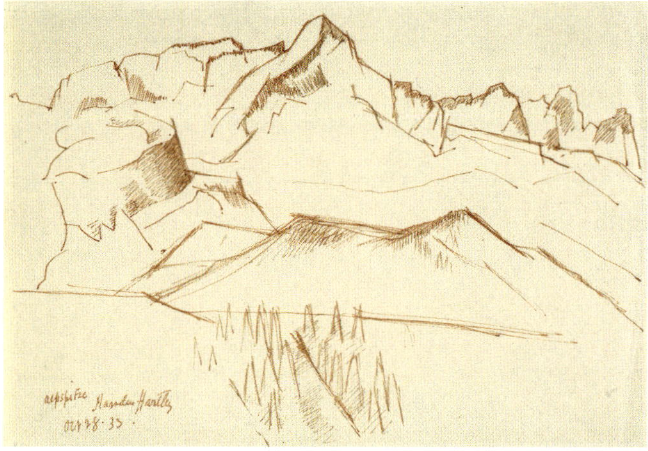

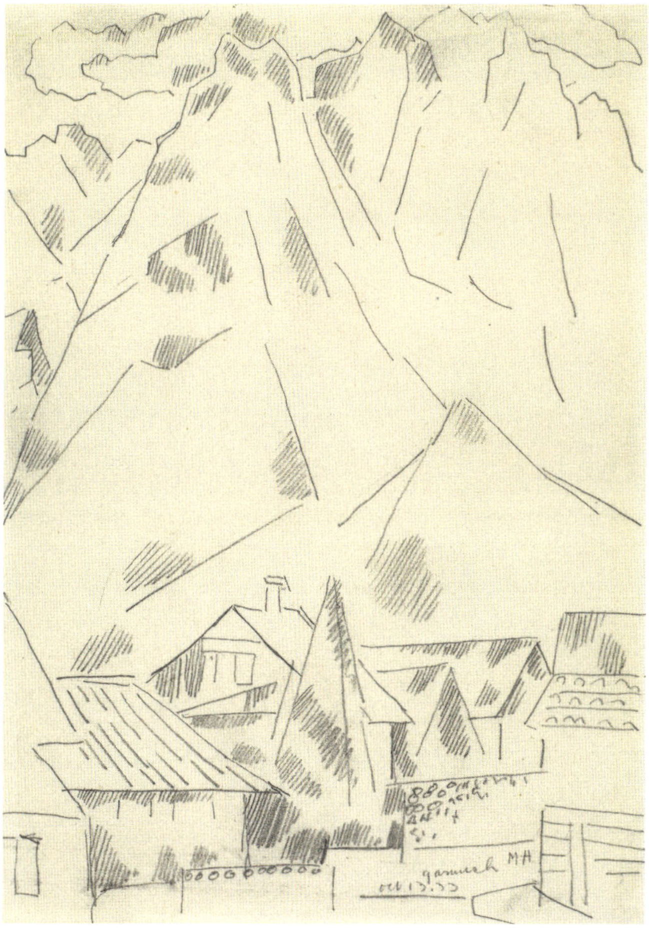

123 Untitled (The Alps), 1933
124 Alpspitze, 1933

122 Garmisch, 1933

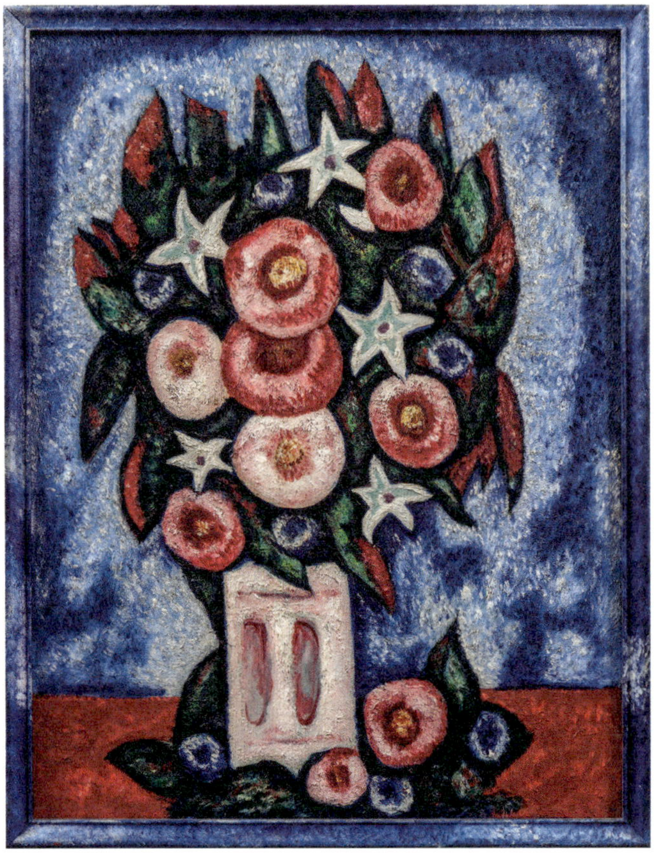

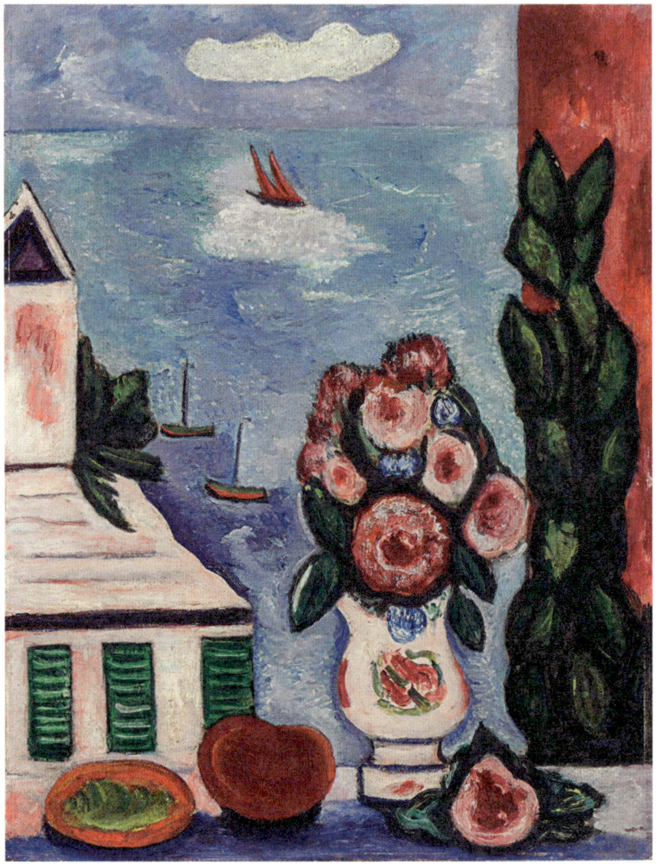

71 Night and Some Flowers, 1935-1936
70 Still Life, c. 1935

72 Red Flowers and Sailboat, c. 1935-1936

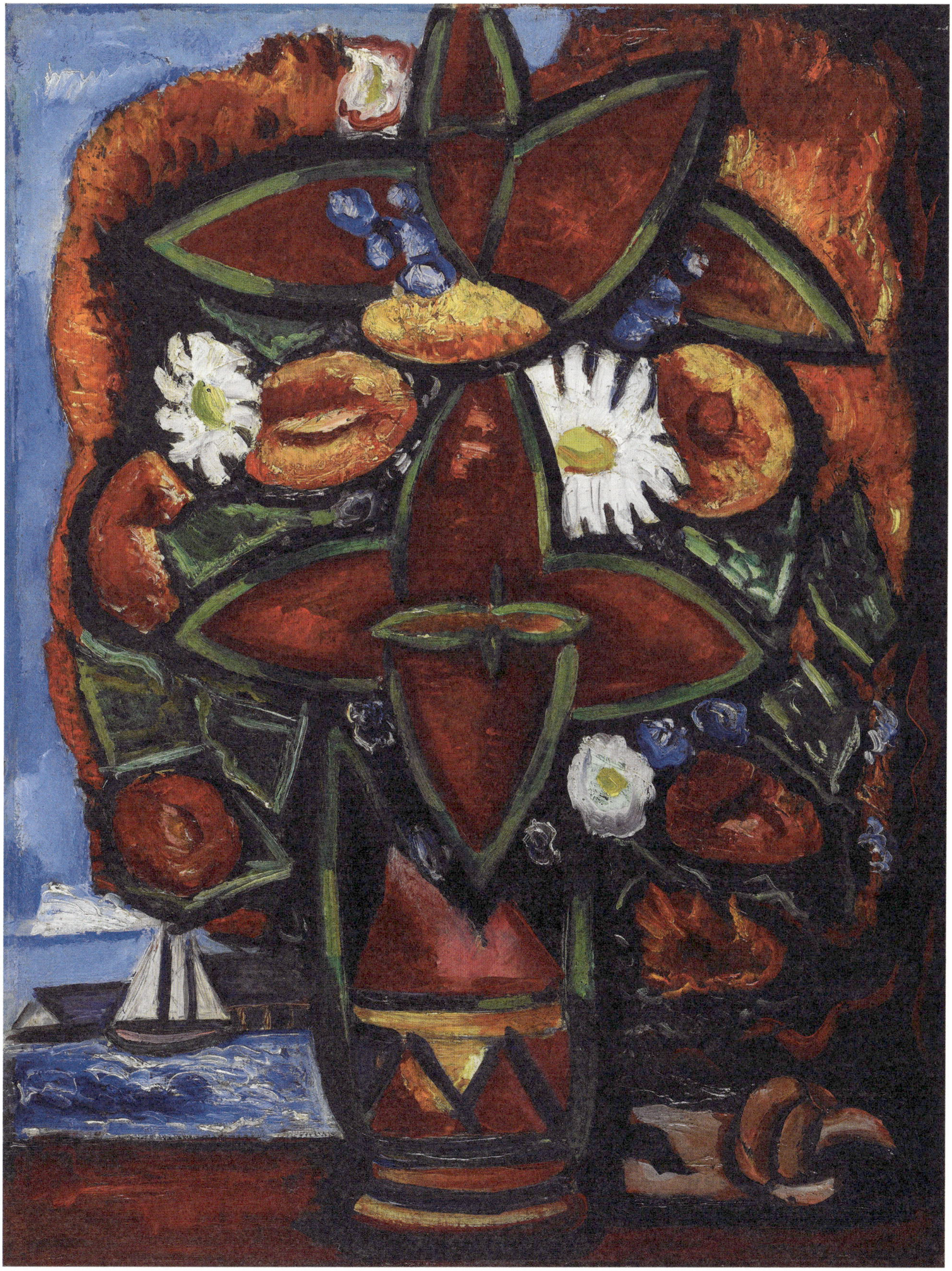

Paul Cézanne: Through-Line

By Randall R. Griffey

Rooted in and responsive to an exceptionally wide range of seemingly ever-evolving philosophical, literary, and artistic sources, Hartley's diverse oeuvre betrays very few unbroken through-lines easily. Rather, it can seem full of surprising and sometimes inexplicable plot twists and turns. Indeed, several of his critics, both during and following his lifetime, have faulted Hartley for apparent lack of focus and indecisiveness. Take, for example, Clement Greenberg's assessment in 1944 on the occasion of Hartley's memorial retrospective at MoMA: "Hartley as half lyricist and half architect, then half fauve and half expressionist; this was his difficulty and the source of the unevenness for which he is blamed. The many different influences, impulses, and aspirations woven into his art sharpened these contradictions."[77]

Notwithstanding the profound impact of a myriad of artists and writers on Hartley's work, especially the earlier American painters Winslow Homer and Albert Pinkham Ryder, arguably none surpasses Paul Cézanne in importance. As testament to and material evidence of Hartley's reverence for the Post-Impressionist, the Maine native died with several Cézanne-related memorabilia among his personal effects. These included two photographic portraits – one in which the Frenchman stands regally in a top hat and coat, the other where he sits, hands folded, in front of his *The Large Bathers* (*Les Grandes baigneuses*) (1895-1906; now Barnes Collection) (fig. 2) – and an unused postcard with a reproduction of *Houses in Provence: The Riaux Valley near L'Estaque* (c. 1883; now National Gallery of Art, Washington, D.C.).[78]

The French Post-Impressionist was a critical aesthetic through-line coursing in and out of the American painter's art from nearly the beginning of his career to the very end, taking different shapes and guises over time. In the 1910s, Cézanne's work served as part of what Hartley would later describe as the "artist's education" that he desired and received in Paris.[79] In years following, particularly in the more unsettled and uncertain periods in Hartley's career (the 1920s, in particular), the Frenchman's distinctive quasi-architectonic reinterpretation of nature in painting provided the American with a reassuring, authoritative stylistic guidebook of sorts, one he emulated at times with rather derivative results. Later in his career, as Hartley reinvented himself as "The Painter from Maine" in the heyday of Regionalism in American art, Cézanne, whose paintings of his home region of Aix-en-Provence propelled him to great fame, served the Mainer, somewhat ironically, as a role model, as Hartley sought more recognition and reward by demonstrating his "American" bona fides to critics and larger audiences by likewise painting his native place.

As several scholars have explained, including Patricia McDonnell, Hartley seemingly began engaging with Cézanne's imagery and ideas about art even before experiencing first hand any of the Post-Impressionist's art.[80] An important early study of Cézanne by German critic Julius Meier-Graefe seems to have provided Hartley a critical introduction. Furthermore, as Bruce Weber has noted, Hartley also studied Cézanne initially from reproductions, some of which Alfred Stieglitz sent to him.[81] Throughout this early period, during which Hartley worked mostly in North Lovell, Maine, he kept a well-known (but possibly apocryphal) Cézanne quote on his studio wall for inspiration and guidance: "When color reaches richness form attains fulness" (*Quand la couleur est à sa richesse, la forme est à sa plénitude*).[82] Stieglitz debuted Cézanne at his influential New York gallery, 291, in the form of three lithographs in an exhibition that ran from 1910 to 1911, but no evidence confirms Hartley's attendance there.[83]

A still life showing two pears cuddling like lovers on a draped compote is among the earliest manifestations of Hartley's emergent study and emulations of Cézanne's work in that genre (cat. 13). Compositionally unpretentious and modest in scale, the painting seems to be a rejoinder the Frenchman's oft-quoted declaration, "With an apple I will astonish Paris," though the American here deploys a different fruit. However, Hartley's paint is typically meatier and brushstrokes thicker than the Frenchman's, characteristics that imbue his canvases with a sense of physical directness and immediacy.

Pears dates close in time to Hartley's first encounter with paintings by the French Post-Impressionist. In late 1911 (or early 1912), he visited the private New York collection of Henry and Louisine

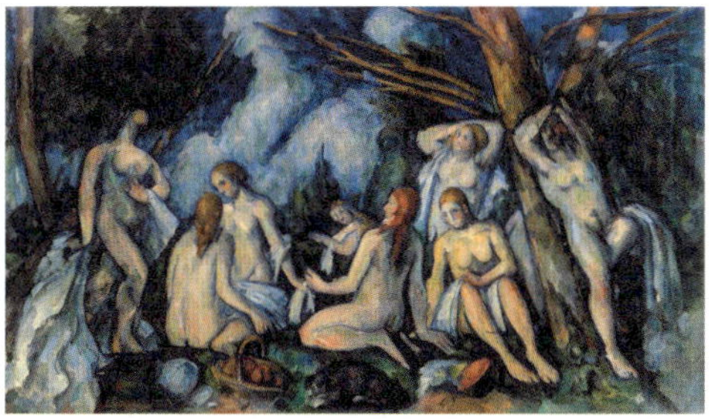

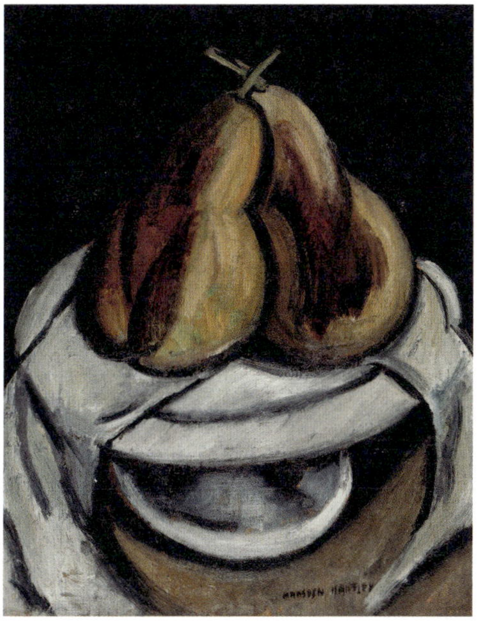

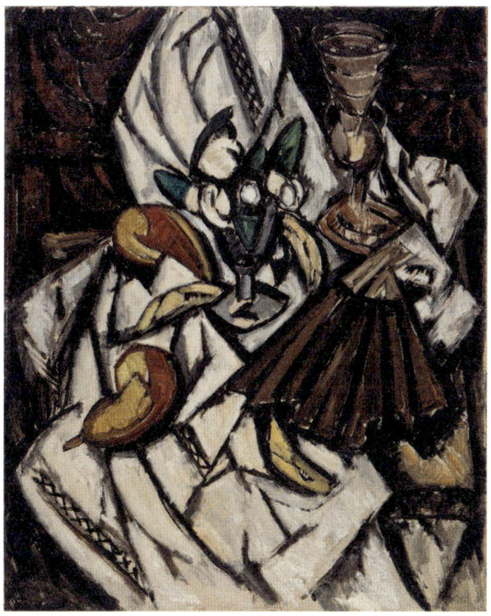

Fig. 2 Paul Cézanne: *The Large Bathers*, 1895-1906
13 *Pears*, 1911
14 *Still Life with Fan*, 1912

Havemeyer, where he encountered several still lifes, in addition to portraits and landscapes, an experience after which he was "afire with the hope of getting to Paris," as he later recalled.[84] With Stieglitz's support, Hartley ventured to Paris for the first time in April 1912 and remained in the City of Lights initially for five months, during which he augmented his study of Cézanne with other modern French artists, including Picasso, Braque, and Matisse. *Still Life with Fan* (1912) (cat. 14) exemplifies the synthetic style that many of his Paris-period canvases betray: the solidity of Cézanne put into somewhat uneasy relationship with the fractured and beveled forms of Cubism.

As Patricia McDonnell has argued, "For Hartley, Cézanne's breakthrough did not center on his formal innovations per se but on his institutive expressiveness, something Hartley then called 'vision.'"[85] However, Cézanne's sway over Hartley waned considerably as Germany gradually superseded Paris in his imagination and art by mid-1913. When wartime conditions forced Hartley to return to New York in December 1915 and after critics received his Berlin-period paintings coolly when Stieglitz showed them the following spring, the artist set upon something of an odyssey to regain direction. A key stop on along this journey in 1918-1919 was New Mexico, a place that prompted him to proclaim and to theorize a "New Realism" rooted in landscape painting, a fresh course that precipitated a return to Cézanne.[86] In both paint and pastel, Hartley rendered the particular topography the desert hills and arroyos with prismatic clarity modeled partly on the Post-Impressionist's technique. Hartley's landscape subject appear concentrated in the center of the composition, such as *New Mexico Hills* (1918) and *New Mexico No. 2* (1919) (cat. 44), which most readily betray Cézanne's precedent, particularly the Frenchman's late renderings of Aix's Mont Sainte-Victoire (fig. 3).

Hartley returned to Germany after the war, and, once again, Cézanne's imprint on his painting faded temporarily. The 1920s constituted arguably the most unsettled period in Hartley's career, one that enhanced his long-standing feelings of detachment and rootlessness. In this regard, the popular myth of Cézanne as a solitary genius held irresistible appeal, so much so that Hartley, in 1925, moved to the south of France, eventually to Aix, where Hartley

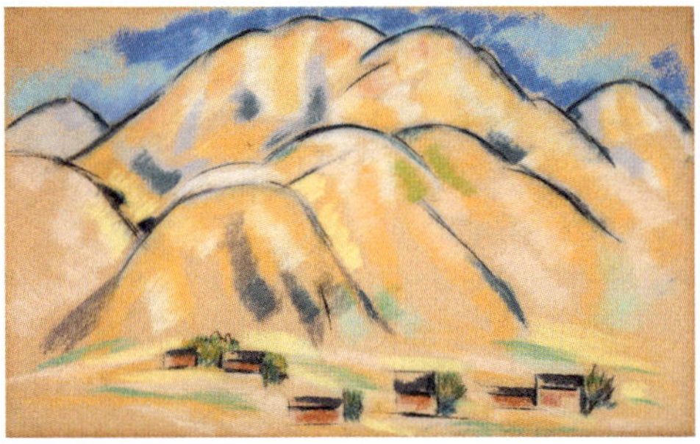

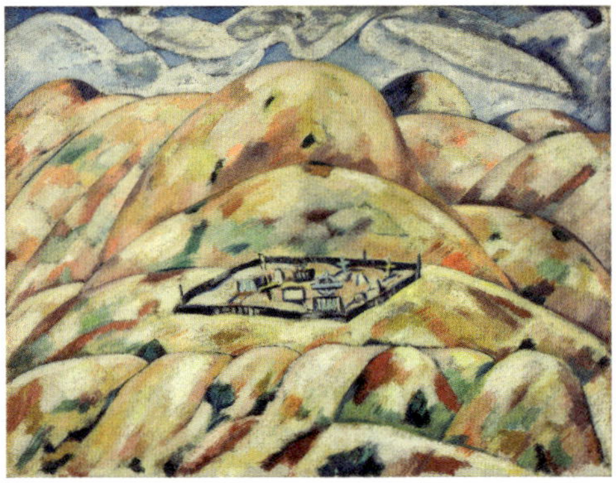

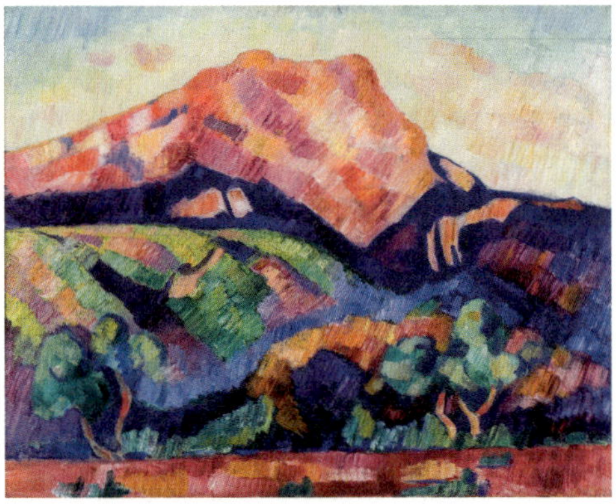

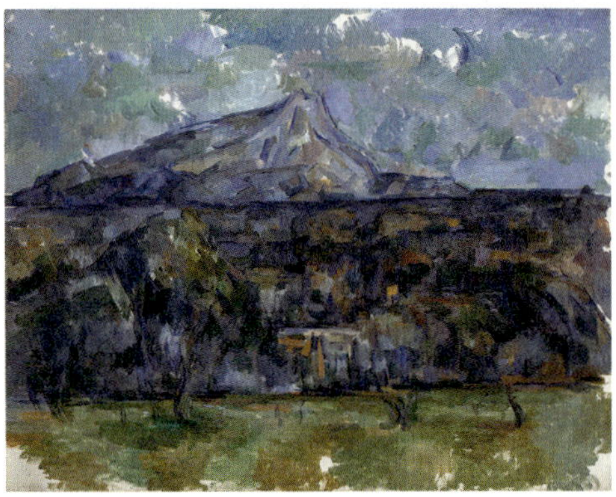

115 *New Mexico Hills*, 1918
44 *New Mexico Hills No. 2*, 1919
54 *Mont Sainte-Victoire*, 1927
Fig. 3 Paul Cézanne: *Mont Sainte-Victoire*, c. 1902-1905

remained in worshipful communion with the French master for several months.[87] Walking figuratively and sometimes even literally in the French painter's footsteps, Hartley produced new landscapes and still lifes in oil, watercolor, and drawing that unabashedly divulge the American's debt and fidelity.

One in a series of paintings of Aix's geological landmark and Cézanne's signature landscape subject, *Mont Sainte-Victoire* (cat. 54) veritably pulsates with color and stacked, staccato brushwork. The painting, like others closely related to it, ranks among the most joyous pictures Hartley ever produced and, with hindsight, it portends his later adoption of Maine's Mount Katahdin as his own geological subject. However, for Stieglitz – and other advocates of homegrown modern American art – such new work by Hartley only underscored the artist's continuing lack of roots in his native soil and culture. While Hartley rather resented and resisted expectations to paint "American," he increasingly felt greater need for critical and commercial success and desire for acclaim. Painting in such clear emulation of the Frenchman would not aid him in achieving these interconnected goals.

Dating to the summer of 1930, when Hartley painted in the White Mountains of New Hampshire, *White Top Mountain* (cat. 58) seems restrained, even repressed by comparison with the chromatic and impastoed *Mont Sainte-Victoire*. Hints of Cézanneque technique remain, but these here give way somewhat to a resurgent naturalism in Hartley's painting, a new direction reinforced by the verdant subject and palette of *Landscape No. 35* (cat. 59). Productive interludes in both Mexico (1932-1933) and Bavaria (1933-1934) interrupted Hartley's brief but portentous reengagement with American landscape, one that he reprised in a more sustained series of paintings inspired by Dogtown, Massachusetts.

Over the course of the 1930s, opportunities for Hartley and other artists to study major works by Cézanne on public view in New York dramatically increased. In 1929, Louisine Havemeyer gave The Metropolitan her collection of mostly nineteenth-century French painting. The Museum celebrated this impressive haul with an exhibition in 1930, a show Hartley attended and one that reacquainted him with several of the works he saw in the family home years earlier. The opening of the Museum of Modern Art in 1930 likewise enhanced Cézanne's exposure in the city, especially after the museum acquired the collection of Lillie P. Bliss, which included a strong group of works by the Provençal.

The profound and enduring impact of Cézanne was fundamental to Hartley's late career, from his final exhibition with Stieglitz in 1937 to his death in 1943, though it is less explicitly manifest in his style than in years past. Throughout this period, Hartley promoted himself as the "Painter from Maine" and, by 1939, painted and exhibited almost exclusively landscapes, still lifes, and figures connected to his home state in a direct, rough-hewn manner critics increasingly lauded as "American."[88] In many ways, Hartley modeled his gambit for acclaim on Cézanne's artistic identity as a painter whose devotion to his native region segued into status of national icon and, even more, international renown.

Cultural circumstances in and around the year 1939 surely stoked Hartley's hopes that his campaign could be successful. That year marked the centenary of Cézanne's birth – January 19, 1839 – an anniversary commemorated with a host of new exhibitions, tributes, and publications in both Europe and the U.S.[89] "Next Thursday marks the hundredth anniversary of the birth of Paul Cézanne, the father of modern painting – that wholly unpredicted, greatly controversial, superbly defiant break with the past," critic R. E. Turpin announced in the January 15, 1939, edition of *The New York Times*, in an article headlined triumphantly: "Cézanne Still Dominates the Era He Launched."[90] The occasion was a source of such national pride that France issued a commemorative stamp that confirmed his lofty place in the French cultural pantheon.

For Hartley, the Cézanne centenary sparked a new spate of painterly responses to the Frenchman's art and legacy, manifestations that went beyond superficial considerations of style. Among other effects, it spurred his motivation to venture once and for all to Mount Katahdin in Baxter State Park to claim it as his corollary to Cézanne's Mont Sainte-Victoire. *Mount Katahdin, Winter* and *Mount Katahdin, Autumn, No. 1* (cat. 86-87) rank among the earliest painted variations of the theme of the subject Hartley executed from sketches and memory following his one and only trip to the mountain (in

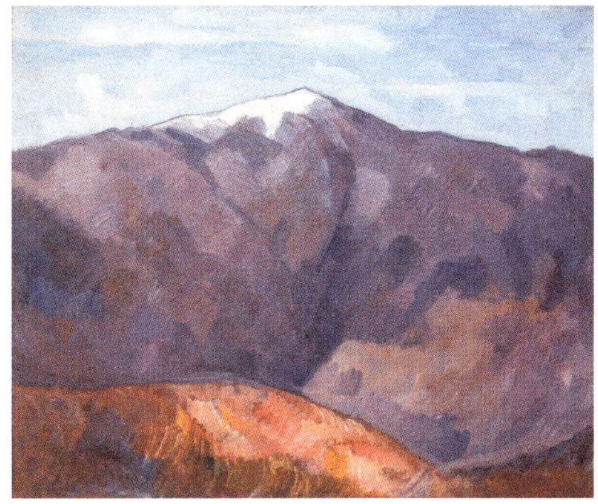

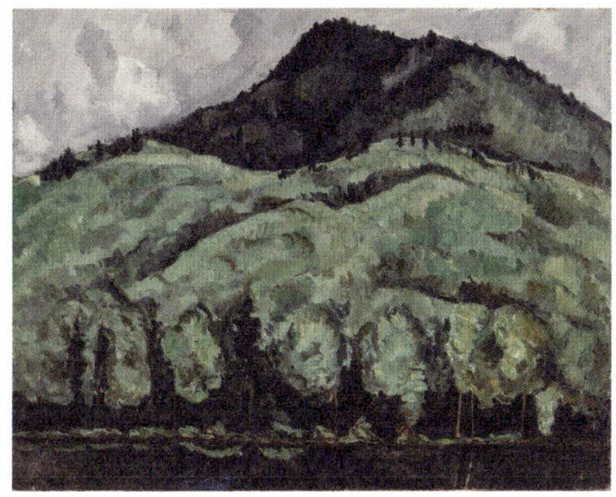

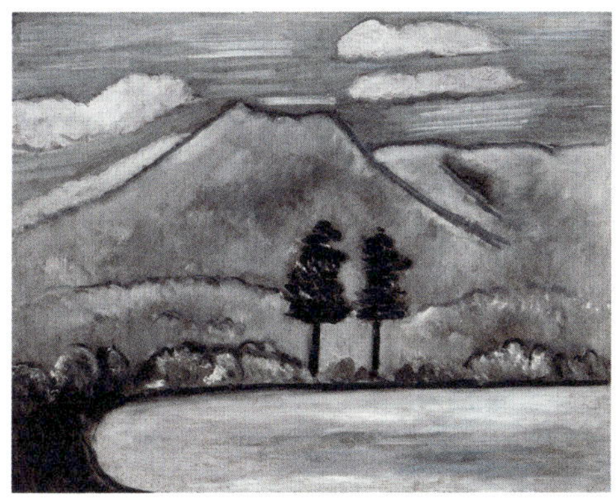

58 *White Top Mountain*, 1930
59 *Landscape No. 35 (Beaver Lake, Lost River Region)*, 1930
86 *Mt. Katahdin, Winter*, 1939-1940

October 1939). As *Mount Katahdin* (cat. 103) and *Mt. Katahdin – November Afternoon* attest, the painter returned to the subject many months, even years, after his expedition, culminating in a series of about a dozen paintings in which Hartley explored over time a compositional scheme consisting of four component parts: lake, foothills, mountain, and a strip of sky often with rocklike clouds, a combination that reprises his earliest paintings of Maine. While the seasons and meteorological conditions change from picture to picture, the mountain remains isolated and resolute, qualities with which Hartley identified.

Hartley's most explicit and specific response to Cézanne late in his career is *Canuck Yankee Lumberjack at Old Orchard Beach, Maine* (cat. 96). Showing a deeply tanned male bather standing centrally against stacked expanses of beach, sea, and sky with arms and legs akimbo, the painting is based on sketches that Hartley made at Old Orchard Beach, a working-class summer destination south of Portland known as a venue for bawdy behavior. *Canuck Yankee Lumberjack* unambiguously conjures Cézanne's *Grand Baigneur* (fig. 5), a painting Hartley would have known from visits to MoMA, where it entered the collection in 1934, and one he likely saw again at the New York World's Fair of 1939-1940. Thus, Cézanne's impact on Hartley extended beyond landscape to figure painting, especially the hulking and, in hindsight, provocatively homoerotic male figures that played such a key role in securing his late-career success with critics and museums.

Hartley entered The Met's collection in 1942 with *Lobster Fishermen* (cat. 99), a painting the Museum acquired out of *Artists for Victory*, an exhibition fueled by wartime patriotism. The painting imagines a scene in coastal village of Corea, Maine, of rugged lobstermen gathered on the harbor docks and accompanied by regional accoutrements: traps, ropes, and shack houses extending into a flattened distance. Portrayed as secular saints, these workers on break are Cézanne's card players (fig. 4) recast as Maine fishermen, who are likewise unassumingly heroic exemplars of rural life.

Hartley's entrée into The Met's collection with *Lobster Fishermen* was part of a wave of critical and professional success his Maine painting afforded him, as many critics and curators were convinced of their sincerity and native-ness, and that this one-time prodigal painter had finally and fully returned

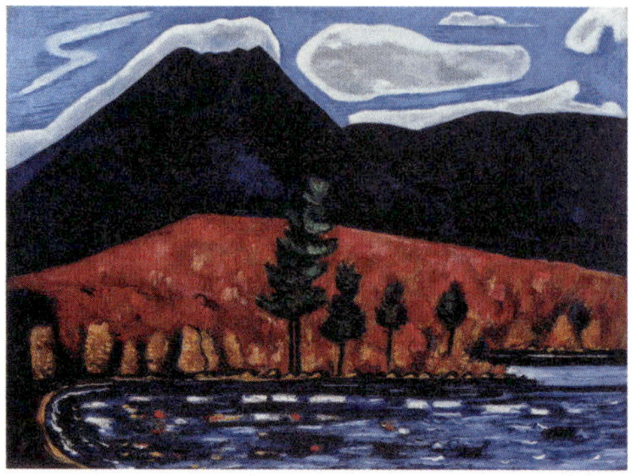

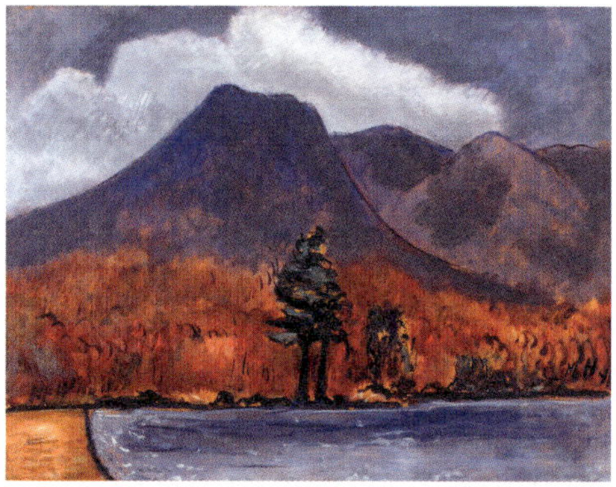

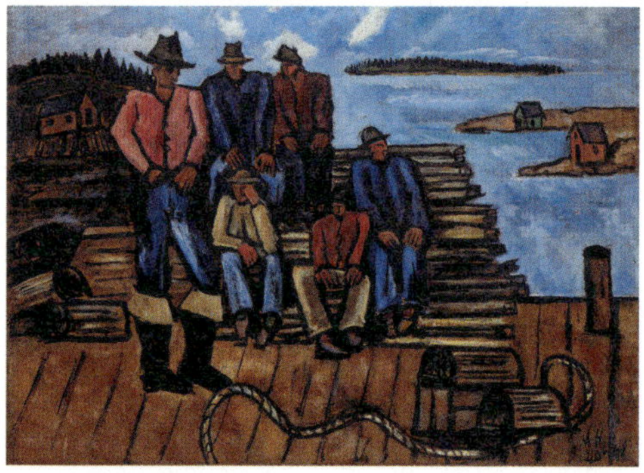

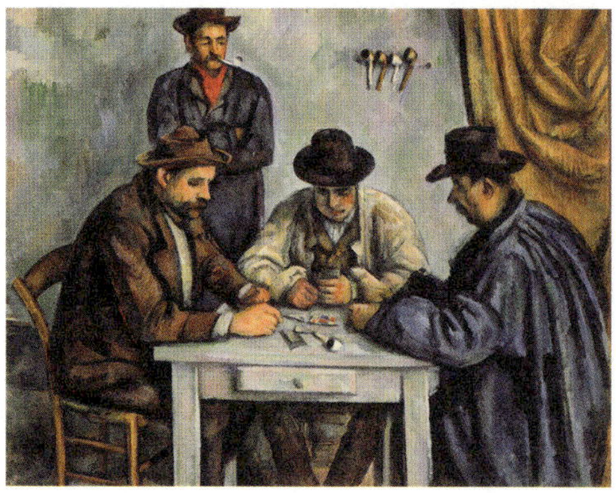

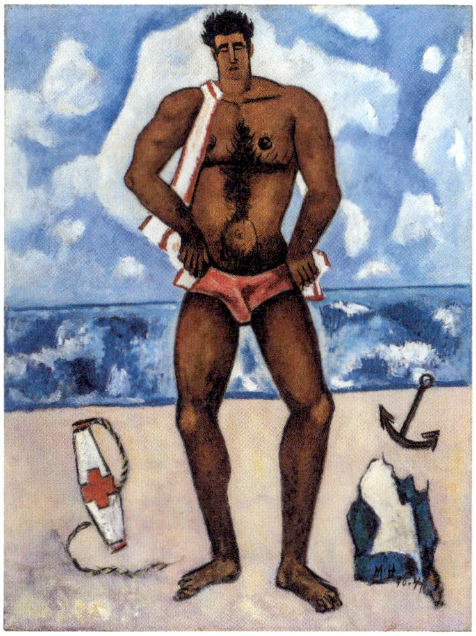

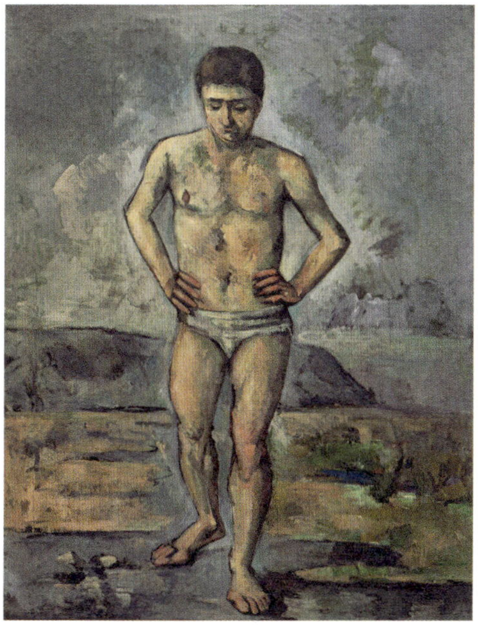

home. Writing to his niece and confidante Norma Berger in late 1942, Hartley, after years of neglect and hardship, proclaimed, "I have a high position as a painter – as high as anyone ... When I am no longer here my name will register forever in the history of American art."[91] The irony of Hartley's claim to greatness is that it presumes his posthumous renown would be based on his late Maine work, not the earlier, previously maligned Berlin-period abstract paintings, such as *Portrait of a German Officer* (cat. 22, p. 33), a painting that subsequently became a mainstay of modern art textbooks. However, at the time of his death, Hartley felt assured he had successfully followed Cézanne's precedent by becoming, in essence, a regional painter recognized widely as a great modernist.

87 *Mount Katahdin, Autumn, No. 1*, 1939-1940
103 *Mount Katahdin*, 1941
99 *Lobster Fishermen*, 1940-1941
Fig. 4 Paul Cézanne: *The Card Players*, 1890-1892

96 *Canuck Yankee Lumberjack at Old Orchard Beach, Maine*, 1940-1941
Fig. 5 Paul Cézanne: *The Bather*, c. 1885

Randall R. Griffey is Curator in the Department of Modern and Contemporary Art at The Metropolitan Museum of Art, where he has curated numerous exhibitions, including *Marsden Hartley's Maine* (with Elizabeth Finch and Donna M. Cassidy).

Summer Evening

Ashes of rose
Fade in the east sky

Thru the quivering poplars
Sun flashed swallows fly

Broad the blue stream flows
Under the arched bridge

Down the gleaming sun goes
Over the earth's edge

A flush in the sun's wake
A ripple – behind a swan
On the tremulous lake
And the day – Is gone!

1904

Salutations to a Mouse

If a mouse makes a nest
Of one's written words,
Is there else to do but accept
The flattery?
I have deemed it wise to do so.
I have thanked him
Sufficiently
As he scurried in and out
Of the room,
He has faced the Winter
With a nest of my words.
I did not suspect them
Of such worth against the cold

1919

Swallows

The Blueback swallows with their
saffron breasts
Punctuate the rooftree – and they
make pretty commas
On the wires,
And place suberb accents above
the blowing corn –
How would it be to skim like them,
The surface of all things,
To graze the cheek of every beauty,
And press one's lips to the sky,
with a sudden frenzy –
To dot the pale vowels on the
pages of the sun
With swift points of beetle-blue
They turn their breasts up to
the sky
Swinging arrow-like, upon a skipping
wind,
These countless commas with
painted wings.

1919

The eagle wants no friends,
employs his thoughts to other ends –
he has his circles to inscribe
twelve thousand feet from where
the fishes comb the sea,
he finds his solace in unscathed
immensity,
where eagles think, there is no need
of being lonesome –
In isolation
is a deep revealing sense
of home.

1923-1929

Whoever dies – dies for the love
of beauty –
no matter what the shape the sense
is there,
for there is obviously beauty –
everywhere –

The mole with its 22 tentacles smells
out the loveliness of the worm beneath
the earth –
the weasel sucks its victim's blood
then eats its brains –
what morsel to wrap a thin tongue
around!
Even the rat knows sweet tenderness
of love –
the raccoon reaches its young to
wash the food it eats.
Everything dies for love of
something better
a loose – or a lost ideal –
precision of the letter.

1939

To the Nameless One

You, who have power over
everything obscure
Listen – come over here, sit by
my side
and let me say the things I want
to say –
I want nothing in the way of artificial
heavens!
The earth is all I know of wonder.
I lived and was nurtured in the
magic of dreams
bright flames of spirit laughter
around all my seething frame.

1940-1943

This Portrait of a Seadove – Dead

Seadove in a shroud
of sand, all shiny with
thick clips of sun –
seadove in a shroud
of sand, and the last word
spoke – alone
I did not carry messages
for love or war, to end their
ways,
I only bore flicked wave caresses
took them to a timely place;
I gave them to my brood to drink,
a draft of silence on the brink
of death I gave, telling them also
to be brave,
have grace
to face
the loneness of their days.
I shut my eye on a kiss
of sun,
and this I give to
everyone.

1936

Marsden Hartley wrote just as much as he painted. In the catalogue texts both his poems and essays are quoted. A small selection of poems from various phases of his life is shown here. A larger selection is included in the exhibition. Marsden Hartley's poems have been published in *The Collected Poems of Marsden Hartley, 1904-1943* (1987), edited by Gail R. Scott.

On the Necessity to Poetize Sensations in Order to Comprehend Them: Marsden Hartley as a Writer

By Edyta Frelik

In 1909, Marsden Hartley was already thirty-two years old when he was discovered by Alfred Stieglitz, the most important early promoter of modern art in America. A photographer and gallery owner, Stieglitz surrounded himself with aspiring artists and literary friends, who all shared a common passion for the avant-garde. The writers often provided an intellectual substrate from which the painters, sculptors and photographers in the circle derived ideas for their works. Several of these artists not only read, but also practiced different types of writing themselves, and Hartley would become the most prolific and accomplished of them. From the start he emphasized that he was part painter and part writer, always dividing his working days equally between the easel and his writing desk. Coming from a small-town working-class family, he was full of complexes and insecurities, which he sometimes dressed in ambivalent self-irony. For instance, he once wrote in a letter to Stieglitz: "I don't know how much I shall ever write – I shall never deteriorate into a writer any more than I shall deteriorate into just a painter."[92] At the same time, he proved his trust in the value of his mostly self-acquired knowledge of literature, art history and philosophy when he daringly tried his hand at reviews, critical essays, autobiographical prose, and, most importantly, poetry. By the time he first submitted a selection of his manuscripts for publication in *Camera Work*, the "photographic quarterly" published by Stieglitz which was in fact an art-literary magazine, he was well versed in the philosophical ideas of America's most important nineteenth-century thinkers, transcendentalists Ralph Waldo Emerson and Henry David Thoreau, and one of the country's greatest poets, Walt Whitman.[93]

Over the years, Hartley amassed a large collection of books on the most diverse subjects, of which one, mysticism, holds special significance here. The reason is that, on the one hand, he acknowledged that certain emotional states are essentially incommunicable, but on the other, as an artist dedicated to giving expression to the experience of spiritual elevation, he had no qualms about resorting to words in order to increase the chances of his painting being understood correctly. One fine example – included in the present exhibition – is *Raptus*, a work from 1913 which was admittedly inspired by a passage on mysticism in philosopher and psychologist William James's book *The Varieties of Religious Experience*. Explaining to Stieglitz the nature of his own spiritual exaltation, he wrote: "I feel myself in a 'higher' place – there is a something here struggling always toward the light – I can't name it – I only see it."[94] In the painting this is manifested by the abstractness of the composition, which consists of triangular configurations of concentric circles and lines. Their symbolism is literally *readable*, for inscribed across the lower half of the picture is the word "raptus," which in this context means the ecstasy felt when one is transported to heaven. The efficacy of verbal language in visual works is a matter of opinion but Hartley clearly believed in words and used them often in his paintings. He once referred to *Raptus* as "a portrait of a word."[95] Words were Hartley's principal medium when he wrote. None of his colleagues pursued their literary interests and ambitions with greater determination and doggedness than him, and nobody found it peculiar that he devoted as much time to composing poems and essays as he did to painting and associating with artists. As a writer, he relentlessly, and to an extent successfully, sought acceptance and recognition among men and especially women of letters. He had the acclaimed American poet Ezra Pound invite him to contribute to *The Egoist* (initially thrilled, Hartley never delivered the commissioned essay), and others' recommendations, including those of Gertrude Stein, Marianne Moore, Harriet Monroe and Mabel Dodge, opened for him the pages of such leading "little magazines" as *Poetry, Contact* (fig. 6) and *The Little Review* and such prestigious commercial periodicals as *The Nation* and *Vanity Fair*. During his tenure with Stieglitz's galleries he not only matured as a painter, producing some of his most important early works, but composed notable poetry and prose texts, some of which were both anthologized and published as books. Following a collection of essays (*Adventures in the Arts*, published in 1921), his verses appeared in 1923 as *Twenty-five Poems* (fig. 7). Hartley continued to write for the rest of his life, at times obsessively and profusely, but increasingly channeled his creative energies into building his reputation as a painter.

After a long publication hiatus, two more collections of poems came out, *Androscoggin* (1940) and *Sea Burial* (1941). He died in 1943 without fulfilling his desire to become the poet laureate of Maine, his native state. Between Hartley's first posthumous retrospective at the MoMA in 1944 and the 1980 show at the Whitney, his literary output was ignored or overlooked by art historians and critics, his stature as one of the great moderns resting fundamentally on his visual output. Then, two volumes of the artist's essays and poetry, *On Art* (1982) and *Collected Poems* (1987), appeared, providing an important corrective lens. The fuller picture of Hartley as a key modernist figure was further enhanced by the publication of his autobiography, *Somehow a Past* (1997). But a large part of his literary output remains unpublished, raising questions not just about its prospects but, more importantly, about its relevance and quality. In fact, the significance of the texts which have appeared in print seems equally uncertain as their critical treatment continues to be scarce and sparse.

It is rather unlikely that Hartley will ever be elevated to the pedestal occupied by the great modernist poets and writers, a position that he securely holds among the most important painters of the era. That makes it all the more imperative to probe his writings for clues not just about his literary ambitions and abilities but also about how his texts can expand our understanding of his art and its sources – his intellect and his imagination. Many of his peers and younger writers acknowledged that: for instance, in a piece written for *The Black Mountain Review* William Carlos Williams, a leading poet of the Imagist movement, states that Hartley's writing style was "delightful" and it "fascinated" him.[96] Yet, such declarations did not translate into wider recognition and interest, making his perennial lack of confidence both more agonizing and more evident. Even though he did not publicly expose his anxieties and torments, he had many to cope and live with. Reflecting his financial and emotional instability, Hartley's creative surges and declines fluctuated more expressly in his writings than in his paintings, where strain or elation could only be indirectly signaled by means of color and line. Perhaps not so ironically at all, that indirection produced paintings with an emotive unequivocal-

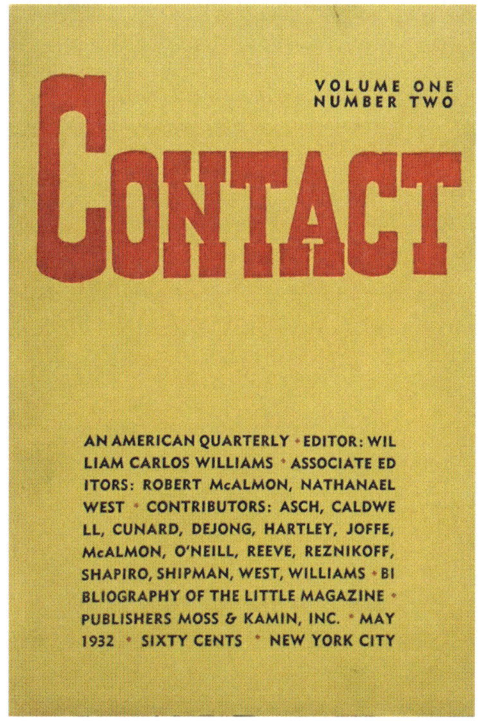

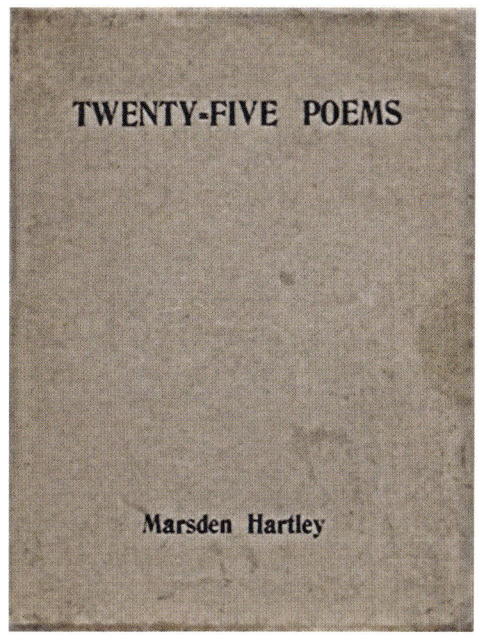

Fig. 6 Front cover of *Contact*, Volume one, Number Two, 1932
Fig. 7 Front cover of *Twenty-five Poems*, 1923

ness of far greater intensity, originality and sincerity than was the case especially with his longer and more complex poems, where the verbose, imitative or overebullient style takes the edge off of the otherwise perceptive, lucid and astute observations or reflections. Hartley's voluminous and varied output testifies that behind his compulsion were poetic intelligence and intuition; we must not forget that he was largely an autodidact who impulsively and voraciously but often also indiscriminately embraced various ideas that he came across during his travels and encounters with people.

Susceptible to influence, he had enough self-possession to persist in his spiritual and aesthetic explorations, but not enough self-confidence to trust his own critical acumen. He craved positive feedback, and when it was not forthcoming his self-doubt and vacillation often aggravated his depressive disposition, as did his chronic lack of material security and proneness to physical ailments. Conversely, words of praise coming from recognized arbiters of taste enraptured him and were magnified by him out of proportion. For instance, when the American writer and mentor for many of the most important Modern artists Gertrude Stein commended him for having "really done it" and accomplishing "what in Kandinsky is only a direction,"[97] he took her words as meaning literally that he was now officially "the most important man of the moment in art" who had "gone miles beyond them all – Picasso included."[98] Perhaps luckily for Hartley, she never revealed any interest in or even awareness of his writing, for everybody knew what she thought about painters writing poetry after she bluntly took Picasso to task with these famous harsh words: "You are extraordinary within your limits but your limits are extraordinarily there."[99] On the other hand, however, Stein's somewhat surprising insistence on keeping traditional artistic domains separate was not very far from Hartley's own views on this matter, though only with regard to others. For instance, in a letter to Stieglitz about Dante Gabriel Rossetti he criticized the English Pre-Raphaelite poet, whom he called "great," for having attempted to also be a painter. His case, Hartley wrote, proved "that if you sing a thing you can't dance it – or if you write it you can't paint it."[100] No stranger to inconsistency and self-contradiction, he saw himself in a reversed perspective – that is, as a painter-dancer who had a thing or two to sing and had to sing them.

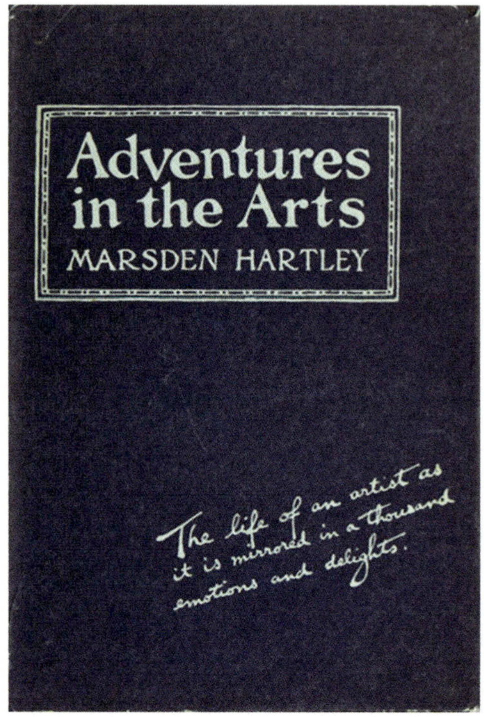

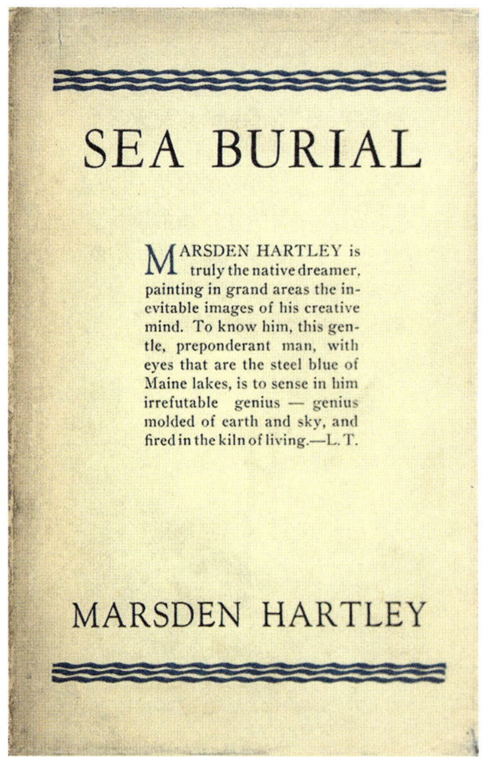

Fig. 8 Front cover of *Adventures in the Arts*, 1921
Fig. 9 Front cover of *Sea Burial*, 1941

His urge to create could not be suitably fulfilled by painting alone, but also had to be expressed verbally. Color and line may suffice to give perfect visual form to emotion, but the line of thought can only be drawn out in words.

Hartley often reflected on the nature of artistic expression and its limits not only in his essays and letters, but also in poems. A fine example is "If It Were the Eye":

If it were the eye
that solely were to satisfy
then we could easily say
what all but faultless blazonry
but when the mind begins to work
then everything goes dark
as very often is the way
the heart no longer knows to breathe
spitting instead of pumping blood
as it does.[101]

In another one, "Yielding the Initiative," he offers an even more articulated exposition of his approach to writing poetry:

We undress the words, frisk them
give them a bath in a respectable
solution
they come out completely clean –
pasteurized
then they must go back to the old
job
of being sweet and pretty and
gracious and dangerous
useful for murder and lying
therefore useful in business, in
society, even in poetry.
The music is sure, but the word
has gone hunting for another
meaning across some fashionable
meadow
another meaning that will look
like honesty – sincerity –
the initiative has been yielded
without mercy.[102]

Hartley of course knew that yielding the initiative to the word did not guarantee finding adequate verbal expression for thoughts and emotions on a par with painting. Nor did he really intend to surrender his individuality in the name of the autonomy of language. He subscribed to the view that pictures *show* things by means of their medium, but poems *say* things because words give voice to speaking subjects. Hartley did not have a "trained" voice, so the one we hear in his poems not only is not strong and clear, but its timbre and other characteristics vary in ways that make his prosody unpredictable and erratic, especially when he tries to emulate effects that impressed him in others. For instance, he admired the ecstatic voice of the English poet Francis Thompson, whom he considered "the last great poet" despite his "stylistic extravagances" and "archaisms" and who held special appeal for Hartley also because he imbued his rhapsodic verses with mystic spirituality.[103] It was an essential quality Hartley strived for in his own poems, which he wanted to "express high feelings" and "mysticism pure."[104]

Assuming that spiritual elevation compelled using words that reach beyond the ordinary, Hartley all too often doused his fiery effusions with exaggerated celebratory diction, in the end reducing authentic emotion to affectation and turning poetic élan into run-of-the-mill mannerism. On one occasion he rather dramatically slipped into inadvertent and malapropos melodrama when he decided to rekindle in verse the grief he experienced when Karl von Freyburg, a young German officer with whom he was romantically involved, was killed in the first days of World War I. Hartley almost instantly immortalized his lover in the painting *Portrait of a German Officer* (1914, cat. 22, p. 33), one of his most recognizable works. A quarter of a century later he wrote "K. von F. – 1914 – Arras-Bouquoi," a companion poem which glaringly fails where the painting reaches artistic heights in how it both displays and conceals its subject. Unable to contain his suffering, Hartley falls into cliché that is heavy-handed and lacks in subtlety and refinement, bearing no trace of its visual analogue's originality, discretion, poise and elegance.

Hartley's predilection for pathos, melodrama and exaggeration was noted by William Carlos Williams, who observed: "He might better let his wit go into discovery, into showing what there is, with the candor of his drawings ... rather than overlooking them with emotion which, in a sense makes them sentimental."[105] It is doubly ironic that as a painter Hartley was more adamant about holding his own and thus was more inclined to disparage his critics, accusing them of making "emotional excursions into this field, which is in most instances foreign to them" and belittling their discourse as mere "verbal entertainment ... compounded of wearisome and inappropriate detail."[106] At the same time, as a poet he took a more pragmatic approach and tried to win approval of those in authority by demonstrating that he was capable of writing in styles that were new and trendy. For instance, when Marcel Duchamp and Man Ray formally incorporated themselves as leading New York Dadaists, he joined their organization with the following disclaimer: "If I announce on this bright morning that I am a 'Dada-ist' it is not because I find the slightest need for, or importance in, a doctrine of any sort, it is only for convenience of myself and a few others that I take up the issue of adherence. An expressionist is one who expresses himself at all times in any way that is necessary and peculiar to him."[107] In addition to the essay in which he made this declaration, he also wrote a Dadaist poem, which he titled "Diabolo." Was he the devil's advocate of a cause he did not really believe in? His involvement with the movement was short-lived and inconsequential. He withdrew when his hopes for being sent to Europe as the organization's foreign correspondent did not materialize. At another time, when an objectivist number of *Poetry* was announced, he rushed to inform its editor, Harriet Monroe, that the series of poetic "tabloids" on New York City he was composing might be appropriate for the issue. Luckily, he was more serious about writing poetry than his fling with Dadaism suggested.[108] Heeding Williams's call for "no ideas but in things," he produced some of his most successful poetic works by restraining his verbal exuberance and placing, as he did in his painting, greater emphasis on "efficacy of form" and "conscious structure." Repudiating the inward-searching subjectivity of the Romantics, he declared: "Subjects never matter" and "the subject calls for handling, not for enthusiasms."[109] Although he did not directly invoke T.S. Eliot's notion of "objective correlative," he paid a very special tribute to him by inscribing three lines from "Ash Wednesday" on the back of one of his paintings from the *Dogtown* series. In poems in which he implemented his new "mechanistic" poetics, expounded in two brilliant essays, "The Business of Poetry" (1919) and "Dissertation on Modern Painting" (1921), Hartley's commitment to "brevity," "tensity" and "precision" pays off. Take, for instance, his short poems in which feelings subtly mark their presence in minimalist descriptions of little events, situations, people, animals, or objects – "hiccoughs of old ladies who have sat on a porch," "chitter of chipmunk skipping on a wall of stones," "two grey herons flying," an "evening moth [that] sips at mouth of some flowers" or "a mouse [that] makes a nest of one's written words." Delivered in a relaxed and unselfconscious voice, these unpretentious vignette poems express a wide range of emotions – joy, serenity, sorrow, solitude, alienation – without labeling them.

Hartley spent the final years of his life in his home state, Maine, at long last finding peace of mind and a sense of accomplishment. In a series of "memory" portraits, both of historical figures (Abraham Lincoln, Albert Pinkham Ryder, John Donne) and local "Yankees," landscapes and seascapes, and studies of coastal objects he called "sea signatures," he evolved a line that was firm but not strained or aggressive, a simple, natural gesture that allowed him to squelch restlessness with poise, and ease despair with stoic repose. Similarly, in verse he found a voice that brought into harmony emotions and experience. The casual "rawness" of the late pieces collected in *Androscoggin* (1940) stands in sharp contrast with the exalted tenor of many of his earlier poems, their relaxed directness a clear indication of Hartley's reconciliation with his own past, with the world around him, and with language.

How reflecting on the past may reflect on the present, causing both to be transformed – re-imagined and re-visioned – is the subject of one of Hartley's most successful longer poems, "Lewiston Is a Pleasant Place," a meditation on time and change triggered by a childhood recollection:

I admire my native city because
it is part of the secret sacred rite
of love of place.
My childhood which was hard, it is always
hard to be alone at the wrong time,
brought seizures of intensity to the years;

the harsh grinding of the mills rang in
my ears for years – and a sordid sort of
music
came out of it.
...
The mills and factories that were once
gigantic
in the vision of a child, monstrous,
terrifying,
prison-like, are now mere objects on the
horizon,
just as the garages and the filling stations
have become.

The Androscoggin flows by them all,
giving them
power through the solemn canals,
minding none of
them, going onward because it has
business with the sea.[110]

It would probably be an exaggeration to say that with his late poems Hartley fully matched the achievement of his best paintings, but, this one shows, he was finally able to convince, if not the world, then at least himself, that pictures and poems can be reciprocally conjoined and even complementary. Infusing into both a subtle but distinctive, signature-like flavor, he curbed his tendency to overemphasize the abstract, ideational side of experience and found a way of approaching the "spirit substance" of things by means of remembrance and invention. How he arrived there can be best gleaned from a much earlier autobiographical-critical essay, titled "Concerning Fairy Tales and Me," with which he opened *Adventures in the Arts*. Reminiscing about his early days, Hartley first writes:

"I had a childhood vast with terror and surprise ... Not that my childhood was so bitter, unless for childhood loneliness is bitterness, and without doubt it is the worst thing that can happen to one's childhood. Mine was merely a different childhood, ... I was constantly confronted with the magic of reality itself, wondering why one thing was built of exquisite curves and another of harmonic angles. It was not a scientific passion in me, it was merely my sensing of the world of visible beauty around me, pressing in on me with the vehemence of splendor, on every side."

He then describes how he sought his "way out from incoherency toward comprehension" until he was "by reason of [his] peculiar personal experience, enabled to extract the magic from the moment, discarding the material husk of it precisely as the squirrel does the shell of the nut." He reaches the high point with what can be read as his most profound and memorable testimony, testament even: "I am preoccupied with the business of transmu-tation – which is to say, the proper evaluation of life as idea, of experience as delectable diversion. It is necessary for everyone to poetize his sensations in order to comprehend them ... It is a fairy-tale in itself if you will, and everyone is entitled to his or her own private splendor, which, of course, must be invented from intelligence for oneself."[111]

Edyta Frelik is Assistant Professor in the Department of American Literature and Culture at Maria Curie-Sklodowska University in Lublin, Poland, and is the author of *Painter's Word: Thomas Hart Benton, Marsden Hartley, and Ad Reinhardt as Writers* (Peter Lang Editions, 2016).

Eight painters' views on Marsden Hartley

Alex Katz, b. 1927, USA

Marsden Hartley produced various types of work with mixed results. He used the enclosing black line that was popular at that time – Matisse, Picasso, Beckmann, Léger, Mondrian, Rouault and others used it. When he failed, the drawing remained local. He also misfired when he got carried away by the subject matter. When he developed his ideas into painting, he really took off. His vision is as strong as Cézanne's. It is hard to see what Cézanne and Hartley saw in any other way than they did. Both of them dominated my vision. I remember Cézanne's show at the Philadelphia Museum. I was disappointed with some of the paintings, but when I left the museum everything looked like a Cézanne. I did not want a house on the shore of Maine, because I could not see it any other way than how Hartley saw it. He makes unforgettable images with a first-class painting technique. He never found truth, but he did find himself and made many sensational paintings with substance, energy and power.

Shara Hughes, b. 1981, USA

I don't actually know if I liked Marsden Hartley's work the first time I saw it. It took me a few times of looking at a couple of different pieces to appreciate it. Eventually, something struck me: the genuineness of his work. Looking at Hartley's paintings made me realize that you could drop the subject matter and still make a great painting. I think that's really what drew me to him, because at the time, in my own work, I was thinking too much about what the subject matter needed to be, or how I needed to explain myself through a story. Actually, it doesn't really matter what you're painting, because at the end of the day you're constructing something that inspires people to think or see differently. Hartley's work feels so touched, so genuine, wrestled with and honest. But they're not simple paintings at all, even if the subject matter is. A pile of logs, how could that be interesting? He makes it so beautiful.

He makes a dark cloud with a triangular white outline of it and a dark background. All of the clouds have that. It's almost like, when he remembers looking at a storm, he remembers the flash, and then he remembers it being dark. He's trying to do both of those at the same time. It's almost how we remember, and it's how he is remembering it. That's what's great, because we're looking at a still picture. To remember a storm is to remember an action. And it's making a gesture, at the same time. That idea of movement and gesture in still life – it's incredible.

More than anything, I'm drawn to his landscapes. I'm drawn to how they're made: the mark-making and the invention of form, how he finds a solution for where those landscapes end up. The process of looking at them is like witnessing their creation. You can tell he's not really looking at a landscape in real life. He's in his studio, making a painting, getting it right for what the painting needs. You see how he keeps going over one line, and it gets thick and heavy. It's almost as if he keeps saying, "Yes, this is how it needs to be." The thicker and heavier those lines get, the more you believe in the painting. His mark-making is so direct. Sometimes, he does not get it right, but that makes the part that he has gotten right look so much better. It's all supposed to be happening on the same painting for a reason. The marks are so specifically there for a reason – to interact, to describe each other.

David Salle, b. 1952, USA

For a painter, the question raised by Marsden Hartley's work is simple: How was he able to give his paintings a feeling of such overt emotionality? By what means? Hartley's subjects were on the whole readily available, quotidian, even generic. The same subjects were painted by hundreds of other artists. But if we were to hold up one of his flower paintings, or one of his renditions of the Maine coast line next to the same subject painted by those others, Hartley's versions are immediately recognizable and clearly distinct; they have their own aura. They are different. How does one account for this difference, for this Hartley effect? The story of how Hartley evolved as an artist, of how he arrived at his unique and inimitable styling of genre subjects, and their transformation into personal symbols of remarkable depth, has something to do with his early encounter with Modernism, at a time when that word was as much a crusade as the name of a style.

The will toward the abstracting of an image, toward simplifying and paring down forms so as to reveal their essences and imbue them with a sense of solidity that is at the heart of so much painting in the first decades of the 20th century, extended to Hartley certain permissions. Sometimes one needs to find external permission to be able to do that which we already know we want to do, to go down a road that we are in fact already traveling. Hartley's drive, his wish, was to merge a sense of the irreducible and elemental with his subjects from nature, to locate the classical ideal within a regional, anecdotal art. Under the Modernist codes, the means to arrive at this depth of meaning was a sometimes brutal paring away, a simplification of forms to a point of awkwardness. This in turn brought Hartley's focus to the mark-making itself. The *way* a form is described, what the brush-strokes themselves look and feel like, is a form of assertion, a way for the self to be present.

Hartley combined some of the fundamental precepts of Modernism – the impulse toward abstraction; the emphasis on simplification and/or fragmentation of forms; the wish to represent more than one instant in time – with the pursuit of a personal symbolic language large enough to hold his enormous well of poetic longing. One feels that the majority of Hartley's painting, if not all, speak in a symbolic register, that quotidian subjects are made to stand in for complex states of mind. One of Hartley's themes is the wish to bond with nature in a pure, open way, and how that feeling for nature is connected to erotic love. This idea shows up with special significance in his paintings of the male body.

The connection between the head, the heart and the brush is what makes Hartley Hartley. The brush is evidence of the mental pressure brought to bear on the subject. It shows how to enliven the subject and make it matter. This is achieved through his layering of marks and different size brushstrokes that almost work in contradiction to the sense of solidity and formal mass that he gives to, say, a cloud. Hartley's clouds are particularly weird, satisfying, and wonderful because they are so very un-cloudlike and yet become more 'cloud-y' than realistic clouds.

I have quoted elements from various Hartley paintings in my work, sometimes over and over again. Why did I feel like I could use them? It has to do with this approach to form that I'm trying to describe, an approach to which I'm very sympathetic. I have also used Hartley as a way to access certain subject matter – the dead bird, for example. I use the dead bird both as a reference to the overt emotionality of Hartley, and as itself. I admit it's a kind of cheating. But I'm also building a new context into which that feeling can land.

Karin Mamma Andersson, b. 1962, Sweden

When you travel to American cities like Cincinnati, New Orleans or San Francisco, there will almost always be a painting by Marsden Hartley in one of the museums. At first the name didn't register with me, but gradually, as I came across more and more of his paintings, I had to ask myself: Who is this artist? I suppose I've always had a penchant for melancholy painters. Hartley's pictures from the coast of Maine, which he painted late in life, are very dark in tone and mood. He depicted the storm, and the great waves when they hit the coast – these are among the hardest things to paint convincingly, and he does it so well.

I don't know if he was religious, but he is a very spiritual artist. As in the paintings of the Swedish painter Carl Fredrik Hill I get a sense of a huge spirituality that isn't religious from Hartley. All the same you clearly feel the presence of something divine in the pictures.

I think he must have felt a great longing for his own landscape in Maine, a feeling with which I can identify. I come from northern Sweden and he was from the northern USA. I recognize the feeling of missing something when you don't have the northland landscape around you. There's a sense of belonging in the land itself, the soil, the smells, the birds. Everything that moves – what you could call the spirituality of the place.

Across all the genres he moves through, from the abstract at one end to the figurative at the other end, I can still see a connection. Hartley constantly challenged painting and stamped it with a special poetic quality that is so hard for us painters to bring out. It's strong, uncompromising and personal painting. You feel that it's the same artist who has produced all the pictures. His touch and his understanding of colour are the same. He never compromises on his palette. When you see a Bonnard painting you can always see it's by Bonnard, whether it's early or late. The same applies to Hartley – he has his own scale.

Sam McKinniss, b. 1985, USA

Perhaps the most troubling aspect to viewers of Marsden Hartley's weird, wonderful oeuvre is the unnerving variety of styles. It can seem like he never quite knew what he was looking to do. This variety, however, is at least semi-representative of the panoply of modern isms that vied for artistic dominance during his lifetime, each in their own way, the philosophical/aesthetic systems for approaching and asserting one's rights to the canvas. In Europe he was a Cubist, other times he was a Fauvist, and then he was also somewhat of a mystical Symbolist cavorting around the American Southwest and Mexico, only to conclude his career by returning, finally, to Regionalist pictorial art made in Nova Scotia, Cape Ann, Massachusetts, and Maine. By the end, he had managed to personally subsume all these differing, competitive styles, synthesizing them into a unique and energetic vision for art on this planet. As one of Hartley's heroes, the Transcendentalist Walt Whitman, would have sung from the mountaintop, he was large, he contained multitudes.

In 1918, Hartley declared, "I am an American discovering America." I understand that. Like most Americans, he was possessed by an almost pathological self-regard. For some reason, none of the work is easy. His canvases are most often modestly sized. Manageable proportions, and yet unmanageable, stressful. Form, reputation and content were real headaches. I detect these painful concerns clustered together in the crude shapeliness of surf, rocks, trees, human beings, building exteriors, interiors, *stuff* – the scratched paint handling, the wild vicissitude between abstraction and figuration betraying inborn conditions of uncertainty, difficulty, congenital dissatisfaction. I love the Maine land- and seascapes, the way his conifers resemble jagged, sharp, black teeth, bared at the edges of merciless skies. America is a confounding reality to possibly everyone, outsiders and citizens alike. It is especially so to anyone attempting to gain understanding of its landscapes, peoples and spirit with any profundity beyond superficialities, beyond run-of-the-mill pride or exceptionalism.

As has been noted by Randall R. Griffey, curator at the Metropolitan Museum, Hartley's 1940-1941 picture, *Canuck Yankee Lumberjack at Old Orchard Beach* (cat. 96, p. 105), bears striking compositional resemblance to Paul Cézanne's *The Bather*. Cézanne's near-naked man is all pasty, pale French Post-Impressionism surrounded by dreary gray seascape, whereas Hartley's semi-nude is suntanned, hirsute, wearing sexy pink briefs, in a red, white, and blue beach scene littered with symbolism. The guy's striped towel is very hot, I think, tossed over one shoulder and slung across his back to dry his butt, which must be damp. Hartley's version is all fun in the sun, iconic, patriotic, but lonely. The pure, bright Atlantic roils away in the background, beckoning and rejecting the old-man painter, "Come hither/ steer clear."

David Hockney, b. 1937, England

I probably didn't see any work by Marsden Hartley until I got to America in 1964. Hartley was a bold painter, very bold. And I always liked him. His work always interested me. He was born only 30 years after the invention of photography, and in a way he knew what the nature of photography was. He knew that you couldn't really paint like photographs. Remember, in America, about 1865 or '70 – a generation earlier, when Albert Bierstadt was painting the Rocky Mountains and so on – they were using photographs, the photographers had gone out West taking photographs. It was very new then. They probably thought that looking through a camera was the truth. Bierstadt deliberately took away the brush mark. But Hartley was always virtually a modernist. He was born about four years before Picasso and must have admired Picasso all his life. He knew instinctively to stay clear of dull academic painting. The reason he had come to Europe is exactly that: all the painting was being done in Europe. A lot more painting was being done in Europe than in America. European modernism was fantastic.

He moved on from place to place and changed his way of painting, because he knew the world is full of variety. It is. It's a marvellous place, full of variety. His landscapes are very marvellous, I think. He didn't use much perspective. He was always bold with his forms. The late figure paintings look like big hunky guys to me. I haven't done anything like that, with big chests. They're very good. They're probably a little fantasy as well, a bit like Tom of Finland.

The world is very, very beautiful if you look at it. But most people don't look very much, do they?

They scan the ground in front of them. They walk, but they don't really look at things incredibly well, with an intensity. I do. And Marsden Hartley did.

Tal R, b. 1967, Israel

It's a general thing for painters that the subject of the painting is an alibi. You paint a landscape, but, of course, you are not the landscape. You're a person going shopping, going to the beach, reading books, having a fight, making love – and then you paint a landscape. If you're a good artist, then whatever you know, whatever the heart and mind are full of, is going to sneak into the painting.

There is always life in Hartley's work, and it's so obvious that he is overwhelmed by it. Whatever style he walks into, whatever landscape, whatever flower, whatever view from a window, it's like a Cavafy poem – there's something else going on there. The way I see it, the personal material, the obsession, the idea, what drives an artist, should always be this heavy hand that pushes away the style. It's bigger than all the individual components. It wants something. That kind of need is much more important than how you use colours. They will follow. Colours don't pull need. It's the other way around, need pulls colours. Whenever you see Hartley trying, even when he tries Kandinsky's way, you could say that, in a way, he doesn't succeed. In another way, he really succeeds, because there's always the heavy hand of something else in his painting – his own, whatever, story, his own obsessions, his own wandering.

To give an example, the painting *Summer Clouds and Flowers* from 1942 (cat. 107, p. 118) shows a vase of flowers in a window with a ship in the background. If you try telling someone that you want to paint a vase with flowers and, in the background, the sea, perhaps a boat, maybe the sun, any art-school teacher would say it's suicide. But, in fact, it's the most brilliant painting. It actually is everything a painting is ever about. A kind of a view, a kind of falling into this open and melting space. It's one of the most beautiful paintings I have ever seen.

Every great painting speaks with two tongues. A person who speaks with two tongues isn't nice. That's a bad person. However, a great painting always speaks with two tongues. It says, I'm a flower, and it says, I'm not a flower. Hartley's paintings are always like that.

Dana Schutz, b. 1976, USA

I have a special affinity for Marsden Hartley's paintings of really brawny men in these oddly disjunctive spaces, which he painted in his final years. The men are huge and almost carved out, but at the same time you feel a real tenderness in the way they are painted, in how the light settles on their bodies. They are incredible, beautiful and strange paintings.

There is a specific painting by Hartley that I love called *Christ Held by Half-Naked Men* (cat. 101, p. 106). It's of a group of muscular men that are all very ruddy and pink. They are wearing denim jeans, and they are holding a much smaller figure, a green-grey Christ. It almost looks like a puppet or a doll and has a squared-off bosom and a very small head. He is holding a halo that also could be a palette or a blazing tambourine. It's the most bizarre painting just in the simplicity of how it's organized. The rhythmic sea of red and blue; the small, green figure wearing what almost looks like star-spangled underwear.

Hartley's subjects could seem everyday, but nothing about them feels everyday. Maybe there is something about desire for the subject, or a sense of feeling toward it. His paintings have an immense sculptural quality to them. I have always loved how each brushstroke has its own weight and direction, and begins to build up the subjects. Waves become rocks, clouds are suspended like mammoth dinner plates, and trees resemble dried paintbrushes. Everything is tectonic, object-y and potent.

I think of Hartley's paintings as very American. The symbolic nature of his landscapes, especially, but there is also a relationship to European painters, such as Edvard Munch or Chaim Soutine, by way of symbolic expressionism. Yet, while the expressionism of Munch and Soutine appears writhing, hovering in a painterly ether, Hartley's is always concrete and connected to the object.

In the great painting *Fishermen's Last Supper* (cat. 98, p. 89), the scene feels like it's happening on a boat right before the moment it capsizes. Everything within the picture is atilt and unsteady. The only thing that is steady in the intimate tableau is a small painting of a boat, hanging on the wall in the background. The family, the set table – the construction of Hartley's painting itself – are about to flip, expressing impending tragedy and upended personal narrative.

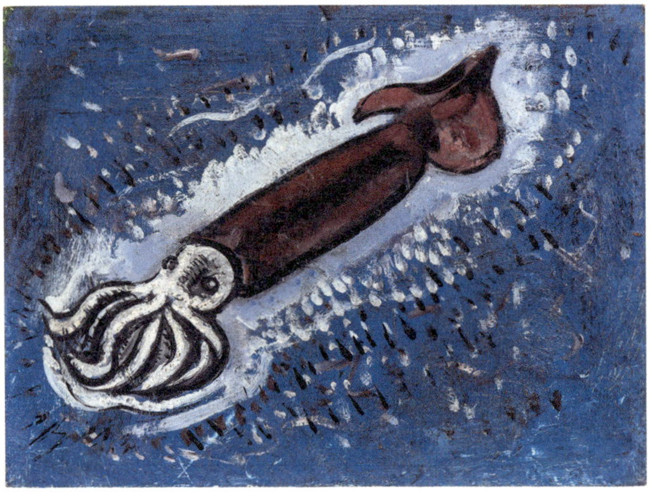

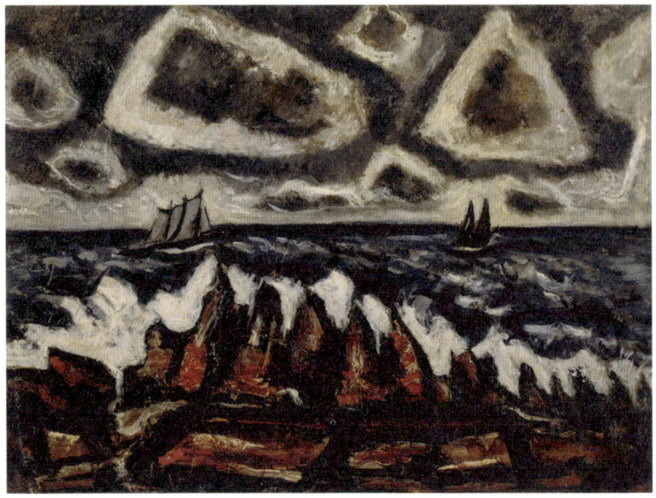

73 Squid, 1936
76 Northern Seascape, Off the Banks, 1936-1937

74 Dry Nets and Lobster Buoys, 1936

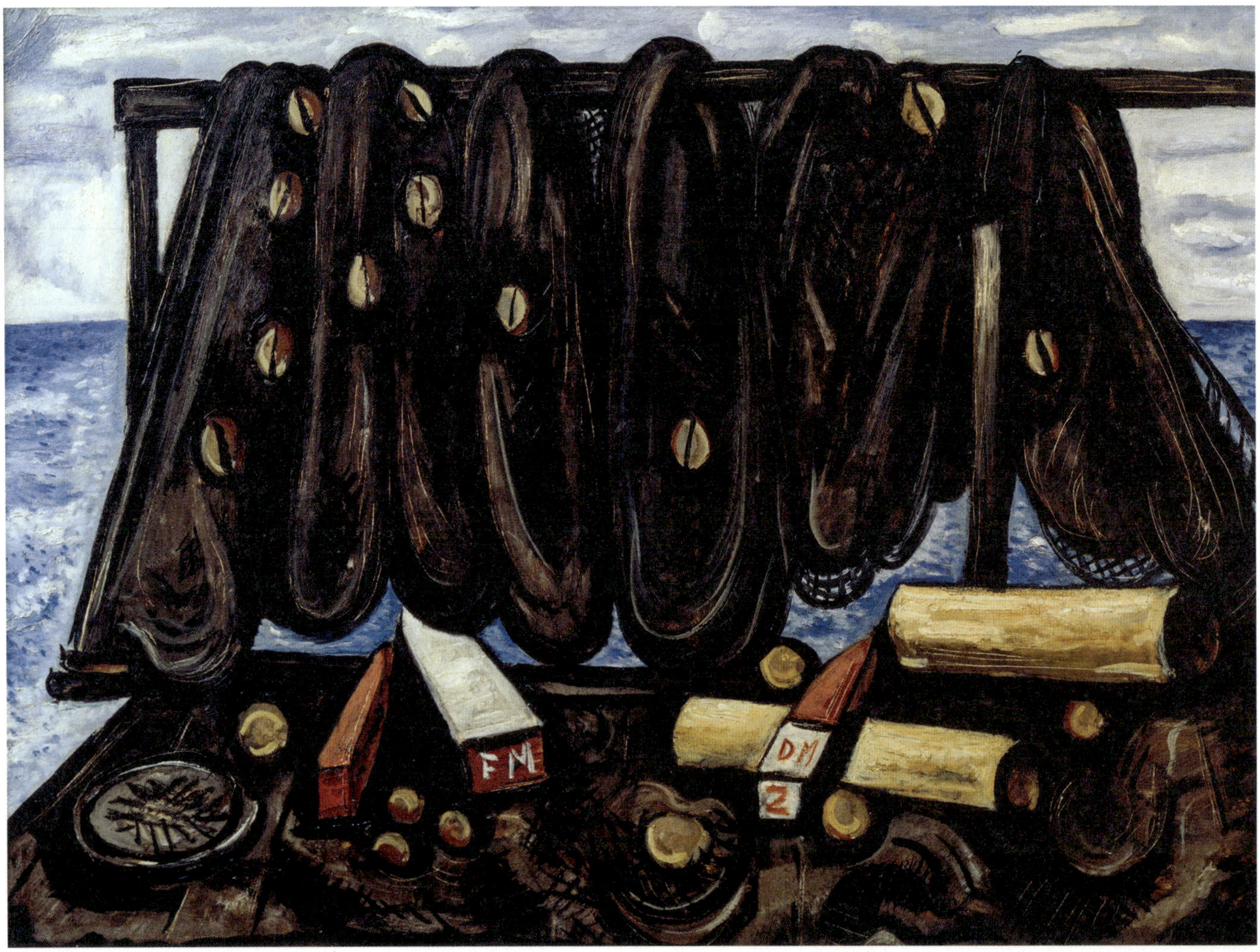

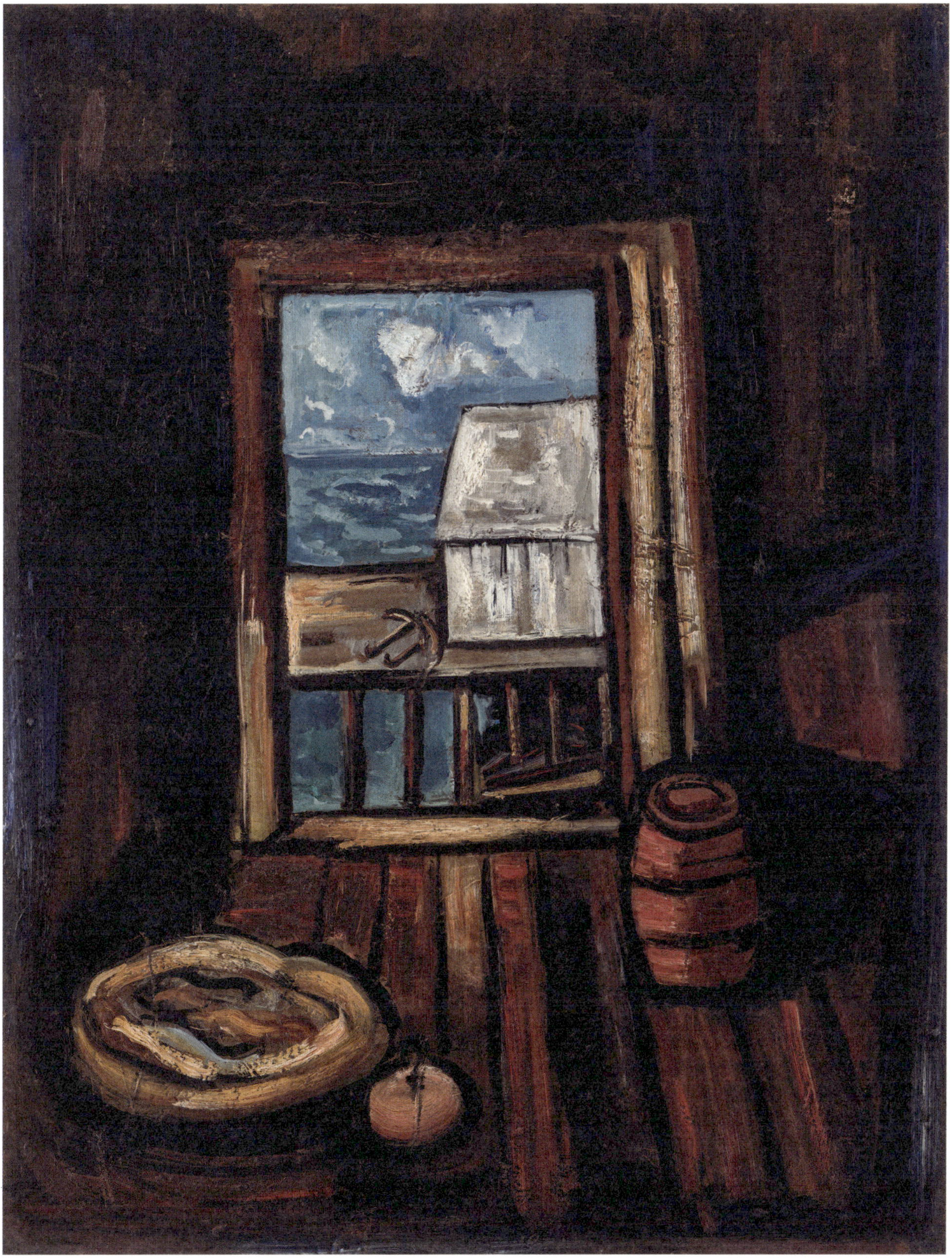

75 Jetty Seen Through a Window, 1936

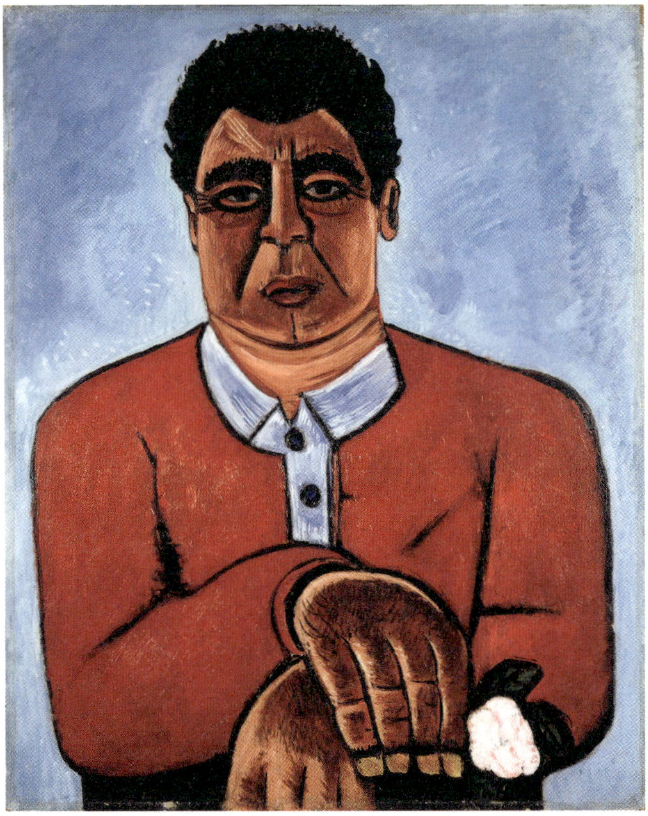

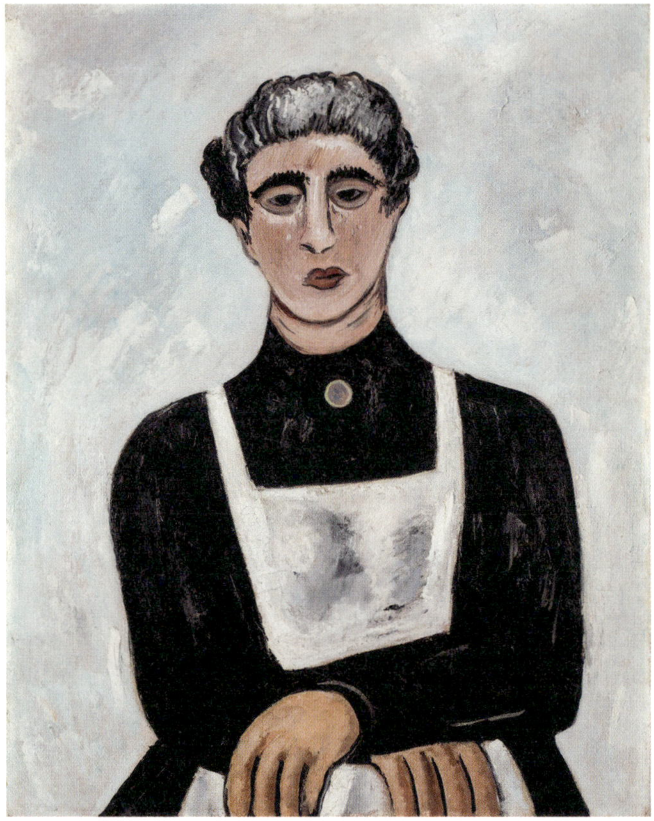

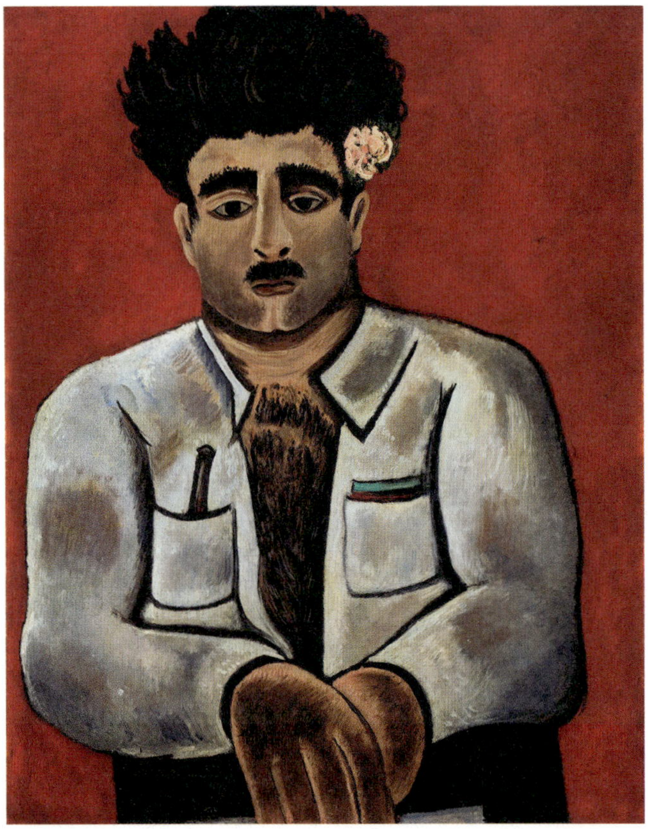

80 Cleophas, Master of the “Gilda Grey”, 1938-1939
81 Marie Ste. Esprit, c. 1938-1939

82 Adelard the Drowned, Master of the “Phantom”, c. 1938-1939

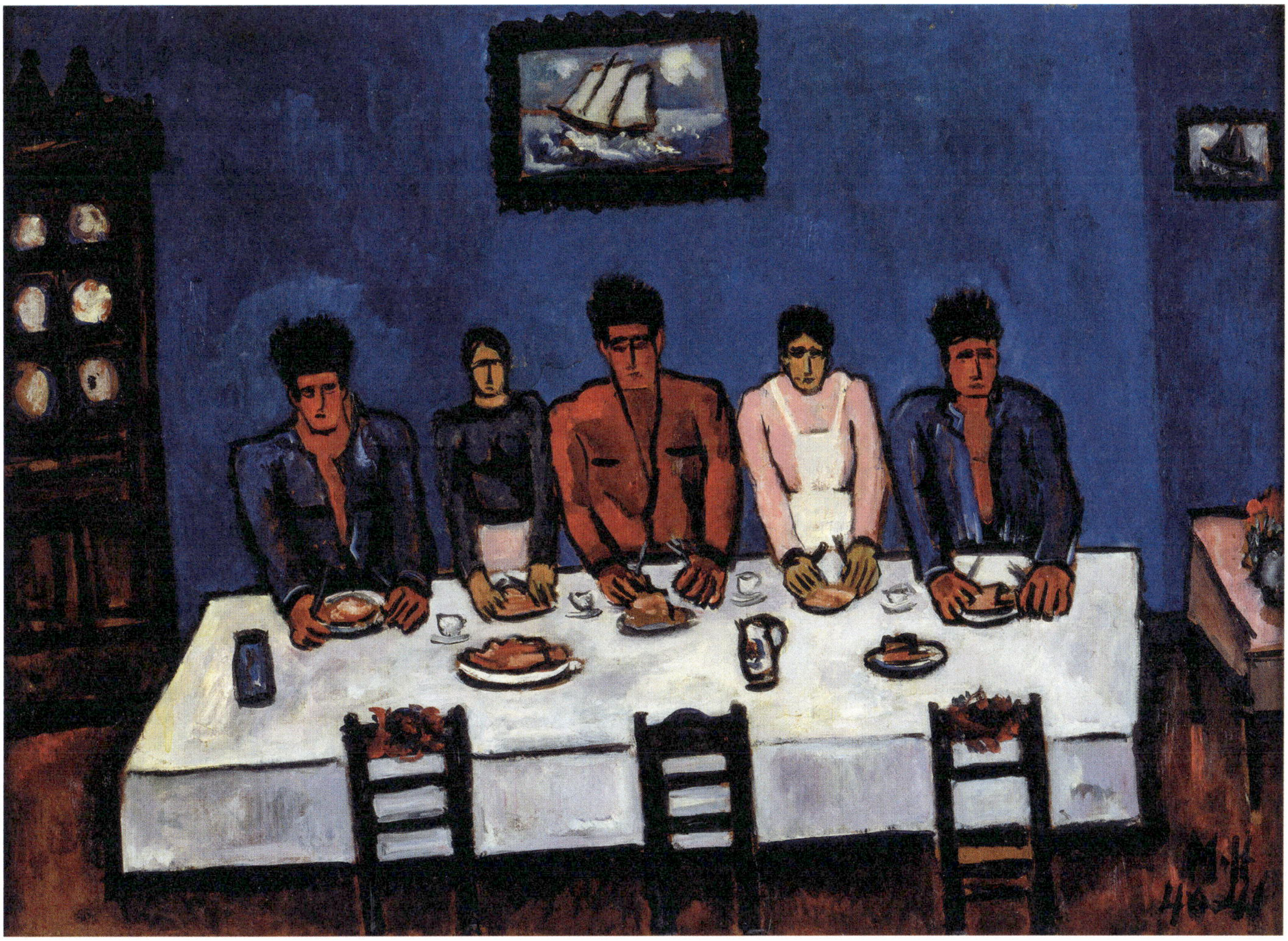

98 Fishermen's Last Supper, Nova Scotia, 1940-1941

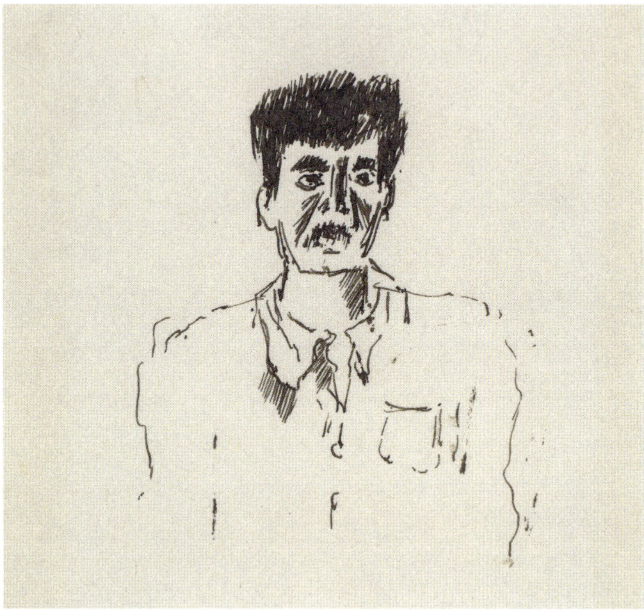

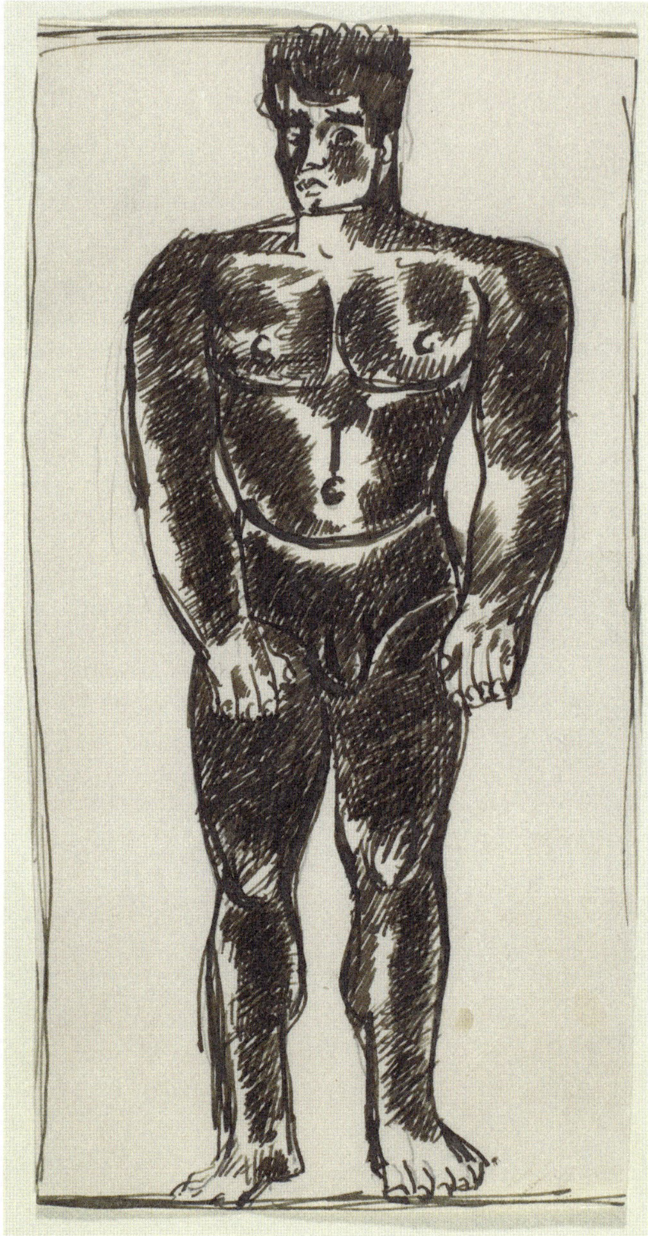

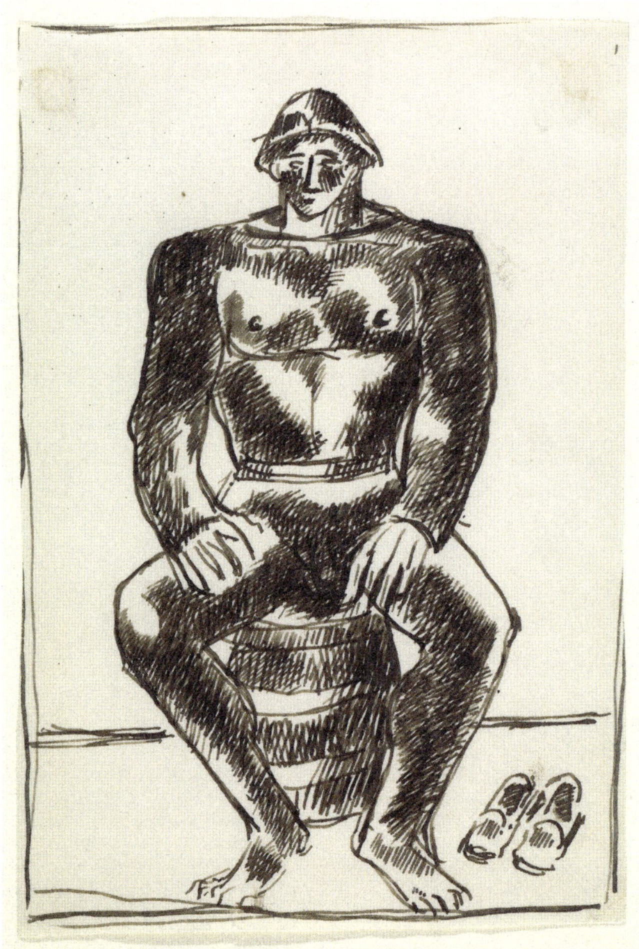

128 Untitled (Sketch of a Man, Head and Shoulders), 1938-1941
127 Untitled (Standing Male Figure No. 1), 1938-1941

129 Untitled (Male Figure Seated on Barrel), 1938-1941

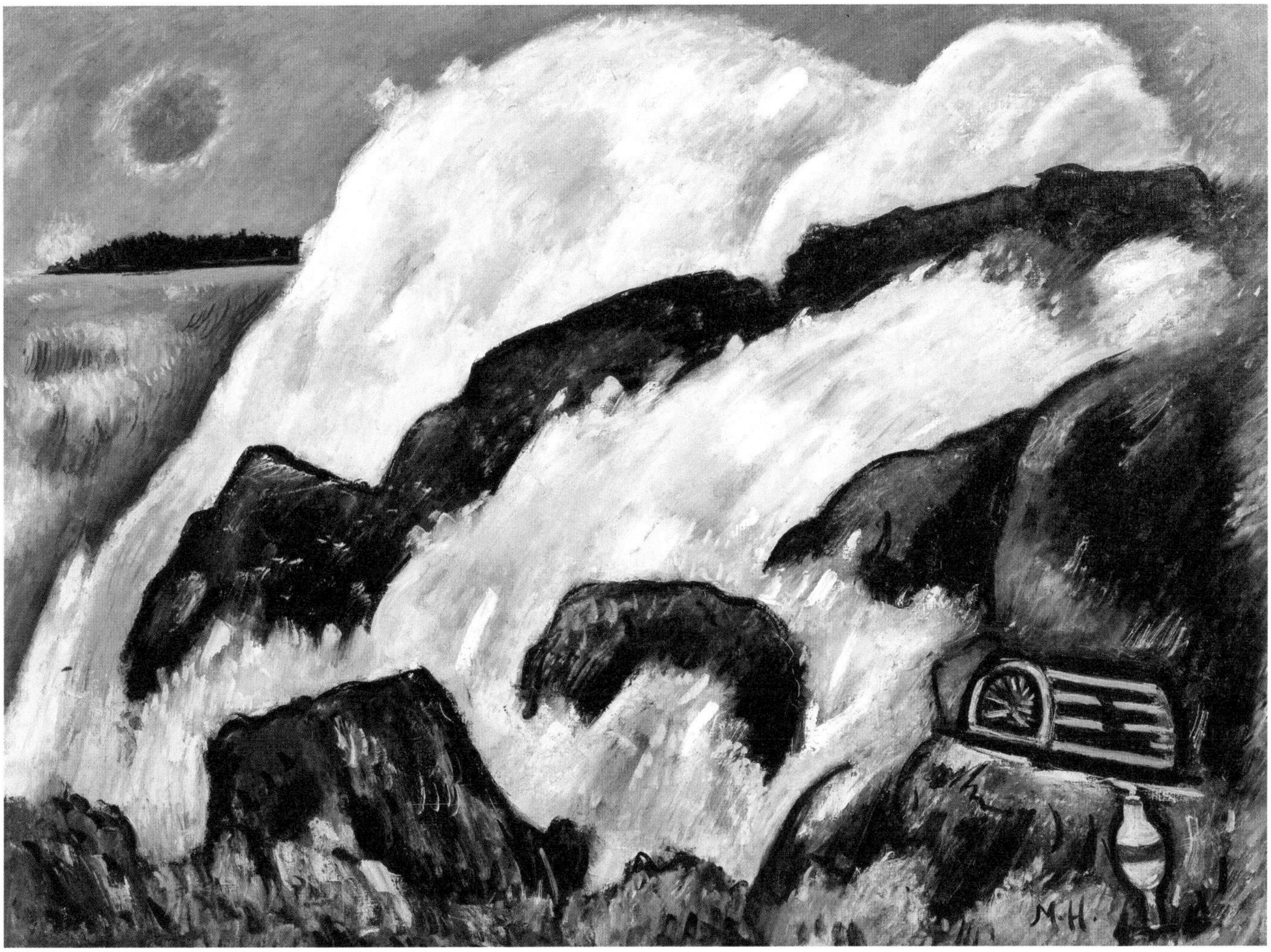

77 After the Hurricane, 1938

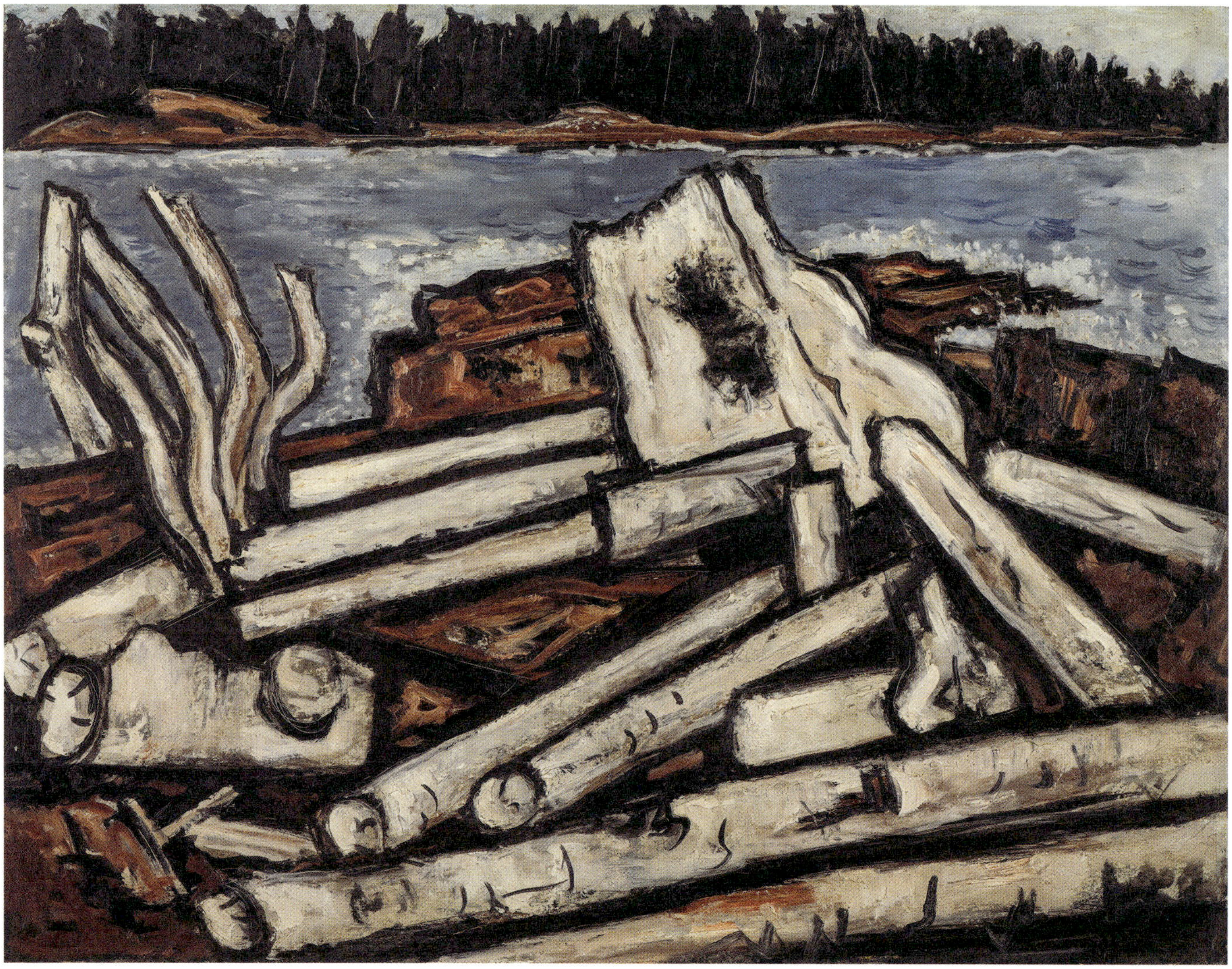

79 Ghosts of the Forrest, 1938
88 Abundance, 1939-1940

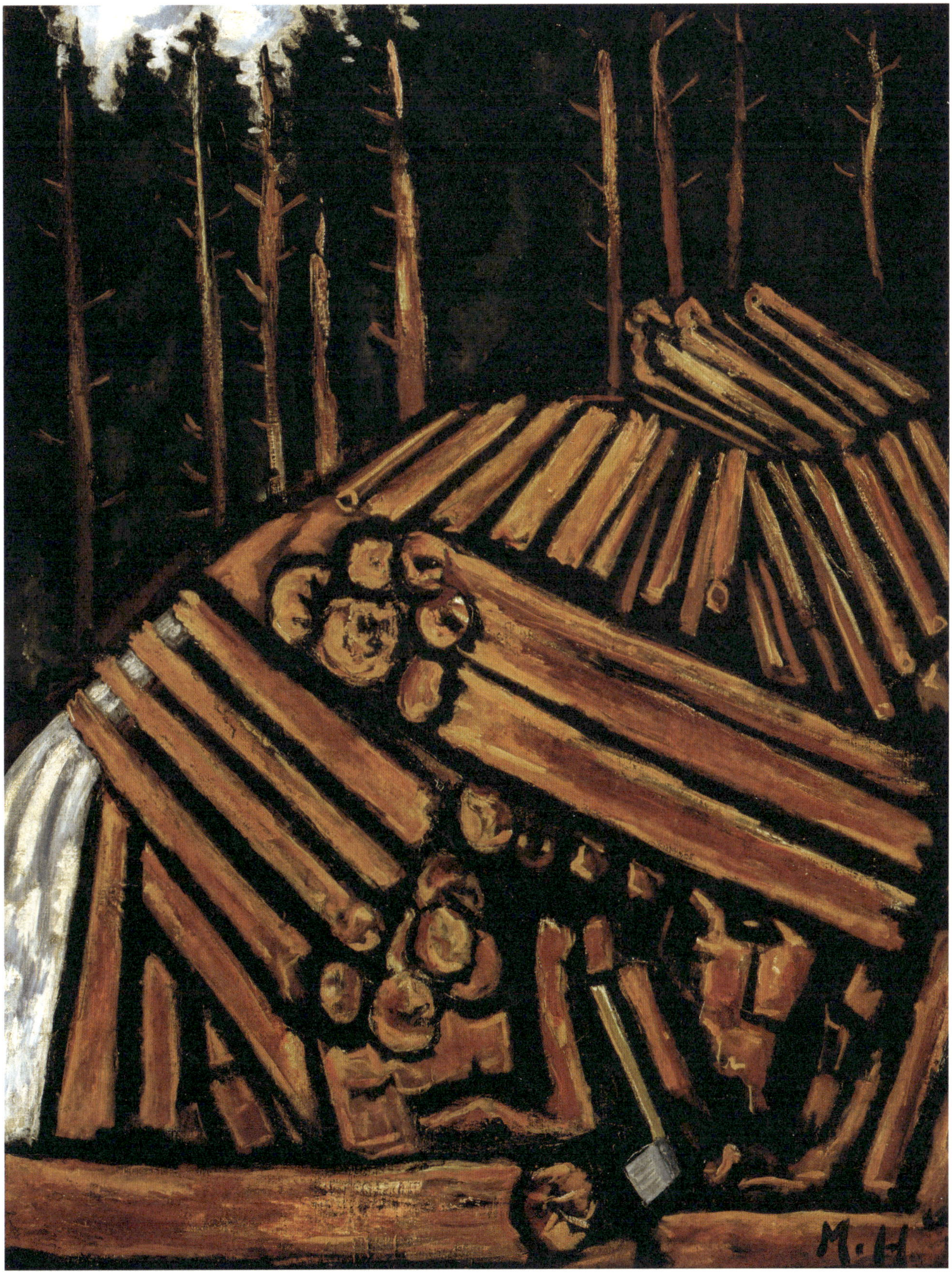
M.H

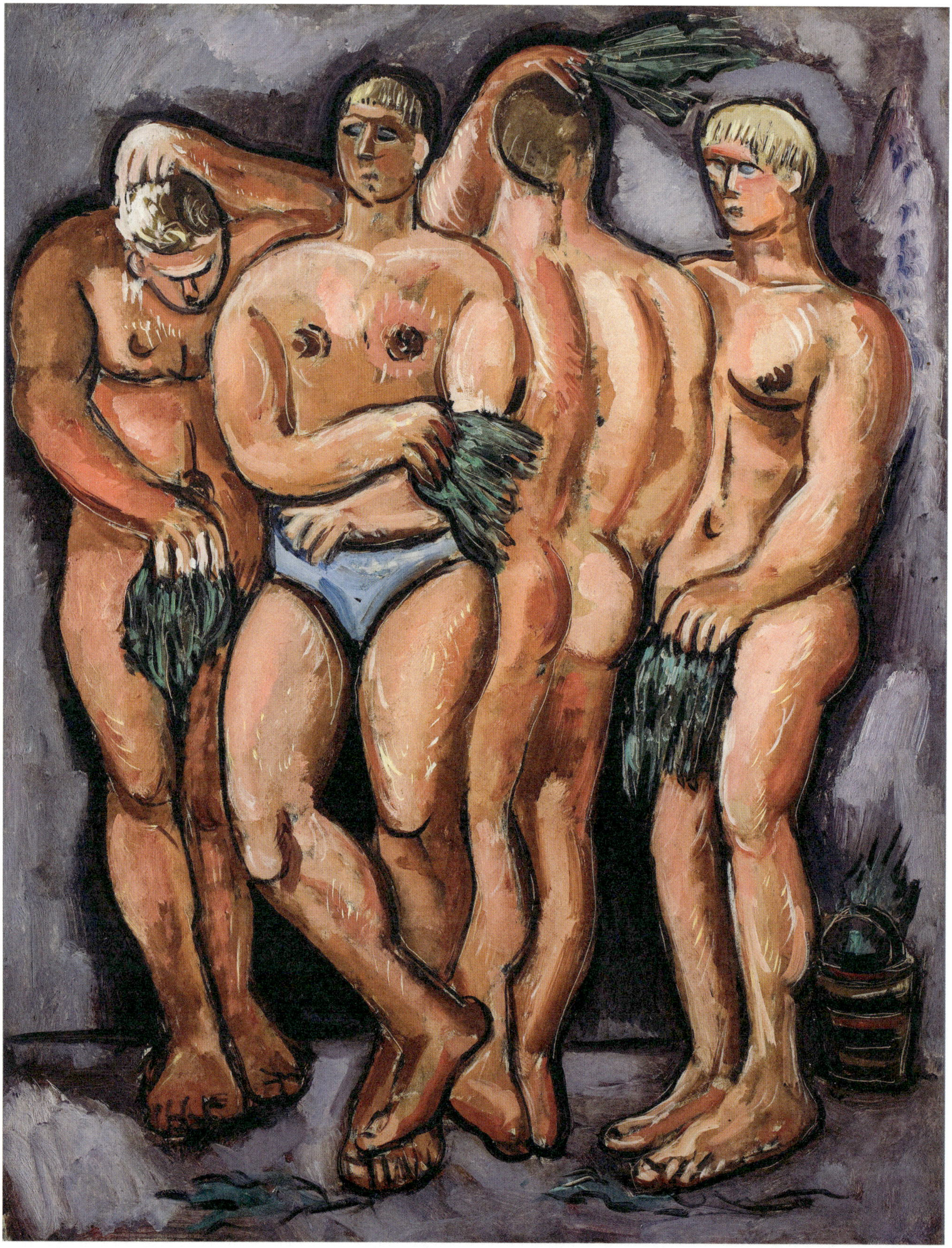

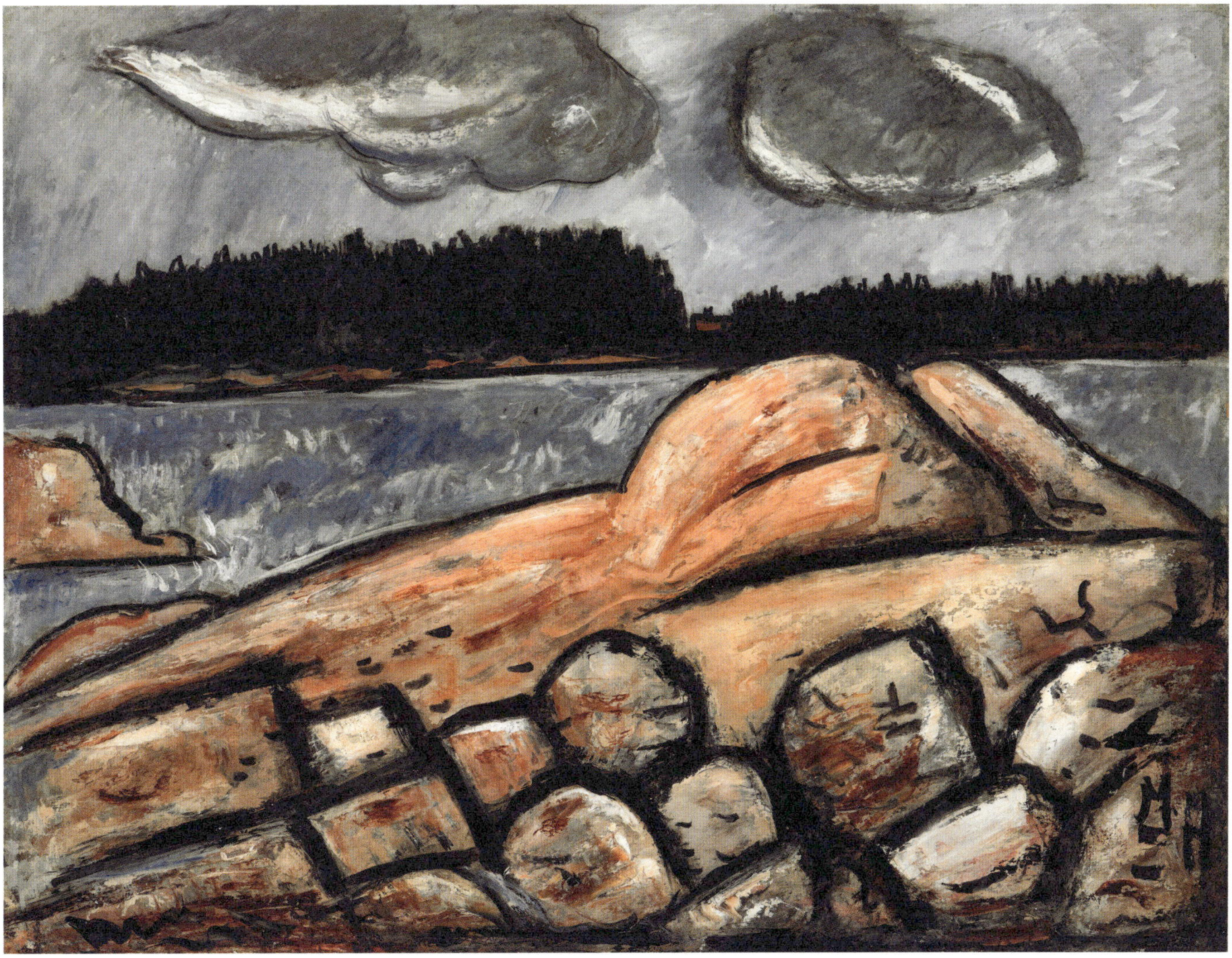

83 Finnish-Yankee-Sauna, 1938-1939
84 After the Storm, Vinalhaven, 1938-1939

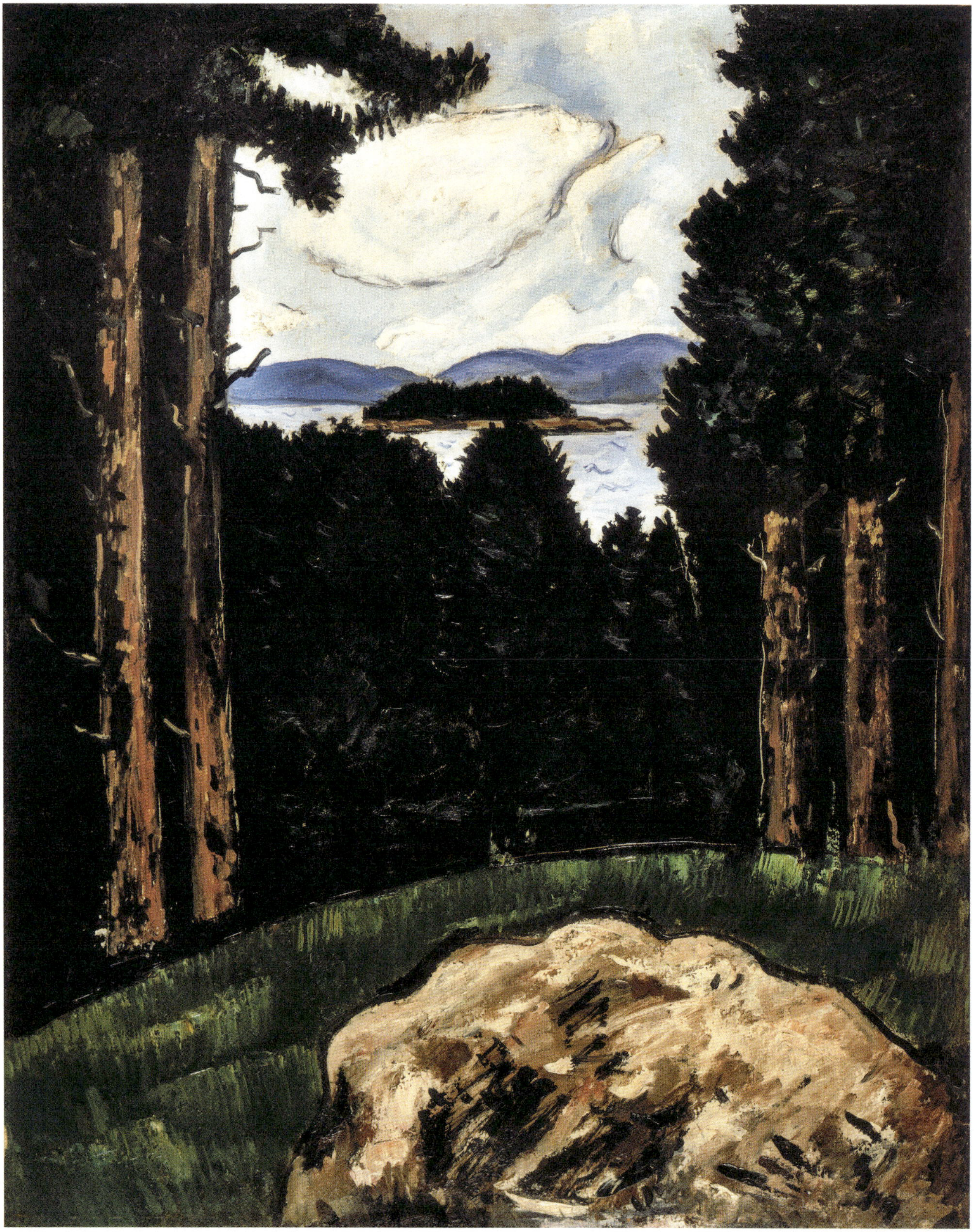

78 Camden Hills from Baker's Island, Penobscot Bay, 1938
91 Madawaska – Acadian Light-Heavy, 1940

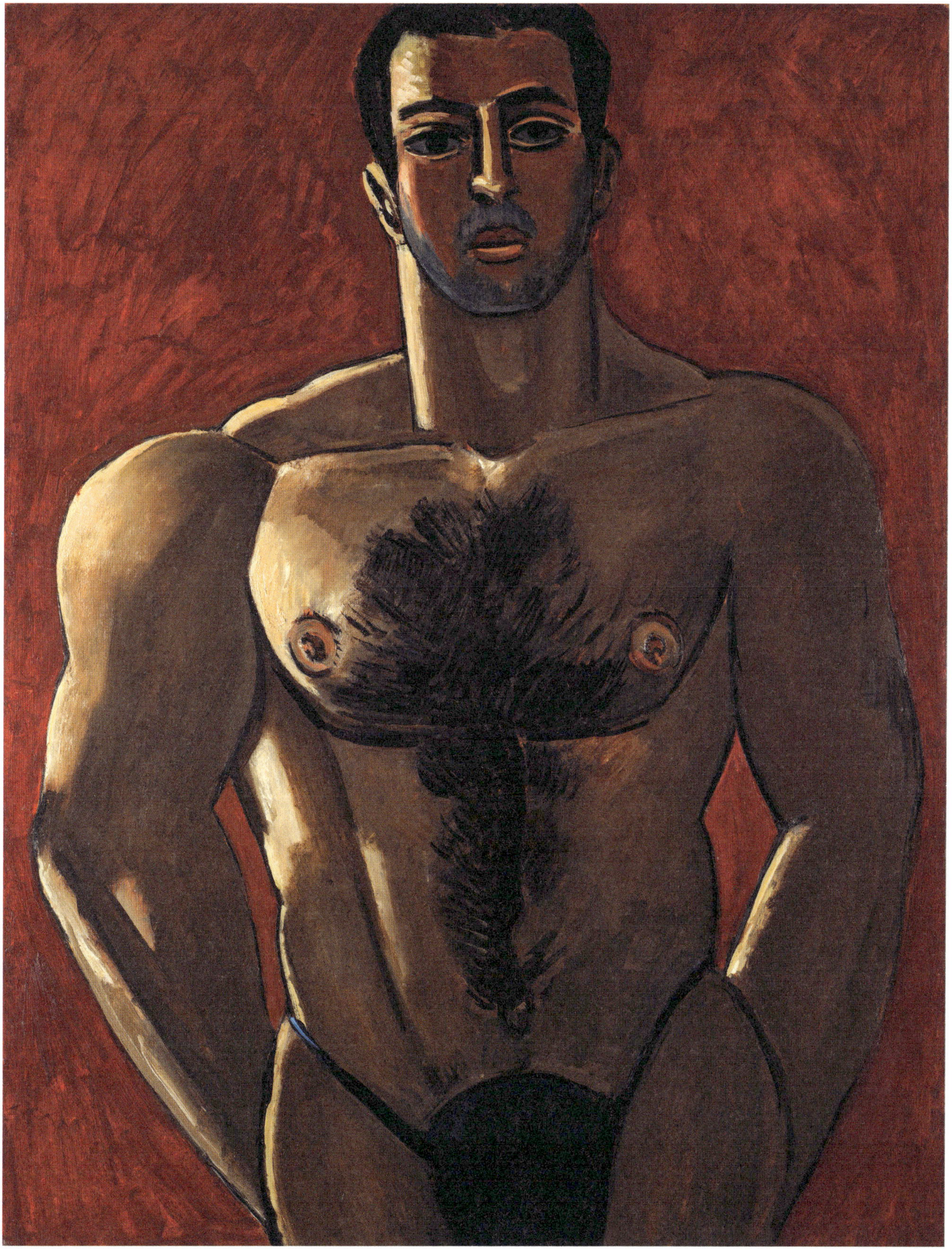

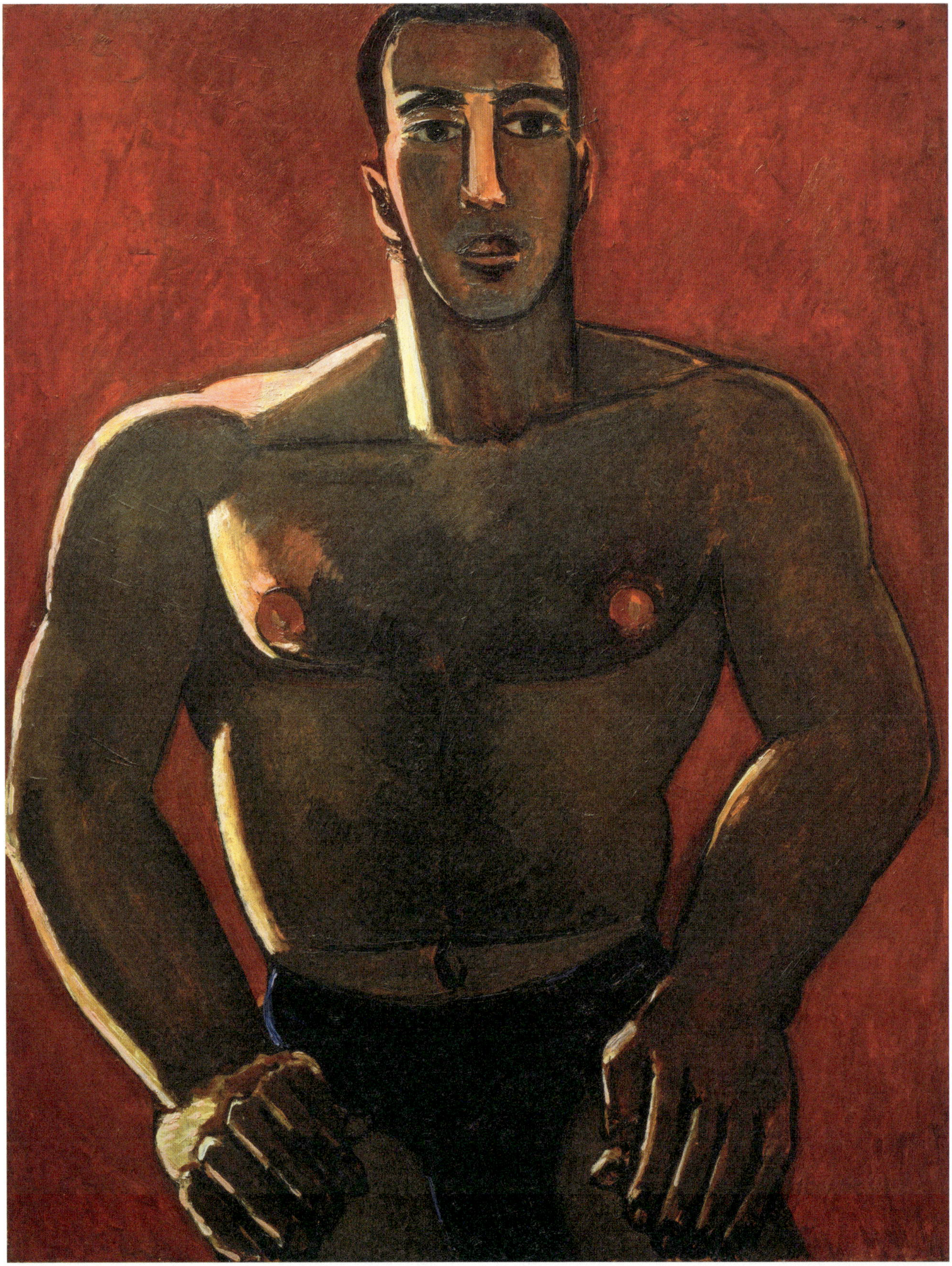

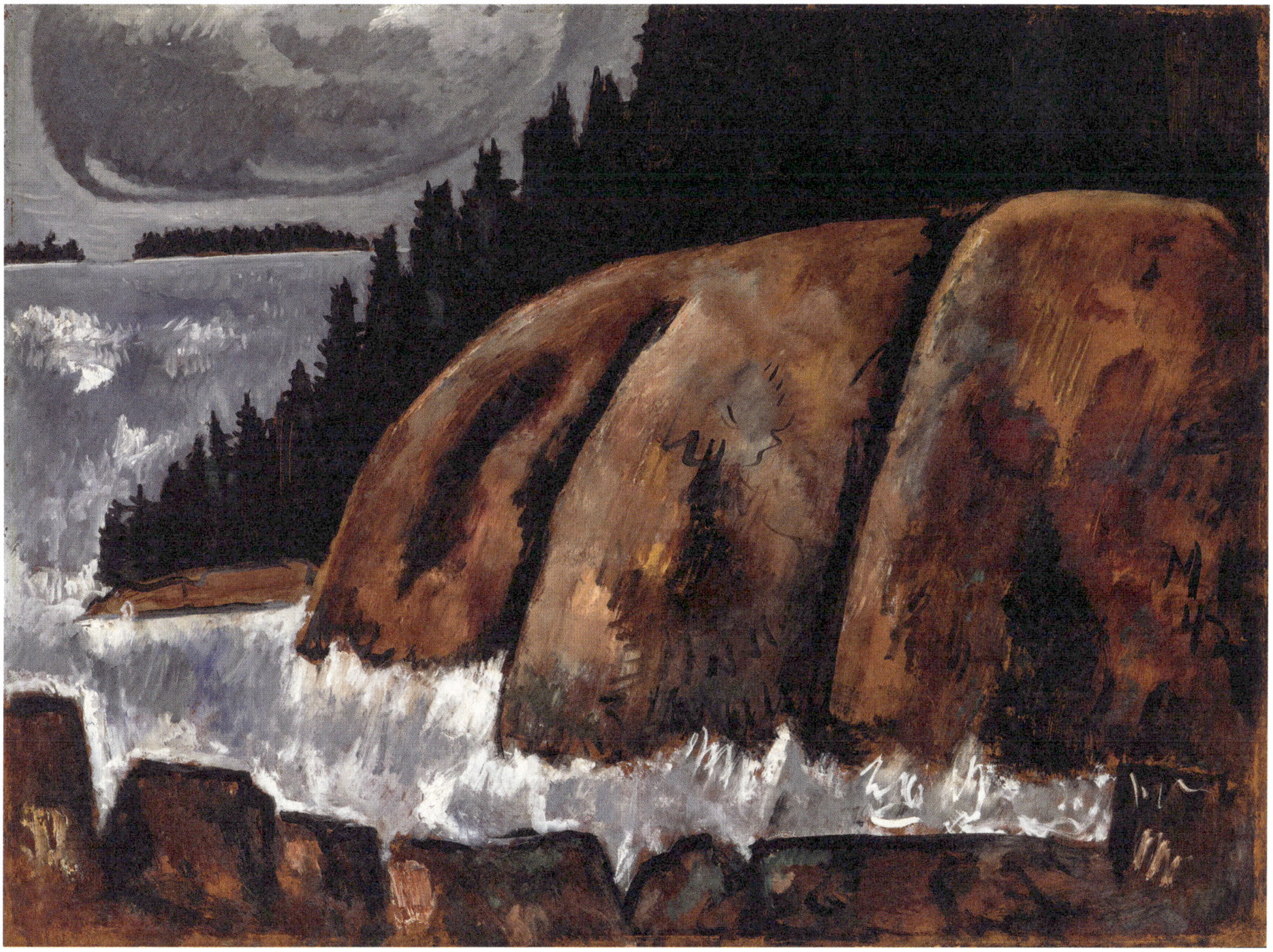

92 Madawaska – Acadian Light-Heavy, 1940
111 Hurricane Island, Vinalhaven, Maine, 1942

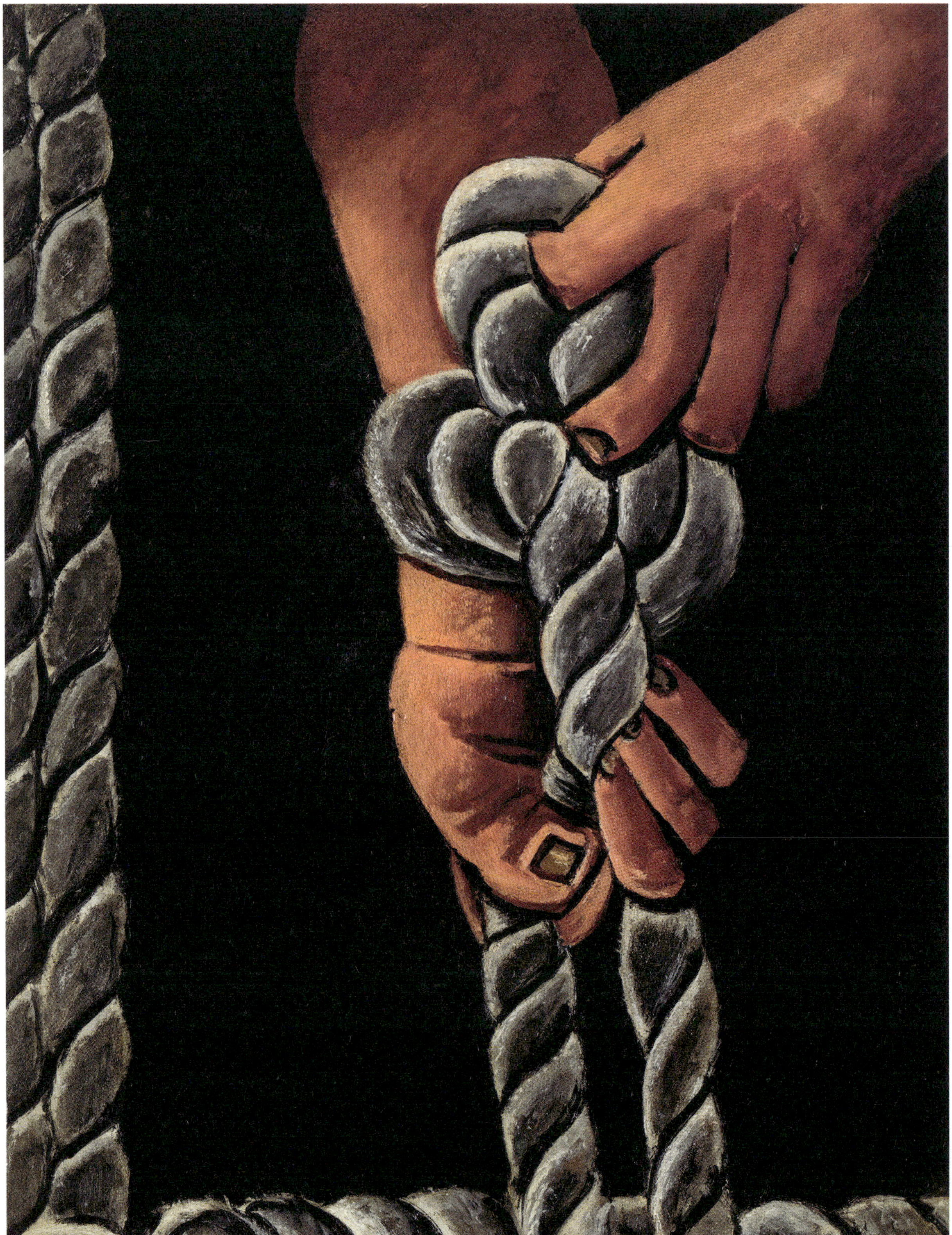

89 Knotting Rope, 1939-1940
93 Madawaska, Acadian Light-Heavy, Third Arrangement, 1940

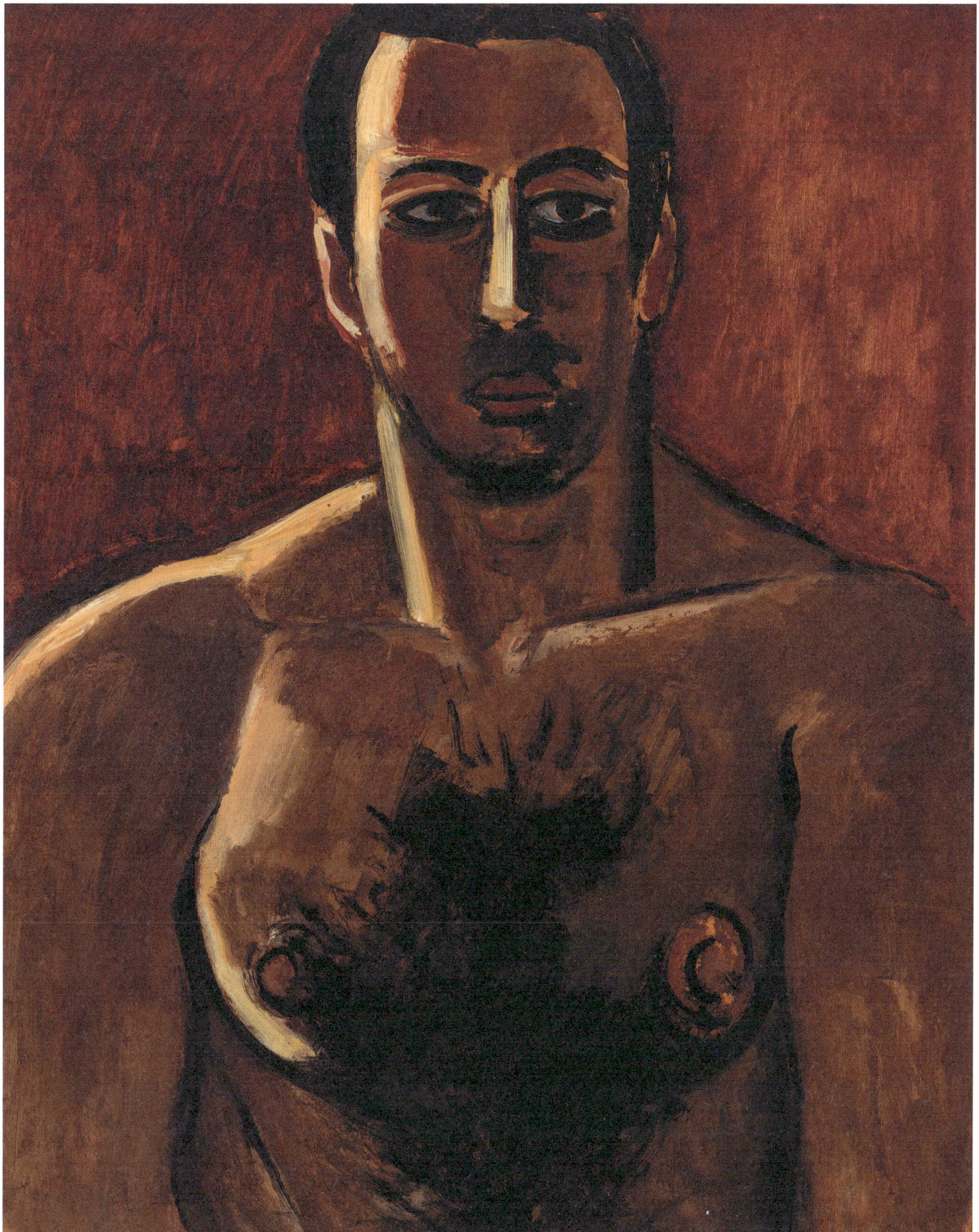

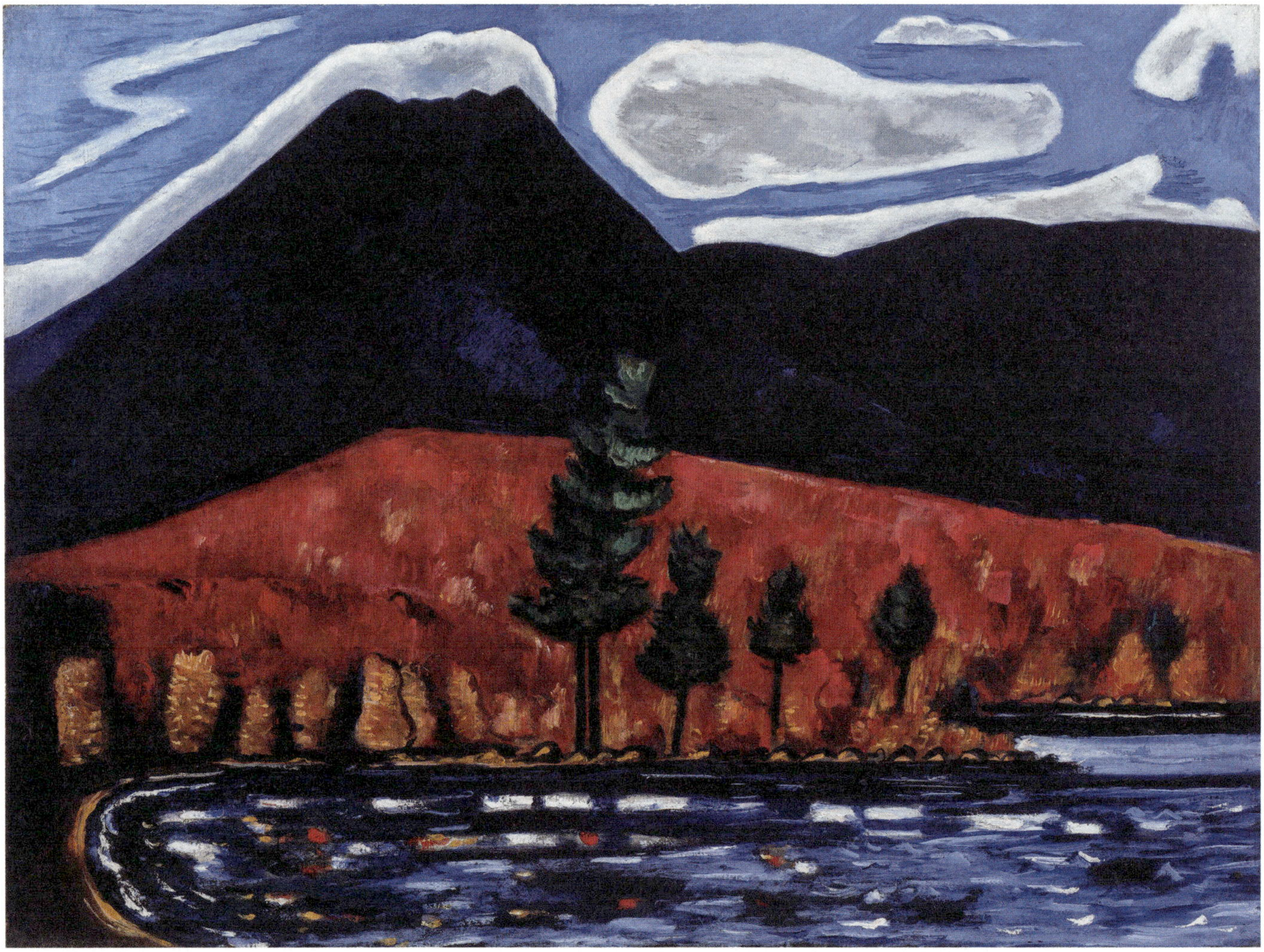

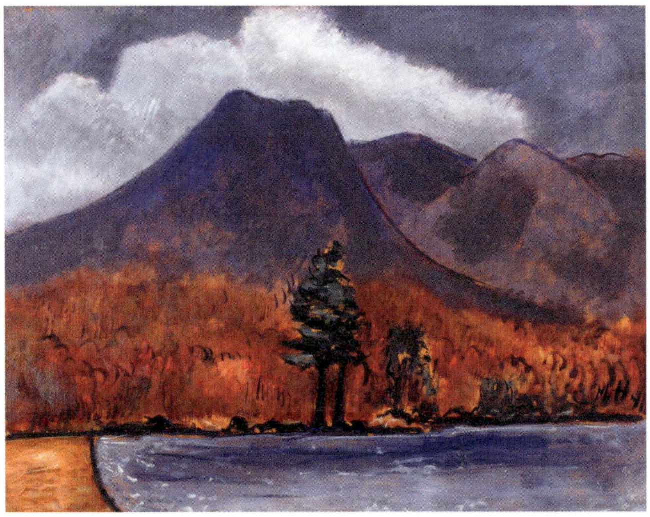

86 Mount Katahdin, Autumn, No. 1, 1939-1940

103 Mount Katahdin, 1941

87 Mt. Katahdin, Winter, 1939-1940

130 Untitled (Mt. Katahdin), 1939
131 Untitled (Mt. Katahdin), c. 1939

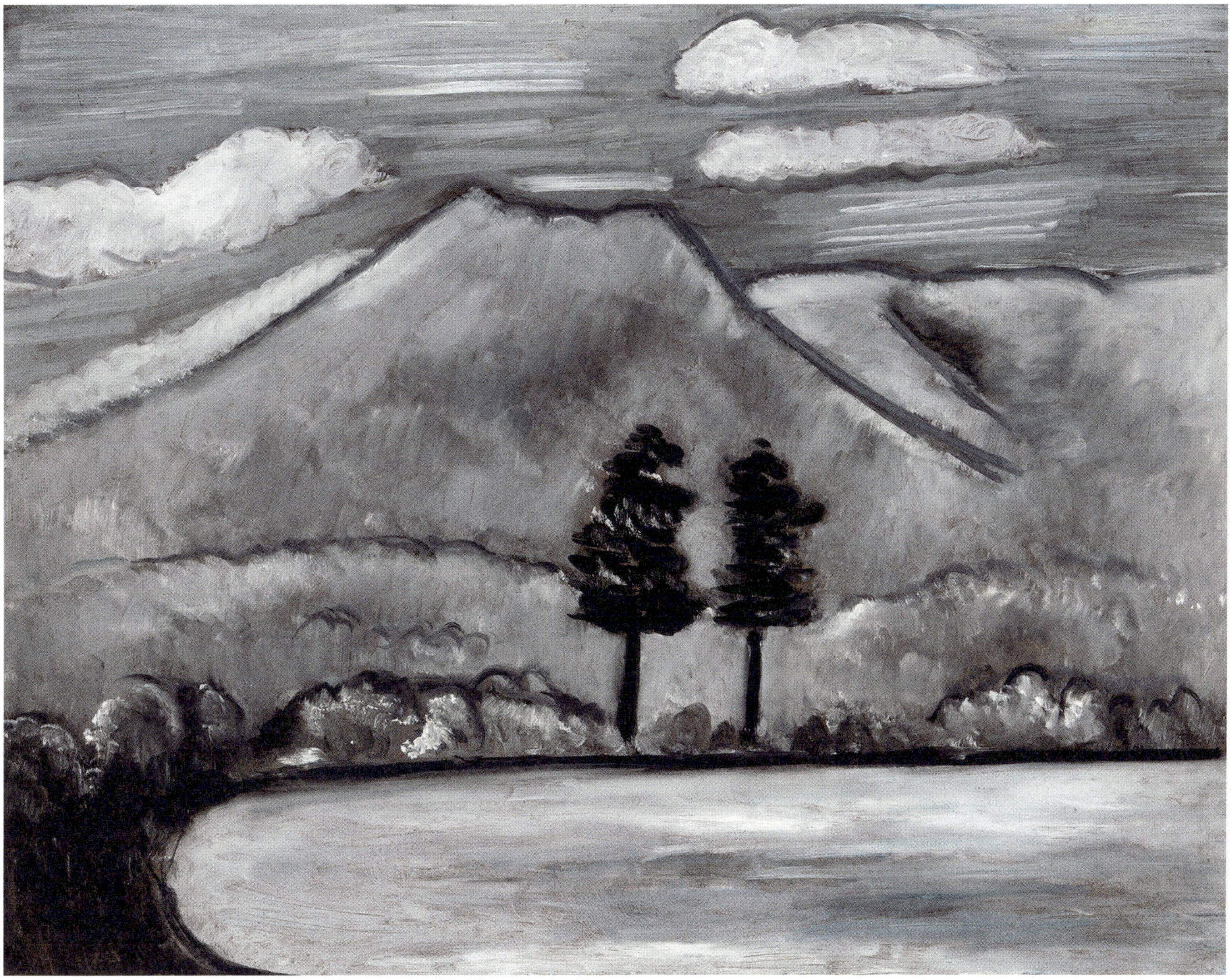

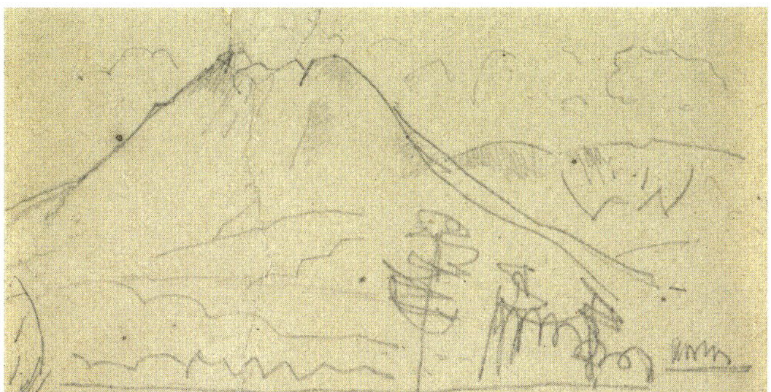

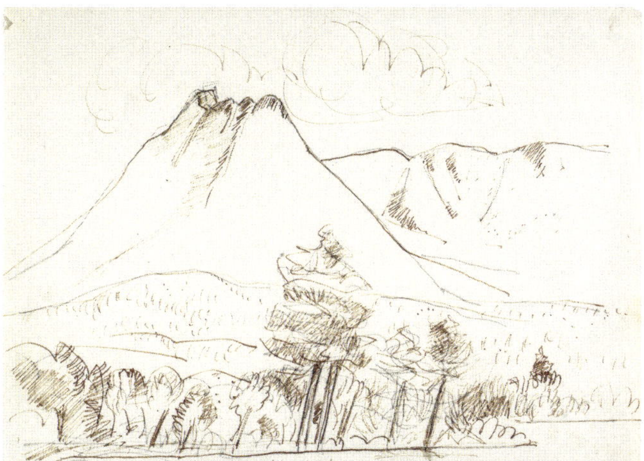

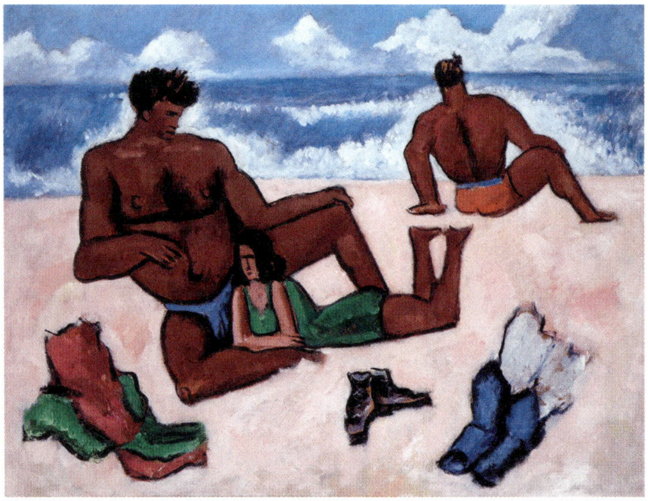

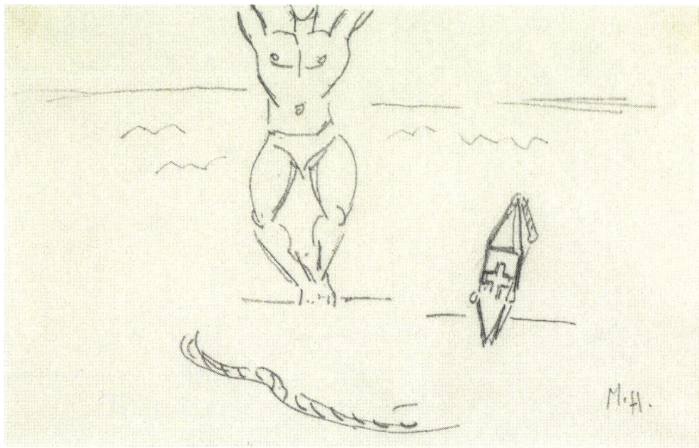

90 On the Beach, 1940
133 Untitled (Male Figure, Rope, and Buoy at Old Orchard Beach), c. 1940

134 Untitled (Two Male Figures – One Standing, One Seated), c. 1940
135 Untitled (Two Male Figures), c. 1940

96 Canuck Yankee Lumberjack at Old Orchard Beach, Maine, 1940-1941

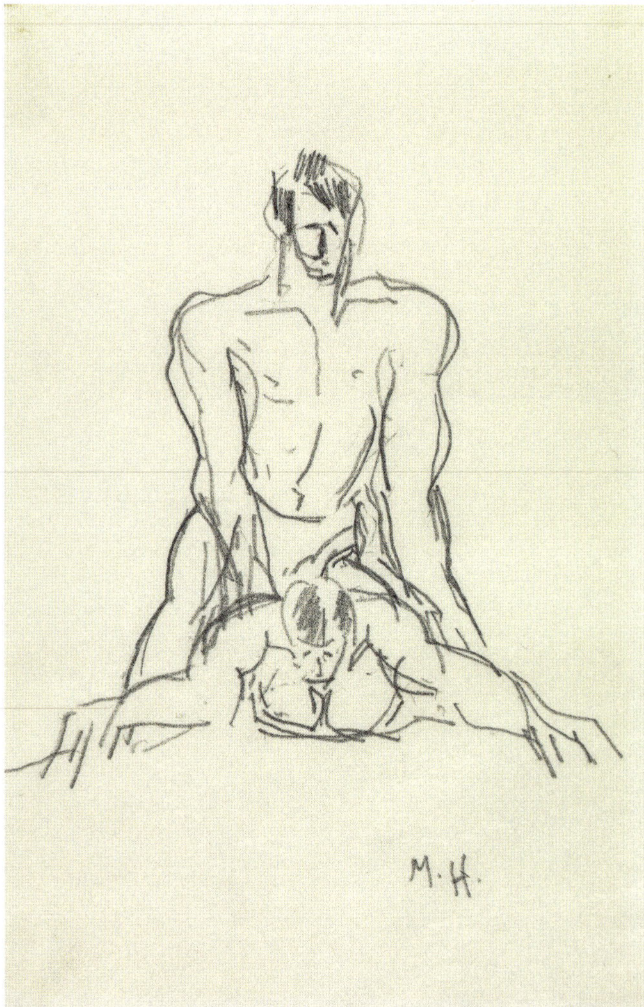

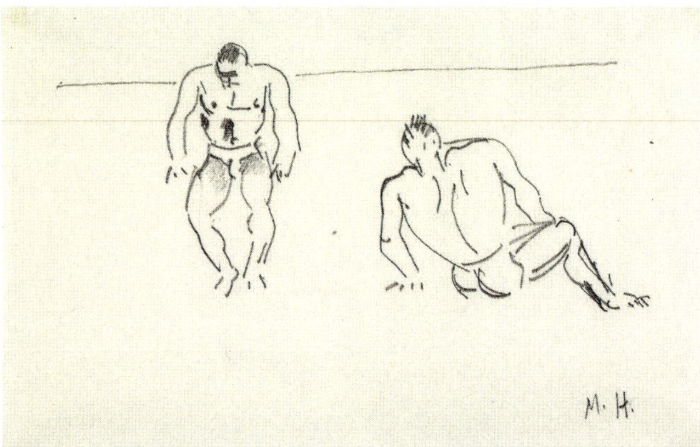

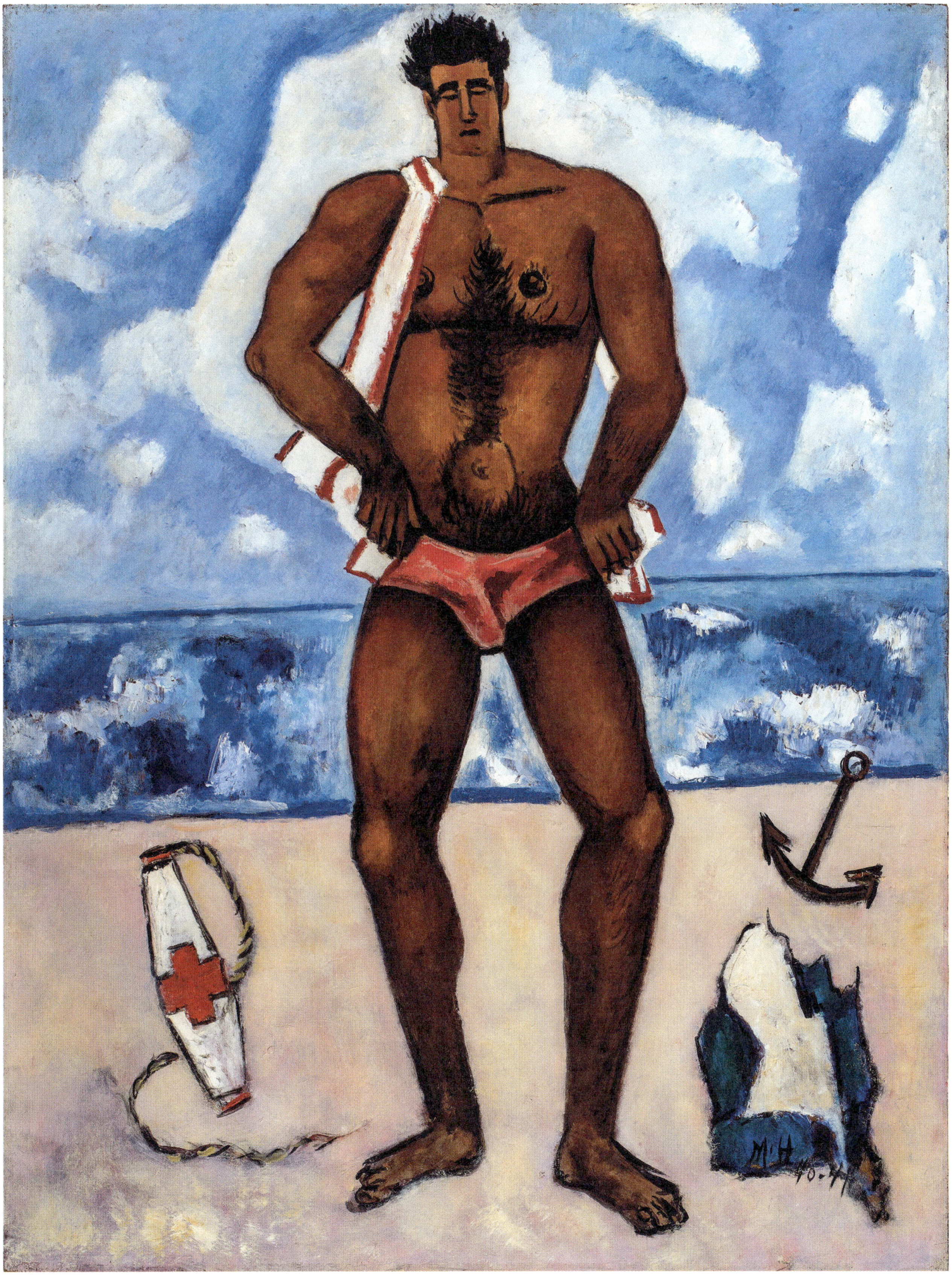

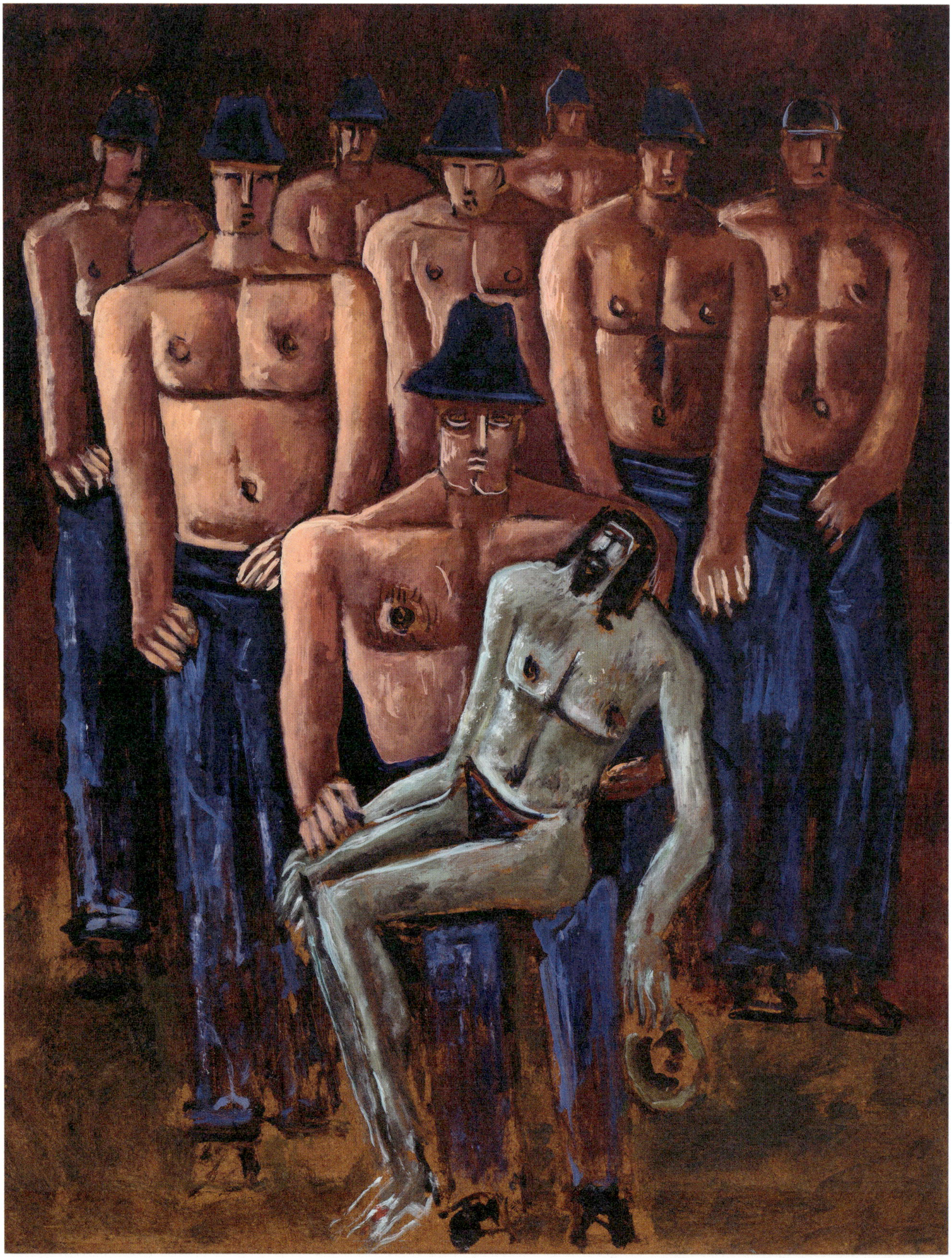

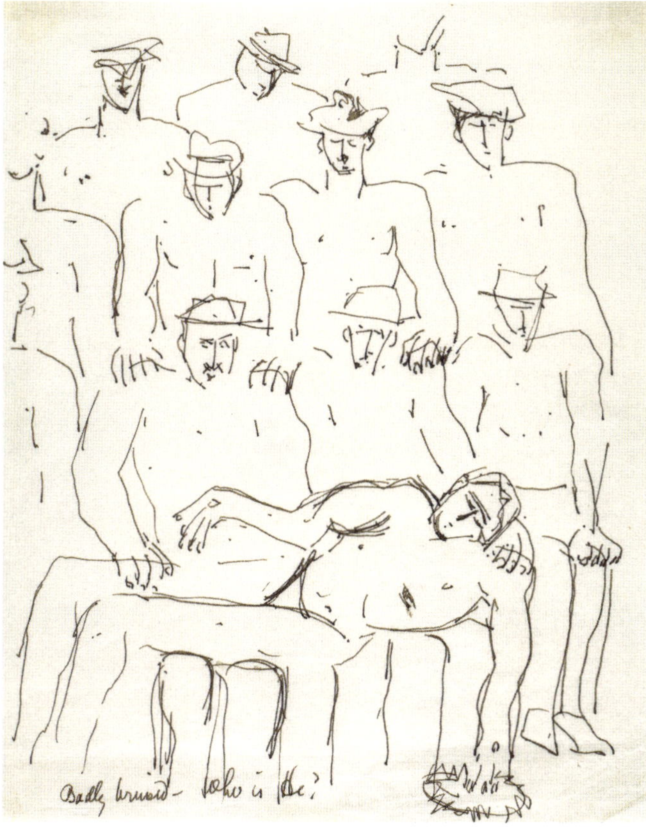

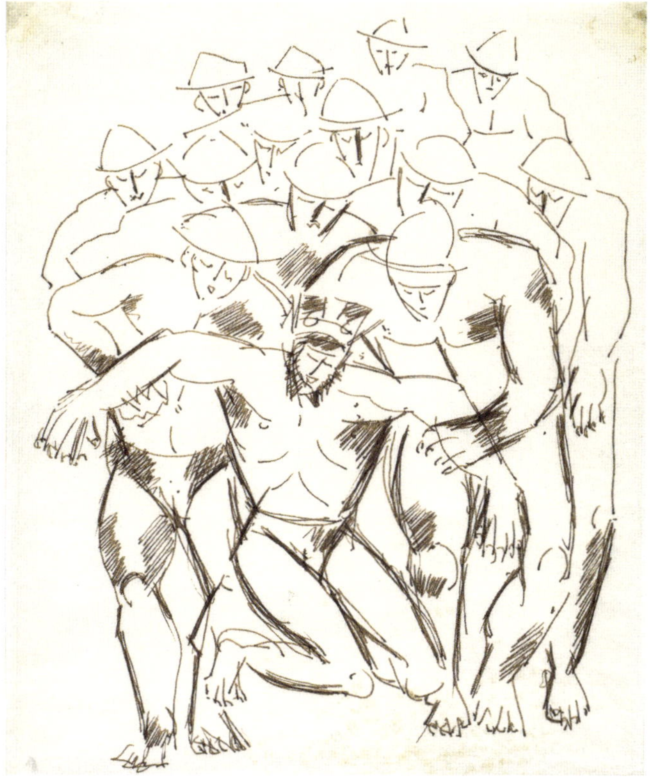

101 Christ Held by Half-Naked Men, 1941

140 Badly Bruised – Who Is He? (Study for "Christ Held by Half-Naked Men"), c. 1942
141 Untitled (Study for "Christ Held by Half-Naked Men"), c. 1942

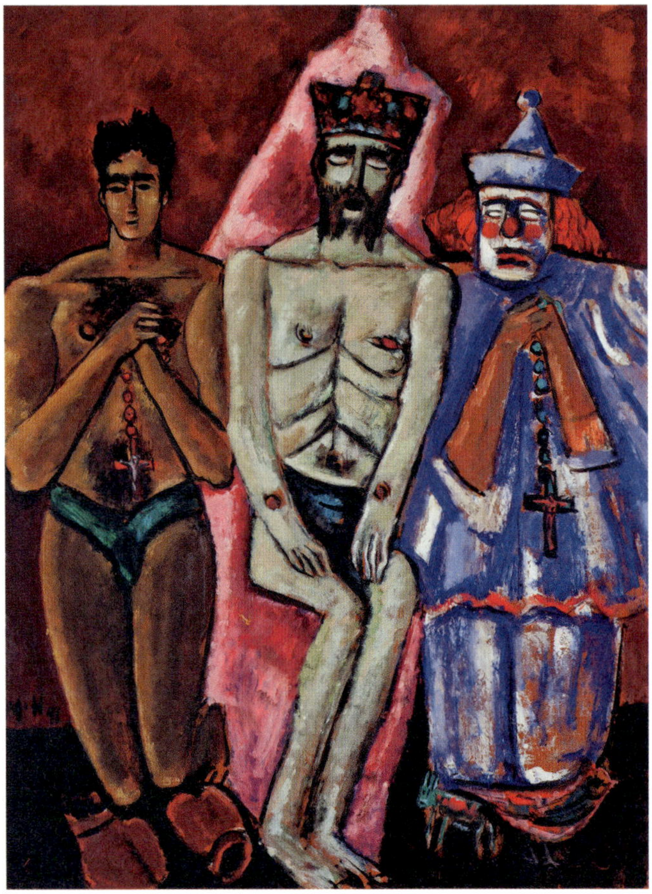

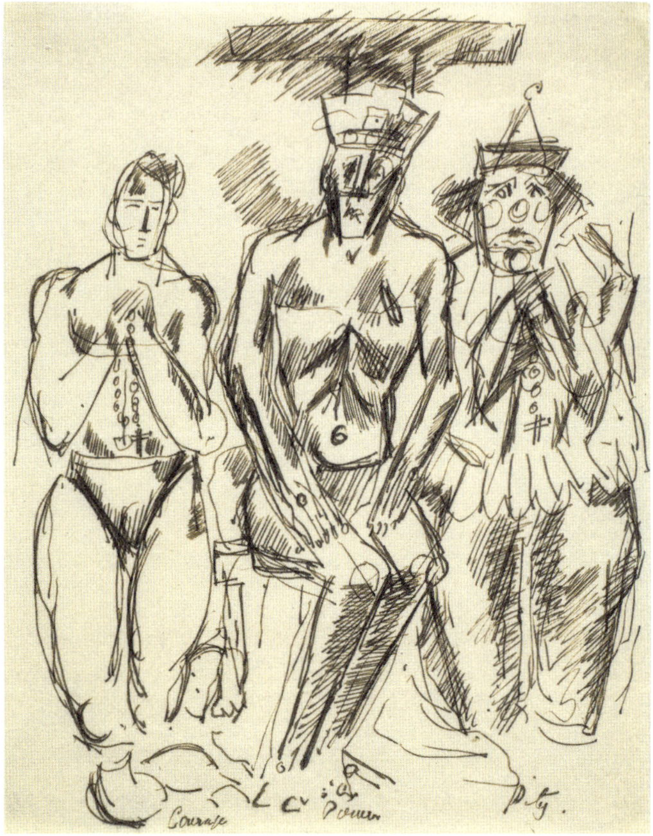

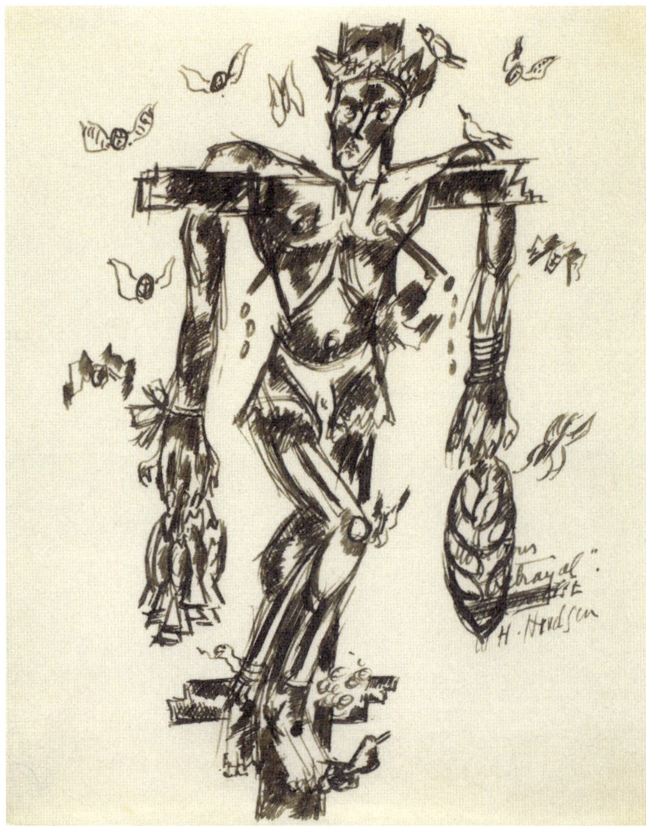

100 Three Friends, 1941
139 Courage, Power, Pity (Study for "Three Friends"), 1942

138 Monstrous Betrayal, 1941-1943

85 Sustained Comedy, 1939

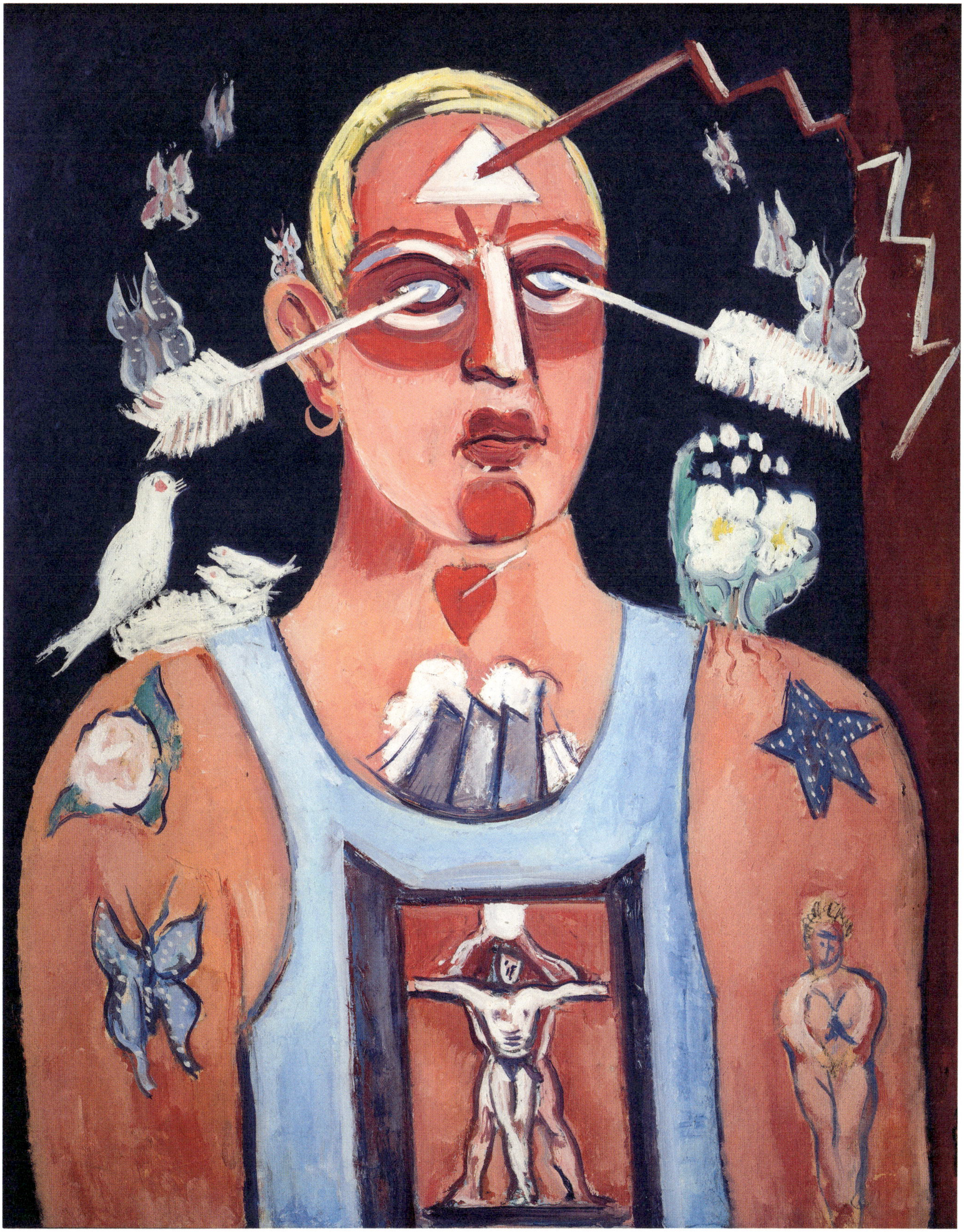

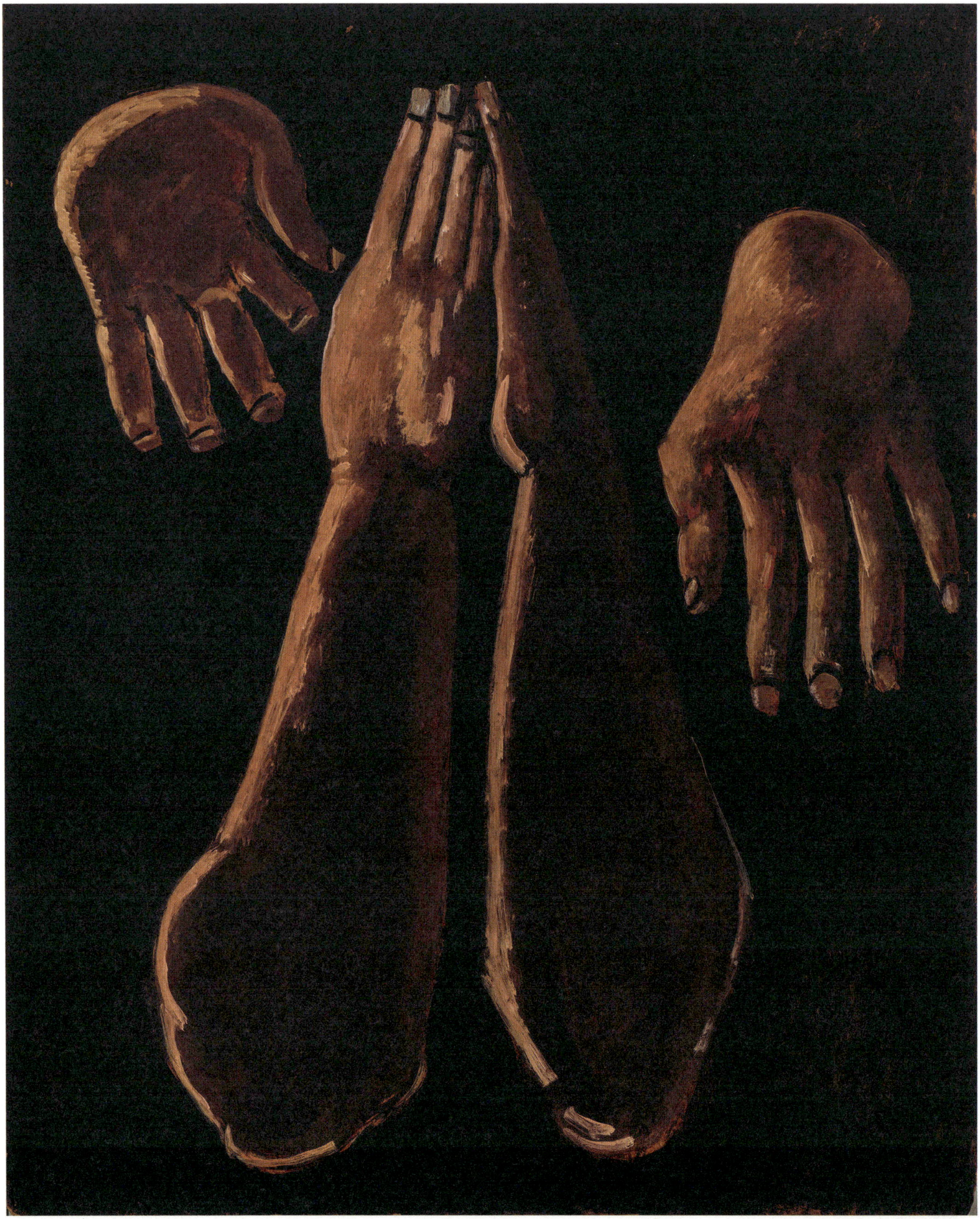

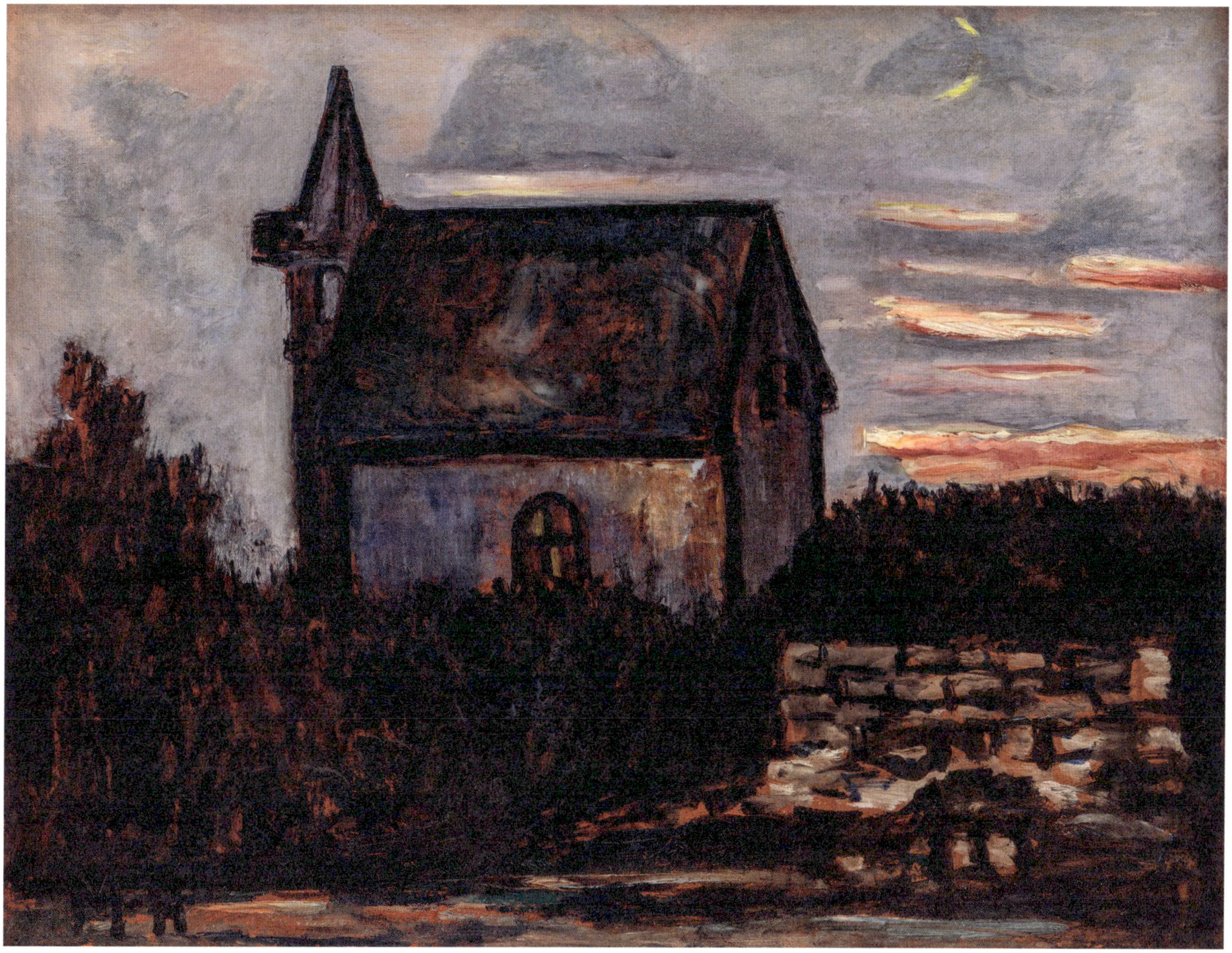

95 Hands, 1940
94 Church by the Barrens, Indian Harbor, Maine, 1940

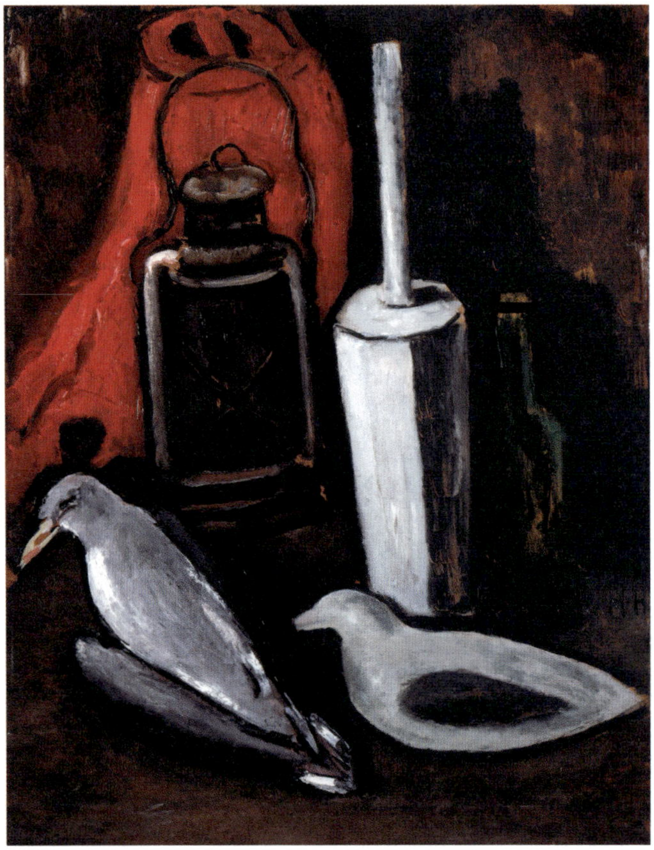

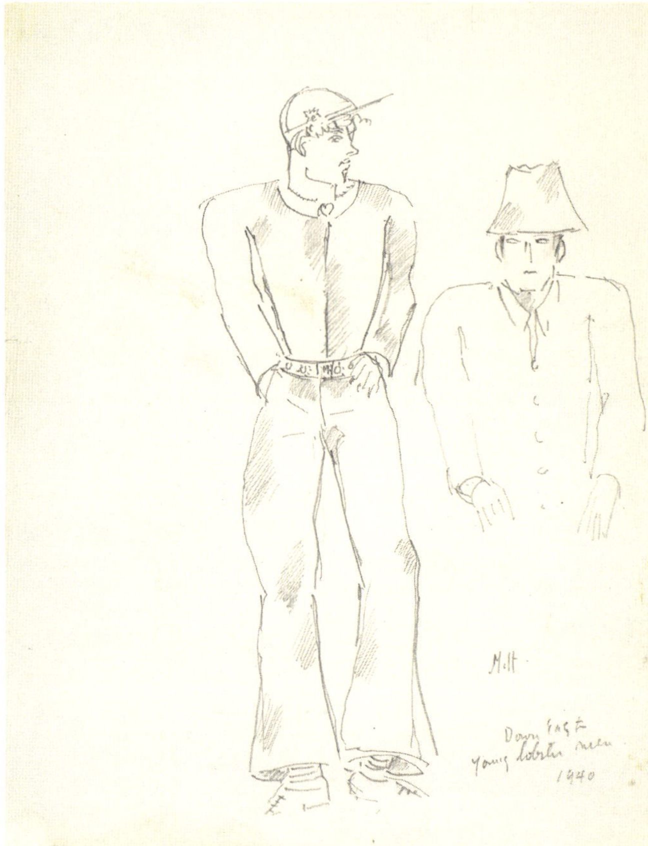

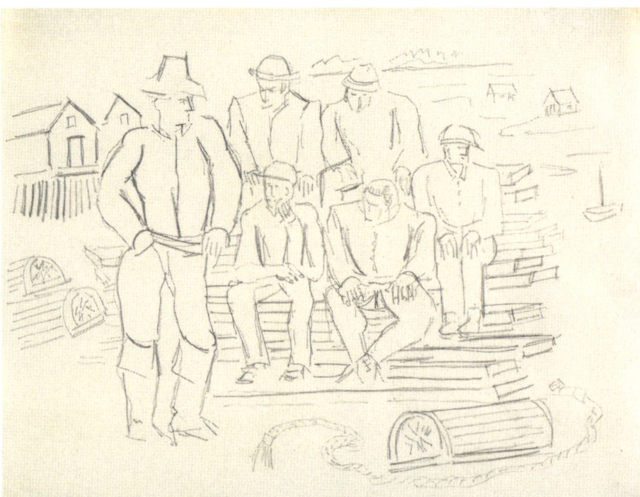

102 Maine Coast Still Life, 1941
136 Down East Young Lobstermen (Study for "Down East Young Blades"), 1940

137 Untitled (Preliminary drawing for "Lobster Fishermen"), c. 1940

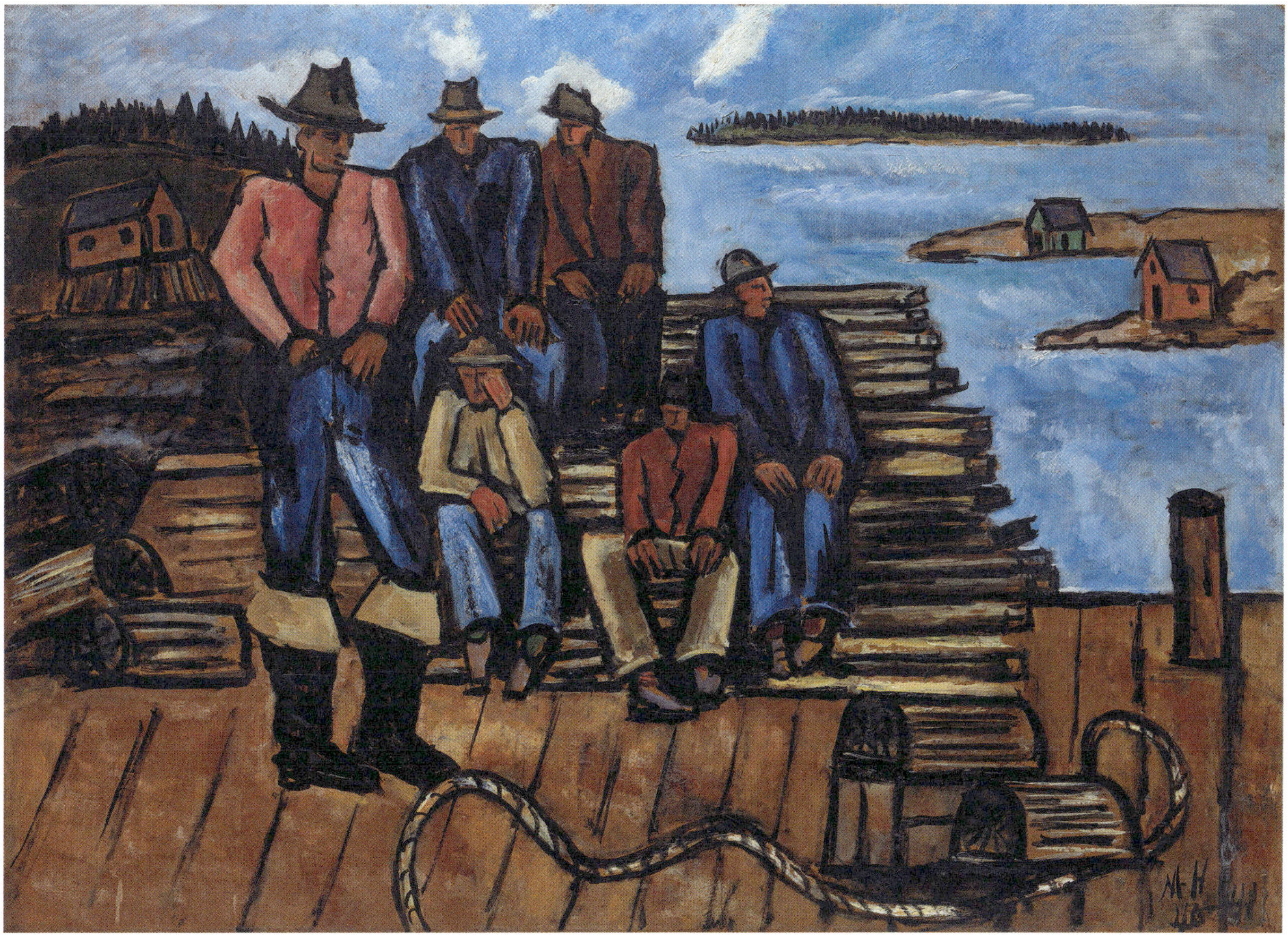

99 Lobster Fishermen, 1940-1941

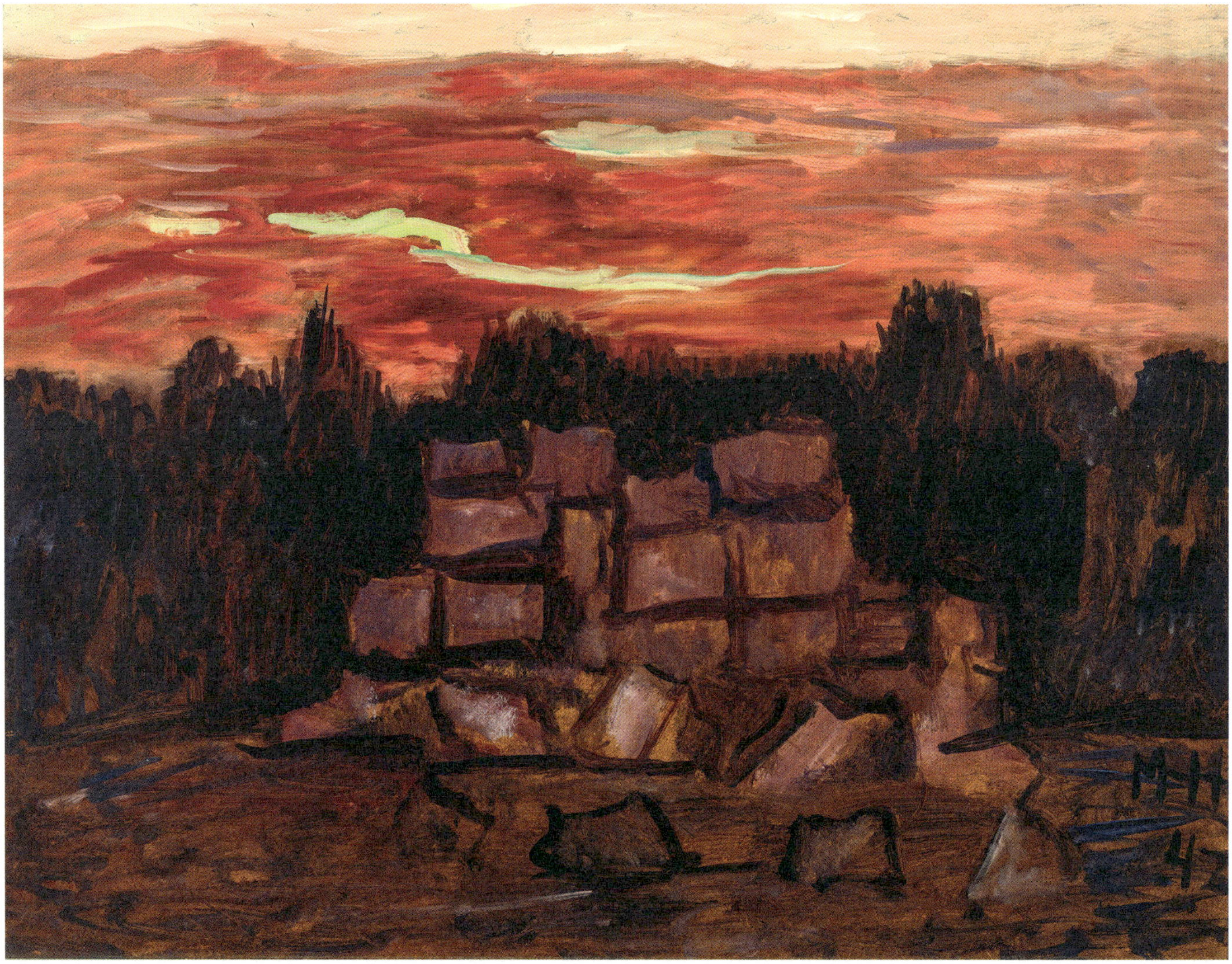

104 Sundown by the Ruins, 1942

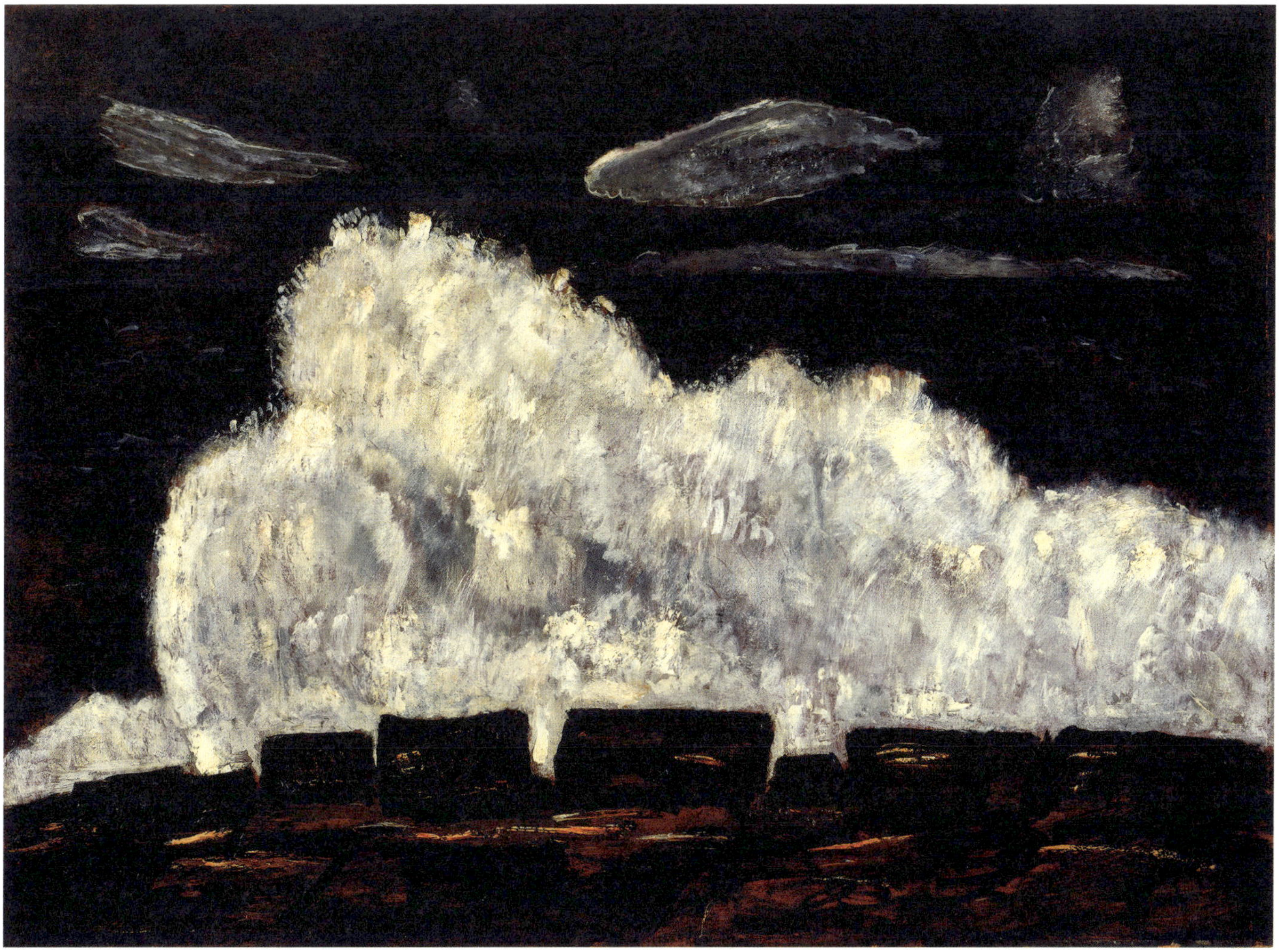

106 Evening Storm, Schoodic, Maine No. 2, 1942

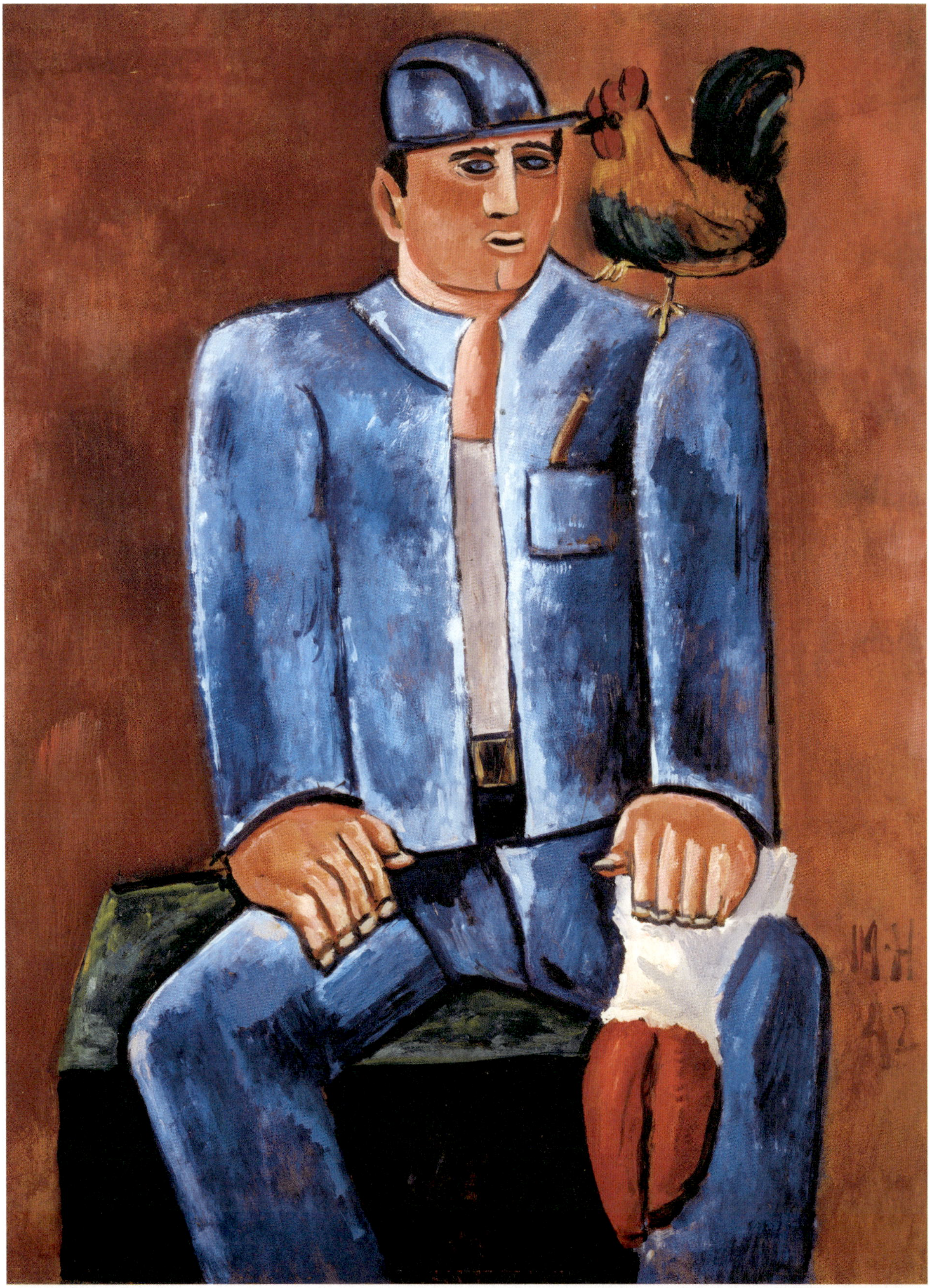

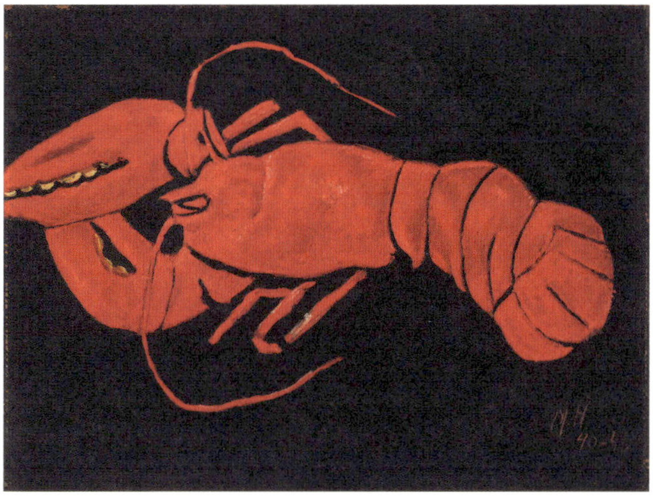

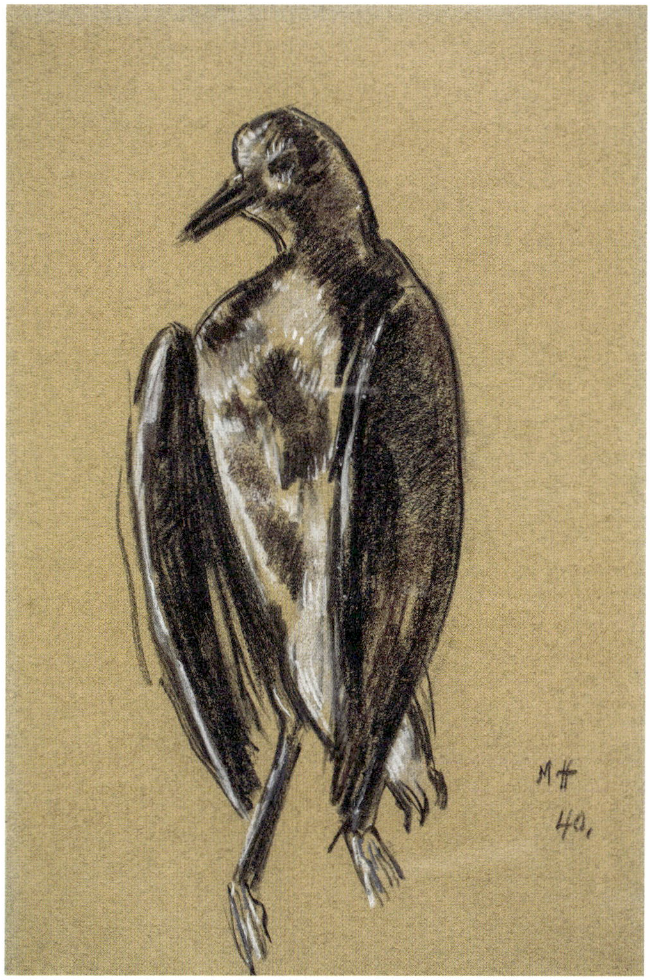

109 Young Seadog with Friend Billy, 1942

97 Lobster on Black Background, 1940-1941
132 Dead Plover, 1940

110 White Sea Horse, 1942
113 Migration, 1943

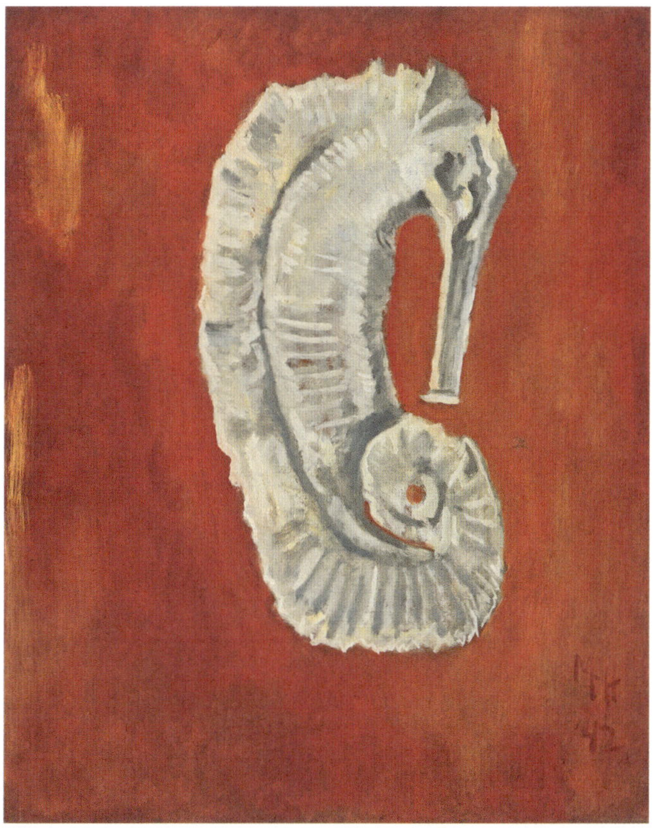

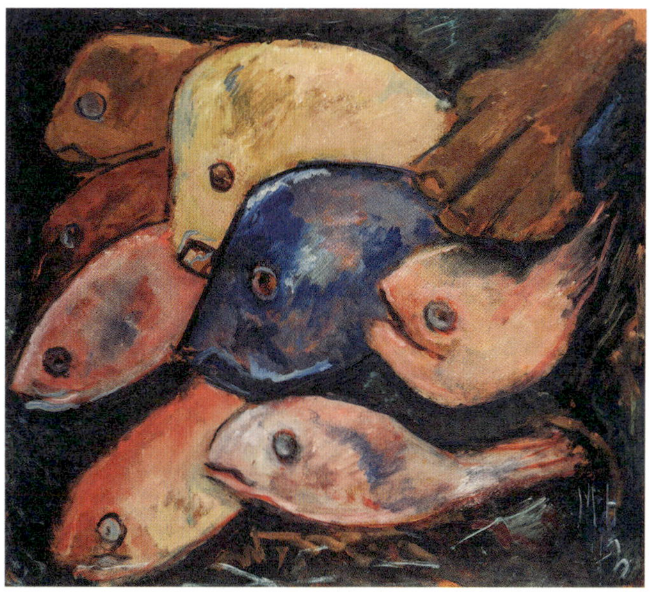

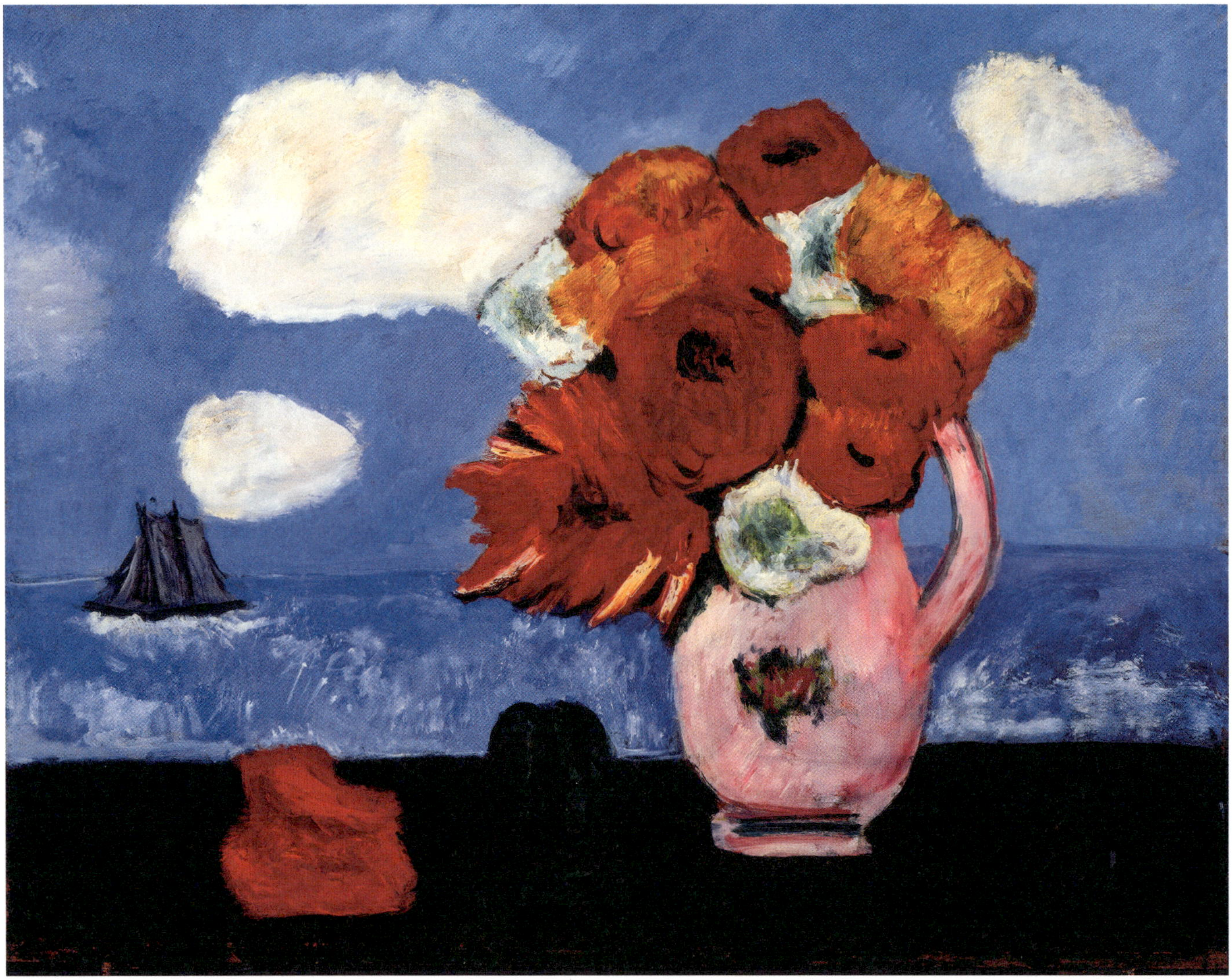

107 Summer Clouds and Flowers, 1942
108 Summer, Sea, Window, Red Curtain, 1942

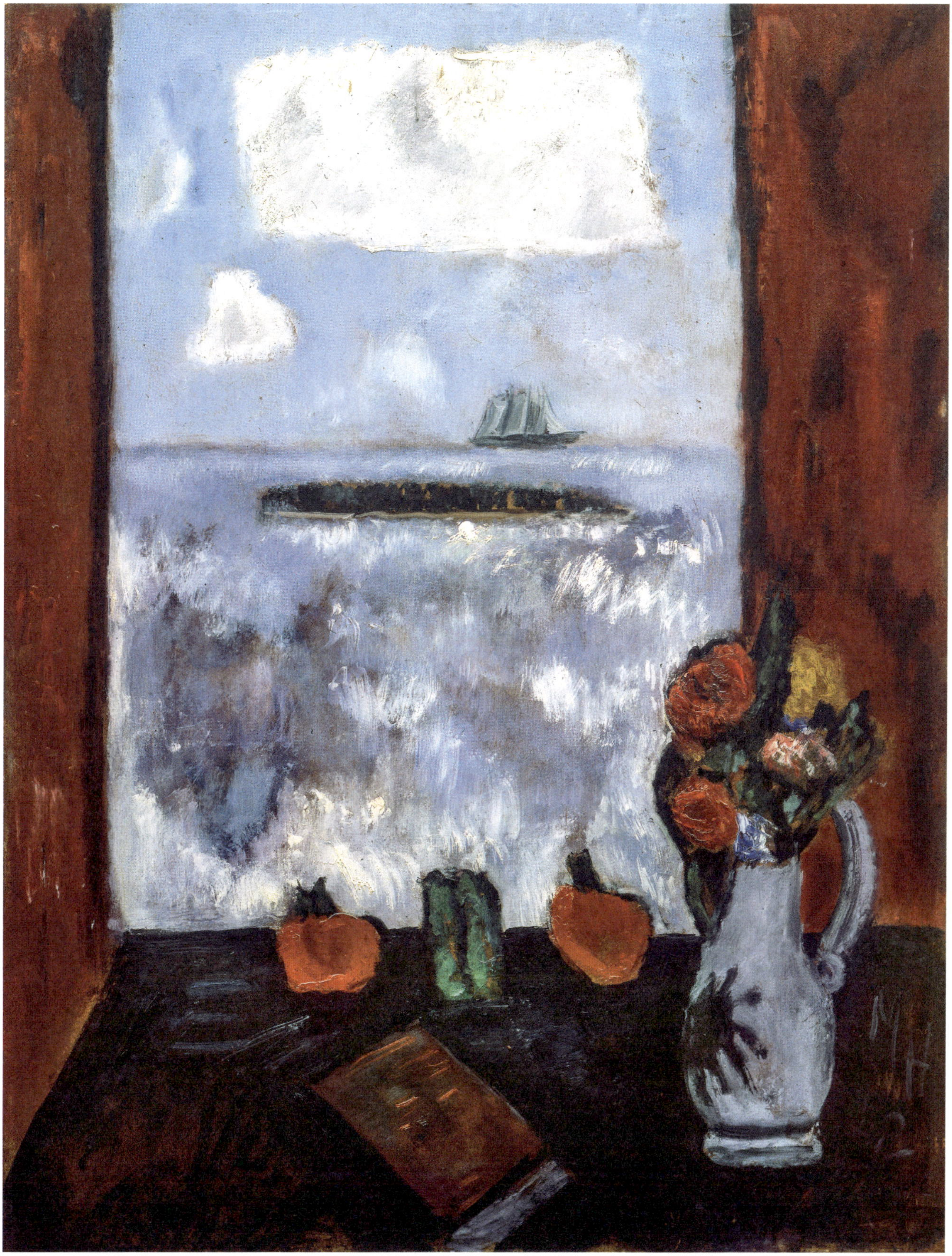

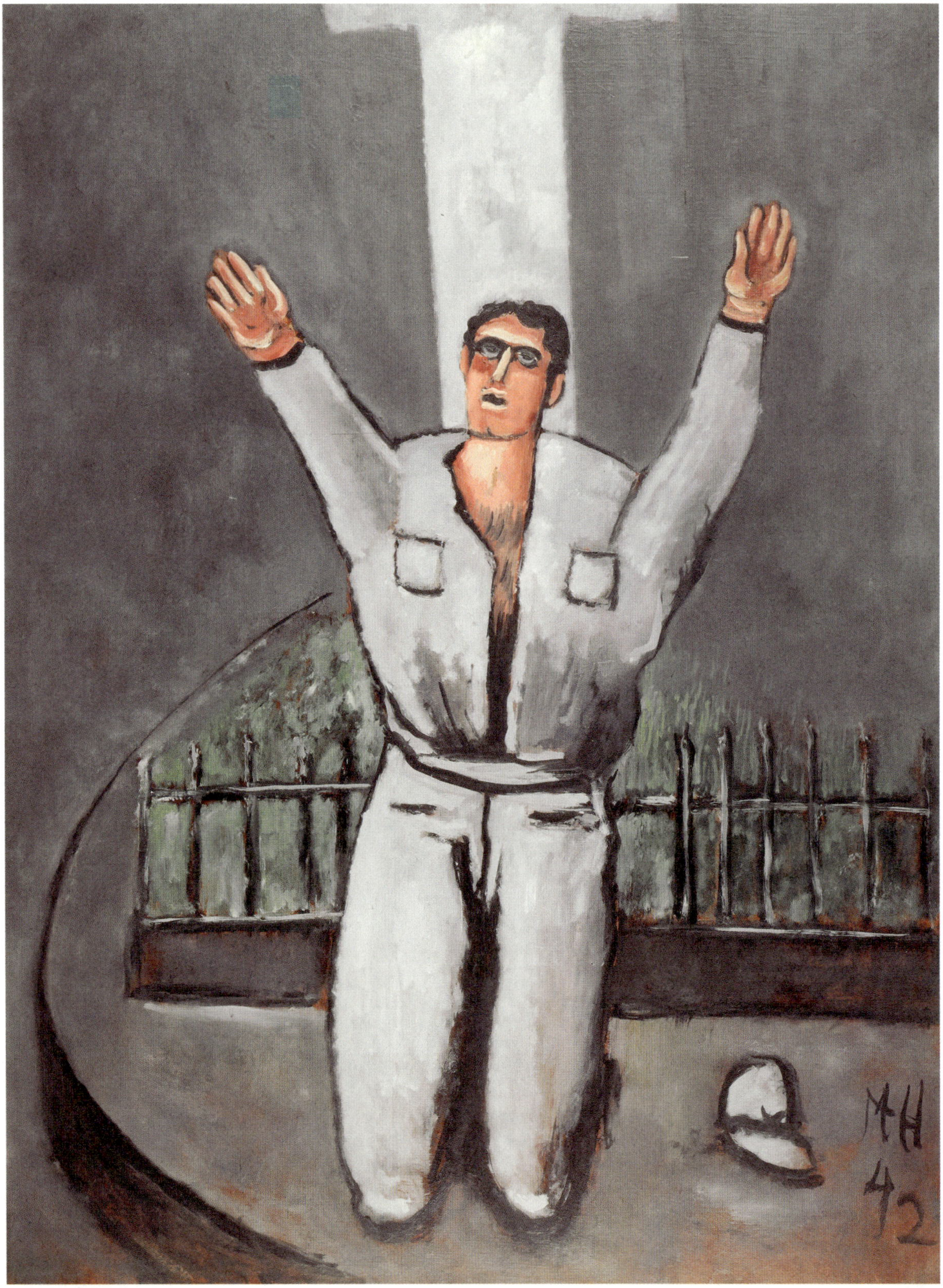

105 Prayer on Park Avenue, 1942
112 Roses, 1943

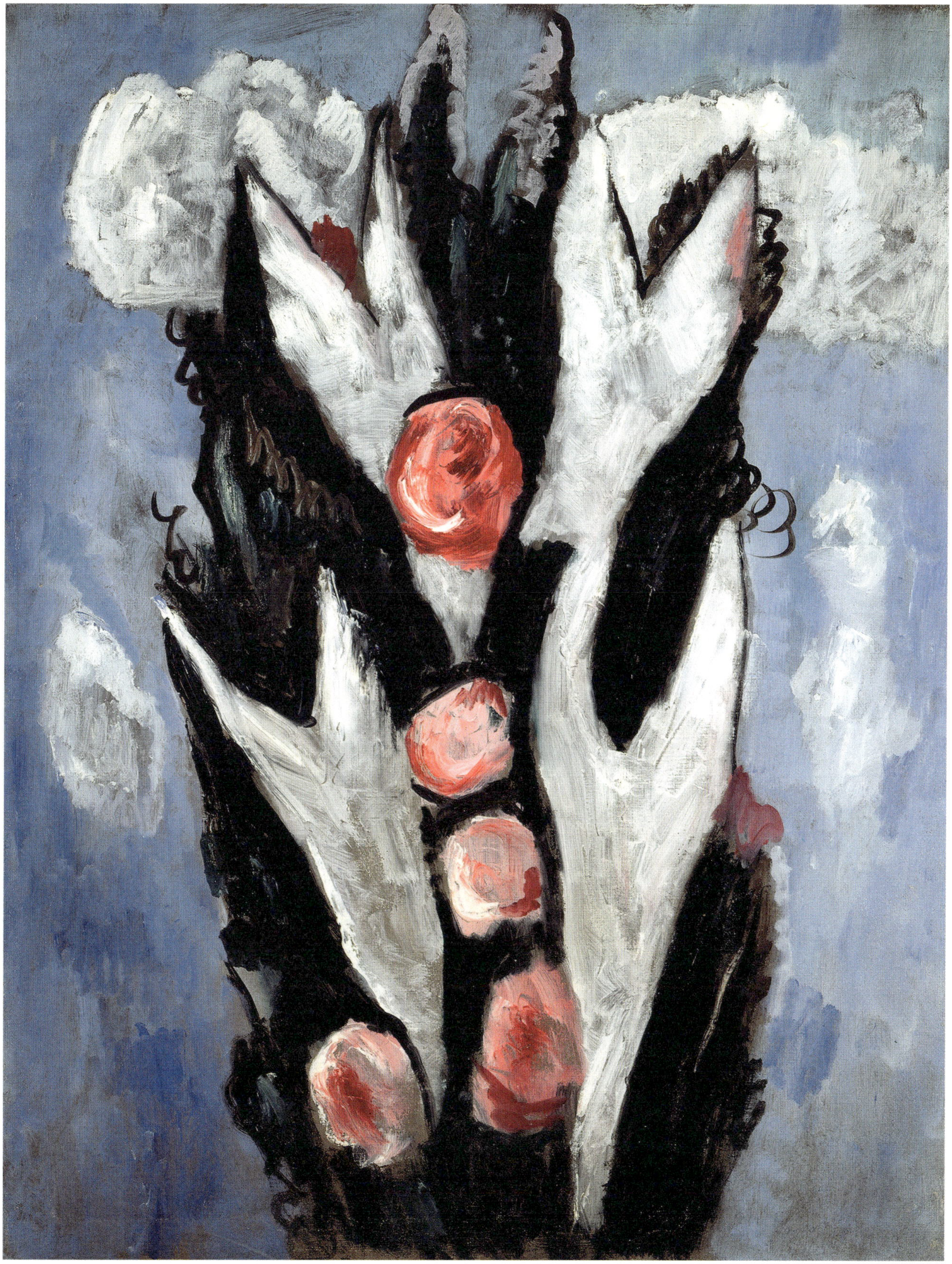

Flat Men, Round Feeling: On Homoeroticism in Marsden Hartley

By Jonathan D. Katz

Marsden Hartley's male nudes can't be confused with those of any other artist. They are defiantly awkward, at once both top heavy, and beefy, as if the bodies were all torso, posed with limbs akimbo or with little attention to how joints actually articulate appendages. They seem to encode a crude version of macho, a schoolboy's ideal that masculinity really is but a concatenation of muscles, body hair, and blank, imperious stares. Rendered as curiously flat, they seem all surface, articulating no sense of an individuated, interior life. Even when his figures are placed in homoerotic poses or situations, as in his many beefcake subjects or his notably weird *Christ Held by Half-Naked Men* (cat. 101), there is nary a hint of queerness, as it was then understood – absent either markers of effeminacy or overtly eroticized male bodies. And genitals, on the rare occasions when they do appear, are reduced to an afterthought, scaled to the schoolboy, or made to disappear.

This curiously citational, notably uncarnal celebration of masculinity wars with the more legibly homoerotic imagery of his predecessors. John Singer Sargent, for example, tended to eroticize his male sitters, as in the Boston Public Library murals or his frankly homoerotic image of a young black elevator operator, *Nude Study of Thomas E. McKeller* from c. 1917-1920 (fig. 10), posing spread eagle, its blatant eroticism enabled by racial difference (although tellingly, this picture was never displayed publicly in Sargent's lifetime, though it did adorn his private quarters). Exploiting the prospect of paint as a volumetric analog to flesh, these paintings stand in marked contrast to the planar rectitude of even Hartley's most embodied men. In telling contrast to Hartley's manly men, Sargent instead knowingly placed men in the traditional positions of female models, as in his extraordinary oil, *Male Model Resting* from c. 1895 (fig. 11). Here Sargent adopts the posture of an odalisque, a pose traditionally deployed towards the revelation of female secondary sexual characteristics – arm below the head to reveal the breasts, legs parted just enough to sug-

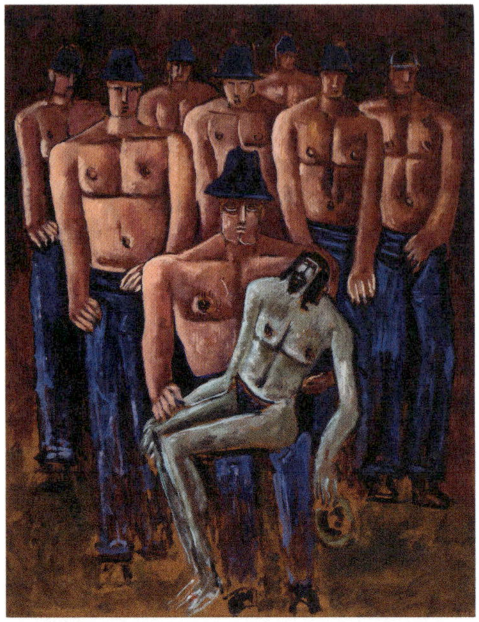

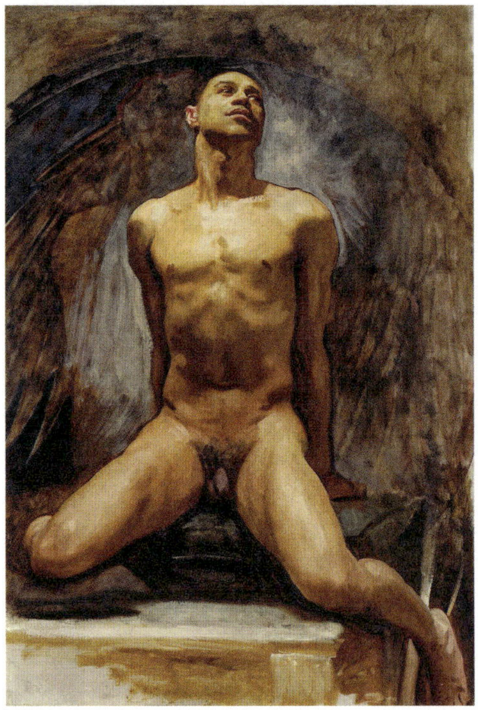

101 *Christ Held by Half-Naked Men*, 1941
Fig. 10 John Singer Sargent: *Nude Study of Thomas E. McKeller*, c. 1917-1920

Fig. 11 John Singer Sargent: *Male Model Resting*, c. 1895
92 *Madawaska – Acadian Light-Heavy*, 1940
91 *Madawaska – Acadian Light-Heavy*, 1940

gest her sex – wielded here to depict his manservant. Such feminized masculinity is literally unthinkable for Hartley.

Often, when Hartley paints a man, as in his late, great images of *Madawaska – Acadian Light-Heavy* from 1940 (cats. 91-92), the figure crowds the frame, pushing all context and situatedness off the canvas. In the transformation of the figure from a more natural build towards this aggressively burly, strapping man, we can see a recognizable male form grow increasingly iconic, the latter image now massively muscular, square-jawed and cut, all sharp angles with almost no human roundness. This hieratic image of a man moreover frustrates any projection of interiority, his face a blank. As he grows more angular and muscled, he seems to get bigger, even though the canvases are of the exact same size. Centrally, this now iconic man ceases to be relational, to be comparable to one of us, to be a human male, with the usual flaws of our kind. He now stands like a Kouros, an object to be gazed at, carrying himself with extraordinary self-possession in a military posture, his hands hidden behind his back, a far cry from the relatable, psychologically coded hip grazing fingers of the more familiar male form. In this transformation from a man into an image of a man lies Hartley's particular genius. These are men we can stare at endlessly, but neither know nor touch. They are less men than an imago of the masculine.

Equally, Hartley's citations of the ideal of masculinity couldn't be more different from the homoerotic horseplay in the work of his good friend Charles Demuth. In his strikingly frank *Three Sailors on the Beach* from 1930 (fig. 12, p. 124), eros is made flesh and men touch, the obverse of Hartley's isolated figures with their suppressed eroticism. Demuth also freely plays with homoerotic desire in works such as *On "That" Street* from 1932 (fig. 13, p. 125), the title a reference to a street at the Brooklyn Naval Yard where "queers" in the language of the time, went to pick up "trade." Trade here signifies not only men who would take the dominant or top position with a queer, but who were considered, because they were sexually consonant with the dictates of masculinity, unmarked by the fact that they were having sex with another man. In *On "That" Street,* Demuth depicts two queers soliciting the attention of the trade, i.e., the sailor on the right. The queers, both of them with hands stereotypically on their hips, include a young,

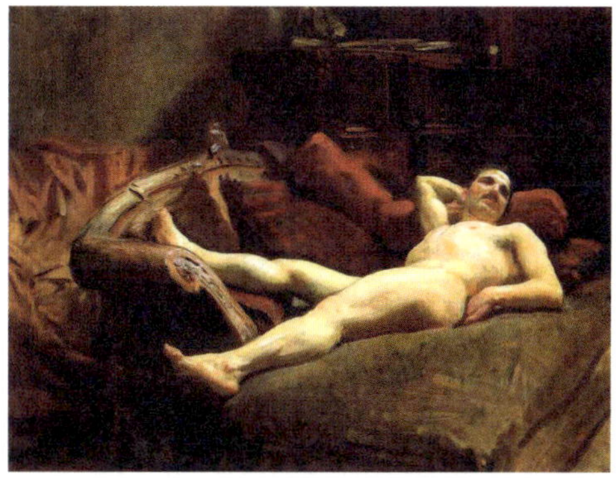

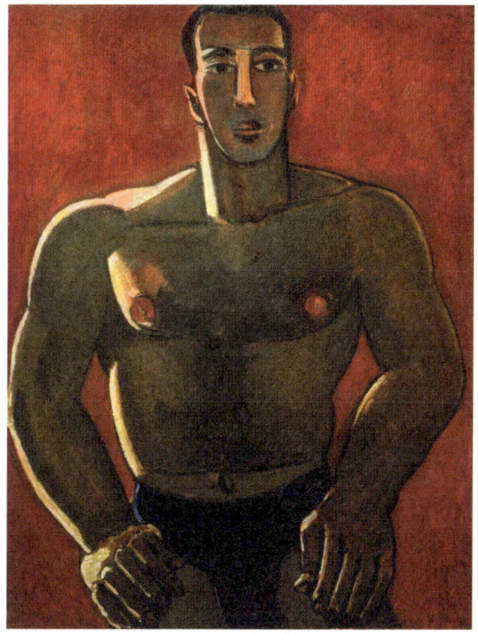

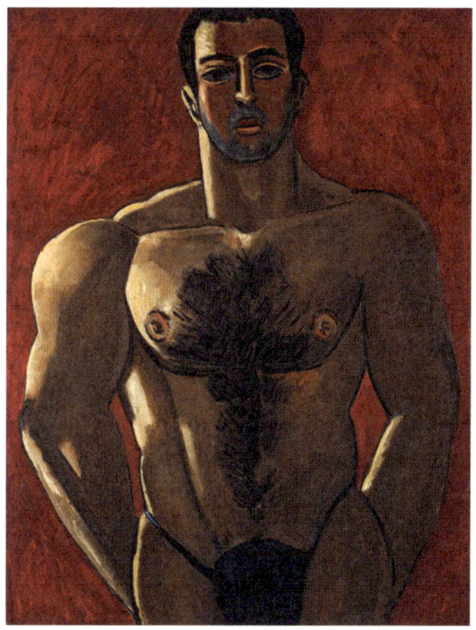

effeminate sailor and Demuth himself. The Demuth figure is staring none-too-happily at the queer sailor because the latter has inserted himself into what should have been an easy and a clear cut transaction. To sailors on shore leave, older queers offered the promise of free lodging, food, and maybe even a little spending money in exchange for sex. And since that sex entailed being the active partner, as long as the trade was not emotionally involved with a queer, by the standards of that moment, he was untainted by any charge of homosexuality, as he was the dominant partner, doing what men do. But a young queer sailor, with no money and no gifts to offer, threatens to short-circuit the dynamic, underscored as the trade looks at Demuth and Demuth looks at the queer sailor in a roundelay of disappointed expectations.

We can see the queer/trade dynamic recorded somewhat more dispassionately by a non-queer artist, George Bellows, in his revelatory print, *The Shower-Bath*, aka *Men's Bath* of 1917 (fig. 14). One of Bellows more popular prints, it went through three different states despite the fact that the central image features precisely such a queer/trade coupling. As in the Demuth, the queer stereotypically places his hand on his hip, while thrusting out his buttocks and offering a leering grin. The trade, on the other hand, looks like a less attractive version of one of Hartley's male nudes, with a beefily built torso, his face a blank mask. But what really gives the game away is that the trade's towel masks his erection. So common, indeed, even accepted, were these queer/trade relations in the context of the necessity of public bathing (few people had private warm water at the time) that Bellows could make this homoerotic dyad the exact center of a public print, and still sell a number of copies, something one would be hard pressed to do today.

The particularities of American queer/trade culture in the first decades of the 20th century is the ground for Hartley's images of masculine men, and extremely rare images they are, for they offer, in a word, trade – men who would occasionally have sex with queers. As we've seen queer images are not all that uncommon, but images of trade, especially trade absent queers, are rare, for by definition what makes a man trade is in fact exclusively his relationship to queers. The ramifications of this very different organization of sexual culture can be glimpsed in

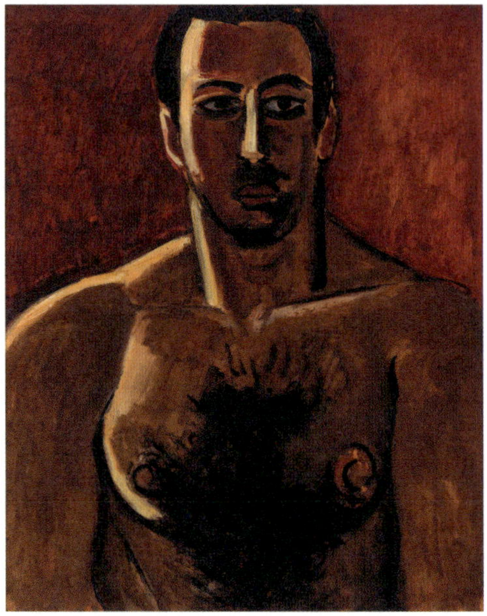

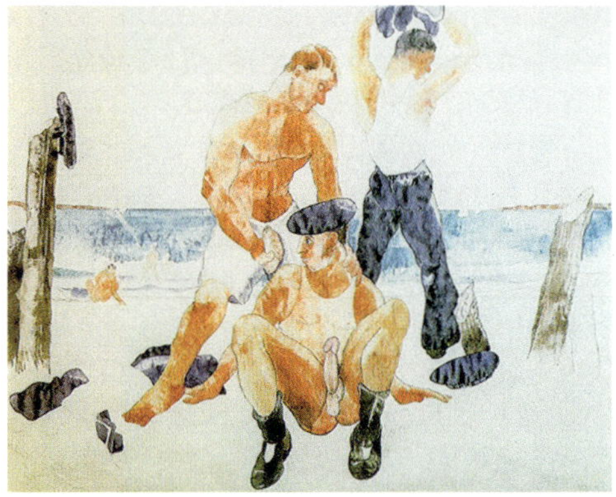

93 *Madawaska Acadian Light-Heavy, Third Arrangement*, 1940
Fig. 12 Charles Demuth: *Three Sailors on the Beach*, 1930

Hartley's works. Trade occupied a codified position in this dynamic, one that, especially in an era that more firmly policed the boundaries of acceptable male/female relations, allowed men sexual release with other men, as long as they adopted the position of top and eschewed any emotional connection. One telling corollary of this integrated arrangement was that as a consequence, paradoxically, queers faced less hostility from dominant culture at this moment, for not only was a sexual pass by a queer not generally met with violence, it was moreover made acceptable then precisely because it was an endorsement of the subject's unimpeachable masculinity. Today, by contrast, the so-called "gay panic" defense seeks to codify an ostensibly justifiable violent response to any insinuation of a shared sexuality. As co-conspirators in the release of sexual energies outside the sanctified terms of marital, reproductive sexuality, queers and trade needed each other, their familiarity a logical result of their mutuality.

While we understand the valence of trade's relationship with queers, the story of the queer's emotional life is less often addressed. A singular consequence of this different sexual culture was that while queers could have a great deal of sex with trade, mutual love was flatly foreclosed (the rare trade that did indeed reciprocate an emotional bond was called a husband and as such occupied one rung below that of traditional trade). Hartley's male portraiture in fact constitutes one of the richest archives for coming to understand the subjective dimensions of a sexuality inescapably bound up with the refusal of real mutuality, of the denial of any emotional component, of being always the desiring party, but never in turn desirable. Indeed much of Hartley's familiar pessimism might be best understood in light of this dynamic, as too his sense of being something of an outsider to life, watching and yearning but never expecting real fulfillment.

I'm of course arguing that Hartley's hieratic images of masculine men are trade, but that poses a problem, for many of these images are solo portraits, and trade without queers is unmarked, merely a form of normative masculinity. Even when a group of men are figured, clearly none correspond to the typology of the queer. Yet Hartley himself underscored the degree to which his autographic trove of flatly rendered, hieratic masculinity corresponds to his desire for trade and the emotional toll such

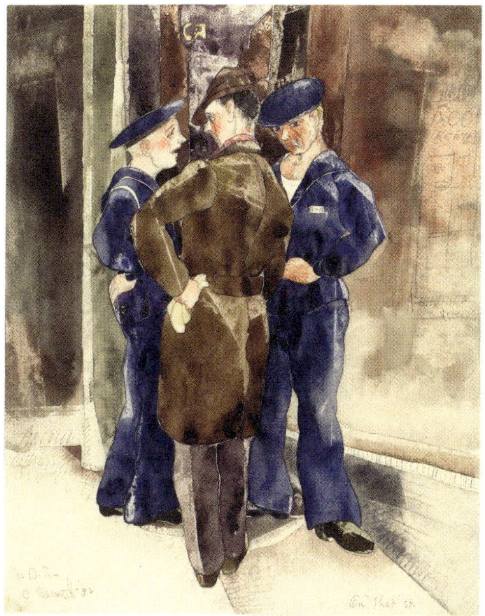

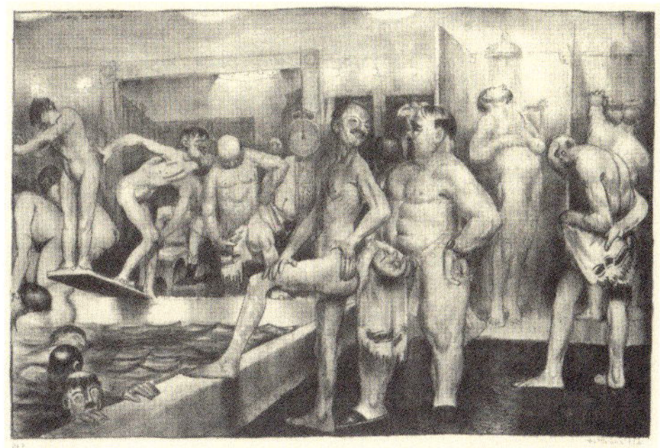

Fig. 13 Charles Demuth: *On "That" Street*, 1932
Fig. 14 George Bellows: *Shower-Bath, First State*, 1917

unreciprocated longing engendered. He penned a short, untitled poem in a collection called *Bach for Breakfast* from the 1920s that analogized flatness to the physical sex act, and roundedness to a fully reciprocal love, including the physical, but going well beyond it:

Holding in reserve
a certain tendency to speed
accentuation,
mistaking nevertheless the pistol shot
for the race,
paying the huge penalty of ultra-previous
enthusiasms, love squashed flat
into patterns of adoration,
all flatness misconstrued for
serene quantitative –
"I see, in time, there is yet
time to make it round,
pumpkins in round heaps of fire,
bodies made round"
his hat still sitting,
rakishly,
above his ears.[112]

The poem is difficult to parse – as it perforce had to be in an era when same-sex desire was literally illegal – but its erotic imagery is nonetheless self-evident. The speaker acknowledges mistaking the pistol shot for the race, namely mistaking orgasm for the full scope and complexity of a relationship. As a consequence, he notes that he is "Paying the huge penalty of ultra-previous enthusiasms," in short, that he recognizes a habitual pattern in which he falls for someone only to find himself closed out, or as the poem puts it, "love squashed flat into patterns of adoration, all flatness misconstrued for serene quantitative – ." In place of the quality of emotional richness, Hartley here notes he must settle for merely scoring the number of encounters, the "serene quantitative" quality the poem leaves hanging.

But then the poet breaks through, speaking directly and in the first person, acknowledging that "there is yet time to make it round" to find a richer, fuller reciprocal relationship that would be like "pumpkins in round heaps of fire," or the absolute

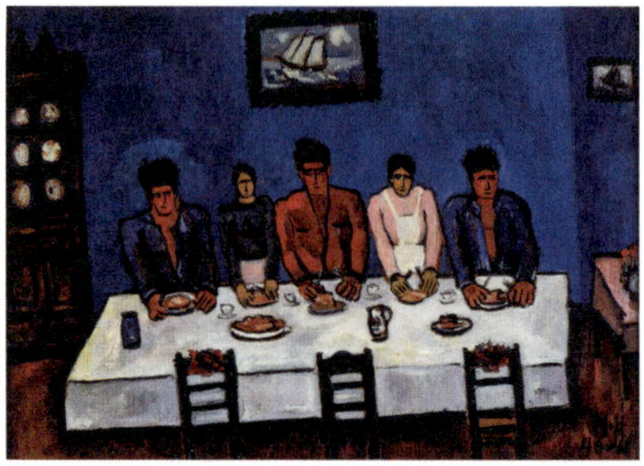

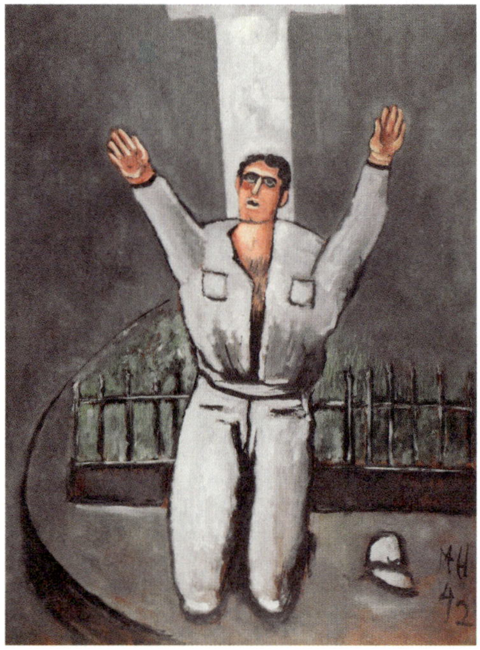

98 *Fishermen's Last Supper, Nova Scotia*, 1940-1941
105 *Prayer on Park Avenue*, 1942

togetherness in extremis that is love. But then, drawn back to the present circumstance, the poem ends by the poet admiring the trade with his rakish hat, physical desire once again flaring. Hartley concludes the poem with the grounded observation that, in the face of his soaring fantasy, he cannot alone make this desire round, for the circumstances of same-sex sexuality at the time militated against it.

By the time of Hartley's late, great male figures, the world of queer/trade he knew so well was on the cusp of a shift to our modern system of sexual differentiation, one in which queerness is measured not by the way you "gender" yourself via position in the sexual act, but exclusively via the biological gender of your sexual partner. And with this change in definition, a genuinely companionate homosexuality was emerging, a real partnership. And yet, in the face of his protests about the flatness of the emotional life available to him, Hartley continues to flatten his men, perhaps even more in his later works than the earlier ones, as in *Three Friends* (1941) (cat. 100, p. 108), or *Young Sea Dog with Friend Billy* (1942) (cat. 109, p. 116). What's more, this distant, appreciative but flat and solely scopic relationship to the object of desire, to the masculine male of trade, becomes transformed in Hartley's work into a particularly disembodied form of religious fervor.

As untheological as it sounds, Catholic contemplation of Christ on the cross becomes a model for depicting trade, for both are distanced, yearning, largely non-reciprocal interactions activated by but one side of the relationship. This scopic desire is of course fundamentally erotic in both, but of the peculiarly sublimated eros of Catholicism in which one eats the body and blood of the beloved only to find a hard wafer in one's mouth. Hartley's images of trade seem to grow increasingly into religious allegories, as in that image of mournful betrayal by the sea in *The Fisherman's Last Supper, Nova Scotia* (cat. 98) or *Prayer on Park Avenue* (cat. 105) in which the male figure is depicted in supplication at the literal foot of a cross, arms akimbo as if crucified. But no other painting is as equally, as indissolubly, both a religious and erotic allegory as *Christ Held by Half Naked Men* (cat. 101). It is modeled of course on a pieta, and likely one of its most famous versions, by Michelangelo. But in place of the lap of the Virgin stand serried rows of shirtless, hypermasculine trade, looking like nothing so much as muscle boys posing in a gay bar. And as one figure tenders the curiously shrunken and doll-like Christ on his lap, he looks past him towards the viewer as all the other half naked men follow suit. Notably flat and angular, the men are ciphers, pure exteriority, while the Christ, holding what seems to be his bloody crown of thorns, is shaded the greenish blue of the recently dead. It is an image of pathos to be sure, but it is also an image of longing, not least because Christ's elongated, narrow face arguably resembles that of the painter himself. The many men stare at us as we stare at them, their tender care of Christ in contrast to their imperturbable machismo.

There, finally, near the end of his life, do we find Hartley's fantasy of trade's tender, loving same-sex caress realized, made plausible, or at least forgivable, through a short, but necessary detour into religious iconography. But the men are still hugely muscular, flat and hieratic, while the Christ is small, limp and, not least, dead. In a short poem entitled "There Are No Rocks and Trees," Hartley writes, "There are no rocks and trees that take / the place of people / the people that are rich and round and large / strong with a nation's agitation / deep with a lovingness profound –."[113] Here are men who, like most trade, stand somewhere between rocks and trees, and people. They are large but not round, strong and perhaps "deep with a lovingness," but even here it couldn't be fully realized, their figures tree-like, their eyes staring unblinkingly ahead. To be queer in early 20th century America was to realize that it was not yet time to make it round.

Jonathan D. Katz is a pioneering figure in the development of a queer art history and currently a visiting professor at the University of Pennsylvania. Has among other exhibitions curated *Hide/Seek: Difference and Desire in American Portraiture* at the Smithsonian National Portrait Gallery.

Pedestrians of the Solid Earth: Marsden Hartley and the Matter of Kinship, 1930-1943

By Elizabeth Finch

Every artist is some sort of a relative of some artist because it is only in the expansive field of art that such relatives are to be found.
– Marsden Hartley, 1938[114]

On the second of December 1930, the newly established Museum of Modern Art opened the exhibition *Painting and Sculpture by Living Americans*. Rather than weigh in on a prevailing style, the project's organizers aimed for impartiality and arrived at miscellany, "choosing artists," as Alfred H. Barr Jr. demurred in the introduction to the exhibition catalog, "regardless of school."[115] For Marsden Hartley, one of thirty painters included in the show, the stakes were high. Having recently returned to the US after an extended stay in Europe, he faced the daunting task of reigniting a career during the Great Depression and the heyday of American Regionalism. *Portrait of a German Officer* (1914), the masterwork from Hartley's first European sojourn, appeared in the exhibition under the poignant alias *Portrait of My Friend*, but there was no way to conceal that its abstraction was out of step with the times (fig. 15).

Hartley responded to the situation by writing, painting, and traveling his way to a solution. By his death in 1943, the perpetually restless artist had successfully remade himself as the "painter from Maine."[116] Central to this late-career transformation was Hartley's assembly of a strategically chosen group of artists, past and present, to whom he proclaimed creative allegiance. While Hartley had long written about the artists he admired, his commitment to this activity increased in the 1930s and became more focused on Americans. Identifying artist "relatives" occurred in tandem with a search for subjects that could further his expressions of selfhood, and aspects of his expressionistic vision would resonate with artists of the generation that would succeed him.

Two artists caught Hartley's attention in the MoMA exhibition. One was the self-taught John Kane, who gained acclaim in the late 1920s after years of toil in the industrial heartland. For Hartley, Kane's Scottish origins and hardscrabble existence in Pittsburgh, America's Steel City, confirmed their kindredness. Hartley's essay on Kane reiterated the popularly held view that he was the American equivalent of Henri Rousseau.[117] If Albert Pinkham Ryder was the only "American master" of interest, as Jackson Pollock once quipped, Kane was an American "primitive" reincarnated.[118] For Hartley and others, including the Abstract Expressionists, such figures epitomized timeless authenticity, and the mining of such sources, fictive and idealized, was the work of the twentieth-century American artist in search of native inspiration.

The other artist Hartley singled out was Mark Tobey, an acquaintance from his first years in New York, two decades earlier. They had since led itinerant lives. Hartley chose Maine as the place to which he returned. For Tobey, that place was the Pacific Northwest, and in the 1930s he pursued an otherworldly take on figuration that would evolve, by the mid-1940s, into the mystically inclined abstraction for which he is best known. After the MoMA exhibition Hartley wrote an essay in which he acknowledged Tobey as a fellow "searcher and a revealer of the inner condition."[119] In Hartley's worldview, such lofty attributes required the rejection of pretension and fussiness. Like the artist from Maine, Tobey was nothing less than "a pedestrian of the solid earth."[120] In the age of the automobile, walking was synonymous with the grounded creativity that defined Hartley's contrarian appraisal of the two artists' relevance.

Around 1938, Hartley struck up a friendship with Milton Avery, an artist twelve years his junior. The two likely bonded over their working-class roots and their burgeoning interest in painting coastal scenes. After seeing one of Avery's exhibitions, Hartley wrote to the younger artist, praising his "authority ... in the world of the imagination."[121] Avery and his wife Sally were convivial hosts and by the time Hartley came into their lives they had long-standing friendships with a tightknit group of artists that included Adolph Gottlieb, Barnett Newman, and Mark Rothko. Yet Hartley never joined this ambitious cohort, which began to disband as the careers of its respective members gained momentum and a distance emerged between Avery's commitment to figuration and theirs to abstraction.

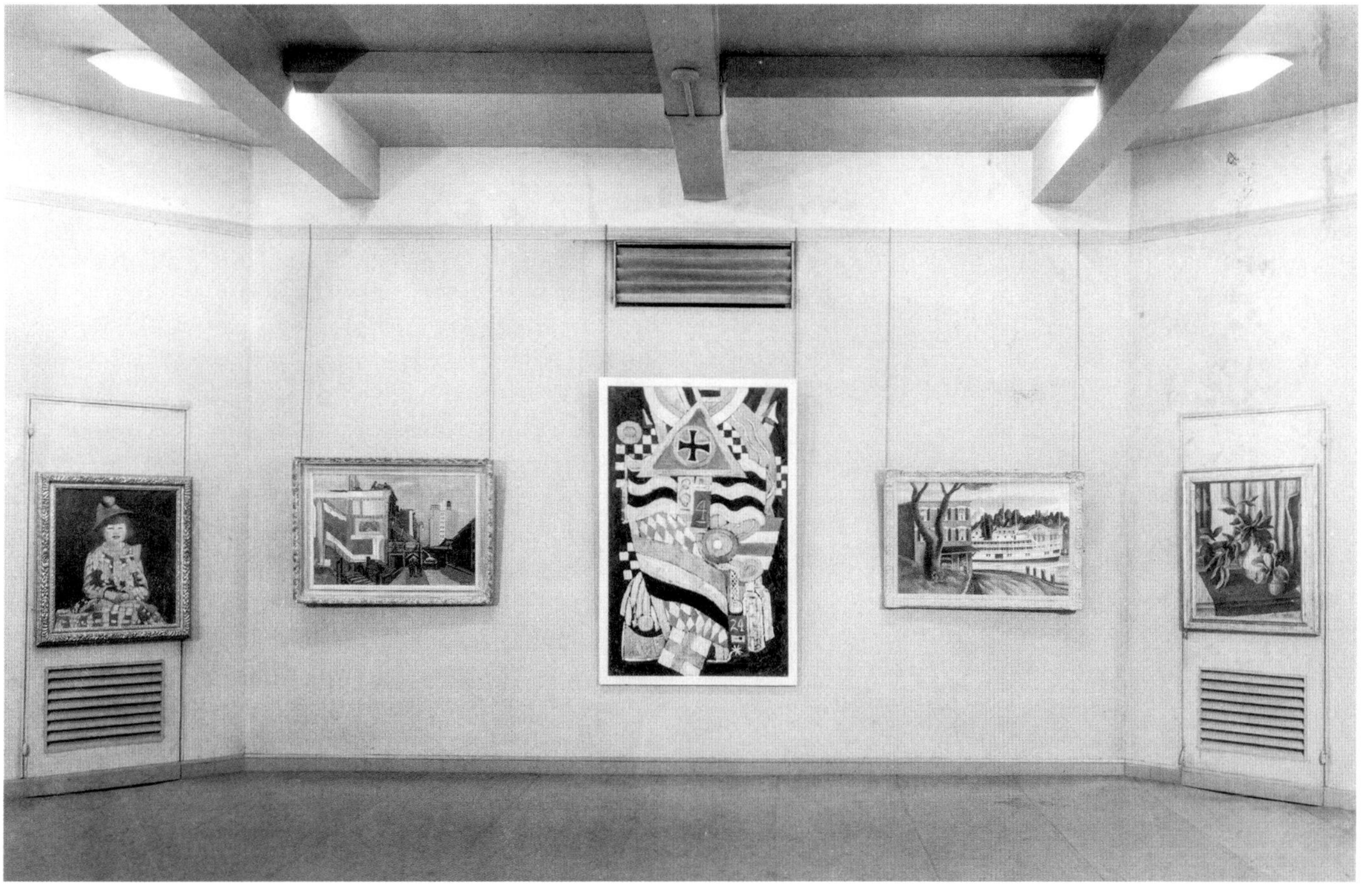

Fig. 15 Installation view from the exhibition *Painting and Sculpture by Living Americans*, Museum of Modern Art, New York (1930) with Marsden Hartley's work *Portrait of a German Officer*

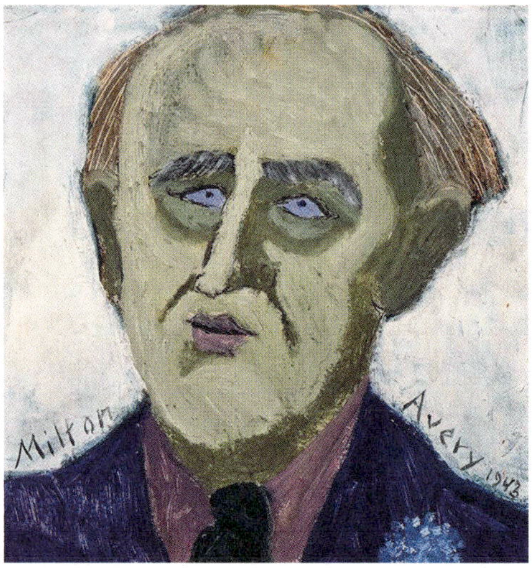

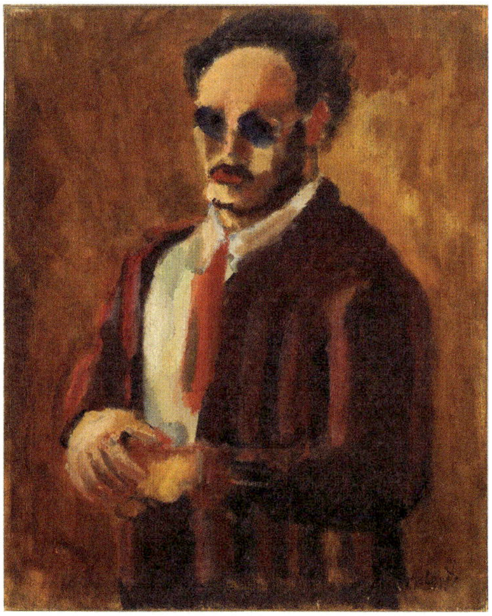

Fig. 16 Milton Avery: *Portrait of Marsden Hartley*, 1943
Fig. 17 Mark Rothko: *Self-portrait*, 1936

In 1943, the year of Hartley's death, Avery painted two portraits of his friend and mentor. Avery's signature rests prominently on Hartley's shoulders in one of these works (fig. 16). Likewise, the piercing blue eyes in Avery's various self-portraits highlight a trait he presumably shared with Hartley and emphasized in emulation of him. Yet Avery's inspiration for this homage may have come from Rothko, whose self-portrait with bespectacled eyes in an otherworldly shade of blue dates to 1936 (fig. 17). Rothko's connection to Hartley may be understood through their mutual friendship with Avery and as an existential affinity – a matter of temperament, mindset, and striving for transcendence. In the late 1950s, during the reign of Abstract Expressionism, Avery created several paintings of waves directly influenced by Hartley's iconic take on that subject (fig. 18). Some art historians have noted that the bold abstraction of Hartley's late landscapes, including the wave painting *Evening Storm, Schoodic, Maine No. 2* (cat. 106), or his blocky clouds seen, for instance, in *Summer, Sea, Window, Red Curtain* (cat. 108, p. 119), stylistically presaged the art that emerged in the years just after his death.[122] Clement Greenberg acknowledged as much, writing in 1950 that Hartley had "anticipated the present mood of American art more clearly than any other artist of his time."[123]

The mood at midcentury, in the United States and elsewhere, was expressionistic and increasingly abstract. As a consequence, Hartley's affiliation with Regionalism, which was celebrated at the time of his death, became a detriment soon after. The year 1943 coincided, it should be remembered, with Pollock's game changing *Mural* for Peggy Guggenheim. And the American artists who came to be known as the Abstract Expressionists were reluctant to claim predecessors – their own artist relatives – preferring instead to put forward the appealing idea that their art was entirely new. Complicating matters further was Hartley's fascination with Germany, which persisted into the 1930s, resulting in a visual and written record that remains problematic even as it can be historically contextualized.

In 1974, Philip Guston acknowledged his debt to Max Beckmann, admitting unabashedly that he "loved him, adored him" because he "made a place, and it's very important to make a place."[124] It was a Hartleyesque observation, and Guston's extraordinary painting *Late Fall* (1963) seems to echo the Maine artist's autumnal abstractions of the early 1900s, works that capture the mixture of awe tinged with regret that accompanies shortening days and falling leaves (fig. 19). Guston's brooding figures, too, seem resonant with some of the people Hartley portrayed in the last chapter of his career. Yet Guston cited Beckmann as an influence, not Hartley, and noted he had seen the German exile's 1938 exhibition at the Buchholz Gallery in New York. Hartley was in and out of New York that year and would have kept abreast of the gallery scene, but he never mentioned Beckmann in his writings. Their paintings were, perhaps, too close in expressive affinity to fulfill his criteria for kindredness. The lyrical Avery, whose works echoed rather than rivaled the dark earthiness of Hartley's creations, was a safer bet.

"Everything," as Alex Katz astutely observed on the subject of Hartley, "was given up to the poetic idea of the painting."[125] Eulogizing Avery in 1965, Rothko acknowledged his friend as a poet-inventor, "where the poetry penetrated every pore of the canvas to the very last touch of the brush."[126] The assumptions that overshadowed Hartley's legacy in the mid-twentieth century have dissolved with time, revealing continuities of expressionism that can be traced from the hills of Maine to the streets and studios of New York.

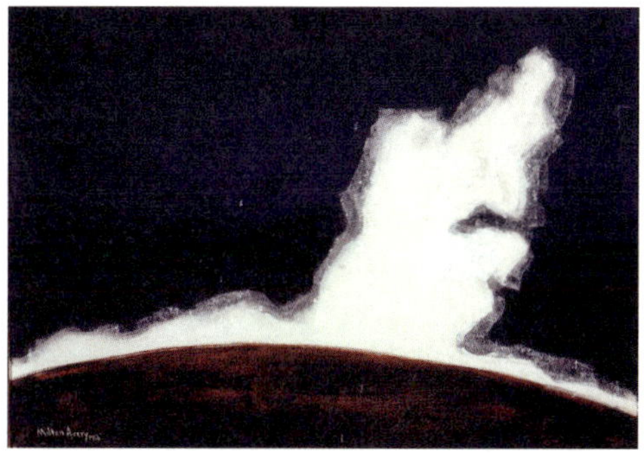

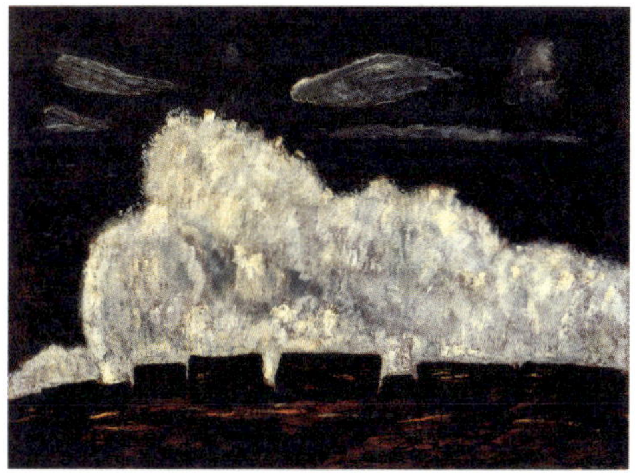

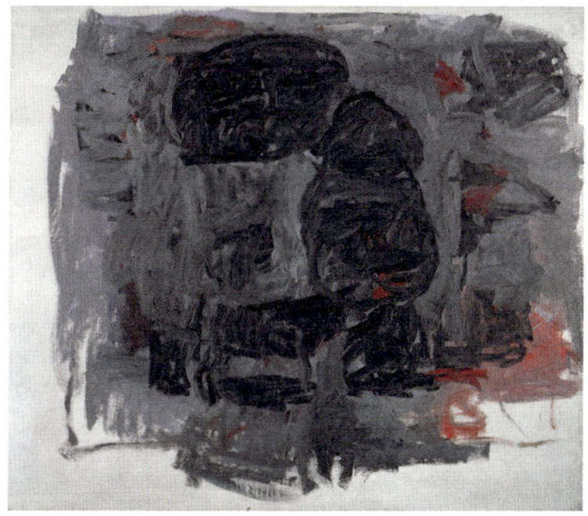

Elizabeth Finch is the Lunder Curator of American Art at the Colby College Museum of Art in Waterville, Maine, where she has curated numerous exhibitions, including *Marsden Hartley's Maine* (with Randall R. Griffey and Donna M. Cassidy).

Fig. 18 Milton Avery: *The White Wave*, 1956
106 *Evening Storm, Schoodic, Maine No. 2*, 1942
Fig. 19 Philip Guston: *Late Fall*, 1963

Pathways to Marsden Hartley – People, Places, Words

In the following we present an alphabetical list of biographical, art-historical and geographical notes which relate in various ways to Marsden Hartley's life and work.

Abstraction
Hartley has been called the first great American modernist, among other reasons because he experimented with various types of abstraction. In Berlin in 1913 he painted "Intuitive Abstractions" – geometrical compositions inspired by Cubism and the art of Wassily Kandinsky (pp. 23-25). In his late landscapes, realistic representation yielded place to more abstract investigations of the picture surface.

Amateurism
Hartley took a strong interest in folk art and in the unschooled and instinctive in art. He begins the essay *The Virtues of Amateur Painting* thus: "Some of the finest instances of pure painting will be found, not as might be imagined by the layman, among the professional artists, but among those amateurs whose chief occupation is amusing themselves first of all."

Armory Show
In February 1913 Hartley participated in The Armory Show in New York (fig. 20). This huge, historically important exhibition showed the best in both European and American art and is known for among other things showing Duchamp's *Nude Descending a Staircase* (1912).

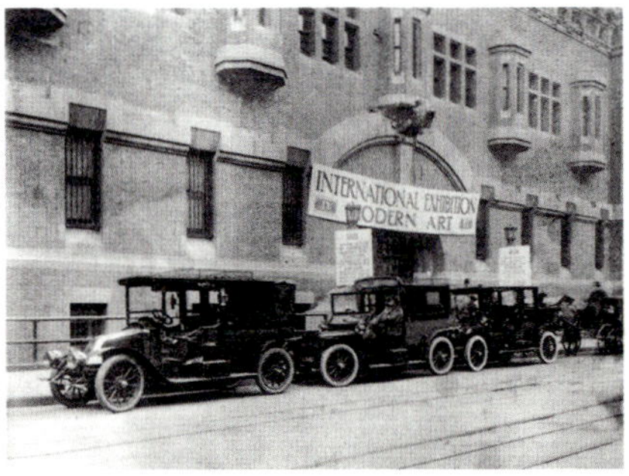

Autobiography
Much of the extensive biographical material we have available about Hartley is from the autobiography *Somehow a Past*, which he began in 1933. The project was inspired by Gertrude Stein's *The Autobiography of Alice B. Toklas*, which appeared the same year, in which Hartley played a very small role.

Bavaria
Hartley visited Bavaria for the first time in 1913, and two decades later he returned to paint a series of pictures of the Alps. In a letter to his niece he wrote: "I have at last registered some Alps ... and I have, I know, gotten them as they are, with as close a fidelity as the eye is capable of and not using a camera ... for what I wanted to get is their inner character."

Bergson, Henri (1859-1941)
The French philosopher was an early source of inspiration for Hartley. In a letter to Stieglitz in 1912 Hartley wrote: "I am convinced of the Bergson argument in philosophy, that the intuition is the only vehicle for art expression and it is on this basis that I am proceeding."

Berlin
The encounter with Berlin in 1913 was love at first sight. In a letter to Stieglitz Hartley wrote of the city: "I like its ultra-modernity and I like the calmness of the people." He painted a number of symbolic portraits of the city, where he stayed until 1915 and to which he returned in 1921-1923 and in 1933.

Bermuda
Hartley spent time on Bermuda in 1916-1917 (and again in 1935) along with his artist friend Demuth, and painted among other things his first "window paintings" and a number of sexualized still lifes. He described the island as "a little bijoux of a place" where his everyday routine was to sunbathe nude and paint.

Blake, William (1757-1827)
Throughout his life Hartley was inspired by the English poet and visual artist Blake, to whom he referred in both paintings and writings. He considered Blake a mystic and therefore without a nationality, precisely as Hartley often described himself.

Cézanne, Paul (1839-1906)
No other painter was a greater source of inspiration for Hartley than Cézanne. Early in his life Hartley had a quotation from Cézanne hanging in his studio: "When colour reaches richness, form attains fullness." Hartley's interest culminated in a journey to Provence to paint "Cézanne's mountain," Mont Sainte-Victoire, in the 1920s (p. 50).

Cleveland
After living for some years with a sister in Maine, Hartley moved at the age of 16 to Cleveland, where his father and stepmother lived. There he took his first art lessons with the local painter John Sermon in 1896. A few years later he was admitted to the Cleveland School of Art.

Corea
Hartley spent the last summers of his life in the small fishing hamlet Corea in Maine from 1940 until 1943, where he painted some of his best pictures. He lived with the Young family, whose daughter drove the aging artist to the places he wanted to paint, for example Schoodic Point. Hartley died on 2nd September 1943 in Ellsworth near Corea.

Crane, Hart (1899-1932)
Hartley met the American poet Hart Crane (fig. 21) in Marseille in the 1920s. In 1932 they spent time together in Mexico City. On the journey home Hart Crane committed suicide, and Hartley dedicated several poems and the painting *Eight Bells Folly: Memorial to Hart Crane* (1933, p. 61) to his memory.

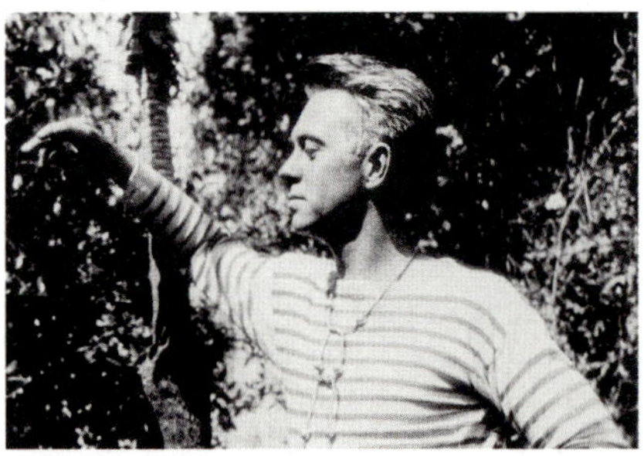

Cubism
Hartley employed Cubist methods in large parts of his oeuvre. His first known Cubist work, *Abstraction* from 1911 (p. 22), is in an analytical style with inspiration from Picasso's and Braque's works from this period. In Paris and Berlin (1912-1915) Hartley continues his Cubist experiments and combined them with his interest in mysticism.

Dada
The New York branch of Dada (fig. 22), Société Anonyme, was founded by Katherine Dreier, Marcel Duchamp and Man Ray. As the secretary Hartley contributed to panel discussions and lectures and wrote the essay "On the Importance of Being Dada."

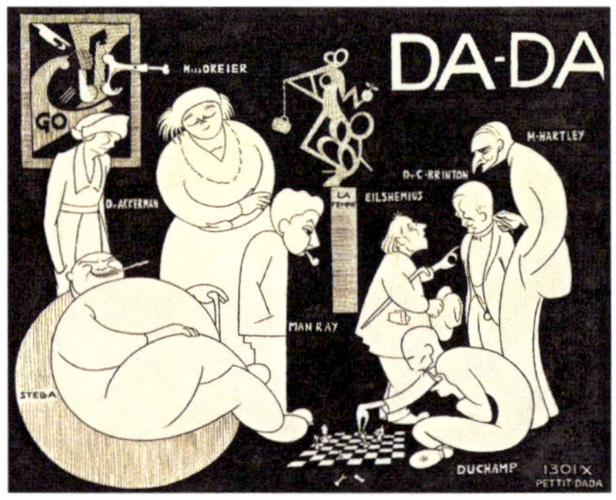

Demuth, Charles (1883-1935)
In 1916-1917 Hartley stayed with Demuth in Provincetown and Bermuda, where they both created works based on among other things the Danish ship *Elsa*, which was anchored in the harbour. Demuth was also homosexual and one of Hartley's close friends.

Depression
Throughout his life Hartley struggled to keep his head above water in the face of both personal and professional adversity. In 1921 he told Stieglitz of his ambition to travel to Florence and to write a book of hate, send it to his friends, and kill himself.

Dogtown
In 1920 Hartley for the first time visited Dogtown, a harbour town near Gloucester on Cape Ann, Massachusetts, but he did not paint the place until the 1930s. In his autobiography he described it as follows: "those huge boulders, mostly granite, stand like sentinels guarding nothing but shore – sea gulls fly over it on their way from the marshes to the sea – otherwise the place is forsaken and majestically lonely, as if nature had at last formed one spot where she can live for herself alone."

Duchamp, Marcel (1887-1968)
Hartley and Duchamp are connected through Stieglitz' famous photograph of Duchamp's work *Fountain* (1917). In the background of the photograph Stieglitz had quite deliberately placed Hartley's painting *The Warriors* (1913). Duchamp and Hartley also worked together in Société Anonyme, New York's branch of Dada.

Education
Hartley's artistic training began in Cleveland and continued in New York, first at the Chase School and later at the National Academy of Design, where he studied for four years from 1900 on. Hartley was awarded a Silver Medal for his still life drawings.

Emerson, Ralph Waldo (1803-1882)
Hartley was given a copy of Emerson's *Essays* by one of his first painting teachers, Nina Waldeck. According to Hartley himself it was the first book he read. Emerson saw the artist as someone who had access to the spiritual dimension in the world and was able to describe this experience in his art.

Erster Deutscher Herbstsalon
Hartley participated in the epoch-making exhibition of the latest modern art in Berlin in September 1913. He showed five paintings, all with the title *Mystisches Bild* in the catalogue. Other participants were the artist group Der Blaue Reiter as well as Rousseau, Arp, Klee and Mondrian and others who have later become prominent figures in the history of art.

Essays
Throughout his life Hartley wrote many essays on art and poetry, some of which were only published long after his death. In 1921, however, he published an anthology of texts under the title *Adventures in the Arts – Informal Chapters on Painters, Vaudeville and Poets*.

Family
Hartley's parents were English immigrants, and he was their only son. At the age of eight he lost his mother and was now "a lone left thing to make its way out for all time after that by itself." His father married Martha Marsden in 1889, and Hartley later took her surname as his first name (fig. 23).

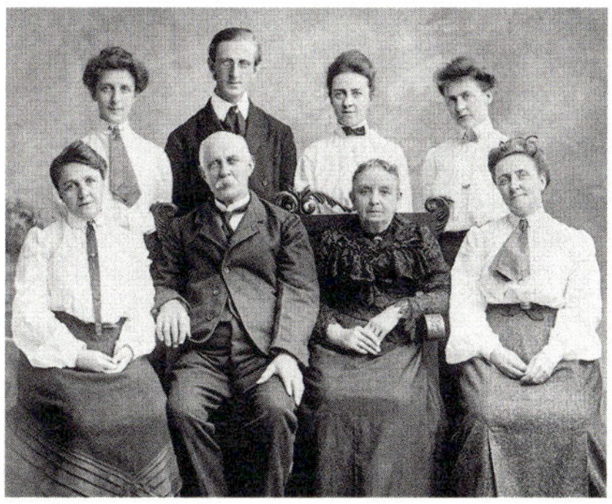

Figure painting
The bulk of Hartley's oeuvre is devoid of human figures. Only indirectly did he paint bodies and faces, for example in the form of saint figures or masks. And only late in life, from 1938 on, did he engage in true figure painting, mainly of muscular men in Maine.

Florence
In 1923 Hartley spent eight weeks in Florence. At the Uffizi he studied Renaissance masters and saw among other works Masaccio's fresco *Adam and Eve Banished from Paradise* (c. 1425) and proclaimed enthusiastically that if he had never seen other paintings he would still have seen "all the art there is."

Freyburg, Karl von (1889-1914)
Hartley met von Freyburg (fig. 24) along with his cousin Rönnebeck in Paris in 1912. Hartley described the relationship of the three as "a beautiful triangle," and several of the triangles in Hartley's works refer to this among other things. Von Freyburg was a soldier and was killed just after the beginning of World War I. Hartley's grief at the loss led to the famous group of works *War Motifs* (1914-1915).

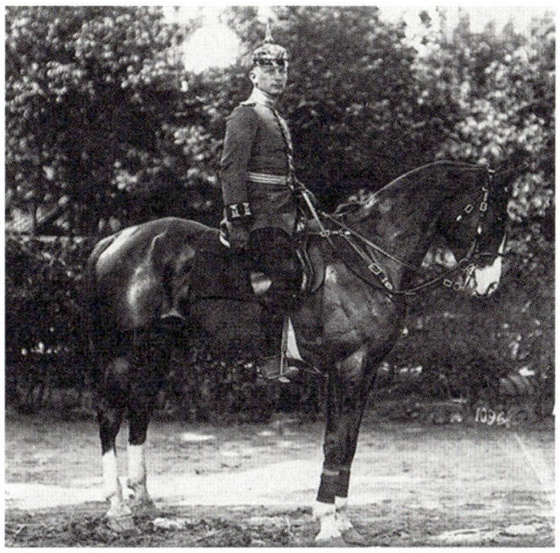

Green Acre
In 1907 Hartley spent the summer at Green Acre, a spiritual and philosophical refuge in Eliot, Maine. There artists, theologians and the like could exchange their views. Hartley studied religion and transcendental philosophy.

Homer, Winslow (1836-1910)
One of the great American painters of the nineteenth century, who like Hartley was from New England and was best known for his marine subjects. Hartley's pictures of the coast of Maine were inspired by Homer's, especially pictures of waves beating against the rocks, like *Evening Storm, Schoodic, Maine No. 2* (p. 116).

Homosexuality
Hartley's restlessness is connected to among other things his identity as sexually deviant in his time. Life as a homosexual and the necessity of suppressing one's identity made it difficult to feel comfortable in the society of the day. Parts of his oeuvre are fraught with an attempt to express and at the same to keep secret his true self.

James, William (1842-1910)
The American philosopher and psychologist was a crucial influence on Hartley. James emphasized personal and internal revelations as the starting point for creating art. Hartley discussed James with Gertrude Stein, who also lent him James' work *The Varieties of Religious Experience* (1902).

Kandinsky, Wassily (1866-1944)
The painter Kandinsky was the great theorist in the artist group Der Blaue Reiter. At first Hartley read translated extracts from his text *Concerning the Spiritual in Art* (1912). The two met in 1913. Hartley's paintings from the period are clearly inspired by Kandinsky, although Hartley claimed to value Kandinsky's theories higher than his paintings.

Kreymborg, Alfred (1883-1966)
The literary figure Kreymborg was one of Hartley's close friends and published poems by Hartley in the literary magazine *Others,* for example in 1919. In 1914 Kreymborg wrote the play *Erna Vitek,* in which he based the role of the composer John Carstairs on Hartley.

Landscape
Hartley was no *plein-air* painter (his last studio in Corea: fig. 25), yet landscape was one of his favourite genres. His interest in landscapes was influenced by transcendentalists such as Emerson and Thoreau, who saw the experience of nature as providing access to the spiritual in the world.

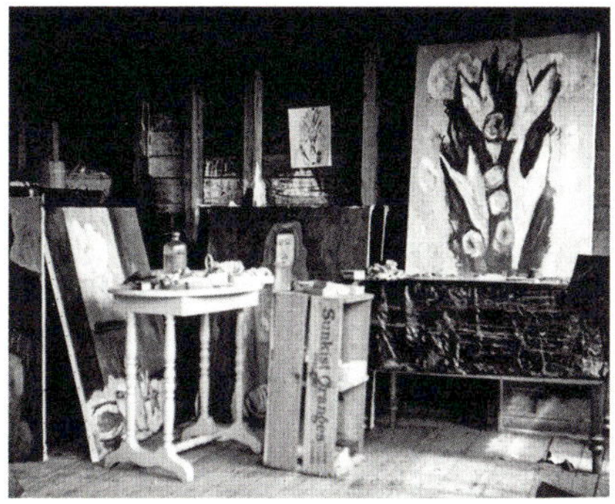

Lewiston
Hartley was born in Lewiston, Maine, on 4th January 1877. The economy of the city was based on textile mills, and Hartley's father was a cotton spinner. In a poem Hartley recollected the city: "My childhood which was hard, it is always/ hard to be alone at the wrong time,/ brought seizures of intensity to the years;/ the harsh grinding of the mills rang in/ my ears for years – and a sordid sort of music/ came out of it."

Loneliness
Hartley's existence was often typified by an abysmal loneliness, a product partly of his homosexuality, but also of his notoriously difficult personality, which drove some generally well-meaning people away. Several times he also proclaimed a hatred of intimacy.

Maine
Hartley's oeuvre begins and ends with pictures from Maine. After many years of absence Hartley returned home late in life, after which his work culminated. He even proclaimed that he wanted to be known as "the painter from Maine."

Marc, Franz (1880-1916)
Marc was a member of the artist group Der Blaue Reiter. Hartley visited him in Sindelsdorf in the Bavarian Alps in 1913. Marc was the most amenable of the German artist colleagues: he wrote several letters to Hartley with praise (fig. 26), and invited him to participate in the epochal Erster Deutscher Herbstsalon in Berlin.

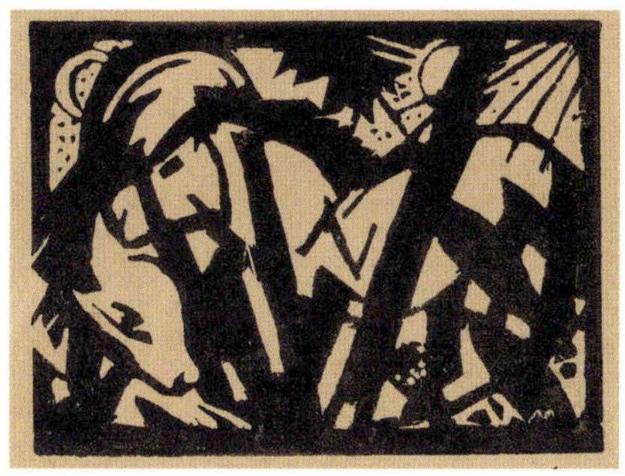

Marin, John (1870-1953)
Hartley often felt neglected and given less than his due by his gallerist, Stieglitz, who according to Hartley preferred Marin, among others. In a letter to Stieglitz in 1919 Marin writes about Hartley's restlessness: "If that rainbow chaser could only have remained [in Maine] – but then, how do I know."

Marsden
Marsden Hartley was christened Edmund. Marsden was his stepmother's maiden name,

which he adopted in 1906. Hartley explained the name change as an affectionate gesture to his stepmother. Another explanation may be that by taking a woman's name as his first name he feminized himself in a discreet way that reminds us of the subtle markings of his homosexuality that appear in his paintings.

Masculinity

It may seem paradoxical that Hartley claimed to be unable to tolerate feminine men, when he himself so definitively belonged to that category. Like his idol Walt Whitman, Hartley loved the working man and in his late work cultivated this ordinary, down-to-earth type in a long succession of works.

Mason family

Hartley lived with the Mason family (fig. 27) in Nova Scotia in 1935 and 1936. He felt close to the family, who consisted besides a mother and father of a sister, Alice, and the two brothers Alty and Donny, for whom Hartley had both brotherly and sexual feelings. The two young men drowned in 1936. Over the next few years until Hartley's death, he painted a succession of glorifying portraits of the family (e.g. pp. 88-89).

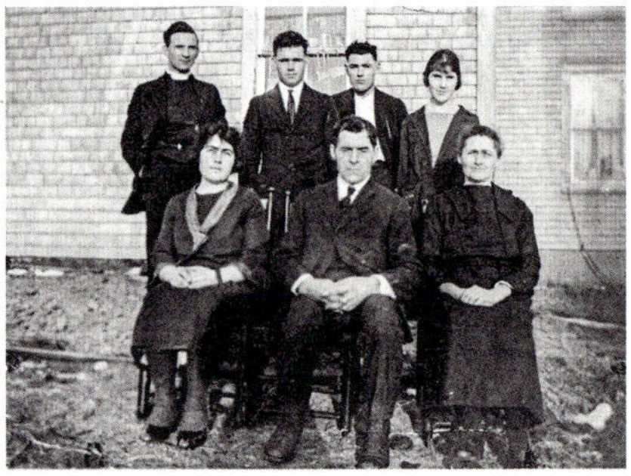

Matisse, Henri (1869-1954)

Matisse was an important early source of inspiration for Hartley, who among other things painted a number of landscapes in a Fauvist style in 1910. Later, though, in the 1920s, Hartley was critical of Matisse and his Fauvist colleagues, who he thought had domesticated their art through repetition.

Mexico

Hartley was awarded a Guggenheim grant for a year abroad, and decided on Mexico, where he stayed from 1932 until 1933. In his autobiography Hartley describes Mexico as the only place "I always shall think of as wrong for me." However, his encounter with works by Mexican artists like Diego Rivera, David Alfaro Siqueiros and José Clemente Orozco was important.

Mountains

The mountain was a mystical object for Hartley and a principal motif in his oeuvre. He painted mountains in Maine, New Mexico, Provence, New Hampshire, Mexico and Bavaria. The culmination of this interest was Mount Katahdin in his native Maine, which he sketched in 1939 and painted over and over again until his death (cf. pp. 102-103).

Mystics

Throughout his life Hartley read works by mystics, including Jakob Boehme, Meister Eckhart and Richard Rolle. Hartley referred several times to mystical thinking in his paintings, but especially in the pictures from Paris and Berlin in 1912-15 and his Mexican pictures of 1932-1933.

New Mexico

Hartley stayed in New Mexico in 1918-1919 to pursue the notion of original American painting. He painted a number of pastels in a Cézannesque style and still lifes of religious figures. Later, in 1922-1923, he recalled the landscapes from New Mexico in his *New Mexico Recollections* (p. 44, 47, 48).

New York

The only place Hartley returned to again and again throughout his life was New York (fig. 28). He had a network there on which he depended to sell his art and put food on the table. Hartley's relationship with the city was particularly ambivalent. The city hardly appears in his art. Only in a few late drawings and in the painting *Prayer on Park Avenue* (p. 120) is there a direct connection.

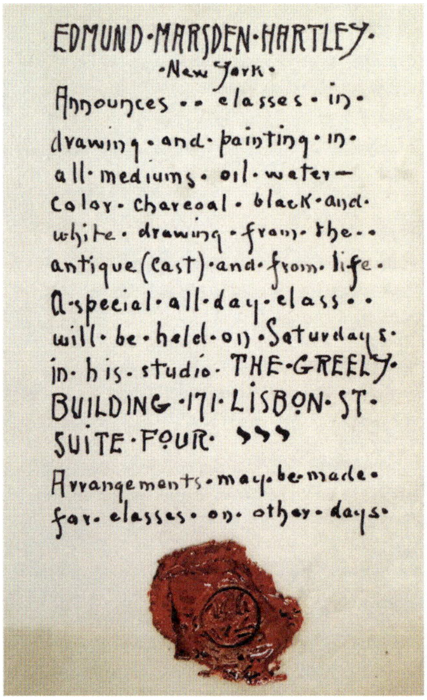

EDMUND·MARSDEN·HARTLEY·
·New York·
Announces ·· classes · in·
drawing · and · painting · in·
all · mediums · oil · water–
color · charcoal · black · and·
white · drawing · from · the··
antique (cast) · and · from · life·
A · special · all · day · class··
will · be · held · on · Saturdays·
in · his · studio · THE · GREELY·
BUILDING · 171 · LISBON · ST·
SUITE · FOUR·
Arrangements · may · be · made·
for · classes · on · other · days·

Numerology

Several of Hartley's paintings incorporate numbers, not least the works from Berlin in 1913-1915. The numbers had obvious mystical connotations for the artist, who at the same time did not think they were crucial to the understanding of his painting. Early in his life Hartley also used sequential numbers in the titles of his works, which reinforced the serial character of the project.

O'Keeffe, Georgia (1887-1986)

Hartley and O'Keeffe had a strained relationship, not least because of Hartley's jealousy over the fact that Stieglitz seemed to prefer his partner's art to Hartley's own. O'Keeffe visited New Mexico for the first time before Hartley in 1917, but his paintings from New Mexico and the later *Recollections* (p. 40) preceded O'Keeffe's first paintings of the landscape from the end of the 1920s.

Paris

In 1912, on his first journey abroad, Hartley arrived in Paris, where he made the acquaintance of Gertrude Stein and the French avant-garde. Several times in the 1920s Hartley went back to the city, where he met among others Ezra Pound and Fernand Léger (fig. 29). In 1924 he exhibited a number of paintings in the city which Marc Chagall among others saw and which recalled his native Maine.

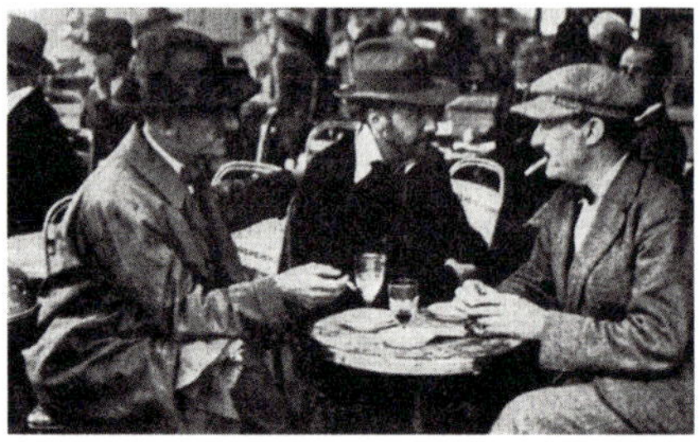

Picasso, Pablo (1881-1973)

Picasso's Cubist works were a great source of inspiration for Hartley, not least during his stay in Paris in 1912-13. He met his idol just once in the latter's studio, and Gertrude Stein is said to have shown Picasso one of Hartley's drawings, which he did not understand – it lacked both eyes and a nose. Later, though, Hartley also became critical of Picasso, opining among other things that the Spaniard had lost his "showmanship."

Periodicals

Hartley's poems were published in many of the leading periodicals for poetry, not least *Poetry: A Magazine of Verse,* which was edited by Harriet Monroe, as well as *The Dial, Contact,* his friend William Carlos Williams' magazine, *The Little Review,* and others.

Poems

His friend Alfred Kreymborg described Hartley as "the painter who writes." Hartley divided his time between writing and painting for large parts of his life, and took an active part in the literary milieu in New York. In 1923 Hartley published the collection *Twenty-Five Poems* in Paris and in the last years of his life the collections *Androscoggin* (1940) and *Sea Burial* (1941).

Portraits

There are many portraits of Hartley by painters such as Ben Benn, Helen Stein and Milton Avery, busts by Rönnebeck and Jacques Lipchitz as well as caricatures by Lee Simonson and Djuna Barnes. Similarly, photographers like Man Ray, Stieglitz, Steichen, Strand and Platt Lynes have depicted him. In literature he appears for example in a word portrait by Gertrude Stein and under pseudonyms in plays by Alfred Kreymborg and Eugene O'Neill as well as in a book by Robert McAlmon.

Poverty

It is evident from Hartley's correspondence that a lack of money was a recurrent problem for the artist. On his birthday in 1934, in deep despair, he had to destroy more than 100 works to save storage space and money. When Hartley died, though, his luck had turned and there were many thousand dollars in his account.

Primitivism

Hartley's life and work are typified by a strong interest in indigenous and exotic cultures. He collected objects of pre-Columbian and Egyptian origin and painted pictures that referred to Native Americans, Mexican saints and African textiles, while he also dressed in exotic costumes for fancy-dress balls (fig. 30).

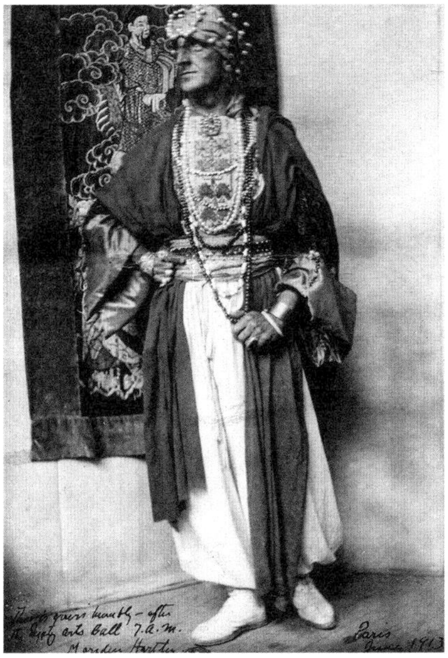

Provence
From 1925 until 1929 Hartley stayed several times in Provence. First in Vence, where he painted the Alps, and later in Aix-en-Provence, where he followed in the footsteps of his great hero Cézanne to paint the mountain Mont Sainte-Victoire (p. 44).

Provincetown
In 1916 Hartley spent the summer at Cape Cod, in Provincetown, Massachusetts, along with the artist Charles Demuth and the playwright Eugene O'Neill (fig. 31) as well as the journalist John Reed and the artist Carl Sprinchorn, resulting in lifelong friendships. He later called this "the great Provincetown Summer.'

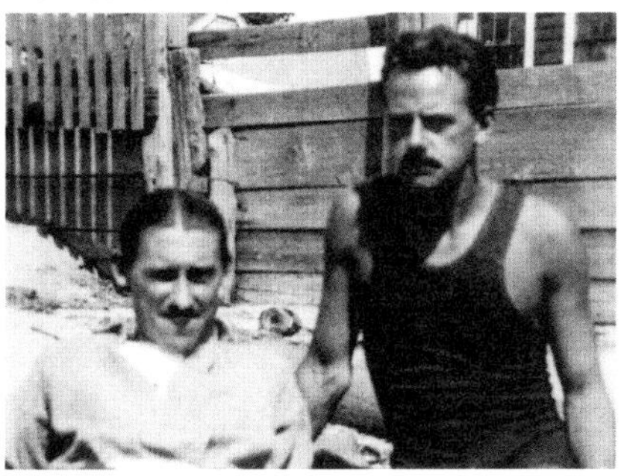

Race
Hartley had a fondness for everything German and thus for the German people as an ideal. At one point he described an enthusiasm for a new type bred in New England with "Vikings appearances, and Yankee behaviors." Hartley's formulations are however by no means systematic and quite definitely left no clear traces in his painting.

Rosenberg, Paul (1881-1959)
The Frenchman Paul Rosenberg was one of the world's leading art dealers and worked with among others Picasso, Matisse and Braque. He began in Paris and moved because of World War II to New York. To consolidate Hartley's late breakthrough, Rosenberg took Hartley into his gallery at 57th Street in Manhattan in 1942, a year before the artist died.

Rosenfeld, Paul (1890-1946)
Paul Rosenfeld was a leading critic in New York and close to Alfred Stieglitz. Rosenberg wrote about Hartley in several contexts. After Hartley's death Rosenfeld described him in an essay as "an extraordinary, an almost gigantic secondary artist."

Rouault, Georges (1871-1958)
The French painter was one of Hartley's great heroes and his works, not least Rouault's religious portraits, had a crucial influence on the late figure paintings in particular. In an essay Hartley described him as follows: "with his faultless technical knowledge, and his deep and powerful humanism – a great spirit – great artist, great performer."

Ryder, Albert Pinkham (1847-1917)
No American painter had a greater influence on Hartley. Ryder was more or less self-taught and stood outside the art world. Hartley saw him as a great mystic. He met Ryder in New York in 1909, after which he painted a succession of dark landscapes directly inspired by his idol (cf. p. 20).

Rönnebeck, Arnold (1885-1947)
The German sculptor Arnold Rönnebeck became one of Hartley's close friends after they met, along with Rönnebeck's cousin Karl von Freyburg, in Paris in 1912. Rönnebeck made portraits of his friend in 1912 and again in 1923, when Hartley lived with Rönnebeck's parents in Berlin.

Segantini, Giovanni (1858-1899)
The painter of the Alps Segantini was one of Hartley's early sources of inspiration. Hartley read about and saw pictures by Segantini in a copy of the periodical *Jugend* from 1903. In Segantini Hartley saw a painter who understood "the inner and outer sense of the mountain."

Scandinavia
Hartley was in Buffalo, NY, shortly after the exhibition "Contemporary Scandinavian Art" had been shown at the local Albright Art Gallery in January 1913, where he may have seen the catalogue, which included pictures by J.F. Willumsen and Edvard Munch. In 1916 Hartley was to have had an exhibition in Copenhagen, which was cancelled because of World War I. In 1939 Hartley corresponded with the director of the National Gallery in Oslo about a possible exhibition which came to nothing.

Stein, Gertrude (1874-1946)
Hartley attended the famous salons of the American author Gertrude Stein after his arrival in Paris in 1912. Stein's apartment at the same time gave Hartley the opportunity to study her collection of leading European artists such as Picasso. Accordingly to Hartley himself, Stein, after seeing his works, pronounced him "at last, an original American."

Stieglitz, Alfred (1864-1946)
Stieglitz was Hartley's gallerist for most years, and at the same time the person who secured the funding for most of his stays abroad. Stieglitz was a crucial figure on the art scene in New York, where he showed exhibitions of progressive European artists like Picasso and Matisse at an early stage.

Symbolism
Hartley's oeuvre has a consistently Symbolist character. In 1921 he wrote: "Symbolism can never quite be evaded in any work of art because every form and movement that we make symbolizes a condition in ourselves."

Thoreau, Henry David (1817-1862)
The Transcendentalist Thoreau's ascetic texts, which describe his life and his connections with nature, were of great importance to Hartley's self-understanding as an artist. In 1846 Thoreau had attempted to climb Mount Katahdin in Maine, the mountain Hartley was so intent on painting, and Thoreau's connection with the mountain was undoubtedly important to Hartley's interest in the subject.

Vinci, Leonardo da (1452-1519)
In Hartley's late essay "The Element of Absolutism in Leonardo's Drawings" he finds parallels with the genius Leonardo. According to Hartley, Leonardo too was a loner who was able to find feminine beauty in other figures than women, and who was capable of balancing his own femininity with his intellect.

Walker, Hudson D. (1907-1976)
For some years at the end of Hartley's life Hudson Walker was his gallerist and an important supporter, both emotionally and financially, in difficult years for Hartley. Walker and his wife donated more than 100 works by Hartley to what today is the Weisman Art Museum, the very largest collection of Hartley's works.

Whitman, Walt (1819-1892)
The American poet Walt Whitman (fig. 32) was of huge importance to Hartley, who early in life described himself as "Whitmanic." Whitman's thoughts on the experience of nature and individuality and the homosexual traces in his poems made him an example of what Hartley strove for in his art.

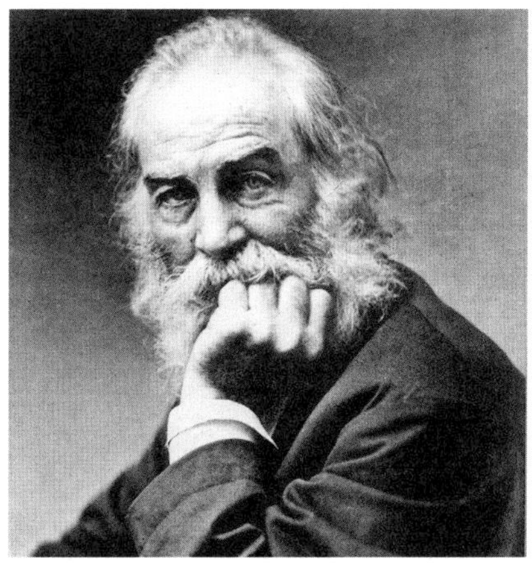

Williams, William Carlos (1883-1963)
The American modernist poet was one of Hartley's close friends throughout his life. Williams published Hartley's poems in the periodical *Contact*. According to Williams Hartley had on one occasion made sexual overtures to him and had been rejected, after which Hartley told Williams that otherwise he "would have made one of the most charming whores in the city."

This index has been compiled against the background of timelines and other biographical information from many catalogues about Marsden Hartley. In addition information has been found in Hartley's autobiography, *Somehow a Past*, and Townsend Ludington's *Marsden Hartley – The Biography of an American Artist*.

PAINTINGS

1
Walt Whitman House, c. 1905
Oil on board
25 × 20 cm (10 × 8 in.)
Private Collection. Courtesy Berta Walker Gallery, Provincetown, MA.

2
Storm Clouds, Maine, 1906-1907
Oil on canvas
76 × 63 cm (30 × 25 in.)
Collection Walker Art Center, Minneapolis. Gift of the T. B. Walker Foundation, Hudson Walker Collection, 1954

3
Maine Snowstorm, 1908
Oil on canvas
76 × 76 cm (30 1/8 × 30 1/8 in.)
Weisman Art Museum, Minneapolis

4
Song of Winter, 1908
Oil on board
23 × 30 cm (9 1/4 × 12 in.)
Courtesy of the Collection of Elizabeeh Redleaf

5
Cosmos, 1908-1909
Oil on canvas
76 × 76 cm (30 × 30 1/8 in.)
Columbus Museum of Art, Ohio
Gift of Ferdinand Howald

6
Landscape No. 36, 1908-1909
Oil on canvas
76 × 86 cm (30 1/8 × 34 in.)
Weisman Art Museum, Minneapolis

7
Landscape No. 20, 1909
Oil on academy board
36 × 30 cm (14 × 11 3/4 in.)
Private Collection of Maurice and Suzanne Vanderwoude. Courtesy Alexandre Gallery, New York

8
Deserted Farm, 1909
Oil on composition board
61 × 51 cm (24 × 20 in.)
Weisman Art Museum, Minneapolis

9
Landscape No. 24, 1909-1910
Oil on academy board
30 × 36 cm (12 × 14 in.)
Collection of Kirk Hopper

10
Waterfall, 1910
Oil on academy board
30 × 30 cm (12 × 12 in.)
Weisman Art Museum, Minneapolis

11
Autumn Cascade, 1910
Oil on board
30 × 30 cm (12 × 12 in.)
Private Collection, Norfolk, VA, USA

12
Abstraction, 1911
Oil on paper on cardboard
42× 34 cm (16 3/8 × 13 1/4 in.)
Weisman Art Museum, Minneapolis

13
Pears, 1911
Oil on wood
41× 32cm (16 × 12 1/2 in.)
Weisman Art Museum, Minneapolis

14
Still Life with Fan, 1912
Oil on canvas
92 × 71 cm (36 1/4 × 28 in.)
Sheldon Museum of Art
Nebraska Art Association, Thomas C. Woods Memorial

15
Musical Theme No. 2 (Bach Preludes et Fugues), 1912
Oil on canvas mounted on masonite
61 × 59 cm (24 × 20 in.)
Museo Nacional Thyssen-Bormemisza, Madrid

16
Portrait Arrangement No. 2, 1912-1913
Oil on canvas
83 × 102 cm (32 1/2 × 40 in.)
The Jan T. and Marica Vilcek Collection. Promised gift to The Vilcek Foundation

17
Painting Number One, 1913
Oil on canvas
99 × 81 cm (39 1/8 × 31 3/4 in.)
Sheldon Museum of Art
University of Nebraska-Lincoln, Anne R. and Frank M. Hall Charitable Trust

18
Painting No. 2, 1913
Oil on canvas
100 × 81 cm (39 1/2 × 31 7/8 in.)
Weisman Art Museum, Minneapolis. Bequest of Hudson D. Walker from Ione and Hudson D. Walker Collection

19
Raptus, c. 1913
Oil on canvas
100 × 81 cm (39 3/8 × 32 in.)
Currier Museum of Art, Manchester, NH. Gift of Paul and Hazel Strand in memory of Elizabeh McCausland

20
Forms Abstracted, 1913
Oil on canvas, with wood frame
101 × 81 cm (39 5/8 × 31 13/16 in.)
Whitney Museum of American Art, New York; Gift of Mr. and Mrs. Hudson D. Walker and exchange

21
Berlin Ante War, 1914
Oil on canvas with painted wooden frame
111 × 88 cm (43 3/4 × 34 1/2 in.)
Columbus Museum of Art
Gift of Ferdinand Howald

22
Portrait of a German Officer, 1914
Oil on canvas
173 × 105 cm (68 1/4 × 41 3/8 in.)
The Metropolitan Museum of Art
Alfred Stieglitz Collection, 1949

23
Berlin Series No. 2, 1914
Oil on canvas
46 × 38 cm (18 × 15 in.)
Courtesy of The Metropolitan Museum of Art. Private Collection

24
Geometric Figure, c. 1914
Oil on millboard
46 × 38 cm (18 × 14 15/16 in.)
Statens Museum for Kunst, Copenhagen

25
Painting No. 50, 1914-1915
Oil on canvas
119 × 119 cm (47 × 47 in.)
Terra Foundation for American Art
Daniel J. Terra Collection

26
Abstraction (Military Symbols), 1914-1915
Oil on canvas
100 × 81 cm (39 1/4 × 32 in.)
Toledo Museum of Art. Purchased with funds from the Libbey Endowment, Gift of Edward Drummond Libbey

27
Painting, Number 5, 1914-1915
Oil on linen
100 × 81 cm (39 1/4 × 32 in.)
Whitney Museum of American Art, New York. Gift of an anonymous donor

28
Painting No. 47, Berlin, 1914-1915
Oil on canvas
100 × 81 cm (39 7/16 × 32 in.)
Hirshhorn Museum and Sculpture Garden, Smithsonian Institution, Washington, DC. Gift of Joseph H. Hirshhorn, 1972

29
Himmel, 1914-1915
Oil on canvas with artist-painted wood frame
120 × 120 cm (47 1/4 × 47 3/8 in.)
The Nelson-Atkins Museum of Art, Kansas City, Missouri
Gift of the Friends of Art)

30
E, 1915
Oil on canvas
121 × 121 cm (47 1/2 × 47 1/2 in.)
University of Iowa, Stanley Museum of Art. Mark Ranney Memorial Fund, 1958

31
Schiff, 1915
Oil on canvas with painted frame
101 × 81 cm (39 3/4 × 31 7/8 in.)
The Jan T. and Marica Vilcek Collection. Promised gift to The Vilcek Foundation

32
A Nice Time, 1915
Oil on board
61 × 51 cm (24 × 20 in.)
Myron Kunin Collection of American Art, Minneapolis. MN

33
Flower, 1916
Oil on board
41 × 30 cm (16 × 12 in.)
Myron Kunin Collection of American Art, Minneapolis, MN

34
Elsa Kobenhavn, 1916
Oil on composition board
51 × 61 cm (20 × 24 in.)
Weisman Art Museum, Minneapolis
Bequest of Hudson D. Walker from Ione and Hudson D. Walker Collection

35
Movement No. 7, Provincetown, 1916
Oil on board
60 × 49 cm (23 1/2 × 19 1/2 in.)

Crystal Bridges Museum of American Art, Bentonville, Arkansas. Alfred Stieglitz Collection, sameje / co-owned by Fisk University, Nashville, Tennessee, and Crystal Bridges Museum of American Art, Bentonville, Arkansas

36
Provincetown, 1916
Oil on canvas board
48 × 39 cm (19 × 15 1/2 in.)
The Jan T. and Marica Vilcek Collection. Promised gift to The Vilcek Foundation

37
Still Life No. 9, 1917
Oil on beaverboard
61 × 51 cm (24 × 20 in.)
Weisman Art Museum, Minneapolis. Bequest of Hudson D. Walker from Ione and Hudson D. Walker Collection

38
Still Life with Eel, c. 1917
Oil on canvas mounted on aluminum
73 × 61 cm (29 × 24 3/16 in.)
Courtesy of the Ogunquit Museum of American Art

39
The Blue Cup, c. 1918
Oil on panel
50 × 40 cm (19 3/4 × 15 5/8 in.)
Columbus Museum of Art
Gift of Ferdinand Howald

40
Santos, New Mexico, 1918-1919
Oil on composition board
81 × 58 cm (32 × 23 in.)
Weisman Art Museum, Minneapolis. Bequest of Hudson D. Walker from Ione and Hudson D. Walker Collection

41
The Last of New England – The Beginning of New Mexico, 1918-1919
Oil on cardboard
61 × 76 cm (24 × 30 in.)
The Art Institute of Chicago
Alfred Stieglitz Collection, 1949

42
The Virgin of Guadalupe, c. 1918-1919
Oil and charcoal on paperboard
81 × 61 cm (31 7/8 × 23 7/8 in.)
The Metropolitan Museum of Art
Alfred Stieglitz Collection, 1949

43
Pitcher and Dipper, 1918-1921
Oil on fiberboard
59 × 46 cm (23 3/8 × 18 1/4 in.)
Hirshhorn Museum and Sculpture Garden, Smithsonian Institution, Washington, DC. Gift of Joseph H. Hirshhorn, 1966

44
New Mexico No. 2, 1919
Oil on canvas
70 × 90 cm (27 1/2 × 35 1/2 in.)
Crystal Bridges Museum of American Art, Bentonville, Arkansas. Alfred Stieglitz Collection, Co-owned by Fisk University, Nashville, Tennessee, and Crystal Bridges Museum of American Art, Bentonville, Arkansas

45
Rubber Plant, 1920
Oil on canvas
81 × 66 cm (32 × 26 in.)
Yale University Art Gallery
Gift of Collection Société Anonyme

46
Landscape Fantasy, 1923
Oil on canvas
72 × 104 cm (28 1/2 × 41 in.)
Grey Art Gallery. New York University Art Collection
Gift of Charles Simon, 1965.58

47
New Mexico Recollections No. 13, c. 1923
Oil on canvas
76 × 102 cm (30 × 40 in.)
Private Collection

48
New Mexico No. 3, c. 1923
Oil on canvas
60 × 105 cm (23 1/2 × 41 1/4 in.)
Private Collection, Norfolk, VA

49
Paysage, 1924
Oil on canvas
81 × 81 cm (32 × 32 in.)
Weisman Art Museum, Minneapolis. Bequest of Hudson D. Walker from Ione and Hudson D. Walker Collection

50
Alpes Maritimes, Vence, 1925
Oil on canvas
80 × 80 cm (31 3/8 × 31 3/8 in.)
Myron Kunin Collection of American Art, Minneapolis, MN

51
Motif from African Textile I, 1925
Oil on board
74 × 30 cm (29 × 9 in.)
Colby College Museum of Art. Gift of the Alex Katz Foundation, 2013

52
Motif from African Textile II, 1925
Oil on board
74 × 30 cm (29 × 9 in.)
Colby College Museum of Art. Gift of the Alex Katz Foundation, 2013

53
Landscape No. 1 (Trees, Vence), c. 1925-1926
Oil on panel
37 × 46 cm (14 5/8 × 18 1/8 in.)
Philadelphia Museum of Art: The Alfred Stieglitz Collection, 1949

54
Mont Saint-Victoire, 1927
Oil on linen
81 × 100 cm (31 3/4 × 39 1/4 in.)
Des Moines Art Center. Gift of Mr. and Mrs. Fred Bohen

55
Two Shells, 1928
Oil on canvas
50 × 61 cm (19 3/4 × 24 in.)
Hirshhorn Museum and Sculpture Garden, Smithsonian Institution, Washington, DC. Gift of Joseph H. Hirshhorn, 1966

56
Leaves, 1929
Oil on canvas
63 × 56 cm (24 13/16 × 22 1/16 in.)
Williams College of Art. Gift of C. A. Wimpfheimer, Class of 1949

57
Still Life No. 4, c. 1929
Oil on linen
24 × 33 cm (9 5/8 × 13 1/8 in.)
Louisiana Museum of Modern Art. Acquired with funding from The Augustinus Foundation

58
White Top Mountain, 1930
Oil on Upson board
76 × 102 cm (30 × 40 in.)
Carnegie Museum of Art, Pittsburgh. Fellows Fund

59
Landscape No. 35 (Beaver Lake, Lost River Region), 1930
Oil on canvas
65 × 8 cm (25 1/2 × 31 3/4 in.)
Philadelphia Museum of Art
The Alfred Stieglitz Collection, 1949

60
Blueberry Highway, Dogtown, 1931
Oil on composition board
46 × 61 cm (18 1/4 × 24 in.)
High Museum of Art, Atlanta
Purchase with bequest of Charles Donald Belcher, 1977

61
Altar Boulder, Dogtown, 1931
Oil on board
46 × 62 cm (18 1/4 × 24 5/16 in.)
Sheldon Museum of Art
University of Nebraska-Lincoln, Bequest of Bertha Schaefer

62
Masks, 1931-1932
Oil on masonite
91 × 51 cm (36 × 20 in.)
Collection Walker Art Center, Minneapolis. Gift of Mrs. Joshua B. Cahn, New York, 1973

63
Popocatepetl, Spirited Morning – Mexico, 1932
Oil on board
63 × 74 cm (25 × 29 in.)
Smithsonian American Art Museum. Gift of Sam Rose and Julie Walters

64
Morgenrot, 1932
Oil on board
63 × 58 cm (25 × 23 in.)
Private Collection

65
Still Life, 1932-1933
Oil on composition board
45 × 54 cm (17 3/4 × 21 1/4 in.)
Smithsonian American Art Museum. Bequest of Edith S. and Arthur J. Levin

66
Tollan, Aztec Legend, 1933
Oil on canvas
80 × 100 cm (31 1/2 × 39 1/4 in.)
Myron Kunin Collection of American Art, Minneapolis, MN

67
Eight Bells Folly: Memorial to Hart Crane, 1933
Oil on canvas
78 × 100 cm (30 5/8 × 39 3/8 in.)
Weisman Art Museum, Minneapolis. Bequest of Hudson D. Walker from Ione and Hudson D. Walker Collection

68
Garmisch-Partenkirchen II, 1933
Oil on board

51 × 76 cm (20 × 30 in.)
Myron Kunin Collection of American Art, Minneapolis, MN

69
Bavarian Alps, Garmisch-Partenkirchen, 1933-1934
Oil on board
76 × 46 cm (30 × 18 in.)
Colby College Museum of Art. Gift of the Alex Katz Foundation, 2008

70
Still Life, c. 1935
Oil on canvas
61 × 46 cm (24 × 18 in.)
Private Collection

71
Night and Some Flowers, 1935-1936
Oil on canvas board
60 × 45 cm
Max & Eleanor Family Trust

72
Red Flowers and Sailboat, c. 1935-1936
Oil on board
62 × 46 cm (24 1/4 × 18 1/4 in.)
Crystal Bridges Museum of American Art, Bentonville, Arkansas

73
Squid, 1936
Oil on academy board
30 × 41 cm (12 × 16 in.)
Weisman Art Museum, Minneapolis. Bequest of Hudson D. Walker from Ione and Hudson D. Walker Collection

74
Dry Nets and Lobster Buoys, 1936
Oil on academy board
47 × 61 cm (18 1/2 × 24 in.)
Albritton Family Collection Courtesy Alexandre Gallery, New York

75
Jetty Seen Through a Window, 1936
Oil on board
61 × 46 cm (24 × 18 in.)
San Francisco Museum of Modern Art. Gift of W. W. Crocker

76
Northern Seascape, Off the Banks, 1936-1937
Oil on cardboard
46 × 61 cm (18 × 24 in.)
Milwaukee Art Museum. Bequest of Max E. Friedmann and Elinore Weinhold Friedmann

77
After the Hurricane, 1938
Oil on canvas
76 × 102 cm (30 × 40 1/8 in.)
Portland Museum, Oregon. Museum Purchase: Ella M. Hirsch Fund

78
Camden Hills From Baker's Island, Penobscot Bay, 1938
Oil on cardboard
71 × 56 cm (28 1/8 × 22 1/16 in.)
Collection Stedelijk Museum Amsterdam. Gift of Hudson D. Walker, New York

79
Ghosts of the Forrest, 1938
Oil on academy board
56 × 71 cm (22 1/8 × 28 in.)
Brooklyn Museum
John B. Woodward Memorial Fund

80
Cleophas, Master of the "Gilda Grey", 1938-1939
Oil on board
70 × 55 cm (27 3/4 × 21 3/4 in.)
Collection Walker Art Center, Minneapolis. Gift of Bertha H. Walker, 1971

81
Marie Ste. Esprit, c. 1938-1939
Oil on academy board
71.1 × 56 cm (28 × 22 in.)
Weisman Art Museum, Minneapolis. Bequest of Hudson D. Walker from Ione and Hudson D. Walker Collection

82
Adelard the Drowned, Master of the "Phantom", 1938-1939
Oil on academy board
71 × 56 cm (27 7/8 × 22 in.)
Collection of the Weisman Art Museum, Minneapolis, MN. Bequest of Hudson D. Walker from the Ione and Hudson D. Walker Collection, 1978

83
Finnish-Yankee-Sauna, 1938-1939
Oil on academy board
61 × 46 cm (24 × 18 in.)
Weisman Art Museum, Minneapolis. Bequest of Hudson D. Walker from Ione and Hudson D. Walker Collection

84
After the Storm, Vinalhaven, 1938-1939
Oil on academy board
56 × 71 cm (22 × 28 in.)
Bowdoin College Museum of Art, Brinswick, Maine. Gift of Mrs. Charles Phillip Kuntz

85
Sustained Comedy, 1939
Oil on academy board
72 × 56 cm (28 1/2 × 22 in.)
Carnegie Museum of Art, Pittsburgh. Gift of Mervin Jules in memory of Hudson Walker

86
Mount Katahdin, Autumn, No. 1, 1939-1940
Oil on canvas
75 × 101 cm (29 3/8 × 39 3/4 in.)
Sheldon Museum of Art University of Nebraska-Lincoln, Anna R. and Frank M. Hall Charitable Trust

87
Mt. Katahdin, Winter, 1939-1940
Oil on panel
54 × 69 cm (21 3/16 × 27 in.)
Courtesy of the Ogunquit Museum of American Art

88
Abundance, 1939-1940
Oil on canvas
102 × 76 cm (40 1/8 × 30 in.)
Currier Museum of Art, Manchester, NH. Museum Purchase: Currier Funds

89
Knotting Rope, 1939-1940
Oil on board
71 × 56 cm (28 × 22 in.)
Private Collection, New York

90
On the Beach, 1940
Oil on masonite-type hardboard
56 × 71 cm (22 × 28 in.)
Ted and Mary Jo Shen Courtesy James Reinish & Associates, Inc., and Meredith Ward Fine Art, New York

91
Madawaska – Acadian Light-Heavy, 1940
Oil on panel
102 × 76 cm (40 × 30 in.)
The Art Institute of Chicago Bequest of A. James Speyer, 1987

92
Madawaska – Acadian Light-Heavy, 1940
Oil on panel
102 × 76 cm (40 × 30 in.)
Private Collection, Courtesy Crystal Bridges Museum of America Art, Bentonville, Arkansas

93
Madawaska, Acadian Light-Heavy, Third Arrangement, 1940
Oil on composition board
71× 55 cm (27 7/8 × 21 3/4 in.)
Whitney Museum of American Art, New York. Gift of Nina and Herman Schneider, Gertrude Vanderbilt Whitney, and Dr. Meyer A. Pearlman by exchange, purchase by exchange, and purchase with funds from the Director's Discretionary Fund

94
Church by The Barrens, Indian Harbor, Maine, 1940
Oil on board
56 × 71 cm (22 × 28 in.)
Max & Eleanor Baril Family Trust

95
Hands, 1940
Oil on masonite
70 × 56 cm (27 3/4 × 22 in.)
Collection of Alex Katz

96
Canuck Yankee Lumberjack At Old Orchard Beach, Maine, 1940-1941
Oil on fiberboard
102 × 76 cm (40 1/8 × 29 15/16 in.)
Hirshhorn Museum and Sculpture Garden, Smithsonian Institution, Washington, DC. Gift of Joseph H. Hirshhorn, 1966

97
Lobster on Black Background, 1940-1941
Oil on fiberboard
56 × 71 cm (22 × 28 in.)
Smithsonian American Art Museum. Gift of Mr. Henry P. McIlhenny

98
Fishermen's Last Supper, Nova Scotia, 1940-1941
Oil on canvas
76 × 104 cm (30 1/8 × 41 1/8 in.)
Collection Friends of the Neuberger Museum of Art, Purchase College, State University of New York, gift from the Estate and Roy R. Neuberger

99
Lobster Fishermen, 1940-1941
Oil on Masonite
76 × 104 cm (29 3/4 × 40 7/8 in.)

Metropolitan Museum of Art
Arthur Hoppock Hearn Fund, 1942

100
Three Friends, 1941
Oil on masonite
104 × 76 cm (41 × 30 in.)
Eskenazi Museum of Art, Indiana University. Gift of Sarahanne Adams Hope in memory of Henry R. Hope

101
Christ Held By Half-Naked Men, 1941
Oil on fiberboard
102 × 76 cm (40 × 30 in.)
Hirshhorn Museum and Sculpture Garden, Smithsonian Institution, Washington, DC. Gift of Joseph H. Hirshhorn, 1966

102
Maine Coast Still Life, 1941
Oil on Masonite
102 × 76 cm (40 × 30 in.)
Collection Walker Art Center, Minneapolis. Gift of Mrs. Archie D. Walker, Josiah Bell Hudson Memorial, 1946

103
Mount Katahdin, 1941
Oil on masonite
56 × 71 cm (22 × 28 in.)
Private Collection

104
Sundown by the Ruins, 1942
Oil on composition board
56 × 71 cm (22 × 28 in.)
Whitney Museum of American Art, New York. Gift of Charles Simon

105
Prayer on Park Avenue, 1942
Oil on Masonite
102 × 76 cm (40 × 30 in.)
Myron Kunin Collection of American Art, Minneapolis, MN

106
Evening Storm, Schoodic, Maine No. 2, 1942
Oil on fabricated board
76 × 11 cm (30 × 4 1/2 in.)
Brooklyn Museum
Bequest of Edith and Milton Lowenthal, 1992

107
Summer Clouds and Flowers, 1942
Oil on fabricated board
56 × 71 cm (22 × 28 in.)
Brooklyn Museum. Bequest of Edith and Milton Lowenthal, 1992

108
Summer, Sea, Window, Red Curtain, 1942
Oil on masonite
102 × 77 cm (40 1/8 × 30 7/16 in.)
Addison Gallery of American Art, Phillips Academy, Andover, Massachusetts. Museum purchase, 1944.81

109
Young Seadog with Friend Billy, 1942
Oil on canvas
100 × 74 cm (39 1/2 × 29 in.)
Karen W. Davidson Collection

110
White Sea Horse, 1942
Oil on masonite
56 × 71 cm (22 1/4 × 28 1/8 in.)
The Jan T. and Marica Vilcek Collection. Promised gift to The Vilcek Foundation

111
Hurricane Island, Vinalhaven, Maine, 1942
Oil on masonite
76 × 101 cm (30 × 39 15/16 in.)
Philadelphia Museum of Art
Gift of Mrs. Herbert Cameron Morris, 1943

112
Roses, 1943
Oil on canvas
102 × 76 cm (40 1/8 × 30 1/8 in.)
Collection Walker Art Center, Minneapolis. Gift of Lone and Hudson D. Walker, 1971

113
Migration, 1943
Oil on board
49 × 55 cm (19 1/2 × 21 1/2 in.)
Jerome F. Dean

WORKS ON PAPER

114
Self-Portrait, 1908
Crayon on paper mounted on paperboard
30.5 × 22.5 cm (12 × 8 7/8 in.)
Smithsonian American Art Museum. Museum purchase through the Robert Tyler Davis Memorial Fund

115
New Mexico Hills, 1918
Pastel on cardboard
77 × 44 cm (30 5/16 × 17 5/16 in.)
Statens Museum for Kunst, Copenhagen

116
Valdez Hills, 1918
Pastel on cardboard
43,2 × 71 cm (17 × 27 15/16 in.)
Statens Museum for Kunst, Copenhagen

117
Standing Male Nude, c. 1923
Pastel on watercolor paper
59 × 41 cm (23 3/8 × 16 1/8 in.)
Weisman Art Museum, Minneapolis. Bequest of Hudson D. Walker from Ione and Hudson D. Walker Collection

118
Seated Male Nude, c. 1923
Pastel on paper
60 × 44 cm (23 3/4 × 17 3/8 in.)
Weisman Art Museum, Minneapolis. Bequest of Hudson D. Walker from Ione and Hudson D. Walker Collection

119
Untitled (Landscape with Forest Road), 1927
Graphite on paper
27.9 × 21.6 cm (11 × 8 1/2 in.)
Bates College Museum of Art, Marsden Hartley Memorial Collection. Gift of Norma Berger, 1955

120
Untitled (Still Life Flowers), 1927
Graphite on paper
22.9 × 30.5 cm (9 × 12 in.)
Bates College Museum of Art, Marsden Hartley Memorial Collection

121
Untitled (Landscape with Trees), 1927
Graphite on paper
22.9 × 30.5 cm (9 × 12 in.)
Bates College Museum of Art, Marsden Hartley Memorial Collection.
Gift of Norma Berger, 1955

122
Garmisch, 1933
Graphite on paper
26 × 18.1 cm (10 1/4 × 7 1/8 in.)
Bates College Museum of Art, Marsden Hartley Memorial Collection. Gift of Norma Berger, 1955

123
Untitled (The Alps), 1933
Graphite on paper
18.4 × 26 cm (7 1/4 × 10 1/4 in.)
Bates College Museum of Art, Marsden Hartley Memorial Collection. Gift of Norma Berger, 1955

124
Alpspitze, 1933
Sepia ink on paper
18.4 × 26 cm (7 1/4 × 10 1/4 in.)
Bates College Museum of Art, Marsden Hartley Memorial Collection. Gift of Norma Berger, 1955

125
Mountain (Alpspitze), c. 1933
Charcoal on paper
32.7 × 40.6 cm (12 7/8 × 16 in.)
High Museum of Art, Atlanta
Purchase

126
Mountain Landscape (Garmisch-Partenkirchen), c. 1933
Black crayon on white paper
40.8 × 31.8 cm (16 1/16 × 12 1/2 in.)
Yale University Art Gallery
Gift of Walter Bareiss, B.S. 1940

127
Untitled (Standing Male Figure No. 1), 1938-1941
Graphite and black ink on paper
23.8 × 12.1 cm (9 3/8 × 4 3/4 in.)
Bates College Museum of Art, Marsden Hartley Memorial Collection. Gift of Norma Berger, 1955

128
Untitled (Sketch of a Man, Head and Shoulders), 1938-1941
Black ink on paper
27.9 × 21.6 cm (11 × 8 1/2 in.)
Bates College Museum of Art, Marsden Hartley Memorial Collection. Gift of Norma Berger, 1955

129
Untitled (Male Figure Seated on Barrel), 1938-1941
Black ink on paper
19.1 × 12.7 cm (7 1/2 × 5 in.)
Bates College Museum of Art, Marsden Hartley Memorial Collection. Gift of Norma Berger, 1955

130
Untitled (Mt. Katahdin), 1939
Graphite on paper
7.6 × 12.7 cm (3 × 5 in.)
Bates College Museum of Art, Marsden Hartley Memorial Collection
Gift of Norma Berger, 1955

131
Untitled (Mt. Katahdin), c. 1939
Sepia ink and graphite on paper
21.9 × 28.6 cm (8 5/8 × 11 1/4 in.)

Bates College Museum of Art, Marsden Hartley Memorial Collection. Gift of Norma Berger, 1955

132
Dead Plover, 1940
Lithographic crayon and chalks on paper
45.1 × 29.8 cm (17 3/4 × 11 3/4 in.)
Weisman Art Museum, Minneapolis. Bequest of Hudson D. Walker from Ione and Hudson D. Walker Collection

133
Untitled (Male Figure, Rope, and Buoy at Old Orchard Beach), c. 1940
Graphite on paper
12.1 × 18.4 cm (4 3/4 × 7 1/4 in.)
Bates College Museum of Art, Marsden Hartley Memorial Collection. Gift of Norma Berger, 1955

134
Untitled (Two Male Figures – One Standing, One Seated), c. 1940
Graphite on paper
12.7 × 20.3 cm (5 × 8 in.)
Bates College Museum of Art, Marsden Hartley Memorial Collection. Gift of Norma Berger, 1955

135
Untitled (Two Male Figures), c. 1940
Graphite on paper
20.3 × 12.7 cm (8 × 5 in.)
Bates College Museum of Art, Marsden Hartley Memorial Collection. Gift of Norma Berger, 1955

136
Down East Young Lobstermen (Study for "Down East Young Blades"), 1940
Graphite on paper
30.5 × 22.9 cm (12 × 9 in.)
Bates College Museum of Art, Marsden Hartley Memorial Collection. Gift of Norma Berger, 1955

137
Untitled (Preliminary drawing for Lobster Fishermen), c. 1940
Graphite on paper
21.6 × 27.9 cm (8 1/2 × 11 in.)
Bates College Museum of Art, Marsden Hartley Memorial Collection. Gift of Norma Berger, 1955

138
Monstrous Betrayal, 1941-1943
Black ink on paper
27.9 × 21.6 cm (11 × 8 1/2 in.)
Bates College Museum of Art, Marsden Hartley Memorial Collection. Gift of Norma Berger, 1955

139
Courage, Power, Pity (Study for "Three Friends"), 1942
Black ink on paper
27.9 × 21.6 cm (11 × 8 1/2 in.)
Bates College Museum of Art, Marsden Hartley Memorial Collection. Gift of Norma Berger, 1955

140
Badly Bruised – Who Is He? (Study for "Christ Held by Half-Naked Men"), c. 1942
Black ink on paper
27.9 × 21.6 cm (11 × 8 1/2 in.)
Bates College Museum of Art, Marsden Hartley Memorial Collection. Gift of Norma Berger, 1955

141
Untitled (Study for "Christ Held by Half-Naked Men"), c. 1942
Black ink on paper
21.6 × 27.9 cm (8 1/2 × 11 in.)
Bates College Museum of Art, Marsden Hartley Memorial Collection. Gift of Norma Berger, 1955

LIST OF FIGURES

Fig. 1 Detail of a nude on the back of *Abstraction*, 1911 (cat. 12) Collection of the Weisman Art Museum at the University of Minnesota, Minneapolis, MN

Fig. 2 Paul Cézanne: *The Large Bathers*, 1895-1906. Oil on canvas, 32 × 219 cm. The Barnes Foundation

Fig. 3 Paul Cézanne: *Mont Sainte-Victoire*, c. 1902-1905. Oil on canvas, 64 × 81 cm. The Nelson-Atkins Museum of Art, Kansas City, Missouri. Purchaser William Rockhill Nelson Trust, 38-6

Fig. 4 Paul Cézanne: *The Card Players*, 1890-1892. Oil on canvas, 65 × 82 cm. Metropolitan Museum of Art. The Bequest of Stephen C. Clark, 1960

Fig. 5 Paul Cézanne: *The Bather*, c. 1885. Oil on canvas, 127 × 97 cm Museum of Modern Art, New York. Lillie P. Bliss Collection. 1.1934

Fig. 6-9 Front covers of Marsden Hartley's publications

Fig. 10 John Singer Sargent: *Nude Study of Thomas E. McKeller*, c. 1917-1920. Oil on canvas, 126 × 84 cm. Museum of Fine Arts Boston. Henry H. and Zoe Oliver Sherman Fund

Fig. 11 John Singer Sargent: *Male Model Resting*, c. 1895. Oil on canvas, 56 × 71 cm Private collection

Fig. 12 Charles Demuth: *Three Sailors on the Beach*, 1930 Watercolour on paper, 34.3 × 41.9 cm. Private collection

Fig. 13 Charles Demuth: *On "That" Street*, 1932. Watercolour on paper, 27.8 × 21.7 cm. The Art Institute of Chicago. Alfred Stieglitz Collection

Fig. 14 George Bellows: *Shower-Bath, First State*, 1917 Lithograph, 56 × 81 cm. New York, Metropolitan Museum of Art

Fig. 15 Installation view of Marsden Hartley's *Portrait of a German Officer*, MoMA, New York, 1930

Fig. 16 Milton Avery: *Portrait of Marsden Hartley*, 1943. Oil on canvas, 32 × 30 cm. The Phillips Collection, Washington, DC. Gift of Louis and Annette Kaufman Trust, 2004

Fig. 17 Mark Rothko: *Self-portrait*, 1936. Oil on canvas, 82 × 65 cm Private collection

Fig. 18 Milton Avery: *The White Wave*, 1956. Oil on canvas, 76 × 107 cm. Herbert F. Johnson Museum of Art, Cornell University

Fig. 19 Philip Guston: *Late Fall*, 1963. Oil on canvas, 173 × 197 cm The Doris and Donald Fisher Collection at the San Francisco Museum of Modern Art

Fig. 20 N.Y.C Armory Show, 69th Regiment Armory, New York, 1913

Fig. 21 Portrait of Hart Crane Marsden Hartley collection / Beinecke Rare Book and Manuscript Library, Yale University

Fig. 22 Richard Boix: Da-Da (New York Dada Group), 1921. New York Museum of Modern Art (MoMA). Katherine S. Dreier Bequest

Fig. 23 Portrait of Marsden Hartley's family. Marsden Hartley collection, Beinecke Rare Book and Manuscript Library, Yale University

Fig. 24 Portrait of Karl von Freyburg. Marsden Hartley collection, Beinecke Rare Book and Manuscript Library, Yale University

Fig. 25 Marsden Hartley's studio, Corea, Maine, c. 1943. Bates College Museum of Art, Gift of Chenoweth Hall and Miriam Colwell, 1996.8.1.b

Fig. 26 Postcard from Franz Marc to Marsden Hartley, 14 March 1913 Marsden Hartley collection / Beinecke Rare Book and Manuscript Library, Yale University

Fig. 27 Portrait of the Mason family. Marsden Hartley collection, Beinecke Rare Book and Manuscript Library, Yale University

Fig. 28 Announcement of Marsden Hartley's art class in New York, 1906. Horace Traubel and Anne Montgomerie Traubel Papers, Library of Congress, Washington, D.C.

Fig. 29 Marsden Hartley, Ezra Pound and Fernand Léger at Café du Dôme, year unknown Bates College Museum of Art, Marsden Hartley Memorial Collection, Gift of Norma Berger, 1955.1.173.t

Fig. 30 Marsden Hartley in costume, June 1913 Archives of American Art, Smithsonian Institution

Fig. 31 Charles Demuth and Eugene O'Neill in Provincetown, MA, year unknown Demuth Museum Archives, Courtesy The Demuth Museum, Lancaster

Fig. 32 Portrait of Walt Whitman, 1870 Bates College Museum of Art, Marsden Hartley Memorial Collection, Gift of Norma Berger, 1955.1.142.a

NOTES

Mathias Ussing Seberg

1 Louisiana's exhibition presents a large number of essays and poems alongside the pictures. Regrettably, the physical limitations of this catalogue do not allow for printing his writings to the extent they deserve. A small selection of poems is available on pp. 74-75. See also Edyta Frelik's text on p. 76.
2 See pp. 82-85.
3 Marsden Hartley, *Somehow a Past: The Autobiography of Marsden Hartley*, ed. Susan Elizabeth Ryan, MIT Press, 1998, p. 50.
4 I am not the only one to have had this thought. Ruth L. Bohan mentions it, noting that Hartley's great idol, Walt Whitman, also changed his name, from Walter to Walt, to achieve greater affinity with his self-image. See Ruth L. Bohan, "Marsden Hartley's Masculine Landscapes," in Bohan, *Looking into Walt Whitman: American Art, 1850-1920*, Pennsylvania State University Press, China, 2006, p. 149.
5 In an extensive study, Marcia Brennan notes that American artists like Hartley, Dove and O'Keeffe deliberately cultivated sexually loaded subjects, which she calls "embodied formalism." See Marcia Brennan, *Painting Gender, Constructing Theory: The Alfred Stieglitz Circle and American Formalist Aesthetics*, MIT Press, 2001.
6 See Jonathan D. Katz's contribution in this catalogue, which discusses Hartley's late figure paintings in the light of the history of gay art.
7 Hartley uses this term about himself in an unpublished vignette about Peter Doyle, Walt Whitman's presumed lover. From the Marsden Hartley Papers, Yale Collection of American Literature, Beinecke Rare Books and Manuscript Library, Yale University (henceforth YCAL).
8 The following passage is marked: "Through me forbidden voices,/ Voices of sexes and lusts, voices veil'd and I remove the veil,/ Voices indecent by me clarified and transfigur'd." See *Looking into Walt Whitman*, p. 144.
9 Jonathan Weinberg, *Speaking for Vice: Homosexuality in the Art of Charles Demuth, Marsden Hartley and the First American Avant-Garde*, Yale University Press, 1993, p. 132.
10 *Somehow a Past: The Autobiography of Marsden Hartley*, p. 181.
11 Patricia McDonnell, *Painting Berlin Stories: Marsden Hartley, Oscar Bluemner, and the first American Avant-Garde in Expressionist Berlin*, Peter Lang Publishing, 2003, p. 37.
12 *Looking into Walt Whitman*, p. 163.
13 *Somehow a Past: The Autobiography of Marsden Hartley*, p. 77.
14 Hartley's *Painting Number One* (1913) hung in Stein's apartment along with other of his paintings. See Barbara Haskell, *Marsden Hartley*, New York University Press, 1980, p. 30. Stein also arranged a studio visit for Hartley with Picasso.
15 *Somehow a Past: The Autobiography of Marsden Hartley*, p. 81.
16 He described his relationship with the two men as "a very beautiful triangle." In Hartley's works from Berlin, the triangle is a frequent motif. See Hartley, letter to Alfred Stieglitz, Berlin, March 1915, in James Timothy Voorhies (ed.), *My Dear Stieglitz: Letters of Marsden Hartley and Alfred Stieglitz 1912-1915*, University of South Carolina Press, 2002, p. 183.
17 This connection proved crucial to Hartley when Marc later invited him to show in the groundbreaking exhibition Erster Deutscher Herbstsalon in Berlin alongside his later renowned German colleagues.
18 Patricia McDonnell, *Marsden Hartley: American Modern*, Frederick R. Weisman Art Museum, University of Minnesota, Minneapolis, 2006, p. 13.
19 *Somehow a Past: The Autobiography of Marsden Hartley*, MIT Press, 1998, p. 90.
20 Widely assumed to have been bisexual, Kaiser Wilhelm is known for his love of uniforms, jewellery, dress-up and childish games among men. See Patricia McDonnell, "Essentially Masculine: Marsden Hartley, Gay Identity, and the Wilhelmine German Military," in *Art Journal*, 56, no. 2, (Summer 1997), p. 66.
21 Marsden Hartley, letter to Franz Marc, Berlin, 2 June 1913, in Dieter Scholz (ed.), *Marsden Hartley: The German Paintings, 1913-1915*, D.A.P., 2014, p. 173.
22 Ruth L. Bohan conducts a comprehensive study of Hartley's interpretation of Whitman. See "Marsden Hartley's Masculine Landscapes" in *Looking into Walt Whitman*, p. 143-164.
23 In a letter to von Freyburg, written 24 years after his death, Hartley describes having had a dream that he interpreted as an image of their intended physical relationship. Unpublished letter to Karl von Freyburg, 1938, YCAL.
24 A single work in the series is on a silver-coloured ground: *Painting No. 49* (1914-1915).
25 There are different interpretations of what the E represents. Jonathan Weinberg doubts that Hartley is referring to Rönnebeck in this painting and believes that the E stands for Hartley's given name, Edmund. See *Speaking for Vice*, p. 152.
26 For comparison, see Hans Holbein the Younger's painting *The Body of the Dead Christ in the Tomb* (1521), in which Holbein likewise crops the canvas in relation to the body.
27 See, e.g., Patricia Junker, "Childe Hassam, Marsden Hartley and the Spirit of 1916," in *American Art*, 24, no. 3 (Autumn 2010), p. 43.
28 Patricia McDonnell, *Marsden Hartley: American Modern*, Frederick R. Weisman Art Museum, University of Minnesota, 2006, p. 16.
29 Hartley appears in a play by the Nobel laureate playwright, *Strange Interlude* (1928), as Charles Marsden – a hybrid of him and Charles Demuth.
30 See, e.g., *Untitled* (1918) by Lyobov Popova, in Louisiana's collection.
31 Charles Demuth also made drawings of the ship, Elsa of Copenhagen.
32 As far as I know, the only one who insinuates such a connection is Bruce Robertson, who writes that the ship Elsa was probably full of blond sailors. See Bruce Robertson, *Marsden Hartley*, Harry N. Abrams, Inc., Japan, 1995, p. 72. In his book on Hartley and Charles Demuth, Jonathan Weinberg, who did the first groundbreaking study of the homoerotic content of Hartley's work, writes that homosexual references disappear from Hartley's works after Berlin and only reappear in the 1930s. See *Speaking for Vice,* p. 163.
33 In the Marsden Hartley Memorial Collection at Bates College and YCAL.
34 A few short years after Hartley and Demuth stayed in Provincetown, in 1919, a sex scandal was splashed across the American press, exposing that sailors and gay men sought each other's company at the harbour in Newport, near Provincetown.
35 Heather Hole, *Marsden Hartley and the West*, Yale University Press, 2007, p. 27.
36 During his Berlin years, Hartley was already experimenting with notions of what American art could be, producing the series *Amerika*, based on conceptions of America's indigenous people. See *Painting No. 50*, from Hartley's *Amerika Series,* on page 25.
37 *Marsden Hartley and the West*, p. 7.
38 "American Values in Painting," in *Adventures in the Arts*, pp. 58-59.
39 Marsden Hartley, "America as Landscape," in El Palacio, the magazine of the Museum of New Mexico, Santa Fe, Dec 21, 1918, vol. V, pp. 340-342
40 See Marcia Brennan, *Painting Gender, Constructing Theory – The Alfred Stieglitz Circle and American Formalist Aesthetics*, MIT Press, USA, 2001, pp. 168-169.
41 Townsend Ludington, *Marsden Hartley: The Biography of an American Artist*, Cornell University Press, 1998, p. 160.
42 This was not the first time that Hartley painted landscapes at a remove. Early in his career he painted his *Dark Mountain Series*, which references his hero Albert Pinkham Ryder in New York, and in general Hartley was never a *plein air* painter but decidedly a studio painter.
43 In Paris, 1924, Hartley continued the device from *Recollections*, recalling Maine landscapes, e.g. in *Paysage* (1924).
44 Heather Hole is also interested in this connection. See *Marsden Hartley and the West*, p. 115.
45 Including a number of self-portraits, e.g. *Self Portrait* (1908).

46 See Randall R. Griffey's text for more on Hartley and Cézanne.
47 Gail R. Scott, too, makes note of this, in *Marsden Hartley*, Abbeville Press, 1988, p. 72.
48 This group of works was not included at all in the two most recent retrospective exhibitions, at the Wadsworth Athenaeum (and other venues), in 2004, and the Whitney Museum of American Art (and other venues), in 1980.
49 Donna M. Cassidy, "The Local as Cosmopolitan," in Donna M. Cassidy, Elizabeth Finch and Randall R. Griffey, *Marsden Hartley's Maine*, Yale University Press, 2017, p. 90.
50 Not including the *Paysages* series from Paris, 1924, which recalled the Maine landscapes.
51 Kristina Wilson, "45 Franconia Notch" (catalogue entries), in Elizabeth Mankin Kornhauser, *Marsden Hartley,* Yale University Press, 2003, p. 306.
52 "The distinctly American understanding of nature-as-artistic-originator (rather than solely the imagination or consciousness), with emphasis on an empirical, perceptual source for the artistic statement, is closely tied to underlying principles in the works of Emerson, Whitman, and James, and this exerted an important influence on American artist/critics' views of modernism." Jill Anderson Kyle, "Cézanne, the 'Plastic,' and American Artists/Critics," in Gail Stavitsky and Katherine Rothkopf, *Cézanne and American Modernism*, Yale University Press, China, 2009, pp. 65-66.
53 *Somehow A Past*, p. 144.
54 Ibid.
55 *Marsden Hartley: The Biography of an American Artist*, p. 160.
56 Elizabeth McCausland, *Marsden Hartley*, University of Minnesota Press, 2017 (1952), p. 45.
57 Late in life, Hartley corresponded with the Guatemalan artist Carlos Mérida, who also worked in Mexico City. In a letter, dated 24 January 1937 and posted from Mexico, Mérida thanks Hartley for a letter in which Hartley appears to have praised Mérida's art. Carlos Mérida, unpublished letter to Marsden Hartley, January 1937, YCAL.
58 As Ludington writes, "For Böhme, the seventh realm of divine corporeality – or the materialized word – was where the sounds of individual things contributed to the divine harmony of the spheres. In Hartley's painting the seventh sphere is on the divine hand made corporeal, 7 being a symbol of perfect order and completeness," in *Marsden Hartley: The Biography of an American Artist*, Cornell University Press, USA, 1998, p. 219.
59 Donna M. Cassidy, "The Invisibility of Race in Modernist Representation: Marsden Hartley's North Atlantic Folk," in Patricia Johnston (ed.), *Seeing High and Low: Representing Social Conflict in American Visual Culture*, University of California Press, Canada, 2006, p. 256.
60 *Marsden Hartley: The Biography of an American Artist*, p. 10. Donna Cassidy has several times described how race is a recurring theme for Hartley, not least in his correspondences and essays. See Donna M. Cassidy, *Marsden Hartley: Race, Region and Nation*, University Press of New England, 2005, pp. 303-304.
61 Gail Levin, "Marsden Hartley in Bavaria," in William Salzillo, *Marsden Hartley in Bavaria*, University Press of New England, 1989, p. 24.
62 Ronald Paulson, "Marsden Hartley's Search for the Father(land)," in Gerald Ferguson, *Marsden Hartley and Nova Scotia*, Press of the Nova Scotia College of Art and Design, 1987, p. 30.
63 Hartley subsequently travelled to Nova Scotia, Canada, which, of course, can also be designated as abroad, though Hartley tied the landscape to Maine, so the effect was more one of returning home.
64 The work may have been painted subsequently in Nova Scotia, since Hartley travelled there directly from Bermuda. The Crystal Bridges Museum of American Art, which owns the work, has no information about where it was painted.
65 Window views were a motif in Hartley's work since his first visit to Bermuda, in 1917.
66 *The Collected Poems of Marsden Hartley*, p. 271.
67 *Marsden Hartley: The Biography of an American Artist*, p. 17.
68 Ibid., p. 254.
69 Unusually for him, Hartley painted these from a live model, not from drawings or memory, as was his preferred method.
70 *Speaking for Vice*, p. 192.
71 Randall R. Griffey, "An Ambivalent Prodigal: Marsden Hartley as 'The Painter from Maine'," in *Marsden Hartley's Maine*, p. 127.
72 These works also reveal a strong interest in race. The titles mention the following races breeds: Finnish-Yankee, Madawaska-Acadian and Canuck-Yankee – all three of them European-American hybrids. Hartley was quite enthusiastic about types bred with "Viking appearances, and Yankee behaviours." In that light, the bright blue eyes in *Finnish-Yankee-Sauna* take on a different character, which cannot be ignored. Without a doubt, Hartley's ideal was European-American. As Donna Cassidy and others have described, Hartley's letters include numerous instances of him referring to other races in derogatory terms. This essay has also discussed his early fascination with Hitler. However, Hartley's choice of phrasing is hardly systematic and, as Randall R. Griffey has described, the interest in race and eugenics was ubiquitous in the 1930s, not only among Nazis and their sympathizers. This was the case in America as well as in Europe, and was not necessarily something Hartley had imported from Germany. For more on Hartley and race, see *Marsden Hartley: Race, Region and Nation* and Randall R. Griffey, "Marsden Hartley's Aryanism: Eugenics in a Finnish-Yankee Sauna," in *American Art*, University of Chicago Press, 22, no. 2 (Summer 2008), pp. 64-84.
73 Hartley, cited in *Marsden Hartley's Maine*, p. 31.
74 See, e.g., ibid.
75 *Speaking for Vice*, p. 188.
76 Gail R. Scott (ed.), *The Collected Poems of Marsden Hartley: 1904-1943*, Black Sparrow Press, 1987, p. 250.

Randall Griffey

77 Clement Greenberg, "Review of Two Exhibitions of Marsden Hartley." In *The Collected Essays and Criticism. Volume 1: Perceptions and Judgments, 1939-1944,* ed. John O'Brian, University of Chicago Press, 1986, p. 246.
78 These materials are housed with the Marsden Hartley Collection, Yale Center of American Literature, Beinecke Rare Book & Manuscript Library, Yale University, New Haven, Connecticut (hereafter YCAL).
79 In an essay unpublished in his lifetime about 291, Hartley wrote: "Of course I wanted to go to Paris. I had seen some Matisse, Cézanne, and Picasso and I wanted to see more for I wanted to have an artist's education." See Hartley, *Somehow a Past: The Autobiography of Marsden Hartley*, edited by Susan Elizabeth Ryan, The MIT Press, 1997, p. 66.
80 Patricia McDonnell, "Marsden Hartley (1877-1943)," in Gail Stavitsky and Katherine Rothkopf, et al, *Cézanne and American Modernism*, exh. cat., Montclair Art Museum, 2009, p. 214-217.
81 Bruce Weber, *The Heart of the Matter: The Still Lifes of Marsden Hartley*, Berry Hill Galleries, Inc, 2003. See pages 16-20 in particular.
82 Townsend Ludington addresses this Cézanne quote in Ludington, *Marsden Hartley: The Biography of an American Artist*, Cornell University Press, 1998, p. 71. Hartley mentioned it in correspondence with Stieglitz.
83 The three lithographs by Cézanne in this exhibition were: *Portrait of Cézanne* (1896-1897; black and white), *Small Bathers* (1896-1897; color), *The Bather* (*Large Plate*). See Jill Kyle, "Paul Cézanne, 1911: Nature Reconstructed," in Sarah Greenough, et al, *Modern Art and America: Alfred Stieglitz and His New York Galleries*, exh. cat., National Gallery of Art, 2000, pp. 101-115.
84 Hartley quoted in Ryan, Ibid.
85 Patricia McDonnell, "Changes of Heart: Marsden Hartley's Ideas and Art," in *Marsden Hartley: American Modern. Selections from the Ione and Hudson D. Walker Collection, Frederick R. Weisman Art Museum*, exh. cat., University of Minnesota, p. 11.
86 See Heather Hole, *Marsden Hartley and the West: The Search for an American Modernism*, exh. cat., Yale

University Press; Georgia O'Keeffe Museum, 2007).
87 Hartley reminisced extensively about this period in *Somehow a Past*. See "Cézanne's Aix," in Ryan, 136-141.
88 See Randall R. Griffey, "Marsden Hartley's Late Paintings: American Masculinity and National Identity in the 1930s and '40s, Ph.D diss. University of Kansas, Lawrence, 1999.
89 See Griffey, "An Ambivalent Prodigal: Marsden Hartley as 'The Painter from Maine'," in Donna Cassidy, Elizabeth Finch, and Randall R. Griffey, *Marsden Hartley's Maine*, exh. cat., The Metropolitan Museum of Art, 2017, pp. 105-141.
90 R. E. Turpin, "Cézanne Still Dominates the Era He Launched," *The New York Times Magazine*, January 15, 1939, pp. 6-7, 19, 21.
91 Hartley to Norma Berger, December 20, 1942, Marsden Hartley Collection, YCAL.

Edyta Frelik

92 Hartley to Alfred Stieglitz, Berlin, March 15, 1915, in *My Dear Stieglitz: Letters of Marsden Hartley and Alfred Stieglitz, 1912-1915*, ed. James Timothy Voorhies, University of South Carolina Press, 2002, p. 184.
93 Notably, one of Hartley's earliest surviving paintings is *Walt Whitman's House, 328 Mickle Street, Camden, New Jersey* (c. 1905). Oddly un-modern in its realism, it prefigures his later style by somber tonality and strongly marked contours.
94 Hartley to Stieglitz, Berlin, October 22, 1913, in *My Dear Stieglitz*, p. 118.
95 Hartley, quoted in Jonathan Weinberg, "Marsden Hartley: Writing on Painting," in *Marsden Hartley: American Modernist*, ed. Elizabeth Mankin Kornhauser, Yale University Press, 2003, p. 124.
96 William Carlos Williams, "Beginnings: Marsden Hartley," quoted in Robert Creeley, foreword to *The Collected Poems of Marsden Hartley, 1904-1943*, ed. Gail R. Scott, Black Sparrow Press, 1987, p. 15.
97 Gertrude Stein to Stieglitz, undated, quoted in Susan Elizabeth Ryan, introduction to *Somehow a Past: The Autobiography of Marsden Hartley*, ed. Susan Elizabeth Ryan, The MIT Press, 1997, p. 18.
98 Hartley to Stieglitz, Berlin, October 22, 1913, in *My Dear Stieglitz*, p. 117.
99 Gertrude Stein, *Everybody's Autobiography*, Cooper Square, 1971, p. 37.
100 Hartley to Stieglitz, Berlin, June 12, 1914, in *My Dear Stieglitz*, 139.
101 "If It Were the Eye," in *Collected Poems*, p. 198.
102 "Yielding the Initiative," in *Collected Poems*, p. 194.
103 "Francis Thompson," in *Adventures in the Arts: Informal Chapters on Painters, Vaudeville and Poets*, Boni and Liveright, 1921, p. 215-220.
104 Hartley to Wassily Kandinsky and Gabriele Münter, Berlin, April 1913, in Patricia McDonnell, "Marsden Hartley's Letters to Franz Marc and Wassily Kandinsky 1913-1914," *Archives of American Art Journal* 29, no. 1/2 (1989), p. 37.
105 Williams to Stieglitz, 27 June 1937, quoted in Dickran Tashjian, *William Carlos Williams and the American Scene 1920-1940*, Whitney Museum of American Art.; University of California Press, 1978, p. 52.
106 "The Dearth of Critics," in *Adventures in the Arts*, pp. 237-238.
107 "The Importance of Being 'Dada'," in *Adventures in the Arts*, p. 248.
108 In the last sentence of his essay "The Importance of Being 'Dada'," Hartley calls art "a witty and entertaining pastime." Luckily, it was just a slightly perverse Dada provocation.
109 "The Business of Poetry," in *Collected Poems*, p. 315.
110 "Lewiston Is a Pleasant Place," in *Collected Poems*, pp. 254-256.
111 "Concerning Fairy Tales and Me," in *Adventures in the Arts*, pp. 3-10.

Jonathan D. Katz

112 Marsden Hartley, *The Collected Poems of Marsden Hartley, 1904-1943*, ed. Gail R. Scott, Black Sparrow Press, 1987, p. 96.
113 Ibid., p. 238.

Elizabeth Finch

114 "On the Persistence of the Imagination, The Painting of Milton Avery, American Imaginative," in Marsden Hartley, *On Art*, ed. Gail Scott, Horizon Press, 1982, p. 201.
115 A[lfred] H. B[arr] Jr., "Foreword," *Painting and Sculpture by Living Americans*, The Museum of Modern Art, p. 5.
116 Marsden Hartley, "On the Subject of Nativeness – A Tribute to Maine," in *Marsden Hartley: Exhibition of Recent Paintings, 1936*, An American Place, 1937, p. 5.
117 Marsden Hartley, "John Kane of Pittsburgh," in *On Art*, 192-195. Many of Hartley's essays, including this one, went unpublished during his lifetime, but they undoubtedly shaped his alliances and the direction of his art. The field is indebted to Gail R. Scott for editing this volume of Hartley's writings and for producing one of the first posthumous monographs. See Gail R. Scott, *Marsden Hartley*, Abbeville Press, 1988. This book was preceded by Scott's edited volume, *The Collected Poems of Marsden Hartley, 1904-1943*, Black Sparrow Press, 1987.
118 Jackson Pollock, "Answers to a Questionnaire," *Arts and Architecture* 61, February 1944: p. 14, as quoted in B[ernard] H[arper] Friedman, *Jackson Pollock: Energy Made Visible*, McGraw-Hill, 1972, p. 21. "American Primitives," was the title of a 1930-1931 essay by Hartley. See *On Art*, 186-191.
119 Marsden Hartley, Mark Tobey, in *On Art*, p. 183.
120 Ibid., p. 185.
121 Marsden Hartley to Milton Avery, undated, Milton Avery Papers, Archives of American Art, Smithsonian Institution. The record for this letter erroneously cites a circa date of 1960; 1940 would be a better estimate.
122 Carol Troyen, "The 'Nativeness' of 'Primitive Things': Marsden Hartley's Late Work in Context," in *Marsden Hartley*, ed. Elizabeth Mankin Kornhauser, Wadsworth Atheneum Museum of Art in association with Yale University Press, 2003: pp. 245, 251; see also in this volume, Kristina Wilson, catalogue entry for *Storm Down Pine Point Way, Old Orchard*, p. 327. Scott indicates that Hartley inspired Milton Avery, Mark Rothko, Philip Guston, Robert Indiana, and Alex Katz. See Gail R. Scott, *Marsden Hartley*, p. 9. And William C. Agee posits that Hartley's late landscapes were "surely affected Pollock's work from the mid-1930s right through to his mature period" but, like Scott, he cites no concrete evidence beyond the general phenomenon of "a more painterly and expressionist vein." See William C. Agee, *Modern Art in American, 1908-68*, Phaidon, 2016, pp. 205, 152.
123 Clement Greenberg, note, *Hartley/Maurer: Contemporaneous Paintings*, Bertha Schaefer Gallery, 13 November – 2 December 1950, n.p.
124 Philip Guston, "On Drawing" (1974), in *Philip Guston: Collected Writings, Lectures, and Conversations*, ed. Clark Coolidge, University of California Press, 2011, p. 266.
125 Alex Katz, "Thoughts on Modern and Contemporary Artists and Poets," in *Invented Symbols: An Art Autobiography*, ed. Vincent Katz, Colby College of Art; Charta, 2012, p. 149.
126 Mark Rothko, Eulogy for Milton Avery, delivered 7 January 1965 at the New York Society for Ethical Culture.

Marsden Hartley
The Earth Is All I Know of Wonder

Edited by Lærke Rydal Jørgensen & Mathias Ussing Seeberg
Graphic Design: Anni's
Photo Editors: Sidse Buck & Kim Hansen
Translations: Glen Garner (Foreword & Mathias Ussing Seeberg), James Manley (Karin Mamma Andersson & Pathways to Marsden Hartley)
Proofreading: James Manley
Mathias Ussing Seeberg's text has been peer-reviewed

Cover, front: Marsden Hartley: *Adelard the Drowned, Master of the "Phantom"*, 1938-1939 (detail), oil on academy board, 71 × 56 cm (27 7/8 × 22 in.). Collection of the Weisman Art Museum
Cover, back: Marsden Hartley: *Camden Hills From Baker's Island, Penobscot Bay*, 1938 (detail), oil on cardboard 71 × 56 cm (28 1/8 × 22 1/16 in.). Collection Stedelijk Museum Amsterdam
Page 1: Marsden Hartley: *Leaves*, 1929 (detail), oil on canvas, 63×56cm (24 13/16 × 221/16 in.). Williams College of Art. Gift of C. A. Wimpfheimer, Class of 1949

Litho & print: Narayana Press
ISBN: 978-87-93659-23-0
Printed in Denmark 2019
www.louisiana.dk

The catalogue is published on the occasion of the exhibition
Marsden Hartley
The Earth Is All I Know of Wonder
Louisiana Museum of Modern Art, Humlebæk
19 September 2019 – 19 January 2020

Curator: Mathias Ussing Seeberg
Curatorial Coordinator / Registrar: Eva Lund
Exhibition Architect: Jens Kamp
Graphic Design: Marie d'Origny Lübecker
Conservator / Exhibition Producer: Ulrik Staal Strange Dinesen

The exhibition is supported by

AUGUSTINUS FONDEN

TERRA FOUNDATION FOR AMERICAN ART

Louisiana's Main Corporate Partners

FRITZ HANSEN

NØRGAARD PÅ STRØGET

Realdania

Supports Louisiana's architectural exhibitions

UBS

Supports Louisiana's exhibitions and programs

Photos:
p. 5: Centre Pompidou, MNAM-CCI, Dist. RMN-Grand Palais / image Centre Pompidou, MNAM-CCI; p. 9 bottom: The Vilcek Foundation; p. 11 top: The Metropolitan Museum of Art/Art Resource/Scala, Florence; p. 12 top: Edward C. Robison III; p. 12 m: Kevin Noble; p. 15 top: Albert Vecerka; p. 15 m: Dwight Primiano; p. 15 bottom: Jim Frank; p. 16 top: Brian Zehowski; p. 19 bottom left: Brian Zehowski; p. 19 top left: Brian Zehowski; p. 20: Brian Zehowski; p. 22 bottom left: Brian Zehowski; p. 22 bottom right: Brian Zehowski; p. 22 top right: William J. Kemp Photography; p. 22 top left: Brian Zehowski; p. 23: Currier Museum of Art; p. 24 bottom right: Brian Zehowski; p. 24 top right: Museo Nacional Thyssen-Bornemisza; p 25: The Vilcek Foundation; p. 26: Robert Gerhardt and Denis Y. Suspitsyn; p. 27: The Vilcek Foundation; p. 33: The Metropolitan Museum of Art/Art Resource/Scala, Florence; p. 34 top left: SMK Foto/Jakob Skou-Hansen; p. 34 bottom left: Robert Gerhardt and Denis Y. Suspitsyn; p. 35: Cathy Carver; p. 36 bottom: The Vilcek Foundation; p. 36 top right: Edward C. Robison p. 38: Perry Smith; p. 39 top right: Brian Zehowski; p. 39: William J. Kemp Photography; p. 40 top: Edward C. Robison III; p. 40 bottom right: SMK Foto/Jakob Skou-Hansen; p. 40 bottom left: SMK Foto/Jakob Skou-Hansen; p. 41: Brian Zehowski; p. 42 top left: The Art Institute of Chicago / Art Resource, NY/ Scala, Florence; p. 42 bottom: The Art Institute of Chicago / Art Resource, NY/ Scala, Florence ; p. 43: Yale University Art Gallery /Richard House; p. 45: Brian Zehowski; p. 48 top left: Brian Zehowski; p. 48 top right m: Kevin Noble; p. 50: Rich Sanders, Des Moines Art Center; p. 55: Joseph Hu; p. 59: Albert Vecerka; p. 61 bottom: Gene Young; p. 64 top right: SMK Foto/Jakob Skou-Hansen; p. 66 right: Nan Chisholm; 66 left: JOSHUA WHITE / JWPicturep.com; p. 67: Dwight Primiano; p. 69 m: Brian Zehowski; p. 70 m: Edward C. Robison III; p. 70 m: Rich Sanders, Des Moines Art Center; p. 70 bottom: courtesy Nelson-Atkins Museum of Art, Media Services / Chris Bjuland and Joshua Ferdinand; p. 71 m: Jospeh Hu; p. 71 n: Perry Smith; p. 72 m: The Metropolitan Museum of Art/Art Resource/Scala, Florence; p. 73 bottom: The Museum of Modern Art, New York/Scala, Florence; p. 73 top: Cathy Carver; p. 78 top right: Brian Zehowski; p.89: Jim Frank; p. 93: Currier Museum of Art; p. 94: Brian Zehowski; p. 95: Digital photography by Peter Siegel; p. 97: The Art Institute of Chicago / Art Resource, NY/ Scala, Florence; p. 98: Alexandre Gallery; p. 100: Trujillo Juan; p. 101: Robert Gerhardt and Denis Y. Suspitsyn; p. 103 top: Perry Smith; p. 105-106: Cathy Carver; p. 108 top left: Kevin Montague; p. 110: Paul Takeuchip. 111: JOSHUA WHITE / JWPicturep.com; p. 113 The Metropolitan Museum of Art/Art Resource/Scala, Florence; p. 119: Addison Gallery of American Art, Phillips Academy, Andover/Art Resource, NY/Scala, Florence; p. 114: Robert Gerhardt and Denis Y. Suspitsyn; p. 117 bottom left: The Vilcek Foundation; p. 117 top left: Gene Young; p. 122 bottom: Museum of fine Arts Boston; p. 122 top: Cathy Carver; p. 123 bottom: Alexandre Gallery; p. 123 m: The Art Institute of Chicago / Art Resource, NY/ Scala, Florence; p. 124 bottom: Ritzau Scanpix / The Picture Art Collection / Alamy Stock Photo; p. 124 top: Robert Gerhardt and Denis Y. Suspitsyn; p. 125 bottom: The Metropolitan Museum of Art/Art Resource/Scala, Florence; p. 125 top: Ritzau Scanpix / Bridgeman images; p. 129: The Museum of Modern Art, New York/Scala, Florence; p. 130: The Phillips Collection, Washington, DC; p. 131 bottom: Courtesy Timothy Taylor Gallery, London / SFMOMA; p. 131 top: Photography courtesy of the Herbert F. Johnson Museum of Art, Cornell University; p. 132 bottom: Marsden Hartley Collection. Yale Collection of American Literature, Beinecke Rare Book and Manuscript Library; p. 132 top right: The Museum of Modern Art, New York/Scala, Florence; p. 133 top left: Marsden Hartley Collection. Yale Collection of American Literature, Beinecke Rare Book and Manuscript Library; p. 133 left: Marsden Hartley Collection. Yale Collection of American Literature, Beinecke Rare Book and Manuscript Library; p. 132 bottom right: Marsden Hartley Collection. Yale Collection of American Literature, Beinecke Rare Book and Manuscript Library; p. 132 top right: Bates College Museum of Art; p. 134 left: Marsden Hartley Collection. Yale Collection of American Literature, Beinecke Rare Book and Manuscript Library; p. 134 left: Rockwell Kent papers / Archives of American Art, Smithsonian Institution; p. 134 bottom: Bates College Museum of Art; p. 135 left: Courtesy The Demuth Museum, Lancaster; p. 135 m: Alfred Stieglitz / Georgia O'Keeffe Archive. Yale Collection of American Literature. Beinecke Rare Book and Manuscript Library; p. 135 right: Bates College Museum of Art.